Theology after Liberalism

Blackwell Readings in Modern Theology
General Editors: L. Gregory Jones and James J. Buckley
Duke University, North Carolina; Loyola College, Maryland

Blackwell Readings in Modern Theology is a series of constructive anthologies on important topics in modern theology. Each volume brings together both classic and newly commissioned essays on a particular theme. These essays will provide students and teachers in colleges, universities and seminaries with a critical entry to key debates.

For a full contents listing or for more information visit our website at http://www.blackwellpublishers.co.uk/religion

Published works
The Theological Interpretation of Scripture
Classic and Contemporary Readings
Edited by Stephen E. Fowl

The Postmodern God
A Theological Reader
Edited by Graham Ward

Inquiring after God
Classic and Contemporary Readings
Edited by Ellen T. Charry

Theology after Liberalism
A Reader
Edited by John Webster and George P. Schner

Theology after Liberalism

A Reader

Edited by

John Webster
University of Oxford

George P. Schner
Regis College, Toronto

Copyright © Blackwell Publishers Ltd 2000
Editorial matter and arrangement copyright © John Webster and George P. Schner
2000

First published 2000

2 4 6 8 10 9 7 5 3 1

Blackwell Publishers Ltd
108 Cowley Road
Oxford OX4 1JF
UK

Blackwell Publishers Inc.
350 Main Street
Malden, Massachusetts 02148
USA

Library of Congress Cataloging-in-Publication Data

Theology after Liberalism: a reader / edited by John Webster,
George P. Schner.
     p.   cm. — (Blackwell readings in modern theology)
    Includes bibliographical references and index.
    ISBN 0–631–20563–2 (alk. paper) — ISBN 0–631–20564–0
(pbk.: alk. paper)
    1. Postliberal theology. I. Series. II. Webster, J. B. (John Bainbridge),
1955– III. Schner, George P., 1946–

BT83.595.T44   1999
230′.046 21—dc21   99-043541

British Library Cataloguing in Publication Data

A CIP catalogue record for this book is available from the British Library.

Typeset in 10½ on 12 pt Ehrhardt
by Ace Filmsetting Ltd, Frome, Somerset
Printed in Great Britain by MPG Books Ltd, Bodmin, Cornwall

This book is printed on acid-free paper.

Contents

Part III Methods

Part IV Criticisms

Part V Afterword

Contributors

John Webster
Lady Margaret Professor of Divinity and Canon of Christ Church, University of Oxford

George P. Schner
Associate Professor of Philosophy of Religion and Philosophical Theology, Regis College, Toronto

Hans Frei
Former Professor of Religious Studies, Yale University

William Placher
Professor of Philosophy and Religion, Wabash College

Colin Gunton
Professor of Christian Doctrine, King's College, University of London

Oliver O'Donovan
Regius Professor of Moral and Pastoral Theology and Canon Christ Church, University of Oxford

J. Augustine DiNoia, OP
Professor of Theology, Dominican House of Studies, Washington

James J. Buckley
Professor of Theology, Loyola College, Maryland

Andrew Louth
Professor of Theology, University of Durham

Kathryn Tanner
Associate Professor of Theology, University of Chicago Divinity School

Frans Jozef van Beeck
John Cardinal Cody Professor of Sacred Theology, Loyola University, Chicago

Mary McClintock Fulkerson
Associate Professor of Theology, Duke University Divinity School

Rowan Williams
Bishop of Monmouth

David Tracy
Andrew Thomas Greeley and Grace McNichols Greeley Distinguished Service Professor of Catholic Studies and Professor of Theology and of the Philosophy of Religion, University of Chicago Divinity School

George A. Lindbeck
Pitkin Professor of Historical Theology (emeritus), Yale University

Preface

This reader gathers together examples of some of the very best recent writing in Christian theology which, in various ways, seek to extricate Christian theology from its more problematic involvements with what (for want of a more suitable term) we identify as 'liberalism'. In what sense and with what justification the texts collected here can be typified as 'postliberal' is very much an open question, discussed in chapter 2. Certainly, bringing these disparate writings together in a single volume does not, and is not intended to, indicate a consistent theological school. But it does point to some converging lines of inquiry, as well as some common questions and proposals about the current and future tasks of theology.

The reader has grown out of a graduate seminar which we co-taught for a decade in the Toronto School of Theology on methods, norms and sources of theology. One of the chief goals of the seminar was to encourage reflective awareness of some of the pressures exercised on the various theological sub-disciplines by the conventions of modernity, especially because those conventions are for the most part largely invisible to theological practitioners. Like the school in which it took place, the seminar and its membership spanned the ecumenical divide: one of us is a Roman Catholic, the other an Anglican, and students from all Christian traditions and none joined our debates. It also crossed the (even broader) disciplinary divisions within theology itself: one of us works primarily in philosophical theology, the other in dogmatics, and at one time or another students in scripture studies, church history and the history of Christian thought, philosophy, pastoral studies and doctrine came together, often discovering for the first time that others working in seemingly distant fields of theological inquiry struggled with similar problems. We addressed these problems in two ways. First, we sought to articulate a genealogy of modernity and its various theological, philosophical and spiritual traditions, chiefly by close reading of some of the definitive texts of the modern era. Limitations of space mean that we cannot reproduce these texts here; but chapter 1 offers an account of modernity which furnishes the necessary background to placing the more recent writings which this volume brings together. Second, we looked at examples of contemporary theological texts which, implicitly or explicitly, called into question or subverted or just ignored the dominant models of intellectual practice in theology. A selection of these forms the core of the present collection, supplemented by some critical appraisals of 'postliberal' theology from theologians who take it seriously but nevertheless do not share its orientation.

We are very grateful to all the contributors who have generously permitted their work to be reproduced. We owe a great debt to the many students who took part in our discussions, and who not only encouraged us to think through and rethink the relation of doctrines and methods in theology, but also helped us clarify the way in which we are to understand the fate of Christian theology in the modern era. We are particularly grateful to Naomi Gold and Rory Hinton for help in getting this volume into shape, and to Blackwell Publishers for exercising exemplary patience with two editors who believed themselves to have virtually limitless excuses for not finishing what they had set themselves to do.

John Webster
George P. Schner

Acknowledgements

The editors and publishers gratefully acknowledge permission to reproduce copyright material as follows:

Hans Frei, 'Identity Description and Jesus Christ', from *The Identity of Jesus Christ* (Philadelphia: Fortress Press, 1975), pp. 86–115.

William Placher, 'The *Perichoresis* of Particular Persons', from *Narratives of a Vulnerable God* (Louisville: Westminster/John Knox, 1994), pp. 53–83.

Colin Gunton, 'The Atonement and the Triune God', from *The Actuality of Atonement* (Edinburgh: T&T Clark, 1988), pp. 143–71.

Oliver O'Donovan, 'Freedom and Reality', from *Resurrection and Moral Order* (Leicester: Inter-Varsity Press, 1986), pp. 101–20.

J. Augustine DiNoia, 'Theology in Dialogue', from *The Diversity of Religions* (Washington: Catholic University of America Press, 1992), pp. 109–54.

James J. Buckley, 'Beyond the Hermeneutical Deadlock', revision of 'The Hermeneutical Deadlock between Revelationalists, Textualists and Functionalists', *Modern Theology* 6 (1990), pp. 325–39.

Andrew Louth, 'Tradition and the Tacit', from *Discerning the Mystery* (Oxford: Clarendon Press, 1983), pp. 73–95.

Kathryn Tanner, 'Self-Critical Cultures and Divine Transcendence', from *The Politics of God* (Minneapolis: Fortress Press, 1992), pp. 35–74.

Frans Jozef van Beeck, 'Depth of Self-Awareness and Breadth of Vision: Joining Reflection and Interpretation', revision of *God Encountered: A Contemporary Catholic Systematic Theology. Volume 1: Understanding the Christian Faith* (San Francisco: Harper and Row, 1989), pp. 97–141.

Acknowledgements ────────────────────────────────────

Mary McClintock Fulkerson, 'Feminist Theology: Language, Gender and Power', from *Changing the Subject: Women's Discourses and Feminist Theology* (Minneapolis: Fortress Press, 1994), pp. 61–116.

Rowan Williams, 'Postmodern Theology and the Judgement of the World', from F. Burnham (ed.), *Postmodern Theology* (San Francisco: Harper and Row, 1989), pp. 92–112.

David Tracy, 'The Uneasy Alliance Reconceived: Theological Method, Modernity and Postmodernity', from *Theological Studies* 59 (1989), pp. 548–70.

George A. Lindbeck, 'Toward a Postliberal Theology', from *The Nature of Doctrine: Religion and Theology in a Postliberal Age* (Philadelphia: Westminster Press, 1984), pp. 112–38.

The publishers apologize for any errors or omissions in the above list and would be grateful to be notified of any corrections that should be incorporated in the next edition or reprint of this book.

PART

Introduction

Metaphors for Theology

George P. Schner

1 Metaphors and Margins

Metaphors to be used by

There are two quite different paths of response to the question 'What is Christian theology?' One could describe in precise detail the history of the complex set of human activities and artifacts which would be needed to give actual content to an abstract dictionary definition. It would be like answering the question 'What is life about?' by recounting the contents of one's daily diary. Another kind of answer is given by appealing to a metaphor, an image which gathers up in shorthand fashion all of the factual details, making an empty, general definition concrete in quite a different manner. We are familiar in literature and art with the use of such metaphors when, for example, they tell us 'what life is about' by depicting it as a 'journey along a path', or a 'play upon a stage', or a 'battle for survival'. Of course, such metaphors do not simply sum things up, they also act as *proposals* of how we ought to think about life. In effect, they give guidance about how to order and evaluate a multiplicity of activities and their interrelations.[1]

As is the case with life as a whole, so also with theology: more than one metaphor is possible, though despite their variety these imaginative construals have a resemblance to one another in their use. They all aim at providing a *kind of unity*, and imply an *order and purposefulness* to the web of convictions, the nest of concepts and the flow of argument that make up theological discourse. They also presuppose certain *basic principles*, and imply what sort of person might be the *practitioner* of theology's tasks, as well as presuming a *context* in which the activities would take place and an *audience* to which theological discourse is addressed.

That we are in fact using a metaphor is most obvious to us when the activities in question, in this case the tasks of theology, seem no longer adequately illuminated by an established metaphor.[2] An individual or group begins to speak about what they are doing, to encourage one another, by using a different image (or myth, fable, parable, model) than the received metaphor. As a new construal is used it gradually becomes less odd, more familiar and useful, until it is taken for granted and presumed to be not just one alternative but the only way in which to name properly the activities in question. This collection of essays bears witness to the fact that Christian theologians, in differing ways in their various traditions and cultural locations, are currently aware that various unifying metaphors for their labours are possible, with varying claims on their convictions, activities and results. The two introductory essays are reflections on why this is the contemporary situation, what elements are involved in it, and how an evaluation of possibilities might be made.

Our purpose, then, is neither a description of the activities a theologian happens to engage in, a flowchart of the day's work or a list of rules and resources, nor does it propose a magic solution to theological problems. In fact, it is doubtful whether much of the current discussion about method is actually proposing a way in which, concretely, a theologian ought to function, or whether a prior decision about method actually aids in producing better theology.

The earliest beginnings

The use of metaphors in the earliest Christian writings was at the service of the explication of the 'truths of the faith', God and God's acts, Christ and the church and the Christian way of life. They were used as ways in which to 'carry across' the reality of faith in Christ to believer and unbeliever alike. Rather than retelling the entire story, one could catch up in a single image, most often borrowed from the Hebrew scriptures, the new creation God had made in Christ, locating the new and strange in a familiar context with the use of typology and allegory. Christ is the new Moses, baptism a new Exodus, the Eucharist a new Passover. Similarly, new images had to be crafted to account for the gentiles as fellow heirs, for a circumcision of the heart, and for a transformation of human wisdom that is foolishness. Thus, the scriptures themselves show considerable inventiveness in offering metaphors as bridges between the worlds of both Jew and gentile and the 'new life in Christ'. What little the scriptures say about Christian self-description itself is *embodied with* the general task of character formation, *paideia*,[3] and with efforts to 'account for the hope' that guided Christians, whether as apology or invitation to unbelievers to better understand the Christian way of life.[4]

By way of merely indicating what an assessment of the rich resources available in the earliest Christian literature might contain, let me venture to list certain common characteristics of both Greek and Latin texts across the first five centuries of Christianity. These characteristics, mutually conditioning each other, function together to make the texts what they are, such that it is difficult to list them in any order of priority. The texts in question take very seriously the need to care for the welfare of the Christian community, the probity of its moral and intellectual life, the security of its inner unity and harmony, the safety of its members in face of persecution and false report. We might sum this up as a comprehensive concern to be *pastoral* in a very broad manner.[5] Of equal importance was a maintenance of faithful continuity with the belief of past generations, with what had been 'handed on' by trustworthy teachers, in the form of hymns and prayers, creeds and professions of faith, the example of holy women and men as set down in accounts of their lives, and ultimately in the formulation of rules or precepts, concise statements of various elements of belief expressed in what comes to be considered 'technical' vocabulary. We might sum up this concern as the need to develop and maintain an *orthodox* theology.[6] We can note a consistent concern to speak to and with the regnant political and intellectual powers of the day, to address the 'philosophy and piety' of non-believers, to resist the calumnies of pagan and heretic alike by sound arguments and clear exposition of Christian belief in elegant and persuasive public discourse. From Justin Martyr to Augustine, a common concern weaves its way through early Christian texts, the need to craft *apologetic* discourse.[7]

If there is something in common underlying these characteristics, it is the conviction that the truth of the gospel message – what God has accomplished in Christ and continues to make present through the power of the Holy Spirit – is determinative of both the 'how' and the 'what' of Christian life and discourse. If, without being anachronistic, there can be said to be anything like a 'method' underlying these modes of discourse, it is the double effort, first to develop ways in which to read the New Testament in concert with the Hebrew scriptures, and second, to borrow from the gentile world conventions of speech whose logic and rhetoric could be put at the service of describing and explicating Christian truth, with a complex purpose of pastoral care of the faithful, transmission of the essentials of belief, and public self-defence in face of misunderstanding and persecution.

If one leaves aside those texts which engage in or directly discuss ways in which to interpret the scriptures, there simply are not to be found lengthy discussions about how to proceed in theological discourse, a lack which the modern period will find naive. Origen, in one of the few ancient texts preoccupied with method in some explicit sense, observes:

> Everyone therefore who is desirous of constructing out of the foregoing a connected body of doctrine must use points like these as elementary and foundation principles, in accordance with the commandment which says, 'Enlighten yourselves with the light of knowledge'. Thus by clear and cogent arguments he will discover the truth about each particular point and so will produce, as we have said, a single body of doctrine, with the aid of such illustrations and declarations as he shall find in the holy scriptures and of such conclusions as he shall ascertain to follow logically from them when rightly understood.[8]

Two centuries later, the task of forming a 'connected body of doctrine' was given an extended description at the beginning of the fifth century by Augustine in the four books of his *De Doctrina Christiana*. The fundamental theological task remains the interpretation of scripture, which is to be aided by the study of languages, natural science, history, rhetoric and dialectics, and philosophy. Yet the context in which these labours unfolded had radically changed from the time of Origen to that of Augustine because of two events: the Edict of Tolerance in 311 and the first ecumenical council at Nicaea in 325. Because of the former, the new status of Christianity within the empire allowed (and required) a new interaction of Christianity with the political, literary and philosophical traditions of the culture of the Roman empire, issuing in new possibilities for the style of theological discourse. What is not lost, though inevitably changed, is the foundational role of the interpretation of scripture in the work of theologian and preacher. As to the latter event, with the commencement at Nicaea of the tradition of ecumenical councils and their authoritative discourse, the expansive character of theology in the imperial church is measured now not only by the scripture text first and foremost, but also by conciliar statements and their expositors and defenders who, along with other ancient 'authorities', come to be named the 'Fathers'.

Though the parameters may have been set during the first five centuries, human inventiveness and the changing context of the church generated a rich diversity of discourse, lively controversy arising from the spiritual passions of the times, and technical advancements in language and argument structure in the Middle Ages. The factors which mark the unity of the period include:

1 the addition of six more ecumenical councils, which required a growing sophistication of terminology and argumentation for the exposition of doctrine;

2 the growing divergence of the church into East and West, which resulted in a striking contrast in theological style and content already prefigured in the patristic period;

3 the burgeoning of monasticism in the West, as the locus of education and reform, which provided both the audience and practitioners for theological

discourse, the monastic life being the continuum of unity in theological development despite the shifting fate of the Roman empire;

4 the 'discovery' of Aristotle and his entrance in several phases into theological discourse combined with Christianized Platonism to provide a settled technical vocabulary for theological controversy;

5 the rise of the medieval universities and their master teachers and the grand schemes of the *summae* they produced inaugurated the schools of thought which formed and developed for several centuries.[9]

While the medieval period certainly saw itself in continuity with the basic Christian theology of the first five centuries, and with Augustine most particularly, there grew a preoccupation with speculation and terminological specialization which by the fifteenth century had invented a literature and a form of exposition and argument which seemed distanced from the intent of the early tradition and opened itself to severe criticism on several fronts. An apparent decline in the ecclesial purpose of the scholastic theology of the late Middle Ages was met with a burgeoning enthusiasm for the return to ancient sources through philological research in ancient languages, a renewed interest in Platonic philosophy shorn of its Christian interpretation, and a variety of spiritual and moral reforms both within and outside of established ecclesiastical structures. If the three dynamics of pastoral care, orthodox doctrine and apologetic self-description are indeed three perennial tasks of Christian theology, we might observe that the passage from the late Middle Ages to the Reformation saw, in the Renaissance period and its various forms of humanism and inchoate reformation, innovative efforts to discover new ways to ensure the perdurance of those three aspects.

> To summarize: when we construct the theological history of the Renaissance period, we enter, as it were, into a vast, busy research laboratory in which experiments are carried on and countless results produced, for over a century and a half, by a complex and ambitious project for renewing the tools and methods to be used in bringing the search for the truth back to the main path.[10]

Whether one judges the Reformation as the last moment of that former period of instability or as its resolution, its effects shaped the ground upon which modern theology's preoccupation with methods, norms and sources was formed. The dual emphasis on doctrinal reform (as in Luther) and moral and institutional reform (as in Zwingli) produced the classic theological texts which have given the Reformers their place with the episcopal Fathers and the magisterial Doctors. These innovators, both Catholics and Protestants, through their personal influence and their texts, joined with other elements to bring about not only religious, but also social, culture change, as witnessed by the

◆ 7

many new 'church orders' (*Kirchenordnungen*) in the German states. The introduction of vernacular languages in liturgy and theology, new forms of education (including the founding of seminaries by the Roman church), and the general social upheaval of the period cannot be underestimated as factors influencing the new shape that Western theology was to take. It should be noted, however, that of special importance was the insistence upon the organic unity (somewhat attenuated in late medieval theology) between doctrine and scripture as essential to the efforts to generate the pastoral and moral renewal the church required.[11]

The return to ancient sources, in particular the concern with the original language of the biblical texts in Renaissance humanism, came to fruition in the Protestant Reformation, and was countered by the Roman church's insistence on a revelatory role for tradition independent of scripture. Both emphases would take four centuries to be officially readdressed as ultimately mutually conditioning rather than irreconcilably opposite. In the interval, they ironically opened a space for the development of modern biblical hermeneutics on the one hand, and on the other, for the confidence in, ultimately subservience to, the autonomous rationality of secular natural and human sciences as the sources of true knowledge independent (and corrective of) the scriptures. It is in the areas of theological anthropology and ecclesiology that we would find the changes in doctrine which are generated by, and then come to authorize, these divergent traditions and their contribution to the rise of modernity.

Similarly, the efforts to pass back beyond the seemingly futile argumentation of late scholasticism to the rhetorical power and pastoral appeal of early Christian texts, issued not only in polemical discourse among Protestants themselves, and between Protestants and Catholics, but continually contributed to the rise of evangelical movements dedicated to the reform of both church and society. As in the first centuries of the church, some of these movements attempted reform by removing their members from society at large, creating alternate cultures. Others left behind the specific moral and devotional practices of the church and adopted non-religious principles as more appropriate to the spirit of reform. Thus, the roots of the contemporary abandonment of the political, social and economic realms to secular theory and practice on the one hand, and the desacralization of the church on the other, can be traced to changes in soteriology and sacramental theology beginning in the Reformation.

Staying within the margins

A reading of texts from the first three major periods of Christian history for the purpose of reflection on their 'methods' would show several perduring elements: first, the inseparability in theological discourse of the language of prayer, catechesis and moral encouragement; second, the development of a tradition of explication of the essentials of Christian discourse with a theme of fidelity as precondition for innovation rooted in epistemological convictions concerning the reality of God's agency in Christ, and enduring fidelity of the Spirit for the church; and third, the dialogue with and use of the available modes of reflection and argument, chiefly classical philosophy and rhetoric, which enabled theologians to describe, defend and promote the Christian way of life in diverse cultural contexts. To these three factors there is an obvious fourth which must be added. Despite the major moments of change in theology's own self-conception, patristic, medieval and Reformation theology all considered themselves as *marginal notes*, a metaphor of primary importance in relation to all others.

The metaphor is apt for three reasons. First, those who practised the craft of theology saw their work as some form of *commentary on the scriptures*. Theology does not simply quote scripture, but represents its content, reflects upon its significance, is engaged in discovering and elaborating its meaning, through *meditation on, explication of, and application of* the biblical text. Theology was thus *only* marginal notes, not essentially a system which stood on its own, generating its own life and movement. That is not to say that theological discourse was not an independent *tradition*, a freestanding *dialectic* of positions, a recognizable mode of discourse with an internal grammar and logic. However, it is striking to note, for example, that to graduate from Oxford with a teaching degree in theology in the thirteenth century one had to be prepared not only to comment on the doctrinal areas of theology but equally to interpret the books of the Bible, thereby modelling in an educational context the unity of theological discourse. The same could be said of most of the patristic authors (e.g. Origen and Augustine, with their extensive commentaries as well as apologetic and doctrinal studies) and of the Reformers as well (e.g. Luther and Calvin).

A second reason for the aptness of the metaphor, 'marginal notes', is theology's position not at the centre of church life, but at its margins. Theologians understood themselves to be engaged in an activity neither isolated from nor identical with the heart of Christian life, but at its service. Living at the margins meant that some theologians slipped imperceptibly outside the bounds of the community, and others slipped imperceptibly into the heart of the community, gradually being accorded a status of importance as *authorities*, as much because of their saintly lives as their texts. This marginality also meant that the double activity of incorporating modes of thinking and speaking from the culture and holding fast to, even defending, the particularity of the Christian way of living, especially its language, in the face of the unbeliever or the heretic, required a broad knowledge of human wisdom, a life of prayer and worship, and a familiarity with the living tradition of the church, which combined to give the theologian credibility both within and beyond the church.

The third and most obvious way in which theology can be construed as 'marginal notes' is in its concrete manifestation as *text*, with the term taken both literally to mean *written text* and metaphorically to mean *thought, speech and enactment as text*. Within that general characterization it is noteworthy to consider the passage of theology as text from the form of letters, sermons and exhortations addressed to a specific *audience*, to the form of commentaries and treatises on focused subjects, to compilations of opinions (e.g. the *Sentences* of Peter Lombard) and their systematic exposition as in the great *summae* of the Middle Ages. The Reformers continue to engage in all these various forms of theological writing. Only gradually will the separation of biblical, doctrinal, historical and pastoral theology come about, with the ultimate isolation of biblical study from the rest and the emergence of philosophical principles and argument as central to systematic theology.

To propose the metaphor of 'marginal notes' as an all-encompassing image for some sixteen centuries of texts is obviously to privilege the role of the scriptures in an account of the history of the inner life of the church and its relations with its various host cultures. In the second half of the twentieth century, other vitally important perspectival investigations, such as feminist, liberationist, and post-colonialist theologies, have alerted us to formerly unseen thematic commitments entrenched in post-Reformation European theology which dictate matters of method and embody forms of unchristian deafness, blindness, and insensitivity.[12] They reread the Christian tradition for evidence of two things: first, the 'eclipse' of vital elements which can be, with difficulty, recovered, and second, the resources within and beyond Christianity with which to address that eclipse. Similarly, the collection of essays in this volume is concerned with the double 'eclipse' of doctrine and scripture.[13] The modern period developed and then made obligatory two convictions: method for theology could (and should) be doctrinally neutral, and the scriptures, if used at all, are not the primary determining element of theological discourse, either as to form or content. It took several centuries for the Christian story, and hence the Bible, to be displaced by other overarching metaphors as the architectonic metaphor by means of which human lives and natural events could discover their meaning and purpose.

2   Maps, Models and Machines

Maps, models and machines have existed for a long time in human cultures, but it can safely be said that Western culture began to change radically when they were adopted as leading metaphors (and effective devices) in rethinking the meaning of that complex of human beings, world and God which Western thought has termed *reality*. There is much contemporary investigation trying to sort out the origins of modernity in late medieval nominalism, in Renaissance humanism, and in the initial rise of the new scientific way of thinking with its modern form of mechanism.[14] Gradual changes in the notion of the self and its use of language, the social fabric and its modes of traditioning, and the cosmos as object of human investigation and manipulation progressively reshaped the common sense of Western culture such that Christianity, in its practice and self-description, was required to take on correspondingly new forms. Modernity has redefined the grounds and the context for Christianity's own self-description.[15] As certain notions long taken for granted by Christianity, such as the knowability of God through revelation, the limitation of human knowledge and freedom due to sin, and the rule of God's providence and grace in the world, are shown to be incompatible with modern notions of reality, theology has the choice either to appear irrational or to accommodate itself to the new rules and limits of modern rationality. In either case, it is ironic that Christian believers themselves in developing such new self-descriptions aided in the invention of modernity and its particular form of atheism.[16] The new leading metaphors of map, model and machine require theology to become preoccupied with the typical activities of modernity – construction, accommodation and projection.[17]

If we take the term *map* as a broad notion, not simply as a representation but as a tool for further action, many kinds of maps make their appearance at the beginning of the modern era. A map for time becomes available with household clocks in the fifteenth century and watches in the sixteenth century. Maps for exploration become significantly more accurate with the invention of tools for surveying and especially with the technique of Mercator projection (an accuracy achieved, albeit, at the price of Eurocentrism). Maps of the sky, dependent upon the use of the telescope and on mathematical 'mapping' of orbits, decisively alter our sense of the size and location of our 'world', the earth. The work of Vesalius, also in the sixteenth century, provides the first modern map of the human anatomy, an important foundation of modern medicine and surgery. In the eighteenth century the philosopher Immanuel Kant offers a map of the human intellect which, he claimed, would finally give philosophy the kind of certainty and basis for genuine progress that the sciences then enjoyed.

If maps purport to offer an accurate representation of that to which they correspond, making new discovery possible, then the term *model* sums up the importance to the modern era of instruments and experiments for the same purpose. By employing devices which amplify or alter our (now necessarily called 'naive') unaided sense perceptions, telescopes and microscopes, and any number of such tools, provide powerful means for isolating and identifying the elements of the material world. With such instruments scientists began to create controlled situations in which natural material processes could be examined. Laboratories and experiments produced results which required the 'ancients' to be replaced by the 'moderns' (e.g. Aristotle gives way to Newton), redefined the nature of knowledge itself (e.g. Descartes' insistence on the 'clear and distinct'), and relocated the dynamism of nature in elements and locomotion, rather than in principles and causality.[18]

Finally, modern *machines* replace the activities of home workshops and guilds, producing what we now call 'handicrafts', with the production of completely replicable, reliable and ever improving artifacts. As did maps and models, so also do machines alter the rhythm and preoccupations of human life in Western civilization, shaping a new notion of ordinary life and its expectations. Whether it be plants or animals, the human body, the world itself, or even the cosmos, every material thing could be imagined to be a machine and explored and used in accordance with this metaphor. With the founding of the modern university at the beginning of the nineteenth century, education at its highest level took on the new goals of research and 'advancement' of knowledge, as centres of 'experimentation' with the aim of producing ever better maps for reality and all its parts. At the end of the twentieth century, there was an ever increasing layer of 'machines', technology in the modern sense, between human beings and the natural world. Theology, like most of the so-called humanities, has difficulty surviving in this environment, and risks its very identity in trying to fashion a 'machine' to ensure its productivity and usefulness.

Needless to say there were maps, models and machines in former ages and in other cultures. At a time of serious reconsideration of the entire project of modernity, we must resist two extremes of reaction: neither can we simply vilify the way of life we have inherited without appreciating the benefits which modern technology has brought us, nor can we idealize past ages to the neglect of the genuine wisdom that modernity has brought. However, modernity's mythology encourages us to put ultimate trust in *discovery*, *invention* and *novelty*, with supreme confidence in *technique* of a mechanical sort.

3 Theology as Construction

There can be little doubt that theology is a work of human inventiveness and as such deserves the qualifying adjective *constructed*. That this characteristic should be taken as the leading or chief quality of theology, naming its essential activities and identity, is a proposal grounded in the modern period, in keeping with modernity's preference for construction or projection as the paradigm for all forms of knowledge.[19] The contrast with the early history of theology becomes clear if we contrast the terms 'invention' and 'constructive' with the terms 'tradition' and 'habitual'. In contemporary parlance the former pair tends to be terms of approval, while the latter tends toward a pejorative usage.

Trusting in a received tradition, depending upon an acquired habit, preferring continuity to novelty, lends itself to our becoming ineffective and inattentive, to privileging the past. Trying to be inventive and constructive necessitates attending to circumstances, being purposefully useful or functional, privileging the future.[20] In fact continuity and change require each other: change comes about only in an already established context, and continuity is possible only because of continuous adaptation.

However, the rhetorical appeal of this model is based on the attractiveness of constructive, inventive thinking and the perceived unsuitableness of settled, habitual thinking. This appeal is now part of our common sense in Western civilization, but had to be acquired through the confrontation between the established world of discourse and practice in church and academy, and the 'novelties' of experimentation and the 'new' science of the early modern period. It now seems self-evident that confidence in the conserving character of tradition tends to make us naive, simple-minded or mentally lazy, and that to be sophisticated requires us to leave behind merely polemical argumentation, to adopt rigorous detached invention, and to subject every new invention to further critical scrutiny. To put everything to the test, thereby avoiding what is arbitrary, idiosyncratic, biased or prejudiced, may not preserve any given element of the present, but it will encourage the development of an analytic, self-conscious and deliberate person.

The responsibility of criticism

The announcement of the superiority of construction invites practitioners to become committed to being *critical*, a peculiarly modern theological virtue. The paradigm of this appeal can be seen in the philosophical programme of Immanuel Kant and those who follow his inspiration.[21] One needs only to consult the preface to the first edition of the *Critique of Pure Reason* to discover, somewhat to the dismay of those who have actually read all three *Critiques*, the simplicity of Kant's project:

> Our age is, in especial degree, the age of criticism, and to criticism everything must submit. Religion through its sanctity, and law-giving through its majesty, may seek to exempt themselves from it. But they then awaken just suspicion, and cannot claim the sincere respect which reason accords only to that which has been able to sustain the test of free and open examination.[22]

From the preface to his *Critique of Pure Reason* through to *Religion Within the Limits of Reason Alone*, as the latter title indicates, Kant does not dismiss religious faith, but seeks to purify it for its own benefit by means of rules for discourse and life which he considers to be universal and unquestionable. He searches for them in three successive investigations of the operation of rationality in its various aspects, discovering the principles which ground all knowledge and action (*transcendental* conditions, in his technical vocabulary), as well as the limits prescribed for human endeavours given these irrefragable conditions. The simplicity and innovative character of Kant's project lies, first, in his intention not to offer a 'critique of books and systems but of the faculty of reason in general, in respect of all knowledge after which it may strive *independently of all experience*'.[23] This procedure is different, it should be noted, from the labour of Platonic dialogue or the Aristotelian consultation of the tradition, though not entirely dissonant with classical notions of *mimesis* or *noesis*. Perhaps more importantly, it is a philosophical activity quite unlike the medieval conversation with the 'tradition', texts received as authoritative in multiple ways.

Kant's critique is dependent upon a reversal of expectations concerning how we are to satisfy the rational demand for the *unconditioned*:

> If, then, on the supposition that our empirical knowledge conforms to objects as things in themselves, we find that the unconditioned *cannot be thought without contradiction*, and that when, on the other hand, we suppose that our representation of things, as they are given to us, does not conform to these things as they are in themselves, but that these objects as appearances, conform to our mode of representation, *the contradiction vanishes* . . .[24]

Such a theory of knowledge may seem, Kant admits, to be negative in its effect, inasmuch as it limits speculative reason to the bounds of experience, and thereby denies that there is knowledge of the ultimate principles of reality, such as the dogmatic metaphysicians of his day claimed. He asserts, however, that these two limitations actually achieve two positive results. The first is to relocate the search for such ultimate principles in the sphere of the practical employment of pure reason in which they can be properly thought; the second is to root out an entire range of 'tendencies of a scandalous sort' which eventually

> break out even among the masses, as the result of the disputes in which metaphysicians (and, as such, finally also the clergy) inevitably become involved to the consequent perversion of their teaching. Criticism alone can sever the root of *materialism, fatalism, atheism, free-thinking, fanaticism*, and *superstition*, which can be injurious universally; as well as of *idealism* and *scepticism*, which are dangerous chiefly to the Schools, and hardly allow of being handed on to the public.[25]

Particularly in the preface to the second edition, it is poignant to note the tone of genuine concern for society and culture at large which situates the highly technical philosophical text which follows, and poignant as well to note that either Kant's admonitions have not been fully observed or, if they have been, have failed to fulfil his own hopes to prevent those 'tendencies of a scandalous sort'. In fact, the irony of Western culture as we know it at the beginning of the twenty-first century is to have established materialism, fatalism, atheism, free-thinking, fanaticism and scepticism as varieties of common sense. And, if one considers certain possibilities for the combination of idealism and superstition, one can find these tendencies established as well. By his own stated intentions, then, we must judge Kant's project to have failed, at least for culture at large, if not for philosophers who still engage in a 'critique' of reason, whether pure, practical or aesthetic.

This eighteenth-century commitment to critique transformed tolerant Renaissance scepticism and the Reformation's zeal for renewal into an equally zealous insistence on rational certainty and proof modelled on mathematics, and geometry in particular because of its obviously 'constructive' character. In settled times the inquiring mind can tolerate diversity, the play of sceptical doubt and the heated rhetoric of religious fervour. But in the social and religious upheaval of the seventeenth century, epitomized by the Thirty Years' War, European society saw much to be gained from Descartes' promise of a 'universal mathematics' (i.e. method of learning), or by the invention of Leibniz's 'universal language' which would guarantee accurate and harmonious communication. Similarly, there was much to recommend Kant's claims to establish, once for all, the firm foundations for all forms of knowledge. Such certainty and security were to be bought at the price of a separation of mind from body, individual from society, humanity from nature, and eventually cosmos from God. Of course, there were always alternate views to the dominance of methodical rationalism, and it is not surprising, for example, that the scepticism of David Hume, which is more akin to that of Montaigne than to the hyperbolic doubt of Descartes, was a primary target of Kant's project of 'pure reason'.[26]

As to the task of philosophically rigorous theology, what is at stake is not the mere criticism of this or that practice or belief of a given religion. Modern criticism, having invented the general category *religion,* is committed to a thoroughgoing critique of religion in general, carried out by an independent application of rationality. It proceeds successively to eliminate those doctrines and practices which it considers superstitious and inappropriate for any religion (in the eighteenth-century Enlightenment), to redefine religion as human invention best understood as a phenomenon attributable to a particular aspect of human nature (in the nineteenth century), and to construct alternate ideologies which displace historical religions with mythologies and socio-political structures for the shaping of entire cultures (in the twentieth century).

More recently, even though confidence in a sophisticated, self-conscious and deliberately critical rational self has been overthrown by the continual application of this critical self against itself, the basic logic of Christian theology is proposed as construction in the form of seemingly contradictory activities such as *deconstruction, ideology critique* and *perspectival theologies*, all of which effects recontextualization of rationality in human bodies and in concrete societies with specialized interests. Thus, depending upon how severe the critique must be, the theologian has a range of options: completely raze to the ground the habits, traditions and texts of Christianity and then construct an entirely new discourse and practice, at one extreme, through various degrees of suspicion and criticism which leave something of the tradition to use, to the other extreme of critique which actually returns the theologian to mine the tradition as received.

Construction as *radical inventiveness* tends to give a very strong meaning to the term *creative*. As a word formerly reserved to speak of God's activity alone, it is only in the middle of the sixteenth century that we find an author such as Tasso able to speak of two creators, God and the poet. Nevertheless, human construction as creativity cannot be radical in the sense of 'creation out of nothing'. In its origins, it did require a radical construction of a kind, namely the proposal of a way in which we ought to think about thinking. The ultimate foundation is the method itself: the free, inquiring mind is the self-establishing principle. Thus, when contemporary theology accepts the agenda of modern rationality, it must submit all its taken-for-granted principles, sources and procedures to rigorous scrutiny, and will be found seriously wanting. What was formerly foundational to theology – faith and devotion, revelation and grace, sin and judgement, tradition and scripture, prayer and the reading of scripture – must give way to more *transcendental* foundations upon which such intra-systematic realities will be judged for their adequacy in the work of construction.

The search for foundations

Depending upon the degree to which criticism calls into question or renders unavailable various texts, practices or even experiences of the Christian, the search for new *foundations* becomes an essential part of theology as construction. This search presumes that the matrix of worship, doctrine and creeds, and the traditional moral practices and institutions of the church can no longer provide satisfactory content and rules for both first and second order discourse about God (the language of worship and theology). This conviction depends upon the notion of the independent, rational subject who takes reality as subject to its construction and control (as 'object'), with a coincident suspicion of established patterns of thought and action, and an eclipse of the possibility of God's agency within history. This reconception of who a human subject is, as autonomous, of who God is, as utterly transcendent and increasingly not a Trinity of persons who act, and of the world as an object of human manipulation, imports into the method of construction presuppositions which displace basic Christian doctrines.

Three foundations must therefore be set aside if one is to abide by the requirements of radical construction, since they cannot satisfy the criteria of intellectual authenticity (various forms of rational certainty and similar criteria) and public accountability: (1) revelation (as the 'acts of God'); (2) tradition (as the special efficacy of a religion's language or practice); and (3) religious experience (as the 'presence' of God). In some respects we might call this a thoroughgoing hermeneutics of suspicion, applied to the three locales of a religion's reflection and action: the world of nature, the world of culture, and human interiority. All three refusals have their classic articulation in the four *Observations* which Kant appends to the chapters of *Religion Within the Limits of Reason Alone*. That text is essentially a revised dogmatic theology which translates Christian doctrine into philosophically acceptable terms, chiefly into moral concepts in keeping with Kant's location of religion within the realm of practical reason. The fourth foundation which Kant cannot dismiss entirely, but for which he must propose rules for reinterpretation, are the scriptures.

As we have seen, his argument against the traditional foundations of Christian faith is not bought at the price of abandoning Christianity's commitment to counteract the philosophical dangers of fatalism, naturalism and materialism.[27] Such views of reality, however, result not from a lack of religion, but from the improper use of human reason in its attempt to know what must remain merely limit concepts without hope of being given content from experience. The role of religion in preventing these ultimately irrational theories and their corresponding practices is obscured by religion's investment in claiming forms of knowledge and human agency which divert its attention from sound moral principles, and discredit the believer. The list of religious dangers is as follows:

> (1) [corresponding] to imagined experience (works of grace), [the consequence is] *fanaticism*; (2) to alleged external experience (miracles), *superstition*; (3) to a supposed enlightening of the understanding with regard to the supernatural (mysteries), *illumination*, the illusion of the 'adepts'; (4) to hazardous attempts to operate upon the supernatural (means of grace), *thaumaturgy* – sheer aberrations of a reason going beyond its proper limits and that too for a purpose fancied to be moral (pleasing to God).[28]

It is surely self-evident to contemporary Christians that there are no events, either internal to consciousness or external to it, to which they can point unequivocally as *revelation*, albeit there continue to be reports of miraculous visions and cures, voices heard or strange events of various kinds. It is a common-sense notion that claims to having experienced such things are to be suspected as illusory and subject to scientific inquiry. Our universe is closed to intrusions by the transcendent, and our minds are similarly closed, though inevitably active in producing illusions of the transcendent. Faith, as an interpretation of events and experiences, is subordinate to the natural and human sciences as superior forms of interpretation.[29]

The term 'God' should be recognized for what it is, a 'limit-concept' (a 'regulative' idea in Kant's technical terminology), which marks the end of rational thinking. It cannot be supplied with any content from experience, and hence remains an empty concept without theoretical use. It can, and indeed must, be used by practical reason, though precisely as a hypothesis, that there is a *moral author* of the world who will ensure the proper fulfilment of our moral striving.[30] To preserve a notion of God with neither the necessity of a confession of faith dependent on a community of belief and its tradition, nor the appeal to extraordinary experience of a private sort, Kant has to redefine the nature of *faith* in this 'God':

> Faith (as *habitus* not *actus*) is the moral attitude of reason as to belief in that which is unattainable by theoretical cognition. It is therefore the permanent principle of the mind to assume as true, on account of the obligation in reference to it, that which is necessary to presuppose as condition of the possibility of the highest moral final purpose, although its possibility or impossibility be alike impossible for us to see into. Faith (absolutely so called) is trust in the attainment of a design, the promotion of which is a duty, but the possibility of the fulfilment of which (and consequently also that of the only conditions of it thinkable by us) is not to be comprehended by us. Faith, then, that refers to particular objects which are not objects of possible knowledge or opinion (in which latter case it ought to be called, especially in historical matters, credulity and not faith) is quite moral.[31]

Revelation might be an 'event' of the past, though resulting from erroneous pre-critical interpretation, and there might even be a tradition of belief and practice extending from such presumed, but false, knowledge. The free, responsible and rational human being cannot, however, put any trust in such claims. Recovering revelation as a viable foundation requires accepting this critique, not because it exposes the concept for what it is, a construction, but because the notion of revelation never did have a simple correspondence to 'divine acts', nor did it enter as a moment in an argument for or against religion.

A second foundation which radical construction cannot accept is the received discourse and practice of a given religion as an efficacious tradition. This seems to follow easily from the rejection of the first foundation, revelation. If there is no 'event' which can in any truthful sense be called an 'act of God', then any tradition of discourse which claims to speak about such a reality must be set aside completely, or at least tested carefully for what can be salvaged on other grounds and for other purposes. There are three aspects to this refusal of a foundation in any form of historical tradition. First, there is the temporal problem of never being able to pass from the present to the past except by means of an imaginative reconstruction (never truly possessing first-hand reports), and always with questions about the evidence for and probability of supposed factual accounts (never truly trusting second-hand reports). Second, there is the metaphysical problem that even if one could locate trustworthy historical accounts (and hence 'facts'), they would neither be able to bear the weight of religious claims nor support the qualities of universality and definitiveness which philosophically rigorous religion demands. In the case of Christianity, they cannot adequately support the christological claim of definitive revelation of God in Jesus. Third, there is an existential problem: if there are no revelational events, and no trustworthy or adequate tradition of confessing them to be true and efficacious, to what would believers in the present age commit themselves other than to their interior conviction without any particular content? At best, they would give free consent to an ideal notion, such as 'salvation', and proceed to give content, or expression, to that conviction according to their own 'imaginative' constructions.[32]

Kant sums up the matter:

> Since, after all, *revelation* can certainly embrace the pure religion of reason, while, conversely, the second cannot include what is historical in the first, I shall be able [experimentally] to regard the first as the *wider* sphere of faith, which includes within itself the second, as a *narrower* one (not like two circles external to one another, but like concentric circles). The philosopher, as a teacher of pure reason (from unassisted principles *a priori*), must confine himself within the narrower circle, and in so doing, must waive consideration of all experience. From this standpoint I can also make a second experiment, namely, to start from some alleged revelation or other and, leaving out of consideration the pure religion of reason (so far as it constitutes a self-sufficient system), to examine in a fragmentary manner this revelation, as an *historical system*, in the light of moral concepts; and then to see whether it does not lead back to the very same pure *rational system* of religion.[33]

The rule for all matters concerning the use of determinate examples (stated in somewhat technical terms, following Kant's theory of knowledge)[34] is simple: for the purpose of aiding our adherence to the call of duty, we may employ 'fictions' of various sorts, stories of godly persons who will inspire us, but we must never acknowledge such fictions as real or efficacious on our behalf.

> We must always resort to some analogy to natural existences to render supersensible qualities intelligible to ourselves. . . . The scriptures too accommo-

date themselves to this mode of representation when, in order to make us comprehend the degree of God's love for the human race, they ascribe to Him the very highest sacrifice which a loving being can make . . . though we cannot indeed rationally conceive how an all-sufficient Being could sacrifice a part of what belongs to His state of bliss or rob Himself of a possession. Such is the *schematism of analogy*, with which (as a means of explanation) we cannot dispense. But to transform it into a *schematism of objective determination* (for the extension of our knowledge) is *anthropomorphism*, which has, from the moral point of view (in religion), most injurious consequences.[35]

Kant is never quite able to dispense with Christ, or the scriptures, as modernity will be able to do in the later nineteenth century. As early as the first *Critique*, he acknowledges a certain tendency in humanity which produces a knowledge of God in the form of an 'as if':

For the same reasons, in thinking the cause of the world, we are justified in representing it in our idea not only in terms of a certain subtle anthropomorphism (without which we could not think anything whatsoever in regard to it), namely, as a being that has understanding, feelings of pleasure and displeasure, and desires and volitions corresponding to these, but also in ascribing to it a perfection which, as infinite, far transcends any perfection that our empirical knowledge of the order of the world can justify us in attributing to it.[36]

However, while the passage from projection to fact, from hypostatization to personification, is a progression we are tempted to follow, as we confuse the necessity of a concept of reason with an actual entity in the field of possible experience, it is also a move which always remains forbidden to us.

The third foundation which radical construction cannot accept is an appeal to religious experience. The whole of Kant's *Critique of Pure Reason* is an extended argument against any access to reality other than through the intuitive material provided by the senses, structured by the internal forms of such intuition into experience, and unified by the categories of the understanding into knowledge. Even if there were historical revelation of the transcendent, the human self could not know it. Along with the first *Critique*, both the *Critique of Practical Reason* and the *Critique of Judgment* permit an 'idea' of God, and a 'hypothesis' of a moral, teleological unity constituting the ultimate ground of all reality. But in all three works, such an idea remains just that, an immanent, empty limit of thought. Any characteristics we predicate of the term 'god' are derived from the requirements of the human project, and it will not be long in the history of Western thought until the evident remnants of Christianity still lodged in Kant's philosophy are challenged. From the side of both subject and object, then, there is neither the capacity for nor the possibility of something like religious experience.

Though we have discussed the refusal of three foundations for theology separately, it should be clear that they comprise a single, unified stance:

> Whoever would derive the concepts of virtue from experience and make (as many have actually done) what at best can only serve as an example in an imperfect kind of exposition, into a pattern from which to derive knowledge, would make of virtue something which changes according to time and circumstances, an ambiguous monstrosity not admitting of the formation of any rule. On the contrary, as we are well aware, if anyone is held up as a pattern of virtue, the true original with which we compare the alleged pattern and by which alone we judge of its value is to be found only in our minds.[37]

The foundational function of revelation, tradition and religious experience is displaced by the foundational character of a prescriptive theory of human cognition and volition which by definition cannot admit the recognizable presence of the transcendent in the world, in human culture, in human interiority, a presence which might exercise a determinative influence on human discourse and action. Human freedom and imagination, as two aspects of human self-transcendence, come to function as surrogates for the transcendent itself. In sum, construction as radical invention sets aside the receptive and the habitual in the Christian way of life, whether understood as faith, as tradition or as experience. Thus, the fundamental distinction which marks this construal of theology as construction is the contrast between theology as grounded in *faith as trust* (the Christian self and community as gift from God) and theology as grounded in human reflection, *faith as criticism and invention* (self and community as self-determining). In the extreme, the theologian takes the stance of modernity as unquestionably correct: either there is no transcendent, or if there is, it cannot enter into our reality; and if it can and does we are unable to know or feel it; more importantly, what we know or feel could not possibly bear the weight of the absolute claims which a religion makes. Thus, even if we do experience the transcendent, we are unable to find words to speak of it. One is reminded of the simple but all-encompassing philosophical system of the Greek Sophist Gorgias. Inasmuch as any kind of religion does continue to exist it is because we human beings continue to invent it.

The use of the imagination

The Enlightenment did not propose a privileged use of the imagination, though Kant did account for its function in his revision of scholastic epistemology, following the traditional distinction between reproductive and inventive imagination, giving a vital role to the former in the construction of knowledge, while consistently cautioning against the use of the latter, particularly in matters of religion.[38] Thus, contemporary 'constructive' theologies owe their specification of a prominent role for the imagination chiefly to subsequent developments in nineteenth-century thought.[39] Importantly, the appeal to the imagination (or later to 'experience') is accompanied by a corresponding neglect of the role of 'memory', or its relegation to the role of an impediment which obscures.

Kant did not want to produce a theology independent either of the cognitive limitations demanded by the principles of natural science or the personal integrity demanded by moral principles. Yet he appears loathe to dispense with the disclosive power of the story of Jesus as an example which sometimes seems to instantiate the 'archetype' of the 'truly godly' person resident in us, and likewise he permits, indeed requires, the projection of the characteristics of an agent upon the ultimate principle of reality. This projection is hypothetical, telling us more about our own desires than about God. The accounts of an archetypically 'godly man' yield no extension of our knowledge: they always remain merely allegories at best. In the first *Critique* Kant's caution is clear:

> Although we cannot concede to these ideals objective reality (existence), they are not therefore to be regarded as figments of the brain; they supply reason with a standard which is indispensable to it. . . . But to attempt to realize the ideal in an example, that is in the [field] of appearance, as, for instance, to depict the [character of the perfectly] wise man in a romance, is impracticable. There is indeed something absurd, and far from edifying, in such an attempt, inasmuch as the natural limitations, which are constantly doing violence to the completeness of the idea, make the illusion that is aimed at altogether impossible, and so cast suspicion on the good itself – the good that has its source in the idea – by giving it the air of being a mere fiction.[40]

The remnants of a Christian doctrine of God as judge gradually give way to the 'hypothesis' of some form of ultimacy which relativizes all efforts to construct meaning, yet which must remain self-effacing despite its totalizing claims. To return to the quotation from the second preface of Kant's first *Critique*, instead of materialism, fatalism and atheism, now we must insert such vital criticisms of Western culture, if not of all the world's cultures, such as the 'errors' of sexism, colonialism, rationalism and nihilism. Perhaps the only 'error' which is not to be undone is that of 'historicism'. If all symbolic discourse and reflective distance are dependent on the human invention of a congeries of ideal reader, ideal world, ideal agent and ideal social order, then it becomes impossible ever to establish any absolute claims which authorize both judgement and action. The *a priori* disqualification of any manifestation of the transcendent and the displacement of the making of meaning into the human subject ironically names a world in which culture itself becomes increasingly endangered. The very goal of constructive theology, to relativize and humanize our world (to remedy our 'culture'), is rendered impossible. Louis Dupré explores this irony in a short work, *Metaphysics and Culture*, a valuable introduction to his more complete exploration in *Passage to Modernity*.[41] He asks: is the restoration of transcendence at the heart of culture itself possible in the present conditions? A hermeneutics of culture or a congeries of diverse sciences each proposing a possible unity cannot restore to culture the unity and certainty needed for it to flourish.[42]

Construction and the scriptures

Theology as *radical* construction requires that one set aside the view that scripture texts are authoritative in any sense, and instead subject them to the same critique as revelation, tradition and religious experience. If they are used in the reconstruction of a notion of God, they must be used with caution and no special status. Idolatry is always a possibility, ironically so for a conception of theology that is committed to 'constructing' God. Feuerbach, for example, warns that to the extent that we fail to recognize the concept of 'God' as our own construction, it becomes idolatrous. The criteria for idolatry will shift, as the proposals for rules of criticism, new foundations and valorization of imaginative constructs shift and change. Put simply, the rules for the use of the scriptures are to be derived neither from the texts themselves, nor from the community which habitually uses them as a rule for life, nor from their status as the word of God revealing the transcendent. The texts must be 'decoded', a process which must take place in a location other than the church (whether that new place is considered 'neutral' or 'invested'), and then put to use for a stated moral purpose. Once again it is instructive to consider Kant's suggestions, this time about biblical interpretation, as paradigmatic.[43]

Like the law of the land for lawyers or government guidelines for medical doctors, so the Bible is a canon which guides the clergy. As such it is an organon to rule the church, and also a vehicle which enshrines ecclesiastical faith. The role of critical thinking in the university is to deny to the Bible the magical power which the public tends to attribute to it superstitiously, or to any of the texts, teachings or practices of the 'businessmen' of law, medicine and theology. Kant is generous in permitting the existence of ruled activities in those three spheres of public order as exercised by those mandated to follow such internal principles, but it is clear that a fourth sphere, that of the scholar, has the vocation of purifying the other three. He articulates four rules which are to govern that task of interpretation, and the first encompasses the rest: if a scriptural text contains any claims to *theoretical* knowledge of the transcendent, it may be reinterpreted according to the rules of practical reason, though in no case may it be allowed to contradict practical reason. Thus, for example, the doctrines of Trinity, incarnation, the resurrection and the Lord's Supper are to be so reinterpreted. In a manner reminiscent of patristic efforts at codifying principles for good interpretation of the scriptures (e.g. Augustine in *On Christian Doctrine*, Book Three), Kant is proposing a way to deal 'rationally' with troublesome doctrines and difficult passages. Unlike patristic, medieval or Reformation commentators, he does not, and cannot, appeal to the normativity of God in Christ, the church and its tradition, or the guiding presence of the Holy Spirit. Rather:

> When we are dealing with religion, where the faith instilled by reason with regard to the practical is sufficient to itself, why should we get entangled in all these learned investigations and disputes because of a historical narrative that should always be left in its proper place (among matters that are indifferent)?[44]

If the text makes claims for certain doctrines as 'revealed' we are to remember that faith in such doctrines is of no help towards salvation, our own efforts being all that is necessary. Further, no supplement to our human efforts by way of an external, supernatural cause can be presumed in our explanation, or counted on as incentive to moral behaviour. And finally, if our own efforts and their results do not seem adequate to the demands of our own conscience, we may suppose our efforts to be ultimately justified and fulfilled, though in a manner entirely unknown to us. Kant appeals to the text of the Bible itself to authenticate his rules:

> Even the Bible seems to have nothing else in view: it seems to refer, not to supernatural experiences and fantastic feelings which should take reason's place in bringing about this revolution, but to the spirit of Christ, which he manifested in teachings and examples so that we might make it our own – or rather, since it is already present in us by our moral predisposition, so that we might still make room for it. And so, between *orthodoxy* which has no soul and *mysticism* which kills reason, there is the teaching of the Bible, a faith which our reason can develop out of itself. This teaching is the true religious doctrine, based on the *criticism* of practical reason, that works with divine power on all men's hearts toward their fundamental improvement and unites them in one universal (though invisible) church.[45]

Kant clearly had confidence that critical examination by way of historical study would not endanger the status of the Bible in Christian life, but rather would establish it on firmer grounds. Thus he distinguished among literal interpretation, done by biblical theologians for pragmatic purposes, moral interpretation according to reason, for the betterment of humanity, and interpretation for the purpose of generating church dogma unnecessary to salvation (in contrast to authentic doctrinal interpretation which leads to rational religion).[46]

4   Theology as Imitation

Beyond Kant by means of Kant

Kant's philosophical limitation of Christian belief and thoroughgoing revision of Christian doctrine and rules for scriptural interpretation were neither accepted as definitive nor left unchallenged. It is ironic that his apodictic proposal for a salutary limitation of faith by means of a philosophical anthropology generated vigorous defences of religious faith which proposed alternate philosophical anthropologies, in effect, alternate construals of the nature of modernity. The metaphors of conversation and expression are two lasting alternatives as proposed by Hegel and Schleiermacher. Chronologically they follow immediately upon Kant's work, and engage it directly.

It may seem odd, then, that I pass over five decades of tremendous intellectual and cultural ferment in Europe to consider the work of Kierkegaard. It is exactly fifty years after the publication of *Religion Within the Limits of Reason Alone* that Kierkegaard inaugurates an authorship as daunting and powerful as any of the great philosopher–theologians in the interim.[47] Much of his writing addresses the inadequacies of both Hegel's and Schleiermacher's own proposals. It has, however, been provocatively argued that there remains an indebtedness to, or at least a hidden conversation with, Kant in Kierkegaard's works.[48] Whether that argument can be sustained or not, it seems evident that Kierkegaard greets the challenge of Kant's reformulation of Christianity on the very grounds of that redefinition. He argues for an understanding of Christianity as practical, not chiefly theoretical; he vigorously supports the self-limitation of rationality as one of theology's chief duties; and he links the limitations of human agency with the necessary move to religious faith. In all three aspects he is like, yet vastly unlike, Kant.

The metaphor of imitation, in its extreme, advocates a segregation of Christianity from modernity for the sake of survival as evidenced in proposals labelled 'Wittgensteinian fideism', which emphasize the non-translatable (possibly unintelligible) character of religious discourse and its embeddedness in practice.[49] However, neither Kierkegaard nor Wittgenstein literally proposed a segregation of Christianity from culture based upon a theory of its irrationality or merely pragmatic character. It is only when the intent of the metaphor of imitation becomes an appeal for mere repetition, 'mindless' repetition, that the internal authenticity of Christian belief is endangered, as is evangelization and apologetics. Before abandoning theology altogether and advocating the existence of only one level of Christian discourse, that of prayer, worship and confession, and relegating Christian practice to the realm of the idiosyncratic,

25

another form of repetition must be considered. In a manner reminiscent of pre-modern conceptions of Christianity, Kierkegaard proposes to rediscover Christianity as something 'lived through' in order to be understood, and the self within Christianity as possessing an inner transcending receptivity upon which all agency must rest.

The limits of rationality

In response to Kant, the metaphor of imitation proposes that philosophy can neither dismiss nor improve Christian belief. It cannot construct an alternate anthropology which might rival that of Kant's and thereby re-establish Christian belief as a true way of knowing. Rather, philosophical reflection is put at the service of belief as a kind of therapy.[50] In *Sickness Unto Death* the dialectical analysis of the self produces a description of the human person which leads the reader progressively through every possible avenue, but offers no escape from the realization that all efforts at the construction of meaning lead to despair, unless . . . at the moment that the content of that 'unless' is named, the analysis ceases and the reader must confront what is beyond:

> Every human existence that is not conscious of itself as spirit or conscious of itself before God as spirit, every human existence that does not rest transparently in God but vaguely rests in and merges in some abstract universality (state, nation, etc.) or in the dark about his self, regards his capacities merely as powers to produce without becoming deeply aware of their source, regards his self, if it is to have intrinsic meaning, as an indefinable something – every such existence, whatever it explains, be it the whole of existence, however intensively it enjoys life esthetically – every such existence is nevertheless in despair.[51]

Kierkegaard does not hesitate to name that despair by its Christian name, 'sin', with its opposite being not virtue or human striving, but 'faith'. His philosophical analysis of the human subject, like that of Kant, leads us to a limit, but a limit which can be positively named by traditional Christian categories. If we are to call such writing 'theology', then it includes two aspects: first, the 'philosophical' analysis, claiming to be more accurate than Kant's (and certainly more accurate than Hegel's optimistic phenomenology), and second, the reiteration, in Christian biblical language, in the form of 'paraenesis' or exhortation, with its demand for a specifically Christian response. It could be argued that the prior philosophical moment actually leads nowhere, thus reconceiving Kierkegaard's project as one of deconstruction, possibly nihilism; or, it could be argued that once the fuss of the analysis is done, it is seen to be irrelevant to the real purpose at hand, the repetition of the demand for belief without rational argument. Kierkegaard's invective encourages the latter, and his irony the former:

> But this is just exactly the way they speak about Christianity, these believing pastors; they either "defend" Christianity or transpose it into "reasons," if they do not go further and tinker speculatively with "comprehending" it. This is called preaching. . . . This is precisely why Christendom . . . is so far from being what it calls itself that the lives of most men, Christianly understood, are far too spiritless to be called sin in the strictly Christian sense.[52]

Only if one construes the prior analysis of despair as some sort of 'proof' of the need for faith, or fails to understand that the opposite of sin, of human limitation and failure, is faith and not virtue, let alone rational clarity, would it be necessary to render 'imitation' into 'mere repetition' in order to improve upon Kierkegaard. If there is a truth in the metaphor of imitation which it shares with the theology of previous ages, it is in its commitment to relativizing the efforts of 'bringing one to the faith' by re-emphasizing the sheer gratuity of the grace of conversion and the 'new mind' it brings with it. The meaning of Christian discourse arises in the process of acquiring and practising the Christian way of life, in the 'imitation' of Christ. This need not require the elimination of the possibility of describing 'coming to the faith' and 'remaining in the faith' using a language once removed from actual worship, prayer and the other activities of the Christian life. The danger of the metaphor is to make too sharp a distinction between the language of religion and language about religion: there is an 'observational analysis' which gives us knowledge of Christianity, and a 'participation in a way of life' which gives us, in Kierkegaard's terms, a 'passional sympathy'.[53]

The limits of human agency

Kant's analysis of human freedom placed incredible responsibility upon each individual to fulfil the demands of duty, despite there being no guarantee of a just and happy fulfilment of such efforts other than the mere *hypothesis* of a just Judge and a world hereafter. Nor did he permit a mere repetition of superstitious practices and prayers as a sop to the morally weak. It is not adequate to respond to these two limitations by merely reasserting the existence of God or the efficacy of Christian practice. Kierkegaard engages in a different kind of 'theological' discourse to undo Kant's restrictions. The dynamics of what he proposes can be observed in 'Christ as the Prototype, or No One Can Serve Two Masters', the second part of *Judge for Yourself*.[54] The title itself is instructive, alerting us to the non-dialogical, non-correlational character of theology – there can be no compromise in Christianity – and to the determinative character of Christ for theology – there is no other focus in Christianity. The text divides roughly into three parts: a meditation on the human failure to live by the command 'no one can serve two masters'; a redescription of the gospel story of Christ's life as the 'prototype' of such obedience; an application or invitation to the reader through a proposal of 'imitation' as our response.

The variety of responses to the command are summed up in what Kierkegaard ironically calls 'sensibleness' and he has it speak for itself:

> "To will the impossible," they say, "is madness; reasonable willing is to will what one is capable of doing. But to require the unconditioned is to insist that one must will the impossible, squander one's energies, one's time, one's life on that without making any headway – and this is madness, ridiculous exaggeration."[55]

Christianity must not compromise on the unconditional command in the face of 'sensibleness', for to do so would be to deny its very nature. Instead it must look to Christ, who in his life and very being is the fulfilment of the command.[56] There then follows Kierkegaard's retelling of the life of Christ, offering what might be called an 'intrasystematic' reading by using Christ's own command to us as the key to interpreting Christ's life. Having done so, we are confronted with the command again, and with a comment on our options:

> *Imitation, the imitation of Christ*, is really the point from which the human race shrinks. The main difficulty lies here. . . . If there is emphasis on this point, the stronger the emphasis the fewer the Christians. If there is a scaling down at this point (so that Christianity becomes, intellectually, a doctrine), more people enter into Christianity. If it is abolished completely (so that Christianity becomes, existentially, as easy as mythology and poetry and imitation an exaggeration, a ludicrous exaggeration), then Christianity spreads to such a degree that Christendom and the world are almost indistinguishable.[57]

As a criticism of all our other metaphors and classic authors – looking back to Kant and forward to both Hegel and Schleiermacher – Kierkegaard proposes an uncompromising resistance, which might be read as the dismissal of any rational articulation of faith. He paints a picture of his nemesis:

> The professor! This man is not mentioned in the New Testament, from which one sees in the first place that Christianity came into the world without professors. Anyone with any eye for Christianity will certainly see that no one is as qualified to smuggle Christianity out of the world as "the professor" is, because the professor shifts the whole view point of Christianity.[58]

The professor corresponds to 'objective teaching, doctrine'; is analogous to the 'monastery' of the Middle Ages and its false emphasis on works; encourages, equally through doubt or reasons, the change from 'decision . . . into postponement'; fosters illusion by 'demeanour and assurances'; and is 'weighted and found wanting' despite 'objective scholarship'.

Christianity as practical

A new imbalance in Christianity requires a new remedy, though it is in actuality a retrieval of a traditional practice:

> When the "monastery" is the deviation, faith must be affirmed; when the "professor" is the deviation, imitation must be affirmed.[59]

If the 'professor' is modernity and its rereading and translation of Christian belief into 'objective scholarship' for its own good, then indeed we can honour the importance of a return to the primacy of practice. However, as we shall see below with the appeal to representation or experience, the appeal to practice, to imitation of Christ in this case, cannot dispense with some form of criticism, even if it be intrasystematic criticism. Kierkegaard has given us the example himself, by his reading of the appropriateness of Luther's reassertion of faith over the 'works' of the monastery, accompanied by a re-description of the life of Christ, and applied through the assertion of a rudimentary 'doctrine', namely, imitation. Knowing what remedy to apply requires critical distance from mere repetition, and Christianity prizes the practitioners of that critical distance even as it resists the 'professor'.

5   Theology as Conversation

Conversation as metaphor

The next two metaphors for theology that we will consider, conversation and expression, are committed to *dialogical* activity as the chief metaphor for theological work. Though construction and imitation do not deny the social embeddedness of any human activity as to its agent, its execution or its instruments, their commitments tend either to the reduction of the specificity of religion into other forms of discourse or the segregation of religion precisely because of its specificity, making conversation secondary or even unnecessary. One could measure this tendency by the degree to which the foundations of revelation, tradition, scripture and experience are construed as non-rational and detrimental to human development. The conversation and expression make the relationship to the culture in which a religion finds itself the primary preoccupation for theology. In order to do so they credit Christianity with a defensible identity, and construe culture as both in need of and capable of redemption. Like construction and imitation, conversation and expression give priority to the *active* role of the theologian and believer over the *receptive* moment of the religious attitude, an obvious debt to modernity's emphasis on rationality as constructive.

The style of theology we are considering under the term *conversation* can also be named *correlation*, a comparison or co-ordination of Christianity and modernity, considered as theories of meaning.[60] Correlation entails *translation* and *persuasion*: a rendering of biblical and doctrinal language into a 'neutral' language which bridges the two realms of meaning, and a rhetorical address to the two audiences (depending upon who is the 'church' and who the 'culture'). At the least, theology makes a case for the survival of the Christian way of life in a hostile culture; at best, it makes a case for an appropriate influence of Christian belief and practice upon a more receptive host culture. The kind of correlation depends upon which pole is dominant, and whether the relation has the character of assimilation, translation or mutual adjustment. If there is, indeed, a 'middle ground', a third partner in the conversation between Christianity and modernity, by means of which the correlation can be effected, the most important question to ask is whether it is without embodiment or social location, borrowing Kant's 'universal rationality', or whether it has a specific grounding.

All theological work takes place within some culture or other, and all theologians work within at least two cultures, if *culture* is an apt metaphor for Christianity. It is possible to read the earliest Christian texts as a conversation (sometimes defence, sometimes self-description, sometimes exhortation, all involving differing audiences); medieval theology conversed with its past and its authoritative sources, and spoke to a present audience which either shared its beliefs, or needed persuading out of its barbarism and into the gospel and the church. Reformers and counter-reformers, however much they engaged in diatribe against each other (a form of conversation no doubt), still shared the basic principles of worship, practice and belief with those they criticized. Conversation with the 'other' has been essential to the shaping of Christianity, as evidenced in the formative influence of Jewish scripture, classical philosophy, the powers of the Roman empire, heretical and schismatic groups, Islam and the growing 'secular' powers of medieval Europe. All these interactions provide evidence of the 'conversational tone' of pre-modern theology, a history filled with as much sin as grace.

In learning to live within a culture, Christian believers have to contend most particularly with its *religion*; that is, they have to argue for and embody membership in a culture while worshipping the Christian God and not the 'gods of the nations'. It would indeed be a long story to recount the adventures of Christian missionaries in cultures other than Judaism, beginning with the travels of Paul, and the ways in which 'pagan' religion was resisted and cultural practices accepted, adapted or endured. The perennial question is whether Christians can be good citizens within a given culture and still remain faithful to the Christian way of life, whether they must construct an alternate culture as separate as possible from the incursion of the host culture, or whether a middle ground is possible and needed. In every age Christians risk persecution because of their faith, find ways to survive through patient accommodation, and exercise their responsibility to change their host culture. Missionary activity has devastated cultures on the one hand, and enhanced them with Christian values through evangelization on the other. On these matters, the history of Christianity is complex and unhappy, but it was relatively clear up to the modern period that the 'conversation' was ruled by doctrinal principles which entailed quite definite consequences: there is only one God, known by Israel, fully manifest in the truly human Christ, our Lord and Saviour, now present in the power of the Holy Spirit. These were, so to speak, objective claims as much as they were regulative principles for a way of life, providing the most rudimentary rules for the conversation.

The situation *vis-à-vis* modernity becomes increasingly complex as Christianity is disestablished and the makers of modern common sense provide thoroughgoing reinterpretations of Christianity, which themselves become competing surrogates for the role of religion within Western culture. In face of this situation, those wishing to continue a doctrinally determined theology take on the task of proposing a justification for continued practice and further evangelization in the midst of a culture which has once again become coincident with religion, though not with any particular historical religion. Thus, the issue for contemporary theology is not whether we are in or must take seriously our contemporary culture, but rather, what kind of relationship Christianity will have with modernity and its religion, and *what function 'culture' will have in theological argument*.

It is important to distinguish between the presence of culture as a *context* and *vehicle*, and the use of culture as a *theory* within theological argument. As context, culture is more difficult to locate in an argument. A theologian may want to attend to or criticize a particular aspect of a given culture, speak in a fashion understandable to the culture, to borrow truths, techniques, attitudes from the culture for Christian purposes, alter Christian practice or belief in accordance with the criteria of the culture. When these activities are judged intrasystematically for their congruence with worship, works of charity, scripture, creed, and the wisdom and practice of holy men and women, then the 'dialogue' with the culture cannot be called 'correlation'. When the complex activities of a culture move from being the context to being the vehicle for the embodiment of Christian belief and practice, there is evidence of conflicting interpretations of the result: some call it 'accommodation' in a pejorative sense, others prize it as a 'coming of age' of Christianity; more recently various theologies of 'contextualization' have reasserted the embodied character of Christian faith over against the irrelevance of theology conducted from supposed 'universal' viewpoints.

Conversation again: definitions and procedures, speaker and audience, criteria and goals

As we will also consider in the next metaphor, the appeal to one's culture as a 'way of life' might occur in the guise of an 'appeal to experience'. In correlation, it is an appeal to a *theory* of experience, or more precisely, to the transcendental conditions of experience as the middle ground offering a common language by means of which Christianity and modernity can name their common commitments and revise them so as to function more adequately for human needs.[61] The appeal is to an originary language which names a view of humanity which no culture and no religion can call into question. However, 'common human experience' dissolves two opposites: if made concrete, it loses its character as common and universal, and if maintained as universal it loses its character as experience, becoming instead a proposal about how we *ought* to describe human experiences structurally or teleologically. In the latter case it comes to function as a non-historical 'religion' which proposes the principles of ultimacy, with ethical and aesthetic consequences, to which both Christianity and modernity must submit for criticism. The privileged language need not be philosophy, but rather psychological, social, political or aesthetic theory. Contemporary forms of 'theology as conversation' take for granted that, despite its problems, modernity is to be preserved and, for all its efficacy, Christian belief and practice must be revised to suit modernity. These convictions name a preference for *apologetics* over *evangelization*.

As to other options, the theologian might borrow an account of a given culture rather than a theory, or might construct a specifically Christian theology of culture. In the former case, the conversation will not tend towards correlation, but rather to an ad hoc engagement of descriptions and categories of explanation which may or may not aid the theological enterprise, since thick descriptions such as anthropologists provide only admit of analogical comparisons. In the latter case, the conversation rests squarely on Christian grounds, but is no less a real conversation.

In addition to proposing the middle ground or privileged language which will mediate between Christianity and modernity, the theologian must also propose a theory of both Christianity and modernity, which addresses their origins, history, chief principles, goals and practices. One way to observe how this functions is to consider who is acceptable as conversation partners from both sides. No real conversation would be possible if the Christian partner is a supernaturalist who maintains belief in a two-tiered universe, a fideist who holds belief to be irrational or non-rational, a fundamentalist who does not admit the need for interpretation or ideology critique, or an anti-secularist who advocates a theocratic or revolutionary role for Christian society. The grounds for exclusion from the conversation are not heterodoxy as to Christian doctrine, but religious commitments that are rudimentarily incompatible with modernity.

On modernity's side, those who would be excluded are the materialist who does not acknowledge a religious or spiritual dimension of reality, the extreme pessimist who does not believe in the ultimate worthwhileness of life, and the atheist who cannot admit of a reasonable theistic interpretation of reality which credits the word 'God' with some form of 'objective' reference. Not surprisingly these are the dangerous errors identified by Kant which he hoped his transcendental philosophy of criticism would forever overcome. The degree to which contemporary society has adopted a cultural 'religion' of just these factors, usually announced by the invocation of the trio Marx, Nietzsche and Freud, is the degree to which a great many practitioners of modernity cannot be conversation partners to the revised Christianity. Modernity and Christianity must hold to a faith in the ultimate worthwhileness of life, admit of dimensions of ultimacy, religiosity and theism, acknowledge regulative ideas which can be given symbolic embodiment, and account for the data of non-progressive, even destructive elements in reality and human agency.

Finally, if we consider the goal of the conversation, various possibilities present themselves. The aim might be: a mutual usefulness of modernity and Christianity, in which Christianity restores to modernity a confidence in a transcendent dimension to reality, and modernity restores to Christianity credibility and respectability in the form of a voice or power within civil society. The motivation for the efforts involved would be, beyond a confidence in the intrasystematic identity of both partners, a common commitment to the unity of all Truth, Goodness, Beauty. If, however, what is essential to a theory of modernity is by definition some form of refusal of the transcendent dimension, and the unity of reality that involves, then the efforts at conversation will never achieve their goal. And if, on the side of Christianity, the revision of its doctrines and practice can be shown to render it inauthentic, and in effect to cause it to lose its identity, then conversation is likewise rendered impossible. If, however, the Christian partner brings a unique identity to the discussion, one which cannot be translated into transcendental categories and which has intrasystematic rules which govern it, the conversation cannot move to correlation. For example, if what is unique is revelation, a tradition of worship, belief, practice and determinate religious experience, what sense are we to make of the oxymoronic terms 'transcendental revelation', 'supernatural existential', 'potential obedience', to borrow the terminology of Rahner? Such paradoxical language points to the limitations of human speech about what we cannot resist speaking of: the event of God in the created order. The person and work of Christ, and hence the scriptures, remain the chief test case for the application of various forms of the conversational metaphor. While they can be spoken of in the language of 'symbol' and 'mediation', can they be resolved into instances of more general categories, and spoken of in a neutral language? Once again, methodological issues resolve themselves into doctrinal ones.

Hegel as the paradigm: neither dead orthodoxy nor irrational mysticism

Our classic example of conversation from the nineteenth century is the work of Hegel. From his earliest unpublished works we have evidence of a desire to accomplish something Kant thought impossible: to hold together basic Christian doctrine and practice and the culture of modernity. In an essay drafted in 1793, during his final year as a theology student in Tübingen, the very year that Kant's *Religion Within the Limits of Reason Alone* was published, Hegel proposed the following agenda for a marriage of wisdom and folk religion:

> A. I. Its teachings must be founded on universal reason.
> II. Imagination, the heart, and the senses must not go away empty-handed in the process.
> III. It must be so constituted that all of life's needs, including public and official transactions, are bound up with it.
> B. What must it avoid?[62]

The last question is as vital as the prior three elements, for Hegel returned throughout his career to a criticism of the dead orthodoxy of his theological contemporaries, and the limitation of religion to feeling and intuition, as he understood it to be proposed by Jacobi and Schleiermacher. Though his early *Life of Jesus* shares with Kant a need to translate Jesus into a teacher of morality, and to minimize the miraculous and spiritual in Christ, even in 1795 Hegel announced the grand theme of an all-encompassing system of thought when he translates into a few sentences the gist of the first chapter of John's Gospel:

> Pure reason, transcending all limits, is divinity itself – whereby and in accordance with which the very plan of the world is ordered (John 1). Through reason man learns of his destiny, the unconditional purpose of his life. And although at times reason is obscured, it continues to glimmer faintly even in the darkest age, for it is never totally extinguished.[63]

The articulation of the unity of God, nature and history, and human self-consciousness as a unity of internal relations, will remain Hegel's goal throughout all the stages of his philosophic career. This interpretation of reality is, in effect, a proposal for an understanding of the modern world which will attempt to honour the first three points of his brief outline of argument, namely that rational knowledge of the absolute is possible, religion in its representational, sensible character is an essential moment in such knowledge, and the resulting harmony of wisdom and religion has public efficacy.

In another early work in 1802–3 entitled *Faith and Knowledge* Hegel begins to mark out his differences from Kant, Jacobi and Fichte. In the first paragraph he gives his estimate of the Enlightenment effort to reconcile reason and faith:

> The new-born peace that hovers triumphantly over the corpse of Reason and faith, uniting them as the child of both, has as little of Reason in it as it has of authentic faith.[64]

Both Kant and Jacobi err, the former in denying to rationality its proper fulfilment in knowledge of the Absolute, the latter in limiting faith to the realm of feeling. In the technical language of the day Hegel states the problem:

> Kant's philosophy posits absolute subjectivity and finitude in pure abstraction and thus acquires the objectivity and infinity of the concept. Jacobi's philosophy does not take up finitude itself into the concept; it makes a principle out of finitude in its finiteness, out of finitude as empirical contingency and consciousness of this subjectivity. The sphere common to both philosophies is the absoluteness of the antithesis between, on one side, finitude, the natural, knowledge – which in this antithesis is bound to be merely formal knowledge – and, on the other, the supernatural, supersensuousness and infinity. For both of them what is truly Absolute is an absolute Beyond in faith and in feeling; for cognitive Reason it is nothing.[65]

Fichte does not resolve the problem when he tries to combine, according to Hegel, the objectivism of Kant and the subjectivism of Jacobi. He only succeeds in objectifying the Absolute again, now as the object of 'obligation and striving'.[66] Hegel continues to expose what he considers to be the inadequacies of such systems of thought, when in the *Phenomenology of Spirit* (written in 1806 and conceived as the introduction to his 'system of science') he accounts for various systems of philosophy as manifestations of various incomplete stages of the development of human and divine consciousness. In the *Logic* (1817), the first part of his mature system of three parts called the *Encyclopedia*, he analyzes three inadequate attitudes toward objectivity (and subjectivity of course), focusing on pre-Kantian thought, Kant, and Jacobi and Descartes. The original text of the *Logic* did not take Schleiermacher as a focus of criticism, but a passage from the preface to the third edition in 1830 states the following:

> By their formal, abstract, nerveless reasoning, the rationalists have emptied religion of all power and substance, no less than the pietists by the reduction of all faith to the Shibboleth of Lord! Lord! One is no whit better than the other; and when they meet in conflict there is no material on which they could come into contact, no common ground, and no possibility of carrying on an inquiry which would lead to knowledge and truth.[67]

Many more quotations could be taken from these works, and especially from the *Lectures on the Philosophy of Religion,* to confirm my first, admittedly complex, point about Hegel as a precursor of contemporary theology as conversation. In summary form: (1) his basic commitment is to a comprehensive view which unites Christianity and modernity; (2) criticism functions as a ground-clearing exercise which sets aside inadequate notions of both philosophy and religion, the two being inseparable; (3) the extremes to be avoided are rationalism on the one hand and pietism on the other, because they both deny a unity and teleology essential to God, nature and history, and humankind. Hegel adopts the term 'Spirit' to name this unity and motion of reality, the basic truth common to philosophy and religion. The common ground which will reconcile the culture of modernity with the truth of Christianity is the recognition of the functional truth of the two basic doctrines of Christian belief, the Trinity and the incarnation. Put boldly: you cannot have modernity without Christianity. The still constantly argued question among theologians is: does Hegel have an 'orthodox' Christianity? Is the common ground of 'Spirit' the Christian God?[68]

Hegel and foundations

In a passage striking for its clarity and simplicity, Hegel, in the introduction to the third part of the *Encyclopedia*, entitled the *Philosophy of Mind,* names the complex foundation of his system by giving an example to elucidate what he means by 'Spirit':

> In order to elucidate for ordinary thinking this unity of form and content present in mind, the unity of manifestation and what is manifested, we can refer to the teaching of the Christian religion. Christianity says: God has revealed himself through Christ, his only-begotten Son. Ordinary thinking straightway interprets this statement to mean that Christ is only the organ of this revelation, as if what is revealed in this manner were something other than the source of the revelation. But, in truth, this statement properly means that God has revealed that his nature consists in having a Son, i.e. in making a distinction within himself, making

himself finite, but in his difference remaining in communion with himself, beholding and revealing himself in the Son, and that by this unity with the Son, by his being-for-himself, beholding and revealing himself in the Son, this being-for-himself in the Other, he is absolute mind or spirit; so that the Son is not the mere organ of the revelation but is himself the content of the revelation.[69]

Hegel here presupposes that reality (God, and because of God all that is not God) is inherently self-differentiating, self-conscious and self-reconciling, and that that definition of reality is possible because the truth of God as triune has been revealed. Elsewhere he laments the fact that theologians have become mere 'countinghouse clerks' who 'adopt only an historical attitude toward religion'.[70] In effect they treat this doctrine as a mere historical curiosity, not realizing that

In philosophy and religion, however, the essential thing is that one's own spirit itself should recognize a possession and content, deem itself worthy of cognition, and not keep itself humbly outside.[71]

We must not fail to note, however, that a *cognitive* reappropriation of the doctrine of the Trinity as a foundational principle for the interpretation of modernity is not a *spiritual or practical* reappropriation for the conduct of life. Such a criticism is mitigated if we can show Hegel's project as more than merely intellectualist, that is, if his early desire to integrate rational, affective and practical concerns remains despite his obvious commitment to a philosophical articulation.

The lengthy quotation above also names the second great foundation of Hegel's system, the incarnation, God made manifest in Christ. In the 1827 series of *Lectures on the Philosophy of Religion*, he articulates the necessity of a this-worldly manifestation of the necessary internal self-differentiation of the Godhead, both of which truths make possible his claim that neither thought nor feeling will go away empty-handed. There is a coincidence of the internal necessity (which we know to be so 'after the fact') of God's self-differentiation and the overcoming of the alienation which is the distance between God and creation. Hegel understands that distance to be properly called evil (though perhaps not 'sin') and clearly wishes to preserve the 'revelatory' character of the arrival in human consciousness of the truth of the overcoming of human alienation from God:

Furthermore, the consciousness of the absolute idea that we have in philosophy in the form of thinking is to be brought forth not for the standpoint of philosophical speculation or speculative thinking but in the form of *certainty*. The necessity [that the divine–human unity shall appear] is not first apprehended by means of thinking; rather it is a certainty for humanity. In other words, this content – the unity of divine and human nature – achieves certainty, obtaining the form of immediate sensible intuition and external existence for humankind, so that it appears as something that has been seen in the world, something that has been experienced.[72]

He states the reality of the incarnation boldly: 'the unity of divine and human nature must appear in *just one human being*'.[73]

As with his understanding of the Trinity, so also with the incarnation, there remains the possibility of interpreting his writings as anything but 'orthodox' Christianity. The inner dynamics of the system will be used by others both to leave behind Christian faith (in so-called left-wing Hegelianism) and to leave behind certain beliefs and values of modernity (in so-called right-wing Hegelianism).[74] The question in the case of the singular uniqueness of Christ as both the necessary and sufficient symbol of the unity of subject and substance, finite and infinite, subject and object, and religion and philosophy, is whether the gracious mysteriousness of that unity and its salvific efficacy remains forever a free act of God or becomes a necessary unfolding of the metaphysical structure of reality. In the case of God, however, can one really distinguish between freedom and necessity? Similarly, we must ask: is the suffering and 'infinite anguish' which is the cross, the miracle which is the resurrection, and the surprise of the presence of the Holy Spirit, merely the logical unfolding of the divine essence? Such questions must be posed to the 'common ground' of every effort at conversation between Christianity and culture. Does evangelization have an uncompromised privilege over theological reflection and systematization, because worship has a determining priority over philosophical insight? The final remarks of the 1824 *Lectures* give us pause:

> This conceptual cognition of religion is by its nature not universal, but is rather only the cognition of a community. For that reason three stages take shape in regard to the kingdom of the Spirit: the first estate is that of immediate, naive religion and of faith; the second is that of the understanding, the estate of the so-called cultured, of reflection and the Enlightenment; and finally the third estate is the community of philosophy.[75]

Hegel on mediation and representation, imagination and the scriptures

This final section on Hegel gives attention to the notions of *mediation* and *representation* in religion,[76] the role of the *imagination*, and the brief but suggestive comments he has concerning the scriptures. Hegel uses a relatively small technical vocabulary in a thoroughgoing analogical fashion, a usage reflecting his conviction that all aspects of reality are analogously related. The primary relation is that of a dynamic unity of identity and difference, *mediation* being the process which brings about the unity of apparent opposites. The

Phenomenology of Spirit describes the development of the self in the history of cultures and God's presence to that history, as a story of the process of mediation which brings the individual, finite consciousness into unity with the Absolute. And the 'motor', so to speak, in the *Logic* is the 'negation of negation', the mediating overcoming of opposites through a process of 'becoming' which preserves each prior stage even as it passes beyond to a higher moment of integration (the movement of *Aufhebung*, often unfortunately translated as 'overcoming'). Mediation not only accounts for life and development in religions, as in all instances of human consciousness, but in its function as *representation* (*Vorstellung*) it differentiates religions from philosophy and its grasp of reality in concepts. Among the historical religions Christianity does not simply provide yet another constellation of representations of the Absolute in artifacts and activities of worship: rather, Christianity presents *the* instance of mediation, *the* representation itself in the person of Christ. Thus it can be said that both philosophy and the Christian religion know the same truth, the former in concepts, the latter in the form of images and stories whose content is identical with that of philosophy:

> The fact that the religious content is present primarily in the form of representation is connected with what I said earlier, that religion is the consciousness of absolute truth in the way that it occurs for all human beings. Thus it is found primarily in the form of representation. Philosophy has the same content, the truth; [it is] the spirit of the world generally and not the particular spirit. Philosophy does nothing but transform our representation into concepts. The content remains always the same.[77]

Hegel's conviction that a 'conversation' between modernity and Christianity is not only possible but necessary rests finally on the basic insight that the *content* of both is identical. Within his own system of thought (and certainly in the thought of his followers in the nineteenth century) the challenge to Christianity is whether the inadequacy of its form – its world of representations – must be abandoned. It could be said that the hubris of Hegel's thought, and perhaps of any effort to bring about a harmony of religion and culture, is the presumption that the full unity of human and divine consciousness can be had in this world.

One final passage, from the 1827 *Lectures on the Philosophy of Religion*, provides some of the few remarks Hegel makes about the scriptures. The tension and ambiguity in the passage reflects accurately the instability of the delicate balance between the revelatory givenness of God's self-manifestation and the cognitive achievement of knowledge of God and God's purposes:

> Still, there is also something historical that is a divine history – a story, indeed, that is supposed to be history in the proper sense, namely the story of Jesus. This

story does not merely count as a myth, in the mode of images. Instead it involves sensible occurrences; the nativity, passion and death of Christ count as something completely historical. Of course it therefore exists for representation and in the mode of representation, but it also has another, intrinsic aspect. The story of Jesus is something twofold, a divine history. Not only [is there] this outward history, which should only be taken as the ordinary story of a human being, but also it has the divine as its content: a divine happening, a divine deed, an absolutely divine action. This absolute divine action is the inward, the genuine, the substantial dimension of this history, and this is just what is the object of reason.[78]

For any commitment to conversation or correlation, the question must always be posed as to whether the scandal of particularity can or even should be overcome, both in the case of the scriptures and the church. Theology can no longer be marginal notes to the biblical text, and the community of believers is no longer marginal to culture. This sublation of particularity is not, however, simply out of embarrassment or atheistic irritation. Allow Hegel to voice the intentions of those engaged in conversation with the culture in an entirely different context, which perhaps brings us back to the very first quotation from his early student years, this time in a letter he writes to his friend Niethammer in October 1816:

> The Catholic community has in its hierarchy a fixed center which the Protestant lacks. Moreover, in the former everything depends on how the clergy is instructed, whereas in the latter the instruction of the laity has equal importance. For we really do not have a laity, since *all* members of the community have the same right and role in the determination and preservation of church affairs in doctrine and discipline. Our safeguard is thus not the aggregate of council pronouncements, nor a clergy empowered to preserve such pronouncements, but is rather only the collective culture of the community. Our more immediate safeguard is thus the universities and institutions for general culture.[79]

6 Theology as Expression

Expression as metaphor

All theological work is in some sense *expression*, the manifestation of human subjectivity as 'experience' which is uttered in symbolic artifacts. Theology does not fall from heaven; it is the result of human effort. This awareness can be found in pre-modern sources, in the guise of an identifying address, intimations of the author's limitations, and humble prayer for wisdom before the task of theology. Appeals to the knowledge of those who knew Jesus, to the example of saintly women and men, and to the arguments of the wise, both in and outside of the church, are appeals to human experience as both a source and norm for theology. Prior to the modern period Christians were well aware that something had happened to them (an 'experience'), that they could and must communicate ('express' their experiences), and that certain of these expressions were to be preferred (some individuals and communities were 'experienced' and therefore trustworthy). Even appeals to texts and practices, as 'products' of experience, can be construed as appeals to human expression. Though an odd way of speaking for the evangelists, contemporary Christians speak of the gospels as accounts of the disciples' 'experience' of Jesus, and the early structures of the church as privileging the experience of certain individuals and communities. Once construed as originating in experience, texts or practices can be subjected to ideology critique and 'lost' experience can be imaginatively reconstructed. Thus the metaphor of 'expression' and its companion notion 'experience' criticize and reconfigure the history of Christian theology.

As with construction, so also expression demands a prior moment of criticism which establishes the 'experience' theology will express. The appeal to experience might be to universal conditions of subjectivity (transcendental conditions of experience), human dissatisfaction with the status quo (experience as basis for hermeneutic suspicion), the intervention of the divine into the human realm (experience as revelatory), a personal/social confession (experience as personal conviction), the inexpressible mystical presence of the transcendent (experience as prior to language and symbolic).[80] Depending upon the choice of construal, the notion 'experience' will enter at differing points in a theological argument, and align itself with different doctrinal presuppositions and philosophical theories.

Of these five possible appeals, 'experience as revelatory' is the touchstone for the rest. If religious, and specifically Christian, experience is not 'of God', in the several meanings this prepositional phrase conveys, then the 'expression' that is theology is not what it claims to be. Only radical construction would deny this. The other metaphors all accredit religious experience with a genuine intentionality in which the transcendent is *received* rather than *produced*. To be other than mere self-assertion, an appeal to experience must include a claim to some form of 'objectivity' and 'truth'.[81]

Investigation of the religious dimension of experience must therefore begin with an acceptance of what believers themselves regard as essential to religious faith, namely revelation and divinely granted grace as its precondition. The experience of God as essentially passive resists any effort to be reduced to human projection. In dialectical tension with this givenness of the transcendent and its final inaccessibility is the 'approach' of the human subject towards the transcendent and the consequent expression of both transcendent and the human approach in symbols, especially language. Finally, there remains the question, 'Is it true?' Theories of truth as correspondence or coherence tend to collapse the criteria of truth into the human subject, in the modern reversal of the foundation of objectivity from beyond to within the human person. Religious experience requires criteria of correspondence and coherence which give priority to that which is intended in the experience. Thus, a theory of 'truth as disclosure' provides the more apt model, permitting religious experience, like aesthetic experience, to bring its own *measure* of truth.

Just as Hegel and his like-minded followers have difficulty maintaining the balance of concept and representation, so Schleiermacher and his followers have difficulty maintaining the balance of the immanent and the intentional in experience. The priority of imagination over memory in both cases gives a clue to the modern character of these difficulties, also to be found in the metaphors of construction and imitation.

The immediacy of religion as experience

Like Hegel's *Phenomenology*, Schleiermacher's *On Religion* locates religion within an account of the self-development of the individual and culture. After a critique of certain philosophical and theological views, Schleiermacher proposes an alternate definition of religion and method for discussion more adequate to its reality and more acceptable to its 'cultured despisers'. He proposes a new 'evangelization' based upon his revisionist and apologetic efforts:

> To make proselytes out of unbelievers is deeply ingrained in the character of religion; those who impart their own religion can have no other purpose. Thus it is in fact hardly a pious deception but an appropriate method to begin with and appear concerned about a matter for which the sensibility already exists, so that something may occasionally and unnoticeably slip in for which the sensibility must first be aroused. Since all communication of religion cannot be other than rhetorical, it is a clever engagement of an audience to introduce them into such good company.[82]

The outward trappings of religion, rightly despised for their cold argumentation and useless controversy, should not distract the search for the inner truth of religion. The attempts of philosophers to reduce religion to a mode of thinking or acting, as reflected upon in metaphysics and moral philosophy, of necessity will falsify religion:

> Thus religion maintains its own sphere and its own character only by completely removing itself from the sphere and character of speculation as well as from that of praxis.[83]

That sphere is a third element, more rudimentary than thinking or acting, which is variously called intuition or feeling, and which has the religious name 'piety'.[84] This mode of operation of subjectivity is not self-contained, however, but is clearly intentional for Schleiermacher. In *The Christian Faith* he will speak of 'the feeling of absolute dependence', while in *On Religion* he calls it 'intuition of the universe', 'the highest and most universal formula of religion'.[85] Our attention must be directed away from inadequate empirical, experiential evidence as well as away from theoretical accounts of religion which blind us to the actual presence of the religious within subjectivity. Thus the proper method is autobiographical:

> The matter of religion is so arranged and so rare that a person who expresses something about it must necessarily have had it, for he has not heard about it anywhere. Of all that I praise and feel as its work there stands precious little in holy books, and to whom would it not seem scandal and folly who did not experience it himself?[86]

One can prize Schleiermacher's reassertion of the primacy of piety as immediate self-consciousness in contrast to speculative argument about the existence of God, or the merely hypothetical postulate of a just Judge, Lawgiver and Author of the world which aids our moral resolve. He restores to modernity the possibility of discovering the presence of the transcendent in the depths of the self, surely a traditional practice in Christianity, as the second of two quotations from Anselm at the head of *The Christian Faith* reminds us: 'For he who does not believe, does not experience, and he who does not experience, does not understand'.

The intentionality of experience

Three further elements of *On Religion* must be attended to: the role of the imagination, the social element in religion, and the need for mediation. Inasmuch as religious experience coincides with the very ground of consciousness, it is out of religion, in dialectical fashion, that both a conscious awareness of the self and of the transcendent grows. One's unique identity as a person and the specificity of one's religion are inextricably connected. It is the work of the 'heavenly imagination' of religion to thematize one's basic intuition of the universe, and then, if such is our tendency, to 'personify the spirit of the universe and you will have a God',[87] though our imagination may not do so. Hence, instruction in religion is 'a tasteless and meaningless word'.[88] To the extent that we must receive the specification of our religion from outside of ourselves we adopt a religion which the nineteenth century would call insincere, the twentieth century inauthentic. Still, the work of the imagination carries a proviso:

> A person is born with the religious capacity as with every other, and if only his sense is not forcibly suppressed, if only that communion between a person and

the universe – these are admittedly the two poles of religion – is not blocked and barricaded, then religion would have to develop unerringly in each person according to his own individual manner.[89]

Believers remain attached to a church only as long as they cannot, of themselves, bring to fruition by the imagination the religious capacity they already unknowingly possess. Otherwise, 'you have memory and imitation, but no religion'.[90] In both early and later works, Schleiermacher places great value upon the family as the locus of that initial education to religion which liberates our innate religiosity. For all its givenness at the primordial level of our being, religion involves a process of development, some form of education and elements of mediation. There is no simple passage from experience to expression.

Schleiermacher also contends with the need and reality of mediation in religion as a moment external to the human person:

> Except for a few chosen ones, every person surely needs a mediator, a leader who awakens his sense for religion from its first slumber and gives him an initial direction.[91]

In the controversial fifth speech in *On Religion* he argues for the excellence of Christianity among historical religions (as he will do again in *The Christian Faith*). That role as the highest religion, encompassing all aspects of life, is due to its 'original intuition' that corruption and redemption, enmity and mediation are inseparably bound to each other and are to be overcome. Christ is the mediator *par excellence* of this intuition because of

> the splendid clarity with which the great idea he had come to exhibit was formed in his soul, the idea that everything finite requires higher mediation in order to be connected with the divine.[92]

Christ is therefore the coincidence of both form and content, not unlike Hegel's conception of him, though here it is a matter of Christ's consciousness, rather than his ontological status, in keeping with the priority of experience. The 'content' of that consciousness is the unity of God and humanity. What is paradigmatically perfected in Christ is ours as well, a 'first point of attachment for every operation of divine grace', a

> desire for fellowship with God, never entirely extinguished, though pushed back to the very frontiers of consciousness, which is part of the original perfection of human nature.[93]

It is the entrance of Christ into our consciousness at just this point which brings about the actualization of a Christian life. Schleiermacher concludes:

Indeed, the parallel between the beginning of the divine life in us and the incarnation of the Redeemer comes out here too. In Him the passivity of His human nature in that moment was just such a lively susceptibility to an absolutely powerful consciousness of God, accompanied by a desire to be thus seized and determined, which became changed through the creative act into a spontaneous activity constituting a personality. In the same way our desire is heightened in conversion by the self-communication of Christ till it becomes a spontaneous activity of the self that constitutes a coherent new life.[94]

Within the confines of Christian theology, the imagination is not free to form just any symbolic manifestation of religious sensibilities. For theology fashioned under the metaphor of expression, Christology exhibits well the tensions within religious experience as immanent but intentional. Concerning the use of the scriptures as an element in conversion and a source for determining the imagination, a remark from one of Schleiermacher's sermons is most telling. Committed as he is to an ad hoc borrowing from other disciplines (consider the first nineteen paragraphs of *The Christian Faith*), he cannot logically prevent the application of historical–critical method to the study of the biblical text. In fact, his proposal for theological education encourages it. He does, however, provide for a kind of 'divinatory' insight into what stands behind the text, as it were, to establish a control upon what can be made out of the scriptures when we encounter difficulties in interpreting them:

> How necessary it is, then, that scripture be complemented by something that works from the inside. And what else is there but that continuing work of the Redeemer himself, those living impressions he creates even now immediately in the human soul: This is what must ever come to the aid of the Word in the Christian church, just as in the Redeemer's own life the two were always united and supported each other.[95]

The ability to maintain a Christology which approximates the orthodox theology of the pre-modern period becomes increasingly difficult, if the 'experiential' foundations of its possibility in our own contemporary experience of the presence of the Holy Spirit cease to convince, or if we are left far too much on our own to account for and to assess it.

To complete this brief sketch of Schleiermacher and the metaphor of expression, we recall his discussion of the prolegomena for theology, and theological method, in the beginning of *The Christian Faith*. If clarity is to be gained as to what the 'church' is, it is not accomplished by a deduction of its definition, but by a process of 'borrowing' from other modes of discourse to give dogmatics its proper grounding. First there are propositions borrowed from ethics (we might speak of social sciences or anthropology) to establish the nature of religion as a church; second there are propositions borrowed from philosophy of religion (as a general theory of religions) to establish the particularity of Christianity; and third a borrowing from apologetics (a historical account of the specificity of Christianity as to doctrine and practice) as a justification of the particular historical shape of Christianity. Once these three descriptions of Christianity have been given, dogmatic propositions can be 'tested'. While talk about the world in the natural sciences and talk about divine modes of action in metaphysics are two forms of discourse, tending to the speculative development and systematic organization of dogmatic theology, neither is the basis of ultimate criteria of authenticity. Nor, it should be noted, as we have seen above, are the scriptures the last court of appeal. The limiting rule is as follows:

> We must declare the description of human states of mind to be the fundamental dogmatic form; while propositions of the second and third forms are permissible only in so far as they can be developed out of propositions of the first form; for only on this condition can they be really authenticated as expressions of religious emotions.[96]

7   Theology as Response

Rethinking the previous metaphors

All theological work is in some sense *response*, a construal of the task of theology which cannot only find a place within but also refocus the metaphors of construction, conversation and expression, with a particular affinity for the metaphor of imitation. That refocusing is not meant to eliminate or obscure the aspects of theological work which give rise to each, but rather to retrieve from pre-modern theology a basic stance which marked its strength. That retrieval is based upon theo–logical (doctrinal), anthropo–logical (philosophical), and socio–logical (cultural and ecclesiological) considerations. Precisely as a metaphor, the notion of 'response' is meant to evoke a fundamental attitude that informs all the other aspects of the human inventiveness we call 'theology'. As with the contemporary retrieval of principles of pre-modern biblical interpretation, there is no simple reproduction of former practices in theological work according to this metaphor. We are at a moment of genuine inventiveness, and the essays of this reader testify to the diversity of interest across traditions. The variety is by no means as great as it might be, and not even all those represented here would necessarily agree with every detail of my journey through alternate metaphors. The editors of this reader, however, propose this reading of contemporary theology based upon convictions derived and confirmed in the kind of theological work represented here. It is, like every metaphor, a proposal.

The basic inspiration for the proposal comes, as I have said, from a reading of the history of philosophy, hermeneutics and theology itself in the modern period, especially as that reading was given shape in the work of Hans Frei. My particular account of the alternate metaphors to 'response' has also been inspired by the first seven paragraphs of the first volume of Karl Barth's *Church Dogmatics*.[97] A lengthy discussion of this seminal text would be out of place here for a straightforward reason. The purpose of this reader is not to propose that Barth is a flawless theologian, much less that all theology should become a form of Barthian scholasticism. He does, however, offer an inspiration and a useful articulation of certain basic principles which attempt to negotiate the legacy of modern theology as it has been conducted since the beginning of the nineteenth century and whose roots can be traced to the late Middle Ages. Barth was by no means ignorant of those who had already greeted the challenges of modernity, and he learned from them. He sought a certain inspiration, however, from beyond. He would surely be the first to encourage a new age to labour again according to the same ancient convictions he also prized.[98]

Notes

1   On metaphors, see Colin Turbayne, *The Myth of Metaphor* (Columbia: University of South Carolina Press, 1970); and *Philosophical Perspectives on Metaphor*, ed. Mark Johnson (Minneapolis: University of Minnesota Press, 1981) for a general non-theological background.

2   For a proposal about the importance of metaphorical redescription see Thomas R. Kopfensteiner, 'The Metaphorical Structure of Normativity', *Theological Studies* 58 (1997), pp. 331–46. For an example of the complexity involved in a change of metaphor, namely the rise, development and decline of the Middle Ages, see Louis Mackey, *Peregrinations of the Word* (Ann Arbor: University of Michigan Press, 1997).

3   See David Kelsey, *To Understand God Truly* (Louisville, KY: Westminster/John Knox Press, 1992), chapters 3 and 4.

4   See Rowan Greer, *Broken Lights and Mended Lives* (University Park: Pennsylvania State University Press, 1986).

5   For an analysis of the contemporary problems in theological education resulting from the fragmentation of theology itself, particularly the dissociation of the 'pastoral' from the 'academic', see David Kelsey, *Between Athens and Berlin* (Grand Rapids, MI: Eerdmans, 1993).

6   For a discussion of the emergence of orthodoxy in relation to the transmission of the biblical text, see Bart D. Ehrman, *The Orthodox Corruption of Scripture* (Oxford: Oxford University Press, 1993).

7   For a 'case study' of the apologetic task of theology in the patristic period, see Jaroslav Pelikan, *Christianity and Classical Culture* (New Haven, CT: Yale University Press, 1993).

8   Origen, *On First Principles*, trans. Butterworth (New York: Harper and Row, 1966).

Compare the translation with that of *Ante-Nicene Fathers*, ed. A. Roberts and J. Donaldson (Peabody, MA: Hendrickson, 1995), vol. 4, p. 241. The word translated as 'follow logically' and 'following a correct method' is *indagine*, from the verb *indago*, whose root meaning concerns 'hunting in the woods'.

9   Along with the rest of the volumes in the series, for a basic outline of the medieval period see Jaroslav Pelikan, *The Christian Tradition: A History of the Development of Doctrine*, vol. 3, *The Growth of Medieval Theology (600–1300)* (Chicago: University of Chicago Press, 1978).

10 *History of Theology: The Renaissance*, ed. Giulio D'Ofrio (Collegeville, MN: Liturgical Press, 1998), vol. 3, p. 16. This entire volume is of considerable value for presenting the complex and fascinating history of the late fourteenth to early sixteenth centuries.

11 See Jaroslav Pelikan, *The Christian Tradition: A History of the Development of Doctrine*, vol. 4, *The Reformation of Church and Dogma (1300–1700)* (Chicago: University of Chicago Press, 1984).

12 A fascinating study of ideology critique as applied to biblical interpretation and useful as a test case for theology is the Bible and Culture Collective, *The Postmodern Bible* (New Haven, CT: Yale University Press, 1995).

13 For the statement of these concerns which guides this essay and the reader as a whole, see the following works by Hans Frei: *Types of Christian Theology* (New Haven, CT: Yale University Press, 1992); *The Identity of Jesus Christ* (Philadelphia: Fortress Press, 1975); *The Eclipse of Biblical Narrative* (New Haven, CT: Yale University Press, 1974); and *Theology and Narrative*, ed. George Hunsinger and William Placher (Oxford: Oxford University Press, 1993).

14 For example, Stephen Gaukroger, *Descartes: An Intellectual Biography* (Oxford: Oxford University Press, 1995).

15 For an intriguing study of this development in terms of the relation of philosophy, theology and revelation see Ingolf Dalferth, *Theology and Philosophy* (Oxford: Blackwell Publishers, 1988).

16 See Michael Buckley, *At the Origins of Modern Atheism* (New Haven, CT: Yale University Press, 1987).

17 See David Lachterman, *The Ethics of Geometry* (New York: Routledge, 1989).

18 See Kenneth Schmitz, 'Analysis by Principles and Analysis by Elements,' in *Graceful Reason*, ed. Lloyd Gerson (Toronto: Pontifical Institute of Mediaeval Studies, 1983).

19 In addition to Lachterman (note 17) see Stephen Toulmin, *Cosmopolis* (Chicago: University of Chicago Press, 1990), especially chapters 1, 2 and 3.

20 See Louis Dupré, *Religious Mystery and Rational Reflection* (Grand Rapids, MI: Eerdmans, 1998), pp. 77–91.

21 In the case of each metaphor I will attempt to draw widely from the works of the author being considered, but will not attempt to give a comprehensive exposition of their thought or of the secondary literature on their works. My aim is to encourage the reader to explore these classical texts for themselves. A contemporary theologian who adopts many of the aspects of the metaphor of construction is Gordon Kaufman. See *An Essay on Theological Method* (Missoula, MT: Scholar's Press, 1975).

22 Immanuel Kant, *Critique of Pure Reason*, trans. Norman Kemp Smith (New York: St. Martin's Press, 1929), p. 9.

23 Ibid.

24 Ibid., p. 24.
25 Ibid., pp. 31–2.
26 Immanuel Kant, *Prolegomena to Any Future Metaphysics*, rev. James W. Ellington (Indianapolis: Hackett Publishing, 1977), pp. 1–9.
27 Ibid., p. 103.
28 Immanuel Kant, *Religion Within the Limits of Reason Alone*, tr. Theodore M. Greene and Hoyt H. Hudson (New York: Harper and Row, 1960), p. 48.
29 For the relation of revelation, interpretation and method, see K. Vanhoozer, 'The Spirit of Understanding: Special Revelation and General Hermeneutics', in *Disciplining Hermeneutics*, ed. Roger Lundin (Grand Rapids, MI: Eerdmans, 1997), pp. 131–65.
30 See Immanuel Kant, *Lectures on Philosophical Theology*, trans. Allen W. Wood and Gertrude M. Clark (Ithaca, NY: Cornell University Press, 1978), pp. 109–21.
31 Immanuel Kant, *Critique of Judgement*, trans. J. H. Bernard (New York: Hafner Publishing, 1968), p. 324.
32 See Gordon E. Michalson, *Lessings's "Ugly Ditch"* (London: Pennsylvania State University Press, 1985).
33 Kant, *Religion*, p. 11.
34 For example, see Kant, *Critique of Pure Reason*, pp. 629–65 on the 'canon of pure reason'.
35 Kant, *Religion*, pp. 58–9.
36 Kant, *Critique of Pure Reason*, p. 568.
37 Ibid., p. 311.
38 See Kant, *Critique of Pure Reason*, pp. 180–7. See Rudolf A. Makkreel, *Imagination and Interpretation in Kant* (Chicago: University of Chicago Press, 1990).
39 See Kaufman, *Essay*, pp. 62.
40 Kant, *Critique of Pure Reason*, pp. 486–7.
41 Louis Dupré, *Metaphysics and Culture* (Milwaukee: Marquette University Press, 1994); *Passage to Modernity* (New Haven, CT: Yale University Press, 1993).
42 See Dupré, *Metaphysics and Culture*, pp. 10, 37, 41.
43 See Kant, *Religion*, pp. 100–5.
44 See Immanuel Kant, *The Conflict of the Faculties*, trans. Mary J. Gregor (New York: Abaris Books, 1979), p. 69.
45 Ibid., p. 107.
46 Ibid., p. 121.
47 See, for example, David J. Gouwens, *Kierkegaard as Religious Thinker* (Cambridge: Cambridge University Press, 1996).
48 See Ronald M. Green, *Kierkegaard and Kant: The Hidden Debt* (Albany: State University of New York Press, 1992).
49 Among many other of his works, see D. Z. Phillips, *Faith After Foundationalism* (London: Routledge, 1988).
50 See the references to Kierkegaard, Christianity and religion in Ludwig Wittgenstein, *Culture and Value*, trans. Peter Winch (Oxford: Blackwell Publishers, 1980).
51 Søren Kierkegaard, *Sickness Unto Death*, trans. Howard W. Hong and Edna H. Hong (Princeton: Princeton University Press, 1980), p. 46.
52 Ibid., p. 104.
53 See Gouwens, *Kierkegaard*, p. 59.
54 See Søren Kierkegaard, *For Self Examination, Judge for Yourself*, trans. Howard W.

Hong and Edna H. Hong (Princeton: Princeton University Press, 1990). I am grateful
to P. G. Ziegler for drawing my attention to this work.

55 Kierkegaard, *Judge*, p. 157.
56 Ibid., p. 159.
57 Ibid., p. 188.
58 Ibid., pp. 195ff.
59 Ibid., p. 156.
60 Among other contemporary examples, consult David Tracy, *Blessed Rage for Order*
(New York: Seabury Press, 1975).
61 Transcendental arguments are of two kinds: arguments for what is obvious, and
arguments for what is contested. Once a field of knowables is presumed, the argument
offers plausible conditions for that field. If a different field is presumed, different
conditions will be plausible. If the field is uncontested, the argument has stronger
weight, if contested, the argument is weak. See Kathyrn Tanner, *God and Creation in
Christian Theology* (Oxford: Blackwell Publishers, 1988), chapter 1.
62 G. W. F. Hegel, *Three Essays, 1793–1795*, ed. and trans. Peter Fuss and John Dobbins
(Notre Dame: University of Notre Dame Press, 1984), p. 49.
63 Ibid., p. 104.
64 G. W. F. Hegel, *Faith and Knowledge*, trans. Walter Cert and H. S. Harris (Albany:
State University of New York Press, 1977), p. 55.
65 Ibid., p. 62
66 Ibid.
67 *The Logic of Hegel*, trans. William Wallace, 2nd edn (Oxford: Oxford University Press,
1965), pp. xxiv–xxv.
68 See Cyril O'Regan, *The Heterodox Hegel* (Albany: State University of New York Press,
1994).
69 *Hegel's Philosophy of Mind*, trans. William Wallace (Oxford: Oxford University Press,
1971), p. 17.
70 G. W. F. Hegel, *Lectures on the Philosophy of Religion*, ed. P. Hodgson (Berkeley:
University of California Press, 1984), vol. 1, p. 128.
71 Ibid.
72 Hegel, *Lectures*, vol. 3, pp. 312–13.
73 Ibid., p. 313.
74 John Edward Towes, *Hegelianism* (Cambridge: Cambridge University Press, 1980).
75 Hegel, *Lectures*, vol. 3, p. 247.
76 See Louis Dupré, 'Hegel's Religion as Representation', in *A Dubious Heritage* (New
York: Paulist Press, 1977), pp. 53–72.
77 Hegel, *Lectures*, vol. 1, p. 396.
78 Ibid., p. 399.
79 G. W. F. Hegel, *The Letters*, trans. Clark Butler and Christiane Seiler (Bloomington:
Indiana University Press, 1984), p. 326.
80 I have developed this range of possibilities in G. Schner, 'The Appeal to Experience',
Theological Studies 53 (1992), pp. 40–59.
81 For a fuller discussion of the three cautions which follow see Louis Dupré, *Religious
Mystery and Rational Reflection* (Grand Rapids, MI: Eerdmans, 1998), pp. 1–40.
82 Friederich Schleiermacher, *On Religion*, trans. R. Crouter (Cambridge: Cambridge

University Press, 1988), p. 101.
83 Ibid., p. 102.
84 Ibid., p. 130.
85 Ibid., p. 104.
86 Ibid., p. 84.
87 Ibid., p. 138.
88 Ibid., p. 144.
89 Ibid., p. 146.
90 Ibid., p. 114.
91 Ibid., p. 134.
92 Ibid., p. 218.
93 Friederich Schleiermacher, *The Christian Faith*, ed. H. R. Mackintosh and J. S. Stewart (New York: Harper and Row, 1963), vol. 2, p. 495.
94 Ibid.
95 Friederich Schleiermacher, *Servant of the Word*, trans. Dawn De Vries (Philadelphia: Fortress Press, 1987), p. 111.
96 Schleiermacher, *The Christian Faith*, vol. 1, p. 126.
97 Karl Barth, *Church Dogmatics* (Edinburgh: T&T Clark, 1975), I/1, pp. 1–292.
98 Karl Barth, *Anselm*, trans. Ian Roberston (London: SCM Press, 1960), pp. 39–40.

Theology after Liberalism?

John Webster

The title *Theology after Liberalism* is, it must be admitted, a clumsy compromise. It can quite rightly be objected that using the term 'liberalism' to designate that which this theology is supposed to come 'after' fails to offer much by way of real discrimination, and runs the risk of falling back on an ill-defined term of abuse. Like any epochal or generic term, 'liberalism' is more of a rhetorical and political construct than a historical description, part of a larger strategy of making recommendations about what Christianity is and what Christian theology should be. At best, perhaps, all it can do is indicate very broad family resemblances between (say) the dogmatics and historical theology of later nineteenth-century German Protestantism and, for example, some strands of British theology before the Second World War and after 1960, or the revisionist theologies of the last thirty years in North America. At worst, the term becomes a weapon in the hands of theological terrorists of various factions, who use it (like its close cousins 'modernism' or 'fundamentalism') to dismiss or denounce what outrages them.

The problems are only compounded when we ask whether theology now *can* be 'after' liberalism. If 'theology after liberalism' is a way of recommending a theology which ignores or refuses to engage with those traditions which cluster around the term 'liberal', then theology *after* liberalism is, in effect, simply theology *before* liberalism. Nor may we claim too much by way of historical distance, as if we were able unambiguously to claim that liberalism has now passed and a new theological epoch has taken its place. Like 'postmodernism', 'postliberalism' is on shaky ground if it assumes too readily that it has neatly extricated itself from the entanglements of the past.

Moreover, there is a sense in which all authentically Christian theology is liberal. In the last few months of his life, Barth (rarely numbered among the giants of the liberal theological tradition) wrote thus:

> Being truly liberal means thinking and speaking in responsibility and openness on all sides, backwards and forwards, toward both past and future, and with what I might call total personal modesty. To be modest is not to be skeptical; it is to see what one thinks and says also has limits. This does not hinder me from saying very definitely what I think I see and know. But I can do this only in the awareness that there have been and are other people before and alongside me, and that still others will come after me. This awareness gives me an inner peace, so that I do not think I always have to be right even though I say definitely what I say and think. Knowing that a limit is set for me, too, I can move cheerfully within it as a free man.[1]

Why, then, persist in speaking of theology after liberalism?

Part of the justification must be the lack of a suitable alternative: most options are even less serviceable because they are more misleading. Terms like 'restorationist' or 'neo-conservative' suggest a kind of theological atavism which sees modernity as something to be escaped. 'Intratextual', a term which has been applied to some strands of postliberal theology which have been especially interested in the role of texts in Christian faith and theology, is rather too narrow a term to catch the range of interests found in this type of theology. It also masks some real hermeneutical and doctrinal diversity among those who otherwise have much in common. 'Postcritical', a term used by analogy from its deployment in describing similar work in philosophy, has not found any widespread acceptance. 'Postmodern' is probably the best alternative term available, and, indeed, typologies of contemporary theology occasionally distinguish between radically deconstructive postmodern theology and a kind of theology which is 'postmodern' in rejecting the terms of the pact between Christianity and modernity. However, the term 'postmodern' has by now become almost inseparably wedded to theologies of deconstruction, and cannot serve our purposes here.

'Postliberal' seems, therefore, the least problematic option. It has the virtue of having been used in the sub-title of what is now one of the classic statements of this kind of theological engagement, George Lindbeck's *The Nature of Doctrine: Religion and Theology in a Postliberal Age*. The book is, of course, very far from a manifesto of some closely defined theological party, and many of the contributors to this reader would disagree with one or more aspects of its treatment of the nature of the theological task. Moreover, as we are using it here, 'postliberal' refers to a much broader range of theological work than that of the so-called 'Yale school' (a designation which was itself only partially and temporarily accurate). Nevertheless, 'postliberal', for all its inadequacies, is probably as good a term as we will find to draw out the commonalities between different contemporary theological thinkers in a variety of different contexts. What are these commonalities?

1 Doctrines

One of the major points at which the various trajectories of postliberal theology converge is that of doctrine. Primarily, however, this is not because of a deliberate attempt to establish some measure of doctrinal consensus: there is, once again, no 'school' here, held together by a firm dogmatic frame. Postliberal theology is more a set of projects than a position. It is doubtless true that postliberal theologians are characteristically less critical of inherited doctrinal standards, and some would describe themselves as 'generously' (that is, neither uncritically nor triumphalistically nor bitterly) orthodox. Yet it is not so much an investment in specific doctrines which characterizes postliberal theology as a particular family of approaches to the task of doctrinal construction.

One way of depicting this set of approaches would be to draw a contrast between 'revisionist' or 'critical' and 'positive' theology. From the early 1960s until the mid-1980s, the dominant model of Christian doctrine in most mainstream academic institutions in both Britain and North America can be thought of as a late flowering of the theological traditions of the nineteenth century, and especially of nineteenth-century Germany. In North America, this often took the form of 'revisionism' – that is, the attempt to revise or, perhaps, reconstruct, Christian teachings in the light of what were felt to be prestigious aspects of modern culture, such as the natural or human sciences, existential and phenomenological anthropology, or history, for example. The intent was both apologetic and doctrinally constructive. That is, it sought to persuade the culture that Christian belief is not only viable but also the fulfilment of the aspirations of modern culture. And it also sought to articulate an account of Christian teaching which took its cultural responsibilities and determinants with full seriousness. In British theology, what was largely the same model showed less interest in the philosophy of existence, and assumed a somewhat more historical form. As 'doctrinal criticism', it offered critical analysis of major Christian doctrines in their classic, usually patristic, formulations (above all, the doctrines of the Trinity and the incarnation), seeking to lay bare how the development of these doctrines contained much that was arbitrary. On this basis, the argument was often made that such accidental developments need not claim the loyalties of contemporary believers, who were thus free to attempt other accounts of the same themes in Christian believing. Constructing alternatives to traditional formulations usually involved keeping a firm eye on putative intellectual norms – an interest in the human and historical, certain sorts of analytical philosophy, an interrogative attitude to moral objectivity and, latterly, an awareness of non-Christian religious traditions.

Postliberal theology differs in a number of ways from these projects, which until fairly recently have gone largely unchallenged in English-language systematic theology. Perhaps most significantly, postliberal theology has shown considerable interest in constructive rather than critical dogmatics. As we shall see, this is bound up with an understanding of theological 'method' which is unconvinced that a great deal is to be gained from the investigation of the foundations of theology in a pre-theological or semi-independent way. For the moment, however, it is important to note that those who might be termed postliberal have undertaken a good deal of *descriptive* doctrinal work. This has meant, on the one hand, a commitment to giving renewed attention to the internal structures of Christian doctrine, both in its constituent parts and in its interrelations, and, accordingly, to offering expositions of doctrine which are not directed by apologetic concerns but by a sense of responsibility towards (and, one might say, delight in) the grand ideas of the Christian tradition. On the other hand, this approach to the doctrine has also put forward a criticism that, if modern doctrinal work has failed, the failure has often been at the level of descriptive adequacy – the level, that is, of a failure to dig deep into or to make full use of Christian doctrine. Revisionist or critical accounts of Christian doctrine have often been reductionistic or even clumsy in their construals of Christian thought; postliberal theology has sought to revisit Christian doctrine, asking not so much what might be wrong with it but what resources it may contain to redefine or illuminate current perplexities.

Postliberal theology is, therefore, in an important sense a return to 'positive' theology – theology which sees itself as reflection upon a *positum*, a given, which does not need re-inventing in accordance with some set of cultural verities. This has involved a significant reconfiguration of the place of Christian doctrine and its relation to the other tasks which make up the theological curriculum. In particular, it has meant a new kind of alignment between systematic and historical theology. Revisionist and critical accounts of doctrine, though they did go hand in hand with historical work in theology (notably patristics), were by and large little interested in retrieval of the tradition, and looked elsewhere for the raw materials of doctrinal construction (to philosophy or psychology, for example). Postliberal theology has both emerged from and sponsored a re-reading of some of the great texts of the Christian tradition, in which it has found substantial resources which enable theology to get some purchase on its contemporary problems. Such re-reading of the classics is an aspect of a way of doing theology which gives priority to description over critical inquiry. In a sense, postliberal theology bears similarities to the movement in French Roman Catholic theology in the 1950s called *ressourcement*, in which the sources (especially patristic) of the church's teaching were rediscovered and reinterpreted in ways which broke apart received interpretations of them.[2] But whereas the *ressourcement* theologians (notably, Congar and de Lubac) deployed the results of this engagement against a rigid, anti-modernist theology which looked to the Christian past merely for reinforcements of established positions, postliberal theology is concerned to unsettle the stereotypical readings of the past which have at times been assumed in critical and revisionist paradigms.

Alongside this, postliberal theology often gives high profile to issues of Christian doctrine when it tries to make sense of the fate of Christian theology in modernity. Once again, in this it offers a significantly different style of theological practice. The genealogy of modernity in the dominant styles of academic theology sometimes assumes that the modern era (in which Kant's critical philosophy is often judged to be a culminating moment) is the end-point of a trajectory which stretches back through the Reformation and early modern periods, through the medievals to the patristic and apostolic eras. The trajectory comes to an end in modernity because, to put it simply, classical Christian theology does not contain within itself the resources to mount an effective challenge to its cultural context. The history of modern theology is thus often represented as theology (when it fails) being incapable of facing up to philosophical critique, or as theology (when it succeeds) discovering or inventing hitherto unused means of articulating the Christian faith. Such accounts are noticeably uncritical of modernity. Moreover, they can work on the assumption that the problems of Christian theology in the modern era stem not so much from appeal to the wrong doctrines or from inadequate attention to those doctrines, but simply from doctrine *per se*; the domestic resources of the Christian religious tradition are by definition (by Kant's definition, above all), incapable of meeting the challenge of critical thought.

Postliberal theology tends to offer a rather different genealogy, in which Christian doctrine plays a rather more conspicuous role. On this account, the problems faced by Christian theology in modernity stem not so much from unanswerable philosophical challenges as from mistakes made in Christian theology itself. Above all, postliberal theologians point to the quiet disappearance of appeal to basic Christian doctrine in the realignment of Western culture in the early modern period, so that (for example) trinitarian and incarnational doctrine is often considered to be irrelevant to Christian response to philosophical problems concerning the existence of God.[3] Or the replacement of a trinitarian account of divine agency in the creation and preservation of the world by more generic language about causality can be seen to lie beneath the incoherence of much of Christian theology's later response to the rise of natural science.[4] Or again, certain philosophical problems about Christian accounts of the relation of divine and human agency may stem less from the intrinsic unintelligibility of those accounts and more from inattention (on the part of both theologians and philosophers) to their specifically Christian content.[5] In short, for postliberal theology, good descriptive work in doctrine is crucial to displaying the essential features of the tasks of Christian theology in modernity. Critical problems which may appear insuperable begin to admit of resolution when the theological materials are expounded with the right sort of Christian determinacy.

2   Methods

Postliberal theology can be understood as a series of attempts to recover the significance for Christian theology of Christian specificity, and hence as a way of responding to the pressures of criticism by a *descriptive* move rather than by the elaboration of a better *theory* of theology or Christianity. Because of this, matters of theological method are distinctly secondary, understood as extensions of theology rather than as extra-ecclesial or extra-theological rules of operation, to which Christian theological discourse must conform if it is to have a voice in the public domain of the academy. Methods are governed by criteria of appropriateness to the fields of intellectual practice in which they are used. In Christian theology, this means that methods are procedural applications of doctrine.

The priority of doctrines over methods in postliberal theology is to some extent obscured by the fact that some of the key texts which gave voice to postliberal theology in the early 1980s were apparently heavily methodological in idiom (notably the work of Lindbeck and Frei). It is certainly true that early debates about postliberal theology did concentrate on questions of the nature of religion, hermeneutics, or the relation of Christian theology to other disciplines such as philosophy or interpretative social science. It is also true that some of the initial impetus for postliberal theology derived less from doctrinal resources (with the exception of the rediscovered work of Barth) and more from philosophers such as Wittgenstein and Ryle, social theorists such as Geertz, or literary historians such as Auerbach. However, as postliberal theology has settled, it has become clear both that earlier use of such theories was simply a way of appealing against modern conventions, and that the real drive of postliberal theology is to positive Christianity, and not to yet more methodological abstraction.

Indeed, one of the chief characteristics of postliberal theology has been its lack of heavy investment in prolegomenal or foundational discourse. Postliberal theology tends to start *in medias res*, and the apologetic effort to establish before doing theology the conditions under which theology is 'doable' is largely left to one side. As Frei put it, this is a style of theology which privileges Christian self-description over 'general theory'.[6] Thereby, both Christian self-description and general theory are quite drastically redefined. Christian self-description is not a mode of discourse which requires to be established before the bar of universal reason, a hermeneutics of praxis or some other external norm: it is simply the given on which theology sets to work. General theory is, accordingly, no longer the *sine qua non* for the articulation of Christian faith; the term simply indicates all those different discourses to which theology may make occasional (but not principled) appeal when to do so is convenient for the purposes of talking about Christianity.

Two important features of postliberal theology encourage this lack of investment in method. First, it is an aspect of a turn from critical inquiry as the defining condition of intellectual responsibility. That turn, echoed in many other scholarly fields, is one of the sharp points of difference from the theological models from which postliberal theology distances itself. This distance is not, of course, a matter of returning to a fundamentally non-critical theology of the kind in which whatever bit of Christian culture one finds oneself in is always unquestionably right (though some postliberal theology has often been accused of sponsoring that kind of intellectual stasis). It is more a matter of a conviction that Christian theology itself holds resources (indeed, *superior* resources) which can engender self-critical practice on the part of Christian communities and believers. Those resources (which can be spelled out doctrinally in terms of, for example, the transcendence of God or the permanent gift-character of revelation) can of themselves unsettle Christian drift into idolatry, and do so more effectively than external norms which enable criticism only by threatening to subvert the whole possibility of Christian faith and its traditions.

A second feature underlying lack of interest in independent theological methodological discussion is a shift in postliberal theology towards viewing theology as an aspect of the practice of Christianity. Here two factors come together. First, this shift is bound up with an account of Christianity as more like a culture than a set of philosophical or ethical teachings. Christianity is best understood, not by abstracting its claims from their cultural locale in determinate religious practices, but by seeing it as a highly complex set of activities, borne along by (for example) traditions of language and ritual, and embodied in institutional forms and roles. The emphasis, in other words, is on externality, rather than on religious interiority or intellectual reconstruction of the contents of religious practice. Second, therefore, the locus of theological activity is more naturally the church than it is the academy as currently understood. To avoid misunderstanding, it needs to be stressed that this is not to be read as postliberal theology seeking to retreat out of the public world of the academy into the private, self-referential or sectarian world of the church and its institutions of learning. It is, in fact, a critique of the established conventions of the academy, conventions which dictate that the religious convictions of voluntary communities must be screened out if the academy is to attain universality as the organ of independent, critical inquiry. Postliberal theology is more likely to argue that the modern academy is not a place of pure, value-free inquiry, but only one more institution, organized around conventions which are themselves culturally specific, and so cannot claim to be *the* location of critical practice.

In sum: for postliberal theology issues of the methods of theology are generally subsumed under discussion of the norms and sources of theology. In their turn, moreover, those norms and sources are located in the practices and traditions of Christianity as a positive religion, and external norms (such as content-independent standards of rationality) or external sources (such as common human experience) do not feature very large in its account of the theological enterprise. One important consequence here is that a richer range of intra–Christian sources is brought into play. For example, the spiritual and liturgical traditions of Christian faith have come to enjoy renewed attention in postliberal theology, which has not considered them merely ornamental but rather as ingredient within Christian self-definition, and thus as offering significant clues to the nature of theological rationality. Like methods and norms, that is, the sources of theology are for postliberal theology more Christianly specific than humanly generic.

3 Criticisms

Precisely because it offers a challenge to some of the regnant paradigms of theological practice, postliberal theology has attracted strong criticism. Any criticism always reveals as much about the critic as it does about the object of critique, and the sometimes sharp exchanges about postliberal theological proposals in the 1980s indicated that the emergence of this theology was considered a serious challenge to what had become established modes of practice. Its appeal to an unfamiliar set of theological criteria, the confessional, kerygmatic voice which came through even its most formal statements, and its proximity to what were perceived to be dangerously authoritarian stances, all made it hard to assimilate. But even when misunderstandings have been cleared away, some residual worries need to be mentioned (they are articulated in exemplary form in part four of this reader).

Of these worries, perhaps the most pressing is that of the construal of Christian faith and theology through what seem like closed categories. First voiced as a protest against the deployment of the notion of culture by Lindbeck in *The Nature of Doctrine*, this criticism rapidly expanded into a general alarm that postliberalism was proposing a version of Christianity which repudiated world-openness, tolerance and readiness to receive criticism, and succumbed to the temptations of sectarianism. This criticism has recently been developed into a further concern that ethnographic, descriptive treatments of Christianity such as are found in types of postliberal theology have very little diachronic sense, tending to view Christianity as a finished product, a determinate, mappable world rather than a process of historical construction, a 'reading' of reality. Various impulses could drive such a criticism. From the standpoint of mainline revisionist theology, postliberalism threatens to become simply a retreat into the sclerosis of authoritarianism and confessionalism. From a more radically postmodern viewpoint, postliberal accounts of Christianity lack a sense of the indeterminacy of Christian faith, failing to envisage it as a disorderly scatter of processes of negotiation rather than as a simple, stable entity. In quite another way, some who are in other respects highly sympathetic to postliberal theology may worry that the emphasis on Christianity as culture can lay too much weight on the immanent realities of Christian believing and belonging, and give insufficient space to discussion of divine action (perhaps most of all in postliberal talk of scripture as the church's store of meanings rather than as testimony to divine revelation). At this level, at least, postliberal theology seems to owe much to both Barth and Schleiermacher.

Something of the same line of argument could be pursued to ask about the doctrinal configuration with which postliberal theology often works. In one sense, as we have already seen, there is no such tightly structured configuration. Nevertheless, postliberal theology has been variously criticized for its weighting of doctrines – away from anthropology, for example, and towards ecclesiology. If the former move is out of line with theological revisionism in which anthropology almost always plays a foundational role, the latter move is for some an indicator of the need to develop operative language about the action of God, Christ and Spirit as the context for talk about Christian culture. Whether postliberal theology will eventually produce works of systematic range, consistency and balance remains to be seen.

In the end, the most startling feature of the best postliberal theology (as well as the feature which its critics find most puzzling) is its invocation of theological categories in describing the nature of theology, in narrating its history and in outlining its contemporary responsibilities. To its critics, this invocation almost by definition lifts it out of the public domain, detaching it from those fertilizing influences in the wider culture which have always been essential to theology's vitality. To its supporters, the absence of such invocation in the favoured modes of theology (whether modern or postmodern) is a sign that they are detached from the life-processes which are the proper ambience of theological work. In the witty lexicon at the end of *Ethics after Babel,* Jeffrey Stout defines postliberal theology thus: 'the quest ... to get beyond all forms of modernism in theology; either a *cul de sac* or the harbinger of a new theological age (too soon to tell)'.[7] The essays which follow are an invitation to ponder the issues: read on.

Notes

1 K. Barth, 'Liberal Theology – An Interview', in *Final Testimonies* (Grand Rapids, MI: Eerdmans, 1977), pp. 34ff.
2 See F. Kerr, 'French Theology: Yves Congar and Henri de Lubac', in D. F. Ford (ed.) *The Modern Theologians: An Introduction to Christian Theology in the Twentieth Century* (Oxford: Blackwell Publishers, 1997), pp. 105–17.
3 See M. J. Buckley, *At the Origins of Modern Atheism* (New Haven, CT: Yale University Press, 1987).
4 See C. Gunton, *The Triune Creator: A Historical and Systematic Study* (Edinburgh: Edinburgh University Press, 1998).
5 See K. Tanner, *God and Creation in Christian Theology: Tyranny or Empowerment* (Oxford: Blackwell Publishers, 1988).
6 H. Frei, *Types of Christian Theology* (New Haven, CT: Yale University Press, 1992).
7 J. Stout, *Ethics after Babel: The Languages of Morals and Their Discontents* (Boston: Beacon Press, 1988), p. 301.

PART

Doctrines

Identity Description and Jesus Christ

Hans Frei

This excerpt is from Hans Frei's *The Identity of Jesus Christ,* one of the foundational texts of postliberal theology, which lies behind much subsequent theological work on hermeneutics, the nature of theology and christological doctrine. The book centres on a distinction between an approach to Christology through questions of Jesus's presence (which Frei associates with the subjectivist traditions of liberal theology) and an approach through questions of Jesus's identity. The latter approach emphasizes the priority of the narrative biblical depiction of Jesus, and eschews any attempt to render Jesus in terms other than those in which his identity is enacted in the gospel story.

On the assumption of prior acquaintance with Jesus Christ, our claim is that the proper order for describing the unity of presence and identity in him is to begin with his identity. Our actual starting procedure, however, was the reverse. In speaking first of Christ's presence, it was concluded that any answer to the question, *How* is Christ present? that is not based on the prior question, *Who* is he? would be hopelessly entangled and useless. At best, it would involve endless and inconclusive arguments about the relation of the description of the 'Jesus of history' to that of the 'Christ of faith', in the vain hope that adding these two abstractions together would somehow provide us with the description of one concrete person. At worst, we could expect to end up with the discovery that the endeavour to understand Christ's presence to ourselves is a projection of our own presence.

If one begins with presence rather than with identity, the question, How is

Christ present? is finally answered by the mysterious movement of Christ toward us, coinciding with our movement toward him. The result of this complete coincidence or simultaneity is, in the last analysis, the ultimate dissolution of both our own presence and his. His presence is not his own; indeed, he is diffused into humanity by becoming one with it. And we, in turn, find in him the mysterious symbol expressing our own ultimate lack of abiding presence and identity. In this fashion, humanity in general or a representative portion of it, such as the church, is the community in which Christ and we become one. Humanity (or the church) then *is* Christ present, and to say this is also to claim that it is the only abiding presence we ourselves have. Such a presence, e.g. that of the archetypal and nameless human stranger, and our own become mysteriously diffused into each other, so that they are one and the same. This, of course, is not what Christians believe (even if the fusion of these modes of presence is taken to be the church), but it is a typical consequence of seeking to discern the unity of Christ's presence and identity by beginning with the understanding of the former.

We must, therefore, turn to the description of his identity, the delineation of which is a delicate thing, as we have already seen. We cannot, for instance, inquire into the 'actual' life and character of Jesus inferred from the records. Most scholars agree that the gospels do not furnish us with the requisite information for such a reconstruction. Nor can we probe the intentions and themes or even the cultural contexts of the gospel writers that underlie the story. Our task is, rather, to observe the story itself, its structure, the shape of its movement, and its crucial transitions.

Reading a story, whether the gospel story or any other, has been rightly compared to understanding a work of visual art, such as a piece of sculpture: we do not try to imagine the inside of it, but let our eyes wander over its surface and its mass, so that we may grasp its form, its proportions and its balances. What it says is expressed in any and all these things, and only by grasping them do we grasp its 'meaning'. So also we grasp the identity of Jesus within his story. There are, of course, parts of the New Testament that do not tell a story, but in the gospels, which tell us most of what we know about Jesus, his identity is grasped only by means of the story told about him.

Several demands are put on us when we inquire into the identity of Jesus Christ in the story about him. First, as we have already attempted to show, the story of Jesus is not really the story of all mankind or, at least, of men of a certain type. In other words, we had to meet the claim that Jesus's identity might turn out to be an identity shared with other storied saviour figures. One such is the mythical saviour figure of Gnosticism, who is not really an individual person and therefore can be represented by any number of salvation stories. Another is the fictional 'Christ figure', who can be embodied in many novel-like stories. Christians claim that to identify the Jesus of the gospel story with either of these types causes serious confusion. The identity of the Christian saviour is revealed completely by the story of Jesus in the gospels and by none other.

Secondly, knowing the identity of any person involves describing the continuity of the person who acts and is acted upon through a stretch of time. But it also involves describing the genuine changes, sometimes to the very core of a person's being, that occur both in that person's character and in the circumstances of a story. A good storyteller manages to do both things without experiencing any difficulties in the process, as Henry James suggested in a brief remark: 'What is character but the determination of incident? What is incident but the illustration of character?' A metaphysician, on the other hand, who has to explain how both change and sameness, unity and diversity, can be real at the same time and in the same conceptual universe may have a more complicated time of it. But we are inquiring into the shape of a story and what it tells about a man, in contrast to metaphysical explanations that would tell us what sorts of things are or are not real and on what principles they cohere.

Thirdly, proper attention to the identity of Jesus also forces us to pay close heed to the appropriate technical and formal categories with which to describe identity. The task here is first to determine what the categories are and then to keep them from taking over the show. In other words, the tools for description easily may and often do turn out to govern with such a heavy hand the material to be described that they distort the descriptions intended. Toward the end of chapter 4, we said that in order to determine any individual's identity it is necessary to ask two formal questions: 'Who is he?' and 'What is he like?' It will now be necessary to ask, What is the force of these formal questions or categories for identity description?

What is Meant by a Formal Question?

But before we proceed we need to ask again what is meant by a 'formal question' and why it matters so much for our enterprise. A formal question, such as 'Who is he?' or 'What is he like?' is one to which an answer is necessary if we are to know anything at all about a person. But more importantly, it is a question that will not force an answer that would risk overwhelming either the person or the story. By contrast, we may mention two alternate kinds of identity analysis that do take this risk and thus demonstrate the real importance of a purely formal approach to identity.

One approach involves asking how a person in a story illuminates, or perhaps merely illustrates, this or that problem of our common existence. It may also involve asking what a person is like in comparison to other persons. In other words, the description of an identity involves comparative reference to the characteristics, conditions or destinies of some other persons or of all mankind as they may be viewed from the standpoint of a given cultural or social framework. In our day, the comparative reference is usually to the common qualities of estrangement, self-alienation or some other basically divisive conflict that may appear within the self, between the self and its society, or between social forces. I do not wish to argue that such references are wrong in relation to the story of Jesus; I only wish to say that in this instance the category in terms of which the identity question is framed materially influences the answer, and the description is not a formal one. The *question* rather than the story becomes the governing context with which the person is identified. (In modern theology the thought of Paul Tillich and Rudolf Bultmann are typical instances of this procedure; for Bultmann in particular the question addressed to a text becomes an important principle for its interpretation.)

A second approach that tends to force an answer that distorts either the person or the story by going beyond mere formal identity inquiry is in some measure contrasted with the first. This approach does involve trying to determine a person's identity by referring simply to himself rather than to others or to humanity as an existential concern. But the attempt in this instance is made by adding a kind of depth dimension to the story's surface, which is actually a speculative *inference* from what is given in the story, rather than a part of it. This procedure enables us to write something like the story behind the story so that we can, for example, explain the consistency of Jesus's actions by reference to the consistency of his inner disposition. The story thus becomes merely the outward illustration of his unswerving inward disposition and tells only what is true about the person in any case. Here, to revert to the dictum of Henry James, incident is indeed the illustration of character, but character and disposition are not shaped by incident.

This approach involves a fundamental prior decision, one that limits the category of identity to the description of the person as distinct from the sequence of events in his own unique story. Identity is given a status independent of, prior to, and only tenuously connected with the story. Thus, in this view, an independently derived notion of Jesus's identity really shapes the story to conform to that notion. The story of Jesus, by virtue of its sketchiness, makes such an enterprise possible. Moreover, the results are often illuminating. But it is obvious that in such a process the category of identity serves more than a formal function, for it gives independent content to Jesus's person or character, which then shapes the reading of the story. (There are innumerable instances of this procedure in modern theology. One that raised considerable interest in scholarly circles some years ago is James M. Robinson's *A New Quest of the Historical Jesus*.)[1]

The two approaches we have briefly mentioned here (which sometimes are in effect one and the same) illustrate the peril of tearing asunder the person and his story in identity description and freighting the inquiry after identity with more than formal categories, even before the examination of the story begins. With this in mind, we will seek to confine ourselves as best we can to the purely formal categories expressed in the questions, 'Who is he?' and 'What is he like?'

'Like' in 'What is this person like?' does not indicate comparative reference to others or to humanity at large, but simply a typical state or action of a person that would properly and genuinely constitute or characterize him. Because we seek with this question to come upon a person in his characteristic stance, the question endeavours to pinpoint him in specific actions or in responses to specific occurrences that involve him. In other words, this category or question accentuates a person's *story*, the *changes* (even those to the very core of him) that he undergoes, and his *acts at a given point* or over a limited stretch of time. The question, 'What is he like?' is answered by an intention–action description.

The second category for identity description is embodied in the question, 'Who is he?' A much more elusive question than the first, it focuses not so much on a person's story directly, or on crucial changes in a person, as on the person himself in his ongoing self-continuity, as he acts and is acted upon in the sequence of the story's events. In other words, the second question concentrates on the steady line of *persistence* that is involved in the very idea of a person. His changes are real indeed; yet he remains the same identical person. The question 'Who is he?' is answered by describing the subject as he is in and through his self-manifestations.

The Unity Between Intention and Action

We shall spend more time on the second question, because its implications are harder to grasp. But to return momentarily to the first, it is essential to understand certain of its overtones. The appropriate answer to the question, 'What is he like?' is: 'Look at what he did on this or that occasion. Here he was characteristically himself.' If there is an instance (or instances) for a given person when we can say that he was most of all himself, we should say that his action in that instance does not merely *illustrate* or *represent* his identity. Rather, it *constitutes* what he is. A person *is* what he *does* centrally and most significantly. He is the unity of a significant project or intention passing over into its own enactment.

Above all, in asking what a person is like, it is essential to grasp the intimate unity of intention and action. An intention, unless impeded or frustrated, is no intention and has no mental status at all except as a plan to be executed. The expression 'I intend' is rightly and logically followed by a verb, i.e. an action word. On the other hand, an event that happens accidentally or without intention is an occurrence rather than an action.

Intention and action logically involve each other in verbal usage. 'To perform intelligently,' says Gilbert Ryle quite correctly, 'is to do one thing and not two things.'[2] Hence, each has to be described by reference to the other. An intention is nothing other than an implicit action; but to say this is not to make intention and action one and the same. The necessary use of the qualifying adjectives 'explicit' and 'implicit' in defining each by the other makes that point clear. Wherein, then, does their unity lie?

Their unity, we can only repeat, is the irreversible passage or movement from one to the other, from intention into action. The enactment of intention always differs from the intention to enact; and each person has inside knowledge of how he passes from one state of affairs to the other directly and without a break. Our identity is constituted by the enactment of central and, in that sense, characterizing intentions, but it is not constituted by the intention alone. For in that case the intention or decision to act would account for everything, the actual enactment for nothing. On the other hand, enactment – the positive external occurrence without an ingredient of intention in it – also does not constitute a human identity, just because it does not pertain to a centred self, but only to a piece of overt behaviour.

We need to say one more word about identifying a person in his intentional acts. Earlier we said that this kind of identification, answering to the question 'What is he like?', points more to changes within a person and to the person's story than to the persistence of the person in the person–story interaction. There are, therefore, limits to this manner of identifying a person. The persistence of the same person through all the changing events, and even through his own changes, is a factor still to be dealt with. It leads to the second category or question of identity description, 'Who is he?' which we shall consider in a moment. But first there is the further limitation on the identification of a person in his story, that a person's story is not only the enactment of *his own* intentions or his own identity, but the enactment of others' intentions and even of unintended events as well as those not specifically intended. Things happen *to* a person that enter into the very identification of him; they are enacted or occur upon or through him. Do such external acts or occurrences become embodied in him? Do they become part of his identity, since they are woven into his story? Undoubtedly, yes, and in part by his own response to or incorporation of these happenings.

What is to be stressed here is that our categories for identity description break down at this very point. They cannot describe how external events become ingredient in a person's identity directly, i.e. other than by his own response to them. All that one can do to describe a person in that situation of direct impact by circumstances upon him (and not as refracted through his own response) and how he becomes himself in and through these circumstances is simply to tell the story of the events.

It is useful to point to this limitation in the applicability of the formal question, 'What is he like?' For without the impingement of external occurrences on the person, there is no story and no person, just as there is none without the external enactment of one's inner intention. But whereas the latter contingency is describable in terms answering to our formal question, the former is not. These reflections are of some significance in the understanding of the gospel story. The identity of Jesus in that story is not given simply in his inner intention, in a kind of story behind the story. It is given, rather, in the enactment of his intentions. But even to say that much is not enough. Rather, his identity is given in the mysterious coincidence of his intentional action with circumstances partly initiated by him, partly devolving upon him. The latter kind of occurrence also, in part, shapes his identity within the story.

The Persistence, Elusiveness and Ultimacy of a Person's Life

The focus of the second category for identity description, embodied in the question, 'Who is he?' is somewhat harder to specify. The task is difficult because it is unclear what the pronoun 'who' asks about, beyond some apparently superficial clue, such as a person's name, or else simply the same thing we discussed under the preceding question (a person's characteristic intentional action). Beyond these two alternatives, the question apparently could refer only to that hypothetical, separable and hidden being inside the organism, steadily unchanged, who purportedly pulls the strings by which the body puts act into effect.

But granted our dissatisfaction with all these solutions, not many of us will dismiss as meaningless the question, 'Who is he?' or even the admittedly prejudicial and often overdramatized question, 'Who am I?' At the very least, such questions are useful in pointing us to the necessity of taking into account the *persistence, elusiveness* and *ultimacy* of personal life in the description of a person.

(a) Persistence

Of persistence we have already spoken, referring to self-continuity or self-ascription over a period of time. The question, 'Who is he?' obviously points us to the identity or self-persistence of a person from action to action, rather than (as does our preceding question) to the uniqueness of each action and the possibility of change at the core of the self from one act to the next.

(b) Elusiveness

The elusiveness of the 'who' lies in the fact that one's own acts *now* cannot become objects of knowledge to oneself until they have receded into the past. If we try to describe (even indirectly) what constitutes the bond of selfhood between a self's own actions, we would have to refer to the self as this elusive, present subject. Persistence and elusiveness go together.

(c) Ultimacy

Finally, ultimacy simply means that asking the question, 'Who is he?' indicates that we can *des*cribe no personal–physical states, characteristics and actions except as we *a*scribe them *to* someone. At least this is true in ordinary conversation. And the 'someone' to whom they are ascribed is ultimate because in ordinary conversation no person is a quality, state or action predicable of another.

But there is still something unsatisfactory about all that we have said concerning the question, 'Who is he?' We may indeed agree that the personal pronoun 'who' indicates the subject in his persistence, elusiveness and ultimacy; but these qualities are simply higher order generalizations that hold true for all identity descriptions. But the very point of asking 'Who . . . ?' was largely to escape a common characterization that applies generally to a number of persons and, instead, to pinpoint specific identity. So we are still tempted to ask, 'Yes, but *who* specifically is he?'

To such a question we are forced to give indirect and not fully satisfying answers. Anything more ambitious will deny the elusiveness of the subject-self and, in effect, return to 'the ghost in the machine' position discussed earlier. The specific and unsubstitutable subject-self does come provided with indispensable marks of identification, but they are also so intimately identified with him that they are, in a certain manner, himself. There is no descriptive device that can enable us to be more precisely definite than saying 'in a certain manner'.

The chief, though not necessarily only, means by which the 'who' question is answered are a person's name and his body. In particular, the identifying status of the name is ambiguous, and the only hope for the name's serving the purpose is that the person himself will supply what others cannot – the intrinsic or organic identification between the core of himself and that name which others attached to him arbitrarily and superficially. The hope is that he will act so as to identify himself with his name as given. Only so is it really his name, and only thus is his name the final clue to his identity. With regard to the body, it would seem a bit more difficult to refuse to identify oneself with it.

From the particular identifying action of naming and taking a name, it is but a short step toward another identification with a tangible or intangible community, either the one by which one has been named or some other. Such a community may be as broad as 'humanity' or as narrow as one other human being. However, even though such identification is indispensable for any human being, it always comes close to identification by comparative reference and hence eludes identification of specific and unsubstitutable identity. But the device of naming suggests not only reference to a person's community setting for the purpose of identifying him, but also the use of *words* as the closest and most intimate exercise in the process of identification. The ascription of a name to a person and his self-identification with it are perhaps the most mysterious uses of a word, a mystery in back of which there is no need to go.

A Person is His Word and His Body

Because the subject-self is elusive and cannot be a direct commentary on that performance which is itself, the unity between the self's identity and the *manifestation* of that identity in the person's use of his name or of other words is bound to remain mysterious and indirect for any description. How is it that any word, a mere sound that ordinarily designates public and observable items like chairs and vegetables, can become the vehicle for the communication of *personal* meaning? We cannot penetrate the mystery of it, but we know it can be done without misleading others about what the words refer to. At times a man's speech is literally his embodiment. He is revealed in his words; indeed, he *is* his word. Sometimes this is the case when a person makes promises, sometimes when his speech sets forth the common purpose of his community, and sometimes when he verbalizes the profoundest states of his affective life. In short, a person's self-identification with his words, in particular those that we have come to call 'performative utterances', is perhaps the most acute form of the unity between the subject and his self-manifestation. It is one of the bases for the coherence between public and private meaning in the use of words.

There are, we said, two identifying means by which the subject is manifest. The first is the verbal medium. The second is that of the body with its peculiar and unexchangeable location that is called *mine*. That body is properly referred to as *mine*, as the *manifestation* of myself and as *I*. The body is indeed possessively distinct from me. It is my body to dispose of and direct in action. There is nothing wrong with saying 'I try to keep my body fit' and, by so saying, to indicate the possessive relation to it. But it is equally appropriate to say 'I keep myself fit' and thereby to point to the fact that the body is not merely a possession, but the intimate *manifestation* of myself. Neither the possessive relation to nor that of manifestation of the subject suggests that the body is a mere external accretion to the 'real' self. Not only is the body the self in manifestation; it *is* the self. The body is I, or rather I am the body occupying this particular, unsubstitutable space. So we say 'I' (and not 'my body') walk from here to the corner. There is no way to state more simply the identity of the self as manifest in and yet identical with its embodiment.

Self-manifestation in both word and body suggests that the elusive and persistent subject can only be described indirectly, i.e. in and through its manifestation. But indirectness does not mean failure by any means. In neither case do we point to a vanishing or unintelligible fact. Instead, each form of description of the subject involves a public medium that both fitly *represents* and *is* the subject. The parallel between the 'who' category and our earlier category ('What is he like?') is evident. In each instance there is a strong relation between the inward and the outward: intention is directly linked with enactment, the subject-self with its manifestation. Neither case has a 'ghost in the machine' character, and each illustrates a healthy regard for the intrinsic significance of the outward life. It remains only to be stressed that neither description gets at a more 'basic' view of the person than the other. The person is as fully described by his intention–action pattern as by the pattern of his self-manifestation.

The Self Seen in Alienation from its Manifestation

Both descriptions suggest the compatibility of inwardness and outwardness in personal identity. It is important to stress this point, for there is another kind of formal inquiry into personal identity that is quite contrary to this analysis. This kind of inquiry may also come under the 'who' question, but its outcome is quite different. Yet because it is a common analysis of human identity or existence underlying much technical theological interpretation of the New Testament, it is of importance for us. Recall that we have stressed that intention is implicit action and that the name and the body are identifying marks of the self. But they are not, we said, merely *manifestations* of the self; they *are* also the self manifest. The self does not stand in mysterious and ineffable fashion in back of them. Rather, there is a complex of indirect identity between the self and its manifestation. Obviously, what is assumed here is that there is a real *fitness* or congruence between the self and its manifestation or representation. Now it is just this assumption which is rejected in the other form of posing and answering the 'who' question.

In the analysis of a good many modern philosophers and theologians, from Hegel to Heidegger's early philosophy, from Kierkegaard to Bultmann and Tillich (including some aspects of Marxist thought), there is, at best, a real distance between *true selfhood* and its *manifestation* and, at worst, a genuine incongruence or contradiction between them. Whether the situation *must* be so may be a moot question for some of them; but at least it seems to them to be so *in fact*, when they look at the actual, external or cultural situation of the self related to history.

The path that analysts of this sort are treading is thorny, delicate and narrow. On the one side, lies the assumption of a real fitness, even identity, between the subject-self and its manifestation – an analysis that seems wrong to them. But the obvious alternative, that since the self is in principle incapable of realization in its manifestation, the real self must inevitably stand in back of its manifestation – a ghost in the machine once more – is also rejected with equal firmness.

As a matter of fact, however, a good case can be made out that the latter position is precisely the danger to which such analysts are subject, although they wish, without doubt, to avoid it. What they attempt is to come down between these two undesirable alternatives and suggest a description of the self that is neither back of nor yet fitly embodied in its manifestations. What they suggest is that all manifestations, not only the words and names and psychological structures of individuals, but also the whole complex of social institutions and cultures in which selves interact and are collectively manifested, are distorted manifestations of the true subject self. As one consequence of this analysis, history becomes the ever-dissatisfied or 'self-alienated' quest of the self or of humanity for its true being through the cultural forms of its own distortedness. In this fashion, the self is at once identical and yet paradoxically not identical with its own individual and collective forms of existence.

Certain other consequences follow from such an analysis. In the first place, there are striking affinities between it and some aspects of the Gnostic outlook. We discussed in chapters 3 and 6 the sense of alienation in the world, of wandering through it in search of one's identity, the haunting possibility that the closest one can come to an authentic sense of identity is the fully cognizant acceptance of the state of alienation, realizing paradoxically that one has no identity of one's own. These are possibilities common to the two traditions. Parallel to this sense of alienation is the conviction that, if the self is neither a substantial, self-contained identity accessible back of outer reality nor an identity fitly embodied in its manifestation, then there is no direct way of expressing what one truly is nor even what one thinks and feels about human identity. Myths, indirect communication and forms of language other than the ordinary and public usage of words are the only ways of pointing toward what cannot be expressed directly.

Secondly, the focus of identification in this description is on the mysterious subject who is not in the technical language of this tradition's philosophers and theologians 'objectifiable'. The subject, that is to say, is distorted as soon as it is caught, frozen and represented in outward manifestation. What is true to its own nature in a work of art, in an action, even in a stretch of history and the understanding of it, is the intending, the deciding, the moment of doing, and not the external deposit that results from it. If one tries to understand an intention–enactment sequence, one must concentrate on the intention or the moment of decision and not on the enactment. If one tries to grasp a subject in its manifestation, one must look at the manifestation only to the extent that it mirrors the subject. In hearing a person's words, one must seek to grasp the being or the personal event within these words. But particularly in trying to grasp the meaning of a sequence of historical events, one must go back of the web of external occurrences and grasp instead the original moment of intending and doing, just as it was on the point of *passing* over, but before it had *passed* over, into external embodiment or into a specific act.

Thirdly, we must ask what happens when this analysis of self-manifestation in distortion rather than in fitness (and the accompanying conviction that a subject's being and doing cannot be 'objectified') is applied to the study of the New Testament. We have already mentioned the consequences in the introduction to this discussion. The formal category of identity description under this version of the 'who' question, we said, runs the risk of supplying the material content to the gospel story rather than deriving that content from the story itself. In this type of identity description, the person and the story tend to be pulled apart, and the emphasis is laid on the 'unobjectifiable' subject in back of the story rather than on the story's sequence of external occurrences.

Furthermore, this analysis of human identity tends to confront the person and story of Jesus with a prior judgement that what is important here must be judged by the criterion we have just mentioned: how Jesus and his story bear on the dilemma of the self at once embodied and yet not embodied in the historical, cultural world. That world, we recall, is in this analysis the place of human self-alienation or self-distortion. Authentic existence in the world, the genuine preservation of one's identity, lies precisely in realizing this dilemma and therefore never losing oneself or one's identity by simple identification with the world. This, then, in this alternate form of interpretation, becomes the frame of reference within which the story of Jesus is significant. Jesus himself, in his preaching and action, is seen to manifest a crucial choice against such simple identification with the world; and he, therefore, is the crucial occasion for our own decision as to who we are.

But, once again, have not the 'formal' categories for identification really taken over the person and the story in this analysis? Have not Jesus and his story been forced into a preconceived pattern whether the right or wrong one? We conclude that, instead of this, the proper procedure is first to look at the story, under as few categories and as formal a scheme of categories for identity description as possible, to see what it tells us about Jesus's identity, and we must use the same procedure in examining those who gain their own identity, by implication, in relation to him.

The Enacted Intention of Jesus

What is Jesus like in the story told about him? We stressed earlier that in the gospels, in contrast to Gnostic accounts, the saving activity has no role independent of the story of the individual, Jesus. The story of salvation is the story he enacts – the story of his obedience in redeeming guilty men by vicarious identification with their guilt and literal identification with their helplessness. In chapter 3, one possible pattern was suggested for understanding Jesus's story. It could well be taken symbolically, as the story pattern of man – the wandering stranger without identity. Jesus's virginal conception, lowly birth, wandering ministry, mysteriously ambiguous identity, and even his empty tomb all lend credence to this interpretation. What we must now try to show is that the story as story – not necessarily as history – should be taken in its own right and not symbolically and that, if it is read for its own sake, it suggests that Jesus's identity is self-focused and unsubstitutably his own. He is not the wandering stranger, but the one individual so completely himself that his inalienable identity not only points us to his own inescapable presence, but also is the focus toward which all of us orient our own identity – each one in his own person and place. For he is the assurance that particular identity is not a false front for its own opposite, the loss of identity and presence.

In the New Testament story, Jesus is seen to enact the good of men on their behalf – or their salvation – in perfect obedience to God. It is not, as we have said, that love to men was his only or even his predominant behavioural quality. Rather, he was perfectly obedient, and his obedience to God was one with his intention to do what had to be done on men's behalf. In this way, his mission was identical with love for men.

But do we actually know that much about Jesus? Certainly not, if we are asking about the 'actual' man apart from the story. But that is not our concern. Whether indeed the 'historical' Jesus *intended* the crucifixion and in what sense, whether he went freely to his death and with what motives, we cannot infer directly from the available evidence. The *believer* will, of course, find confirmation of the coming together of Jesus's intention and acts with those of God in God's raising him from the dead. He will claim that whatever Jesus's motives, the resurrection is the seal of God's confirmation upon them. Indeed, the resurrection demonstrates Jesus's acceptability to God as being obedient to God's will. But the resurrection is not, of course, an event subject to critical historical judgement; and even if taken at face value, it, by itself, tells us little about the internal history of Jesus.

We are, in fact, thrown back on the story simply as a story, regardless of whether or not it is well documented. But, then, do we actually have testimony to Jesus's obedience in his story? Here the answer is a decisive 'yes'. The testimony we have is not of a detailed sort. It does *not* light up the motives, the decision-making process, the internal ambiguities, or the personality of the story's chief protagonist. Nor is there, precisely at those points in the story where claim is laid to a knowledge of Jesus's intentions, any evidence whatever that there were others present or that he had shared his thoughts with them. In other words, at those few points at which the story gives an inside glimpse of Jesus's intentions, they are *not* provided in the same way a biographer or historian provides inferential or indirect clues from the witness's testimony or other external data. The insight we are allowed is far more sparse and restrained than that, and yet also more intimate. It is like that of the novelist who tells us from the inside, as it were, of his subject's intentions and the bond by which they lead into action. This is what the gospel story does at one or two crucial points; but it does so in exceedingly spare terms that do not search out the personality, inner motivation, or even the ethical quality of Jesus. The glimpse we are provided within the story of Jesus's intentions is just sufficient to indicate the passage of intention into enactment. And what is given to us is neither intention alone nor action alone, neither inner purpose alone nor external circumstance alone. Rather, he becomes who he is in the coincidence of his enacted intention with the train of circumstances in which the story comes to a head.

So the pattern of Jesus's identification in the story is at once simple and subtle, unitary and complex. When we seek to determine what Jesus was like by identifying the enactment of his central intention, we note that those who told the story about him or commented on it speak of his obedience to God's will (Romans 5:19; Philippians 2:8; Hebrews 5:8). Secondly, when we ask about the manner in which his obedience was enacted, we are brought face-to-face with the *coexistence* of power and powerlessness in his situation. But we also note that there is a *transition* from one to the other. Indeed, the narrative points simultaneously to the pattern of coexistence and transition between power and powerlessness. Jesus enacted the good of men on their behalf in both ways. It is his vicarious identification with the guilty and, at the climax of the story, his identification with the helplessness of the guilty that provide the gospel's story of salvation. Yet this helplessness is his power for the salvation of others. Something of his power abides and is accentuated as he becomes helpless. The pattern of exchange becomes the means of salvation. In the description of Jesus, one has to keep coming back to the ironic truth of the words of the priests and the scribes, 'He saved others; he cannot save himself' (Mark 15:31). These words detail the pattern of the saving action and suggest that, if Jesus had not forsaken the power to save himself, he could not have saved others. Thus, the transition from power to helplessness is at the same time the realization of his saving power. There is, then, not only transition but also coexistence between his power and powerlessness.

Finally, in discussing the complex pattern of Jesus's obedience, it must be noted that the enacted intention of Jesus to obey God and to enact men's good on their behalf meshes with external circumstances devolving upon him. That is to say that the exact circumstances climaxing his story were not completely initiated and executed at his behest. On the other hand, he did not passively await and accept them. In fact, his identity is revealed in the mysterious unity of his own decision and determination with the circumstances and events of his passion and death. He is identified as well by his initiation of circumstances, his response to them and their sheer impingement upon him.

Without this narrative sequence of events that climaxes the gospel story, we should not be able to identify Jesus by an intention and action pattern. But we must add that the circumstances making up the sequence of the story should not be regarded as fated. They are, rather, due to the interaction between Jesus and the initiative of the power he calls 'Father' to the very end. In addition to the coexistence and transition between power and powerlessness, the identity of Jesus that is manifest in his obedience must be seen in the mysterious manner in which his intention–action pattern meshes or interacts with that of God in the gospel story.

He Was Obedient

Jesus was obedient to the will of God. This is the light in which the apostle Paul writing before the composition of the synoptic gospels as we now have them saw what Jesus did. Apparently Paul himself saw the action of Jesus that way in at least partial dependence on a yet earlier tradition (Romans 5:19; Philippians 2:5–11). It is striking that, in all four gospels and in the other writings of the New Testament, it is the motif or quality of obedience that is stressed in regard to the person of Jesus. By contrast, there is, for example, very little mention of his faith. The characterization does not occur at all outside the gospels (except for one uncertain reference in Hebrews 12:2, but even this seems to speak of him as the one 'on whom faith depends from start to finish',[3] rather than the 'pioneer' of faith [Revised Standard Version]). Within the gospels, the references to Jesus's power rising out of his faith are few and ambiguous (Mark 9:23; Matthew 27:43). Undoubtedly Jesus is the ground or source of the believer's faith; but if we trace the movement that goes from his teaching to his personal being, to his power for salvation, and thence to the believer's new relation to him, we cannot say that 'faith' is the common underlying factor in all stages. We simply have no warrant from the sources for this conclusion. To draw it would be to claim an inside knowledge of him that we do not have. This is true not only by virtue of the sparse amount of information the gospel story provides us about Jesus, but also because of the kind of information we are actually given. As a storied figure, it is not his faith, but his mission and his obedience to it to which constant reference is made. He is one who is 'sent'. All the gospels have such self-references on Jesus's part, and the fourth gospel abounds in them. The counterpart of this is his consent to 'him who sent me' (Matthew 10:40; John 13:20) and to the events enacting the purpose for which he was sent (Matthew 26:53–54; Luke 24:26; John 12:27; 18:11).

The implication of what we have said about the primacy of Jesus's obedience as a clue to his identity is interesting. If we were able instead to begin our understanding of him by grasping certain of his inherent personal character-istics, such as his faith – and we might add love, freedom, authoritativeness – we should be able to construct his personality from them. Moreover, the characteristic most profoundly typical of him would then be the clue to his personality and to his saving power. Now, such characteristics may be inferred from the story about Jesus, but what must be kept in mind is that they do not reside at the very centre of the story. In fact, we do not possess any such profound or intimate knowledge of him. The main point is, however, that if we did have such knowledge of him, we should be able to find the centre of Jesus's person within himself rather than in his story, i.e. in relation to the events of his life and the persons with whom he came in contact.

We may illustrate the point by returning to the question of Jesus and the quality of faith. We commonly think of faith as faith *in* something and therefore to be seen only in relation to that object. But when faith is regarded as the central characteristic of a person, then what counts is not that to which faith refers, but the quality of the person's faith itself. What is presupposed in such an understanding is that faith is a spiritual characteristic of him, a disposition that shapes his outlook and behaviour patterns. It is significant that we have no such direct knowledge available from the gospel story by which to characterize Jesus. The story and the early commentary about him show only that he was fundamentally obedient, rather than faithful, loving, free or authoritative.

And the point about his obedience is that it is not, like these other hypothetical qualities, regarded as a quality in its own right in the story. His obedience exists solely as a counterpart to his being sent and has God for its indispensable point of reference. Jesus's very identity involves the will and purpose of the Father who sent him. He becomes who he is in the story by consenting to God's intention and by enacting that intention in the midst of the circumstances that devolve around him as the fulfilment of God's purpose. The characterizing intention of Jesus that becomes enacted – his obedience – is not seen 'deep down' in him, furnishing a kind of central clue to the quality of his personality. Rather, it is shown in the story with just enough strength to indicate that it characterized him by making the purpose of God who sent him the very aim of his being.

We may suggest three consequences that result from this attempt to identify what Jesus was like from the story's depiction of his intentional action. (1) As we have emphasized from the beginning of this essay, the focus of this story, unlike that of Gnostic myth, clearly turns on Jesus as the unsubstitutable, specific individual he is and becomes through the equally specific actions and circumstances of his last days. (2) In very broad terms, Jesus's identity is centred on his moral action in moving towards a certain goal, rather than on his basic, constantly unchanging yet constantly renewed self-understanding. This fact, no doubt, provides a clue to the New Testament's understanding of how others are to see their own identity in relation to that of Jesus. The clue to that relation lies more in moral obedience than in profound self-grasp. (3) Unlike what one finds in so many Christ figures, Jesus has, in his story, a clearly personal centre, a self-focused identity. It is he who makes the pattern of coexistence as well as the pattern of transition between power and helplessness flow together in their complex harmony. They are not a set of paradoxically or otherwise related states or qualities for which he is the empty personal receptacle. These states or qualities do not exist apart from his person. Instead, he makes them instruments of his saving efficacy, making them all internal to his obedience to God. There is no power for salvation in such pre-established, paradoxical qualities as helplessness and power, guilt and purity, either in themselves or apart from him. They become efficacious for salvation because they are *his* and because he holds them together in the enactment of his obedience to God.

The Characterization of Jesus in His Obedience

The characterization of Jesus as obedient man is not simply inferred but is directly set forth at two points at which the story, in very restrained fashion, tells us something 'from the inside' of the intention of Jesus's moving toward enactment. In a certain sense, this direct portrayal is at the heart of the temptation episode right after Jesus's baptism and the descent of the Spirit upon him, when he – still 'full of the Holy Spirit . . . and . . . led by the Spirit' – is depicted as rejecting the satanic temptation to tempt God (Matthew 4:1–11; Luke 4:1–13). Returning from the wilderness 'in the power of the Spirit', he is shown immediately thereafter (Luke 4:14–44) beginning his ministry. The stress, now that he has rejected the temptation to disobedience, is on his obedient enactment of his mission. He does that for which he was sent (vv.18, 43). He cites Isaiah 61:1–2 to his hometown hearers:

> The Spirit of the Lord is upon me, because he has anointed me to preach good news to the poor. He has sent me to proclaim release to the captives and recovering of sight to the blind, to set at liberty those who are oppressed, to proclaim the acceptable year of the Lord. (Luke 4:18–19)

81

Being obedient, he can say to them, 'Today this scripture has been fulfilled in your hearing' (v. 21). At the end of this same chapter he tells his listeners that he must preach the Kingdom of God, 'for I was sent for this purpose' (v. 43).

But if obedience is to be understood as specific enactment of an intention, one needs a sequence of cumulative, unbroken events within a story. We do not have such a sequence at this early point in the gospel story. Jesus's obedience is set forth more clearly in the events of the final stage of his career. In the early portions of the narrative, the accounts present us with self-contained blocks of material, each covering one topic. In the final portion, we begin to get a sustained and unbroken narrative, leading from event to event, starting with the preparation for the Last Supper (Mark 14; Matthew 26; Luke 22). Set into the midst of this sequence is our second glimpse into Jesus's inner life (within the story) when, tempted to plead for a way out of what looms ahead, he confirms his obedience: 'Yet not what I will, but what thou wilt' (Mark 14:36). It marks the crucial *inner* transition point from power and scope to powerlessness. We shall speak of it again in that context. What we must emphasize now is that here, as nowhere else, the story points 'from the inside' to his obedient intention. This is its focus. We should be gravely mistaken were we to put the stress of this incident on the sadness and agony of his terror and decision. They are there, and it would be equally erroneous to ignore them. Without them, as without Peter's bitter tears after his denial of Jesus, we should not penetrate below the surface and into the real centre of the story's figure. The stress, however, is not on the agony so much as on the fact that in the midst of it Jesus determined to be obedient. The writer of Hebrews, apparently speaking about this particular scene, comments that beginning here Jesus actually *learned* obedience (Hebrews 5:7–10). Here, then, is the inner point at which Jesus's intention begins to mark his identity.

But intention, as we have said repeatedly, is nothing in itself without enactment. Enactment does not merely illustrate, but constitutes, intention. Corresponding to the transition from power to helplessness on the *inner* plane is its constituting enactment on the *outer* plane. In a measure, this is nothing short of the whole passion–crucifixion–resurrection sequence. Nothing accomplishes that point of transition from inwardness to outwardness at the point of change from power to powerlessness more clearly than Jesus's words in Matthew's report of the arrest, just after the scene in the Garden of Gethsemane. Staying the hand that would defend him against arrest, Jesus asks: 'Do you think I cannot appeal to my Father, and he will at once send me more than twelve legions of angels? But how then should the scriptures be fulfilled, that it must be so?' (Matthew 26:53–54). Jesus affirms the will of God obediently by both initiating and consenting to the shape of the events that now develop in their mysterious logic.

But we said earlier that Jesus's obedience to God is also his love toward man.

It is so by virtue of the coincidence of the intention of Jesus with that of God. His love enacting the good of men on their behalf is not to be discerned simply and directly as predominant personal deportment, but as the specific vocation entailed by his mission of obedience to God. We need only remind ourselves of the will of God embodied in the mission on which he sent Jesus, the righteous one: it was an errand of grace extended to the world. In the words of the fourth gospel: 'For God so loved the world that he gave his only Son, that whosoever believes in him should not perish but have eternal life. For God sent the Son into the world, not to condemn the world, but that the world might be saved through him' (John 3:16–17). Again, Jesus's use of the words of Isaiah 61:1 (Luke 4:18, cited above) puts his obedience in announcing his gospel in the terms of an errand of mercy. Here, again, the *referent* of Jesus's obedience is the will of God and his purpose, which become embodied in the climactic events of Jesus's self-enactment. The *content* or meaning of that obedience is the pattern of merciful, saving activity drawn largely from the picture of the obedient, righteous servant in Deutero-Isaiah. It is the pattern of exchange (chapters 7 and 8). 'For I tell you that this scripture must be fulfilled in me, "And he was reckoned with transgressors"; for what is written about me has its fulfilment' (Luke 22:37; cf. Isaiah 53:12). In a word, 'the Son of Man came not to be served but to serve, and to give his life as a ransom for many' (Matthew 20:28).

But, once again, it is in the connected narrative sequence of the last events of the gospel story that we look for the coincidence of Jesus's obedience to God and his love toward men, which is the content of that obedience. The most striking instance of that unity of obedience and love comes precisely in the process of his identification in the enactment of his intention. The sequence, we have said, begins with the preparation for the Last Supper. The crucial transition point for the enactment of his obedience through the events is in the garden and the subsequent arrest. Shortly before, in the upper room, he had spoken to his disciples of the cup they shared as the blood of his covenant, 'poured out for many' (Mark 14:24; Matthew 26:28). This is the content or aim of his obedience to God, enacted in the events climaxing the gospel story. To be obedient to God was to pour out his blood in behalf of men. Who, then, was Jesus? He was what he did, the man completely obedient to God in enacting the good of men on their behalf.

Jesus's Power and Powerlessness

The obedience of Jesus must be seen at once in the *coexistence* of his power with his powerlessness and in the *transition* from the one to the other.

About the coexistence of his power and powerlessness, we shall not say much, important though it is. Were it not there at all, it would be difficult to see wherein the actual saving efficacy of his helplessness lies. Moreover, it would be difficult to get any glimpse at all of the complex and yet positive interrelation between God's action and Jesus's action at the climactic stage of the gospel story.

We may note the coexistence of Jesus's power and helplessness when he stands silently before the accusations of the Roman governor. The silence is broken only at the moment of Jesus's own choice, when the governor asks him if he is the king of the Jews. 'You have said so', is Jesus's reply, and thereby he actively turns the governor's question into unwitting testimony to himself, the Christ (Mark 15:2; Matthew 27:11; Luke 23:3). Again, in Luke's account of the crucifixion, we have several sayings that testify to Jesus's abiding initiative in and even over the circumstances that hold him in thrall, so that they come to be, by a subtle reversal, at *his* service. His promise to the thief that he should be with him in paradise; his active placing of his spirit in the hands of God (Luke 23:43, 46) are instances of this sort.

The writer of the fourth gospel took this stress and made it one of the main themes of his interpretative account, to the point of the elimination of Jesus's passive, helpless suffering. He portrays Jesus as actively laying down his life for his sheep; he is not robbed of it: 'I lay down my life, that I may take it again. No one takes it from me, but I lay it down of my own accord' (John 10:17–18). Likewise, in John's account, the last word spoken on the cross is neither the pathetic cry concerning God's forsaking him, not even the commendation of his Spirit into the hands of God, but the announcement that this is the completion and fulfilment of his own activity (John 19:30). Thus, Pilate's proclamatory superscription of Jesus's kingship which he had placed over the cross (vv. 19–22) loses almost every vestige of ironic quality in the seriousness of Jesus's own claim in John's gospel.

So Jesus is and remains powerful to the end, constraining all acts and words, even those of his opponents, to testify to him. Hence, our earlier statement that Jesus's helplessness is a theme in the synoptic gospels must be drastically modified, if not eliminated, when one looks at the fourth gospel. Yet even in the synoptic gospels, the coexistence of powerlessness with saving efficacy is one of closest contact, though they are united in complex fashion and never directly merged. The rulers' words, 'He saved others; he cannot save himself', are perhaps the most striking instance of the complex relation of efficacy and helplessness and of ironic reversal between them. In summarizing and articulating his complete helplessness, the rulers are witnesses to his saving power.

Having spoken of the coexistence of the power and powerlessness of Jesus, we now turn to what is involved in the transition from one to the other. Though Jesus in his helplessness is still the Saviour with power, he is none the less genuinely helpless. The gospel writers show us a picture of the actual *transition* from power to helplessness, a transition held together through the experience of the one undergoing it. To this end the terrible story of Jesus in the Garden of Gethsemane is a vivid example. The transition in the story is from a certain liberty of action to an equally certain elimination of it. This transition is effected through his own decision, as well as through the action of the authorities. The process in the story is irreversible. Once Jesus gives himself over to the authorities, his liberty of action will be at an end, and the result will be almost certain death for him. In his agony he remains obedient to his mission and consents to powerlessness, even unto death.

We have already mentioned that the story of the temptation in the Garden of Gethsemane is one of the crucial turning points of the gospel narrative. There, as perhaps nowhere else, Jesus's intention is depicted as that of being obedient to God. What we are given in this narrative, then, is access to the storied Jesus's intention at a crucial point.

We are not unprepared for what comes to pass after this agonizing scene in the garden. The web of circumstances had already given ominous signs of tightening around Jesus. The atmosphere of the story had become fraught with heavy foreboding from the moment he announced to his disciples that he was going with them to Jerusalem (Luke 18:31–34, cf. Mark 10:32; Matthew 20:17). The scenes of controversy in the Temple in Jerusalem are particularly sharp and seem almost bound to provoke with tragic finality the insight that clarifies the meaning of the whole story of Jesus (Mark 11:18, 27–33). But it is the scene in the Garden of Gethsemane that pinpoints the transition between what went before and what comes afterward. Up to this point Jesus had had freedom and scope of movement. He had been portrayed as a figure of authority and power, but now in the garden, with circumstances narrowed to the decisive point, it became part of his own free agency to enact the coincidence between his own decision and the developing events. From that coincidence would develop the crucial pattern of events in which his identity would be enacted.

Earlier we said that the identity of an individual is described in part by the answer to the question, 'What is he like?' This kind of identity description we called intention–action description. It locates the identity of an individual at the point at which his inward life, coming to outward expression, is linked with or meshes into the train of public circumstances. Such a description of Jesus's identity comes at the crucial point of his transition from authoritative power to helplessness. It is in the sequence in the Garden of Gethsemane that we begin to discover the identity of Jesus through an intention–action description that reaches its climax in the crucifixion and resurrection. The intention of Jesus is nothing without that sequence in the garden, in which it is enacted. The inner intention never comes into direct view again with such intimacy as it does in this sequence. More and more thereafter we are forced to behold him from the distance of outward events – from enactment and circumstance rather than from inner life – except for the isolated and sudden, yet fitting, bereft cry on the cross, 'My God, my God, why hast thou forsaken me?' (Mark 15:34).

The pattern of significance embedded in this intention–action sequence is startlingly illumined by the words of Jesus near the beginning ('Yet not what I will, but what thou wilt') and by the rulers' words at its consummation ('He saved others; he cannot save himself'). In these two sayings and in the events they circumscribe, we see the transition of Jesus from power to powerlessness, a transition made in the full consistency of the same identity carried from intention into action: Jesus was what he did and suffered, the one whose identity was enacted in his passion and death.

Notes

1. James M. Robinson, *A New Quest of the Historical Jesus* (Naperville, IL: Allenson, 1959).
2. Gilbert Ryle, *The Concept of Mind* (New York: Barnes and Noble, 1949), p. 40.
3. *The New English Bible, New Testament* (Oxford: Oxford University Press; Cambridge: Cambridge University Press, 1961).

The Triune God: The
Perichoresis of Particular Persons

William Placher

The following excerpt is the third chapter in the first part of *Narratives of a Vulnerable God*. The book seeks to recover a reading of both biblical narratives and theological doctrines as discourse about a God 'vulnerable in love' rather than one who is distant and oppressive. This requires a criticism of modern interpretations of the doctrine of God and a return to biblical narrative as the source for reinterpretation. In conjunction with this reading, Placher's *Unapologetic Theology: A Christian Voice in a Pluralistic Conversation* (Louisville, KY: Westminster/John Knox Press, 1989) and *The Domestication of Transcendence: How Modern Thinking about God Went Wrong* (Louisville, KY: Westminster/John Knox Press, 1996) would be helpful.

To speak, as Mark does, of the 'Gospel of Jesus Christ, the Son of God', or to talk about the obedience of Christ, as the Reformed tradition has done so prominently, raises obvious questions: What does it mean for 'God' to have a 'Son'? To whom is Christ obedient? Similarly, thinking about the relations between time and eternity leads to questions about the incarnation: Should one simply say that 'God' was born in the first century? If not, what sorts of distinctions need to be introduced?

The natural way in which such issues arise indicates that it makes no sense to pose a sharp dichotomy between biblical narratives and trinitarian metaphysics, as if issues about the Trinity were foreign to a biblical, narratively oriented theology. The argument of this chapter, indeed, will be that precisely reflecting on the identity of the God revealed in the biblical narratives leads to the realization of God's triunity.

Twenty-five years ago, when as an undergraduate I was just embarking on the study of theology, devoting a chapter to the doctrine of the trinity might well have seemed an enterprise so eccentric as to require initial explanation, if not apology. Some more conservative types would simply have declared it unbiblical. For more radical theologians, it just served as a good example of the sort of dogma thoroughly irrelevant to contemporary life. In all, it seemed hard enough back then to argue that God was alive, without tackling the claim that God was triune.

At one level, everything has changed. The three most significant living German Protestant theologians, Wolfhart Pannenberg, Jürgen Moltmann and Eberhard Jüngel, have all come to make the trinity the organizing principle and central theme of their theologies. The last decade has seen important books on the trinity from Latin American Liberationists such as Leonardo Boff and Eastern Orthodox theologians such as John Zizioulas.[1] The corporately written Roman Catholic and Lutheran doctrinal theologies recently published in this country feature prominent chapters on the trinity early on, and the authors of those chapters, Catherine LaCugna and Robert Jenson, have also published major books of their own on the topic.[2] The Presbyterian Church (USA)'s 1991 'A Brief Statement of Faith' uses the trinity as both starting point and structural principle.

But at other levels, has anything really changed very much? In the average congregation, or even ministerial gathering, or even seminary classroom, does not the trinity often still come as bad news rather than good? Just when a Christian or a new theological student was dealing with struggles to believe in God, it emerges that Christians have to believe not only that God exists but that God is, in some complicated way, both one and three. Dorothy L. Sayers wrote a generation ago that, to the average churchgoer, the mystery of the trinity means,

> The Father is incomprehensible, the Son is incomprehensible, and the whole thing is incomprehensible. Something put in by theologians to make it more difficult – nothing to do with daily life or ethics.[3]

So perhaps it is best not to bother with it very much. Pastors out in the parish can hope that Trinity Sunday will fall on either Father's Day or Flag Day, or that they can find some way to finesse the topic as long as no one ever asks them to explain it. As Karl Rahner finally put it,

> We must be willing to admit that, should the doctrine of the trinity have to be dropped as false, the major part of religious literature could well remain virtually unchanged. . . . The catechism of head and heart (as contrasted with the printed catechism) . . . would not have to change at all if there were no trinity.[4]

Even of Calvin, after all, Barth could say that, while he gave 'indeed a thoroughly correct and respectful exposition of the doctrine of the Trinity . . . it is noteworthy that the author's interest in this matter is not exactly burning.'[5]

The doctrine of the trinity needs to be reclaimed, not just among theologians but in the faith and life of Christian people, for the catechism of the head and even the catechism of the heart, and for at least two reasons. First, Christian theology should not begin with a concept of God – perhaps a concept of God as first of all powerful, or as timelessly eternal – derived from some set or other of cultural or philosophical assumptions but from the vulnerable God fully immersed in life who is revealed in Jesus Christ. If Christians begin with the biblical narration of God's self-revelation, however, and consider its implications, they will find themselves thinking about a triune God. It is not that Christians know God first, and then have to add something about the trinity, but that Christians come to know God precisely as triune: the Logos incarnate in Jesus, the one whom Jesus called Father, and the Holy Spirit.[6]

Second, there is the issue of practical import. In his dismissal of the doctrine of the trinity, Immanuel Kant argued the same point that Dorothy Sayers imagined the average churchgoer making. In his words, this doctrine 'has no practical relevance at all, even if we think we understand it. . . . Whether we are to worship three or ten persons in the Divinity makes no difference' for our 'rules of conduct.'[7] But Kant was wrong. If we Christians understand the doctrine of the trinity aright, we will realize that it implies that God is not about power and self-sufficiency and the assertion of authority but about mutuality and equality and love. Moreover, in thinking about a God with an internal 'life' that exists independent of creation, we will not think of timeless immutability as the highest ideal. If we think of God as perfect, such reflections change our model of perfection. That in turn can transform not only the way we think about God but the way we think about Christian communities and our own lives as Christians. 'The doctrine of the trinity', as Robert Wilken has written, 'reaches to the deepest recesses of the soul and helps us know the majesty of God's presence and the mystery of his love. Love is the most authentic mark of the Christian life, and love among humans, or within God, requires community with others and a sharing of the deepest kind.'[8] The doctrine of the trinity is the account of that community and sharing in the life of God.

This chapter will not develop a theology of the trinity, a task far too great for a short book, let alone for a single chapter.[9] The chapter will focus on two issues already mentioned: the relation of trinitarian theology to the biblical account of God's self-revelation in Jesus Christ – the 'particular persons' of the chapter's subtitle; and some of the implications of the trinity for thinking about the nature of God – a topic that will lead to *perichoresis* and back to the vulnerable God strong in love rather than power.

The first of these topics picks up a methodological theme prominent in several of the recent books on the trinity, namely, that one should begin, not with abstract ideas of threeness and oneness, but with the concrete three persons we encounter in scripture.[10] In the first volume of his *Systematic Theology*, Pannenberg even criticizes Barth and Jüngel for starting their trinitarian thinking with abstract concepts of revelation and love rather than 'from the data of historical revelation of God as Father, Son, and Spirit'.[11] Whether or not the comment is fair as a criticism of Barth and Jüngel, the basic instinct behind it seems correct. Christians did not start talking about the trinity because of some fondness for the number three. They did so because they found they had to, in order to say what they needed to say about the particular God they had come to know in three particular ways.

To move from the data of God's self-revealing work to a doctrine of the trinity is to presuppose the principal thesis of what may be the most influential book on this topic in this century, Karl Rahner's *The Trinity*. 'The "economic" trinity', Rahner wrote, 'is the "immanent" trinity, and the "immanent" trinity is the "economic" trinity.'[12] In traditional terminology, the immanent trinity is the threefold character that God has within God's own nature. The economic trinity is what gets described in the biblical accounts of God's self-revelation – Jesus Christ the Son, the Father to whom he prayed, and the Holy Spirit at work in our hearts and in the world.

In the theological tradition, these two trinities, economic and immanent, had tended to move farther apart. The argument began with the idea that all of God's works are the works of all three persons of the trinity.[13] At most, one 'appropriated' various particular works to various persons – creation to the Father, redemption to the Son, sanctification to the Spirit, for instance – but this was just a kind of heuristic fiction: all the works of the trinity *ad extra* were equally the works of the whole triune God. Therefore it followed that there was no correspondence between the instances of activities of God in the world and the intradivine persons, and one therefore could not make any moves from the economic trinity to the immanent trinity. Rahner said that was wrong. First of all,

> Jesus is not simply God in general, but the Son. The second divine person, God's Logos, is man, and only he is man. Hence there is at least *one* "mission," *one* presence in the world, *one* reality of salvation history which is not merely appropriated to some divine person, but . . . proper to him. . . . At any rate, this *one* case shows up as *false* the statement that there is nothing in salvation history, in the economy of salvation, which cannot equally be said of the triune God as a whole and of each person in particular.[14]

Moreover, the separation of economic and immanent trinities defeats the whole point. The issue is God's self-revelation, but, if the triune way in which we know God does not disclose the triune way in which God really is, then God has not revealed God's own self, and a hidden God remains unknown behind the revealed God.[15]

One note of caution does seem in order: God's self-revelation implies a created world to which revelation can be directed, and the Christian tradition has wanted to hold that God can be God even without a created world – so that creation is an act of freedom and grace, not some sort of necessity. Therefore the economic trinity cannot be 'who God is' in the same essential sense in which the immanent trinity is. God could be God without an economy of revelation.[16] But the economic trinity does indeed *reveal* who God is and in that sense corresponds to the immanent trinity. God could be God without revelation to the world, but the revelation to the world is God's authentic *self*-revelation and therefore reveals who God really is. All three persons are at work in all of God's works, but in different manners which we come to know in a way that reflects actual distinctions within the triune God.

The distinctions, after all, keep emerging in the language of the biblical narratives. A brief summary may serve as a useful reminder. The Gospel of Mark declares itself to be, right at the start, 'the good news of Jesus Christ, the Son of God'. 'It is God the only Son, who is close to the Father's heart, who has made him known,' the fourth gospel says (John 1:18): the Word of God who in the beginning was with God and was God. Christ is 'the image of God', Paul writes to the Corinthians (2 Corinthians 4:4),[17] and the Letter to the Hebrews speaks of Christ as 'the exact imprint of God's very being' (Hebrews 1:3). The terms vary, but part of the message, at least, seems clear enough: if you want to know who God is, attend to these stories about Jesus Christ.

What do we learn from these stories? We learn that Jesus Christ is one

> who, though he was in the form of God,
>   did not regard equality with God
>   as something to be exploited,
> but emptied himself,
>   taking the form of a slave,
>   being born in human likeness.
> And being found in human form,
>   he humbled himself
>   and became obedient to the point of death –
>   even death on a cross. (Philippians 2:6–8)

This is what God is like, not as mere message from God, information passed on, but as God's own self come among us as the revelation of who God is.

Then in addition, in the gospel accounts, Jesus consistently speaks of one he calls his Father. He bears witness to the Father (John 8:18, 50) and serves the Father's will (John 10:37). The Father, he says, is greater than he (John 14:28), and the word he speaks is 'not mine, but is from the Father who sent me' (John

14:24). When someone calls him good, he insists that only the Father is good (Mark 10:18).[18] He subjects his will to the will of the Father (Mark 14:36), and prays to the Father. On the other hand, Jesus says that to know the Son is to know the Father (John 8:19). 'The Father and I', he says, 'are one', using the strong Greek word *hen*, meaning one and the same thing, sharing one reality (John 10:30).

The word 'Father' of course raises a good many complex issues today, and the Christian tradition has, to put it mildly, given mixed signals about how this particular symbol functions. The Council of Toledo, in AD 675, spoke of the Son as 'begotten or born out of the Father's womb',[19] the paradoxical language opening up the symbol and challenging any literal interpretation of the male language. Aquinas, on the other hand, appealed to the teaching of Aristotelian biology that the father actively imposes form on the offspring, while the mother passively contributes only the matter, and concluded that only a Father, as pure act, could singularly beget the Word.[20] On this interpretation, the maleness of the Father really mattered.

Faced with this complicated tradition, a good many recent theologians have tried to return to Jesus's own example. Beginning with Joachim Jeremias, biblical scholars and theologians have argued that Jesus himself used the word 'Abba' and that this was an informal, family term rarely if ever otherwise used of God, something like the equivalent of calling God 'Daddy'.[21] Jesus's own references to his 'Abba' were therefore not the reaffirmation of stern and distant patriarchy but shocking, revolutionary language of intimacy with God.[22]

Unfortunately, all three of the historical claims implied by this line of thought seem problematic. (1) Talmudic references to God as 'Abba' show that this usage would not have been unique or necessarily revolutionary in the Jewish context.[23] (2) As Jeremias himself came to admit, 'Abba' was in common use among adults, sometimes as a mark of respect for old men and teachers; 'Daddy', with its childhood connotations, is simply a misleading translation.[24] In fact, the New Testament itself always follows the word with the Greek translation, *ho pater*, the rather formal 'the father'. More informal Greek translations were available – the diminutive *pappas*, for instance – but neither Paul nor Mark used them.[25] (3) Most important, it is simply not clear that Jesus used the term 'Abba'. The word appears, after all, only three times in the New Testament. In Paul's two uses (Romans 8:15 and Galatians 4:6) it refers to the practice of the community – it is Christian believers who cry, 'Abba, Father' – without reference to what Jesus himself did. The one gospel passage (Mark 14:36) refers to a scene in which Jesus is praying to God without any human witnesses. True enough, the use of this Aramaic word untranslated in a Greek text may point backward to something in Jesus's own practice or the life of the earliest Christian communities, but the scanty evidence simply does not warrant historical claims about the centrality of 'Abba' in Jesus's own talk about God.[26]

The debate about 'Abba' illustrates the dangers of putting too much theological weight on particular historical claims about details of Jesus's life or ministry. The next chapter will return to the general issue of historical claims concerning the biblical narratives and argue for a significantly more complex relation between theology and history. In thinking about God as 'Father', the moral indeed seems to be that theologians should not rest too much on any one foundation but should consider the issue in the context of a variety of historical, textual and theological conclusions.

Historically, for instance, Elisabeth Schüssler Fiorenza and others have made a good case that the very earliest Christian communities embodied more equally between women and men than subsequent periods during which the later New Testament books, at least, were written.[27] A cumulative case that does not depend too much on just two or three passages indicates that the gospel created initial communities that in important ways challenged the patriarchal social structures of their time.

In the New Testament texts themselves, moreover, Jesus is, with some consistency, bringing into question what contemporary American politicians would call 'traditional family values'. 'Call no one your father on earth' Matthew's Gospel has him say, 'for you have one Father – the one in heaven' (Matthew 23:9). Following the Jesus who does the will of this Father means abandoning the usual family obligations – not even worrying about your duty to bury your own human father (Matthew 8:21–22). Faithfulness to Jesus's Father in heaven means the abolition or radical relativizing of every human form of patriarchy, and therefore the symbol of the Father in heaven, in this particular context, may oddly challenge patriarchal social structures that embody power in earthly fathers.[28]

Phyllis Trible, among others, makes an important counter-argument: 'To the extent that Jesus disavowed the earthly father in the name of the heavenly father, . . . to that extent Jesus re-enforced patriarchy by absolutizing the rule of the father. To transfer male dominance from earth to heaven is not to eliminate but to exacerbate it.'[29] But does that argument cast the issues too much in either/or terms? Exclusively male language about God does reinforce patriarchal structures. If we speak of God only as 'Father', then fathers will seem a bit like God. On the other hand, a radical challenge to earthly fathers on behalf of a heavenly father can subvert those structures. If there is a God, Moltmann once remarked, then at least human beings cannot play god over each other.[30] Analogously, one might argue, if God is really our Father, then at least no man can play ultimate patriarch. It is surely possible for the same symbol to function in some degree in both ways at once. If it does so, then a contemporary Christian theology sensitive to some of the concerns of feminism might want to introduce diverse images, including female ones, for God into the life of the church – including images already present in the Christian tradition – while also learning from and celebrating the anti-patriarchal messages embodied in the New Testament language about God the Father.

Theologians – and preachers and hymn writers and liturgists – need to explore alternative terms for the persons of the trinity that remain faithful to the logic of trinitarian thought. Elizabeth Johnson cites a number of possibilities: primordial Being/expressive Being/unitive Being (John Macquarrie); God's absoluteness/humaneness/present presence (Gordon Kaufman); love as creative source/self-expressive act/responsive movement (Norman Pittenger); divine being/divine Logos/divine love (Langdon Gilkey).[31] These possibilities may seem a bit cumbersome, but they have at least the advantage of not dividing up the work of the trinity, with one job per person, as does the all-too-common 'Creator, Redeemer, Sustainer'. Both the logic of the tradition and contemporary practice seem to incline toward maternal symbols, 'Mother' among them, for the whole triune God rather than the first person of the trinity – God as 'like a mother', or the formula 'Father, Son and Holy Spirit, one God, Mother of us all'[32] – and it will be interesting to see how such usage develops.

The language of 'Father' and 'Son' will surely continue to be important in the Christian tradition, and in a more diverse linguistic context perhaps 'Father' can function in more complex ways. Anne Carr remarks that women find that the 'official language for God' in the Christian tradition gives them 'an image of God as authoritarian, as a judge "over against" the self, humankind, the world. It is an image of God as power in the sense of control, domination, even coercion.'[33] If Christians think of God as vulnerable in love, then 'Father' language itself may become less problematic.

In any event, Christians will be most faithful to the biblical narratives if 'Father' functions, when used, primarily as a symbol of love rather than of power.[34] Theologically, and for reasons that go beyond these issues of gender too, it is important not to picture the trinitarian Father purely as the impassible Judge to whom the Son offers sacrifice in obedience. That way of telling the story does foster a picture of father as distant tyrant that carries unhealthy lessons about family structure but also distorts the biblically narrated relations within the trinity. The 'Son' does not win over the love of a reluctant 'Father'. '*God* so loved the world that he gave his only Son' (John 3:16). 'In this is love, not that we loved God but that he loved us and sent his Son to be the atoning sacrifice for our sins' (1 John 4:10). God as parent, so willing to be vulnerable in love as to send off a beloved child to die for a sinful creation, is also fully engaged in the risks of love. As Calvin put it, 'It was not after we were reconciled to him through the blood of his Son that he began to love us. Rather, he has loved us before the world was created.'[35]

If the New Testament indeed presents us with the narratives of a vulnerable God, then the 'Father' to whom they refer is at least an unusual sort of patriarch. Perhaps even the use of the word 'Abba' can, by its very foreignness, call

Christians' attention to the special characteristics here embodied, without making specific claims about the usage of the historical Jesus. The One called Abba in the biblical narratives overflows in love. The sending of the Christ and the Spirit manifest this divine love (Romans 8:39). The Jesus vulnerable in love is the image of this One, the exact imprint of this One's very being; indeed, Paul identifies the love of Christ with the love of God expressed in sending the Son (Romans 8:35).[36] This Abba calls us to turn away from obedience to the lords of this world to a new kind of intimacy based on love. We did not 'receive a spirit of slavery to fall back into fear', Paul wrote to the Romans, but 'a spirit of adoption. When we cry, "Abba! Father!" it is that very Spirit bearing witness with our spirit that we are children of God, and if children, then heirs, heirs of God and joint heirs with Christ' (Romans 8:15–17). Heirs do not grovel before intimidating powers but feel at home on the family estate, do not let anybody push them around, and joyfully obey in love the One whose love they have come to know. In most human situations such joy is always tempered by the contrast between the heirs who inherit and the servants and others who get left out, but in this case status as heirs is open to all, and to prodigal children especially. The Middle Eastern patriarch walks through the village in his long robe at a stately pace; Jesus's Abba, indifferent to dignity, runs to greet every returning prodigal.

When we cry, 'Abba! Father!' Paul says, it is the Spirit bearing witness. The Spirit too is part of the story of this God. Mary was found to be with child from the Holy Spirit, two of the gospels tell us (Matthew 1:18; Luke 6:27–35). The Spirit descended on Jesus at baptism and then led him into the wilderness, Luke says (Luke 4:1), from which he returned 'filled with the power of the Spirit' (Luke 4:14). The Spirit provided Jesus with the power and authority with which to perform his works (Mark 3:20–30). The Spirit is the Paraclete – the advocate, the comforter, the defender, the one who makes urgent appeals – whom Jesus promised his Father would send (John 14:16, 26).

This Spirit seems in some ways the most mysterious part of the story. Yves Congar puts it this way:

> The incarnate Word has a face – he has expressed his personality in our human history in the way persons do, and the Father has revealed himself in him. The Spirit does not present such personal characteristics. He is, as it were, buried in the work of the Father and the Son, which he completes.[37]

Having quoted Congar's references to the Holy Spirit as 'he', one should acknowledge that pronouns are a particular problem here. The word for 'spirit' is feminine in Hebrew, neuter in Greek and masculine in Latin; Jerome once cited this as evidence that gender does not apply to God at all.[38] It is tempting to make the Spirit the feminine side of God and thus begin, as it were, to even out gender representation within the godhead, but here Rosemary Radford Ruether seems correct: a trinity with two male and one female persons does not exactly manifest equality, and the traditional image of the Spirit as the person who perfects and completes the trinitarian work while glorifying the Father and Son would invite thinking of a feminine Spirit as 'a subordinate principle underneath the dominant image of male divine sovereignty',[39] thus if anything reinforcing gender stereotypes.[40] Questions of gender in reference to God need to be addressed in other ways.

What is important, in regard to the Holy Spirit, is to preserve personhood. However problematic 'she' or 'he' may be, 'it' is just wrong. The temptation to move to impersonal language in connection with the Spirit is not one to which contemporary concerns about gender gave rise for the first time. Barth proposes that there is a reluctance in us to affirm the Spirit's personhood, since part of the particular work of the Spirit lies in the nurturing of our response to revelation, and therefore the full acknowledgement of the divinity of the Spirit involves conceding that even our response to God is not our work but God's, so that we are not, as it were, even masters in our own house.[41] The work of God for us is not something simply external we observe as interested spectators, nor is it something we do for ourselves. Rather, it achieves completion only when it transforms us from within, and even that transformation is the work of the triune God. We acknowledge that when we affirm the coequal personhood of the Holy Spirit. Barth may have been right, incidentally, to say that Calvin was not very enthusiastic about the trinity, but he was irreproachable on the topic of the work of the Spirit.

Barth regularly referred to God as 'the one who loves in freedom'. That phrase could be used of any of the persons of the trinity.[42] Christ breaks the bonds of the law, sits at table with outcasts and sinners, and freely risks everything in love. The One he called 'Father' overflows with love for creation, challenges every human definition of authority, and so loves even a world of sinners as to send a beloved only child to redeem it. But the Spirit bears a special relation to freedom and love. In describing living by the Spirit in his letter to the Galatians, Paul writes of being called to freedom (Galatians 5:13) and lists love as the first of the fruits of the Spirit (Galatians 5:22). Above all, in those grand discourses which begin in John 14, Spirit and love and truth keep intertwining, with the memory hovering over them of that earlier word that the truth will make us free (John 8:32). As Walter Kasper puts it,

> Everywhere that life breaks forth and comes into being, everywhere that new life as it were seethes and bubbles, and even, in the form of hope, everywhere that life is violently devastated, throttled, gagged and slain – wherever true life exists, there the Spirit of God is at work.[43]

The Spirit manifests God's love in freedom, and when the Spirit has sealed God's work in us, then we ourselves live in love and freedom.

Christ, the very image of God, according to the passage from Philippians already quoted, 'did not regard equality with God as something to be exploited'. Such generosity, such mutual deference, characterizes all the persons of the triune God. Philippians 2 continues by telling of God's exaltation of Christ Jesus

> so that at the name of Jesus
> every knee should bend,
> in heaven and on earth and under the earth,
> and every tongue should confess
> that Jesus Christ is Lord,
> to the glory of God the Father. (Philippians 2:10–11)

The Father's glory lies not in any honours directly given the Father but in this grand, universal adulation of the Son. Yet Christ, as we have seen, subjects his will to the will of the one he calls Abba or Father and serves that One's will in obedience (Mark 14:36; John 10:37). He asks that he might be glorified only that he might in turn glorify the One whom John's Gospel has him call simply 'God'. The Spirit in turn glorifies the Christ and claims nothing from individual authority but speaks of the Son from the Father (John 16:15; 14:26).[44]

We all live in human communities, from nation-states to college campuses to churches to corporations, full of jockeying for position and all kinds of competitiveness. Even within ourselves, we often find the part of us most committed to career at war with the part of us most interested in family, and so on. The triune God, the Bible intimates to us, is not like that. In this unity in diversity mutual love and deference wonderfully yield mutual glorification.

Christians, then, do not believe in just any trinity but in the triunity of these three persons – the Christ who does not grasp at equality but humbles himself, even to death on a cross, the One he called Abba or Father, outpouring love, challenging human assumptions about hierarchy, the Holy Spirit of love, truth and freedom, all one God glorifying each other. That said, the old question remains as to whether Christians are just shockingly bad at arithmetic and unable to realize that three does not equal one.

The answer to that question lies in reflecting on the relation of the three and the one in Christian theology, and at some level that relation remains a mystery. But the word 'mystery' should not be an excuse for intellectual sloppiness. Christians should try to understand what they can, and in this case the theological tradition has offered to explain quite a lot. As we try to understand these matters today, however, analysis of the tradition terminology may not offer a very helpful starting point. The Greek *hypostasis* and *ousia* notoriously do not translate very well into the Latin *personae* and *substantia*, and the English 'persons' and 'substance' may not render either version with much precision. 'I do not know', even Augustine frankly admitted about the Greek theologians, 'what different meaning they wished to give *ousia* and *hypostasis*.'[45]

Moreover, sometime between the ancient world and the world of post-Kantian philosophy and post-Einsteinian physics, the meaning and context of 'person' and 'substance' changed radically in the intellectual tradition of the West. Personhood has come most generally to refer above all to individual self-consciousness, the Cartesian *ego cogito*, and philosophers and physicists alike think of the 'substances' of the world as shaped and defined by the thinking of such 'persons'. That alters both the meaning of 'person' and the relation of person and substance in fundamental ways. The moral is not that we ought to give up the traditional terminology but only that the terms themselves do not initially give us much help in understanding. As a supplement to the terms used of the trinity, the theological tradition has often appealed to analogies. Two of the analogies most often used in the tradition for the trinity, the psychological and the social, may provide a more useful starting point.

In the first half of his great book on the trinity, Augustine laid out the elements of the church's teaching on the trinity as he understood it. Then in the later books he began to explore various analogies to the trinity in human experience. The order of his procedure is worth noting. He is not saying that we find a threefoldness in various aspects of our experience and can therefore infer to a triune God. Rather, his discussions offer an instance of *fides quaerens intellectum*, the great Augustinian tradition of faith seeking understanding. He begins with the faith he has received, and then he struggles, with analogies among other devices, to understand it more fully.

If we are made in the image of God, as our faith assures us, and God is triune, then there ought to be some analogy to that threefoldness within us. In book 9 of *On the Trinity*, Augustine therefore considers the human mind. My mind exists, and it exists in knowing and loving. At first glance, Augustine's model might seem to imply subordinationism, for existence sounds like the substance of the mind, with knowing and loving only its activities. Augustine, however, insists that the mind exists only in knowing and loving, and therefore existing has no priority. The mind is not like a knife that can sit there on the shelf being a knife, waiting to start cutting. In his terminology, 'love and knowledge are not in the mind as in a subject, for they are there substantially as the mind itself is.'[46] The mind's very existence, for Augustine, inheres in its activities of knowledge and love. If nothing else, in isolation it would know and love itself.

But there is also a relation, Augustine thinks, between knowing and loving. One cannot love something without knowing it – that part may be obvious. If you say, 'Don't you love Hong Kong?' or 'Don't you love skiing?' my answer is, 'I don't know I've never been there, I've never done it, how can I talk of love?' Augustine thinks the relation works the other way too. I cannot know what I do not love. Often enough, one hears a remark like, 'You've been around my family, my church, my school, and I suppose you know a lot of information, but you don't really understand, you can't have a certain kind of empathetic feel – because you don't love them.' There are, to be sure, things that 'we rightly disapprove of'.[47] To know them is not to love them. But even then there is a relation between knowledge and love, for we are glad to have censured evil, glad therefore to have recognized it, glad to have known it. We love our knowledge even as we do not love the thing we know.[48]

So the mind exists and knows and loves. And this existence and knowledge and love are not three parts, like the back and the seat and the legs of a chair. The whole mind exists and knows and loves. Nor is this trinity of the mind like a single drink made of water and wine and honey. In that case, even though each of them extends through the whole drink, still each is also a separate substance, a different kind of thing. No, mind and love and knowledge are three things, yet one thing.[49] Moreover, in knowing something, we produce an image of the thing known, as a parent begets a child and as the Logos is the image of the Father. And love unites subject and object in love just as the Holy Spirit for Augustine unites the Father and the Son in love. 'And so there is a certain image of the trinity: the mind itself, its knowledge, which is its offspring, and love as a third; these three are one and one substance.'[50] One can trace that psychological analogy for the trinity through the history of Western Christendom from Augustine to Anselm to Aquinas to Barth.

But another analogy, the social, appears in various forms particularly in the Eastern church and was expounded and elaborated in the Latin West in the twelfth century by Richard of St-Victor. Richard began with love. God is perfect love, perfect charity, and perfect love needs an object. To be sure, God can love the creation, but it would be disorderly to love it supremely, for the creation is not supremely good. 'However, as long as anyone loves no one else as much as he loves himself, that private love which he has for himself shows clearly that he has not yet reached the supreme level of charity. . . . Therefore, so that fullness of charity might have a place in that true Divinity, it is necessary that a divine person not lack a relationship with an equally worthy person, who is, for this reason, divine.'[51] But the highest kind of love is mutual love, and in mutual love it is absolutely necessary that there be both one who loves and one who returns love. 'Therefore, the showing of love freely given and the repayment of love that is due prove without any doubt that in true Divinity a plurality of persons cannot be lacking.'[52]

This analysis yields only a duality. Richard thinks, however, that even two persons in mutual love still do not encompass perfect love. If you were deeply involved in a mutual love, it would still be an imperfection of that love if you were not willing to share it. 'Nothing is rarer or more magnificent than to wish that another be loved equally by the one whom you love supremely and by whom you are supremely loved. So a person proves that he is not perfect in charity if he cannot yet take pleasure in sharing this excellent joy.' The perfection of love requires therefore not only an object of love whose object I am in turn but a third person with whom I am willing to share the perfection of this mutual love. 'Thus you see how the perfection of charity requires a trinity of persons, without which it is wholly unable to subsist in the integrity of its fullness.'[53] Something like this social analogy of the trinity runs down the history of Eastern Christianity from the time of the Cappadocian Fathers and has drawn increasing interest in our time in the West. Indeed, many of the last decade's works on the trinity seem to cast Augustine as the villain of the story and some version of a social trinity as the collective hero.[54]

The adherents of these two analogies, indeed, find themselves regularly in conflict. To those who favour the psychological analogy, drawing the analogy of three human beings sharing mutual love seems to imply the existence of three gods. To those who favour the social analogy, the psychological one seems to imply a God who is one person, albeit with a complicated internal life.[55] Moltmann, who favours the social analogy, says that Barth's trinity is 'a late triumph for the Sabellian modalism which the early church condemned',[56] and George Hunsinger, writing with sympathy to Barth, says that the form of the social analogy in Moltmann's *The Trinity and the Kingdom* 'is about the closest thing to tritheism that any of us are ever likely to see'.[57]

Conceding that any account of such matters involves the risky application of human analogies to a divine mystery, still, the psychological and social analogies for the trinity may not point in quite such different directions as first glance suggests, if one reflects a bit more deeply about the nature of human self and human community. Indeed, the point of the preceding discussion of these analogies is in part that it leads to such reflection.[58]

The human self, to use a bit of jargon that has become a philosophical cliché, is socially constructed. In important ways, I do not find out who I am by introspection in isolation but by how other people define me and how I define myself in interaction with them.[59] In Buber's phrase, 'I become through my relation to the Thou.'[60] Narcissus, after all, who fell in love with his reflection in a pool, and thus, Ovid says, 'with an insubstantial hope, mistaking a mere shadow for a real body', lacks an authentic other and therefore can only die: that is somehow the point of the story.[61] We all know tragic stories of children whose parents keep telling them they are worthless – of course they come to believe it. The expectations and responses of those around us shape all of us; indeed, we become selves, persons, in interaction with others, in a social context.

Something within us resists this human reality. I want to be self-sufficient; I want to define who I am. I want to be in control. Yet interaction with an other is basic to my very identity as a person. Hegel's *Phenomenology* is, among many other things, the story of the pathos of trying to define oneself in relation without losing control of one's identity. It is interesting that one of Hegel's early images for the process is of mortal combat, an image that may suggest just how terrifying Hegel found the issue. If you and I challenge each other to a fight to the death, then whoever wins has established an identity – as victor – in relation with another and yet succeeded in achieving control, for now the opponent is safely dead. Such an ontological achievement seems almost worth the risk of the consequences of losing.[62] But victory in such combat is always Pyrrhic: no sooner do I triumph and thereby affirm myself than I have killed the other and find myself again in an isolation that threatens even my own identity.

So do not kill off your other, but turn to enslavement, and keep a handy other around the house to affirm your identity. Trouble is, what you really want is a slave who will reliably tell you how wonderful you are, in a way that you will really believe. But a slave knows what it is safe to say, and so after a while the slave's praise of the master no longer works. It comes to be like a teacher asking students on the day before the exam how they liked the course. 'It is not an independent, but rather a dependent consciousness that he has achieved. He is thus not assured of self-existence as his truth.'[63] (I leave the masculine pronouns in place: Hegel's self seems to me irreducibly masculine; that may be part of the problem.) What we want is to have an other who is really other but who, we can trust, will never criticize, never threaten. We want to be Narcissus, who had, Ovid tells us, 'a pride so unyielding' that no one 'dared to touch him',[64] but a Narcissus who can reach through the surface of the pool.

To speak of Hegel's pathos is to imply that Hegel was still pursuing Narcissus's dream. The object, after all, turns out to be part of the subject in the end. Contemporary philosophers such as Emmanuel Levinas have protested against the character of Hegel's enterprise. 'The Other as Other', Levinas writes, 'is not only an alter ego: the Other is what I myself am not. The Other is this, not because of the Other's character, or physiognomy, or psychology, but because of the Other's very alterity.'[65] The Other is really other, and not, at the end of the day, only a part or projection of myself. 'The solipsist disquietude of consciousness, seeing itself, in all its adventures, a captive of itself, comes to an end here: true exteriority is in this gaze which forbids me my conquest.'[66] To look another person honestly in the face, Levinas insists, is to encounter someone I cannot control. In Jean-François Lyotard's elegant phrase, Levinas 'attacks Hegelian alterity as only a caprice of identity'.[67] I can really be myself only in relation, and I can be in true relation only if I fully respect the otherness of the other. That means doing a host of things Hegel's assertive self resists: becoming vulnerable, accepting that I am not fully in control, not in a position to control, or therefore to know, how the story will turn out. I would then also have to accept the limits and partiality of my understanding, thereby giving up Hegel's project of arriving at an absolute standpoint from which I can see the truth without partiality. Acknowledging my limits, making myself vulnerable in full relation to an other is the only way I can become fully myself. Such loss of self-independence in relation does not threaten individual identity but precisely creates it.

In another way too we often become most fully ourselves when we at once lose ourselves and find ourselves – the gospel language seems the only appropriate description for the experience – in a community that transcends ourselves. In Indiana, one always starts illustrating this point with an example from basketball. In a team sport, the players who are always asking, 'How am I doing? Am I getting my share of the shots? Am I going to be the star in tomorrow's paper?' never in fact play to their potential. On the other hand, we have all seen the games, and some of us maybe had the luck to take part in them, where the players lost themselves in a team effort that involved a kind of self-forgetfulness that paradoxically made them the best players, as individuals, that they had ever been. One can tell similar stories about artists lost in their work, lovers lost in their beloved, workers lost in the excitement of a common enterprise, contemplatives lost in God. Afterward, perhaps, they look back on themselves and say, 'What a remarkable thing I did there', but part of what was remarkable was that at the time no such thought crossed their minds. One tossed aside the part of oneself that always stands watching on the sidelines, and, in forgetfulness of self, became most truly oneself.

There are limits to how much humans can do this sort of thing. We are sinners, and we have bodies – for the Christian tradition these are two quite different issues, but in different ways they both limit our capacity to find ourselves in losing ourselves. We are sinners, and therefore we can never quite achieve forgetfulness of self. Could even Michael Jordan make the double-backhanded basket purely in the joy of the rhythm of the game, with no thought of the million-dollar endorsement intruding? Perhaps for a moment, but the thought comes back.

Even free of sin, we would still be embodied selves, with inevitable limits.[68] When you break your ankle, I tell you that I am sharing your pain, but you know it is not really true. I may be empathizing, I may feel great distress, but the pain in that ankle is yours and not mine. As I watch you eating the omelette I have prepared for you, my pleasure in your pleasure may be even greater than your pleasure; cooking for appreciative friends can be a greater joy than eating. But it is a different pleasure, the particular sensation of the omelette on your taste buds is yours alone.

Suppose, however, there were disembodied agents who were also without sin, each defining its own identity in genuine otherness, each losing itself in common enterprise pursued without jealousy or conflict, so at one that each was in the all. The classical theological term for such a state of affairs is 'perichoresis', the 'passing into one another' of the divine persons. 'The Father is in me and I am in the Father', Jesus says in John 10 – and a bit earlier, 'The Father and I are one'. Two or three can so pass into one another that they become as one. Gregory of Nazianzus was probably the first to use the term 'perichoresis', although he used it for the interpenetration of the two natures, human and divine, in Christ.[69] A text called *Pseudo-Cyril* used it of the persons of the trinity in the sixth century, but it was John of Damascus who fully developed the theme. As Daniel Migliore nicely explains the idea of perichoresis, the trinitarian persons '*indwell* each other . . . *make room* for each other, are incomparably hospitable to each other'.[70]

The analysis so far presented has taken its start from the social analogy of the trinity, moving from plurality to unity. An exclusive emphasis on the social analogy, however, risks suggesting that the divine persons are just rather like human persons, only very closely interrelated. But John of Damascus made an interesting move that in a way jumps to the other side and emphasizes the unity of God. With all *creatures*, he explained, their individuality is actual, and one can see what they have in common by reason or thought. So Peter is actually distinct from Paul, and we have to impose some uniting conceptual category in order to think that they are both human beings, or Americans, or whatever. In the case of the trinity, however, the Damascene says, the *unity* is actual, and it is the *distinction* that has to be made conceptually. We do not encounter three Gods and determine they must be one, the way we encounter three baseball players and determine they must all be Yankees; rather, we encounter one God and determine that that God is three-personed.[71] Each human person

> is distinct and considered in itself, since it has a great many things to distinguish it from the other. For, truly, they are separated in place and they differ in time, judgment, strength, form or shape, habit, temperament, dignity, manner of life, and all the other distinctive properties – but most of all they differ by the fact that they do not exist in each other but separately.

'With the uncircumscribed God', however, 'we cannot speak of any difference in place, as we do with ourselves, because the Persons exist in one another.'[72] God exists three-personedly, but none of those three persons has independent existence, for they are what they are in relation, so that God is what God is in this interrelation.

Moreover, while the persons undertake different tasks in enacting God's love for the world (the economic trinity we encounter, it will be remembered, corresponds to the immanent trinity), they never act at cross-purposes. 'Every operation', Gregory of Nyssa wrote, 'which extends from God to the Creation, . . . has its origin from the Father, and proceeds through the Son and is perfected in the Holy Spirit. For this reason the name derived from the operation is not divided with regard to the number of those who fulfill it.'[73] In the early church, theologians often used the image of the one Sun from which different rays shone forth to make the distinction between one God and three persons – sometimes they even treated the Father as the Sun and the Son and Spirit as rays coming forth in a way that risked subordinating the second and third persons of the trinity to the first. But Gregory of Nazianzus dramatically reversed the image: so perichoretically united is the work of the three persons that it is like the light from three *Suns* shining to form one *beam*.[74] God is who God is in being God, that is, in doing what God does. And what God does, while authentically revealing the threefold way in which God is through the different roles of the three persons, is always a unified act. It is interesting that people coming, as it were, from opposite sides, from the context of the psychological and social analogies, such as Barth and Moltmann, unite in finding perichoresis to be the key in sorting out the meaning of the trinity.[75] When we think of the Three so united in purpose and activity, beyond all discord, when we think of one God so rich in love, the questions of whether these are three individuals or one melt away. Not three isolated individuals; not one without internal distinction. Each in full selfhood precisely in community; one most itself in its threeness.

Such human analogies may provide a glimpse of how God can be at once one and three, but what does it matter beyond the solving of a puzzle? This chapter began with the proposal that the trinity should not be bad news, one more difficult thing to be believed, but good news of central importance to Christian faith. First, that is so because Christians, in their lives and in scripture, come to know God precisely as triune. We do not know an abstract God first and then have to attach this trinitarian talk, but, from the start, we encounter God in Jesus Christ, in the one he called Father, in the Holy Spirit. Second, knowing God as triune tells something important about God. God is not an isolated, single monarch whose only relation is to rule. God is a community of equals united in mutual love, 'a monarchy that is not limited to one Person', Gregory of Nazianzus wrote, 'but one which is made of an equality of nature and a union of mind, and an identity of motion and a convergence of its elements to unity.'[76] God, to return to the central theme of this book, is defined in terms of love rather than power.

That matters because Christians have so often modelled hierarchies in this world after the presumed divine hierarchy. 'The one God, the one heavenly king', declared Eusebius of Caesarea, Constantine's court flunky, 'corresponds to the one king on earth.'[77] Ignatius of Antioch had earlier appealed to the principle of one God, one bishop.[78] Ephesians makes an analogous argument for the hierarchy of male over female (Ephesians 5:22–23). But the triune God is about equality and mutual concern, a God of love. In the Christian tradition at least, the God of monotheism, as Patricia Wilson-Kastner observes, 'has historically been imaged as a male, patriarchal and dominating'. The doctrine of the trinity encourages us, on the other hand, 'to focus on interrelationship as the core of divine reality'.[79] 'Monotheism', Walter Kasper has written, 'has always been a political program as well as a religious: one God, one realm, one emperor.' But in the Christian vision of the triune God, 'God's unity is fullness and even overflowing fullness of selfless giving and bestowing, of loving self-outpouring; it is a unity that does not exclude but includes; it is a living, loving being with and for one another.'[80] Christians worship that sort of God. For Christians sympathetic with feminist concerns, it can therefore be particularly important not to let the problems of the language of 'Father' and 'Son' stand in the way of significant attention to the implications of the trinity. As Anne Carr has written,

> The mystery of God as trinity, as final and perfect sociality, embodies those qualities of mutuality, reciprocity, cooperation, unity, peace in genuine diversity that are feminist ideals and goals derived from the inclusivity of the gospel message. The final symbol of God as trinity thus provides women [and men too, one hopes!] with an image and concept of God that entails qualities that make God truly worthy of imitation, worthy of the call to radical discipleship that is inherent in Jesus' message.[81]

Writing to the Romans, Paul assured them, 'if the Spirit of him who raised Jesus from the dead dwells in you, he who raised Christ from the dead will give life to your mortal bodies also through his Spirit that dwells in you' (Romans 8:11). Paul lacked most of the categories with which the church later expressed the doctrine of the trinity, and yet he was pointing to the trinitarian shape of the narratives of God's work of salvation. It is the Father of Jesus who raised Jesus from the dead; it is through the indwelling of the Spirit that one comes to know the life given to Jesus in the resurrection. The perichoretic love within the trinity is a love willing to be vulnerable lying at the heart of who God is. In mutual love the persons of the trinity live limitlessly in a life that coheres without opposition between past, present and future, and thus live eternal life.[82]

Perhaps we need to conclude by emphasizing yet again that Christian faith does not concern just any trinity – the point is not equality and mutual love between someone or other, fill in the blanks. The three persons of the God in whom Christians believe are the Christ who suffered on the cross, the one whom Christ called his Father, whose outpouring love sends forth both the Christ and the Spirit, and the Spirit who makes communities of love and freedom. If we Christians are invited to draw diagrams about God, we should not begin with a pyramid with a single divine point at the top. The symbol of the trinity, Elizabeth Johnson writes, indicates that the particular kind of relatedness than which nothing greater can be conceived is not one of hierarchy involving domination/subordination, but rather one of genuine mutuality in which there is radical equality while distinctions are respected. At the heart of holy mystery is not monarchy but community; not an absolute ruler, but a threefold *koinōnia*.[83]

At the end of his journey through Paradise, Dante tells us, he saw 'three circles of three colours and one magnitude; and one seemed reflected by the other, as rainbow by rainbow, and the third seemed fire breathed forth'[84] – interconnected circles representing the equality and reciprocity of the one triune God.

Notes

1   Leonardo Boff, *Trinity and Society*, tr. Paul Burns (Maryknoll: Orbis Books, 1988); and John D. Zizioulas, *Being As Communion: Studies in Personhood and the Church* (Crestwood: St. Vladamir's Seminary Press, 1985).

2   Francis Schüssler Fiorenza and John P. Galvin, eds, *Systematic Theology: Roman Catholic Perspectives* (Minneapolis: Fortress Press, 1991); Carl E. Braaten and Robert W. Jenson, eds, *Christian Dogmatics*, 2 vols (Philadelphia: Fortress Press, 1984); Catherine Mowry LaCugna, *God for Us: The Trinity and Christian Life* (San Francisco: Harper, 1991); and Robert W. Jenson, *The Triune Identity: God According to the Gospel* (Philadelphia: Fortress Press, 1982).

3   Dorothy L. Sayers, *Creed or Chaos* (New York: Harcourt, Brace, 1949), p. 22.

4   Karl Rahner, *The Trinity*, tr. J. Donceel (New York: Herder & Herder, 1970), pp. 10–11.

5   Karl Barth, *Church Dogmatics* I/1 (Edinburgh: T&T Clark, 1936), p. 477.

6   I have begun these reflections on the trinity with the traditional 'second person' as does the Presbyterian *Brief Statement of Faith*. Barth offers a good argument: 'Biblical revelation has a definite historical center, while the doctrine of the Trinity has a definite historical occasion, in biblical revelation. Historically speaking, the three questions answered in the Bible as to Revealer, Revelation, and Revealedness have not the same weight; it is rather the second of these concepts, God's action in His revelation, ... which is the real theme of the biblical witness. ... And so, too, the doctrine of the Trinity historically considered, in its origin and construction, has not been interested equally in Father, Son and Holy Spirit; here also the theme was primarily the Second Person of the Trinity' (ibid., p. 361).

7   Immanuel Kant, *The Conflict of the Faculties*, tr. Mary J. Gregor (Lincoln: University of Nebraska Press, 1992), pp. 66–7.

8   Robert Wilken, 'The Resurrection of Jesus and the Doctrine of the Trinity', *Word and World* 2, no. 1 (Winter 1982), p. 28.

9   To mention just one point, the debate over the *filioque* clause in the creed which has so divided Eastern and Western Christians down the centuries will not be discussed.

10 See, e.g., Wolfhart Pannenberg, *Systematic Theology*, vol. 1, tr. Geoffrey W. Bromiley

(Grand Rapids, MI: Eerdmans, 1991), p. 296; Jürgen Moltmann, *The Trinity and the Kingdom* (San Francisco: Harper, 1991), p. 64; and LaCugna, *God for Us*, p. 2.

11   Pannenberg, *Systematic Theology*, vol.1, pp. 296, 298. Barth does begin his account of the trinity, 'In order to achieve the necessary conceptual clarification of the question of the Subject of revelation . . .' (Barth, *Church Dogmatics*, vol. I/1, p. 348). But he also says that such analysis only 'brings us in a preliminary way into proximity with the problem of the doctrine of the Trinity' (ibid., p. 343).

12   Rahner, *The Trinity*, p. 22.

13   Augustine, *Enchiridion* 38, tr. J. F. Shaw (Chicago: Henry Regnery Company, 1961), pp. 47–9; Basil, Letter 189.7, *Letters*, tr. Agnes Clare Way (New York: Fathers of the Church, 1955), p. 31; Aquinas, *Summa Theologiae* 3a., q.3, a.5, tr. R. J. Hennessey, vol. 48 (London: Eyre and Spottiswood, 1976), pp. 99–100; and Barth, *Church Dogmatics*, vol. I/1, p. 416 – to cite an impressive range of authorities.

14   Rahner, *The Trinity*, p. 23. See also Eberhard Jüngel, 'Das Verhältnis von "ökonomisches" und "immanenter" Trinität', *Zeitschrift für Theologie und Kirche* 72 (1975), pp. 353–65.

15   In Rahner, 'The possibility of a *deus absconditus* . . . who lurks behind *deus revelatus* is banished once and for all. There is no God who might turn out to be different from the God of salvation history' (LaCugna, *God for Us*, p. 211). For an extension of the implications of Rahner's identification of economic and immanent trinities, see Piet Schoonenberg, 'Trinität – der vollendete Bund', *Orientierung* 37 (May 31, 1973), pp. 115–17. Barth anticipated Rahner's basic point: 'The reality of God in His revelation is not to be bracketed with an "only", as though somewhere behind His revelation there stood another reality of God, but the reality of God which meets us in revelation is His reality in all the depths of eternity' (Barth, *Church Dogmatics*, vol. I/1, p. 548). In Robert Jenson's language, if 'God is *our* God antecedently in Himself', then God is 'action and relatedness [and] . . . history antecedently in himself' (Jenson, *The Triune Identity*, p. 138).

16   'If ... we can speak of the trinitarian relations only as enacted and never as eternal, then the only life that God has is the life that is (must be?) shared with creatures' (J. A. DiNoia, review of *God for Us*, by Catherine Mowry LaCugna, *Modern Theology* 9 (1993), p. 216.

17   See also Colossians 1:15.

18   Jesus refuses to assign James and John places on his right and left, saying that such matters are the Father's business (Matthew 20:23). He does not, he says, know how the age will end, for only the Father knows this (Mark 13:32).

19   Quoted in Moltmann, *The Trinity and the Kingdom*, p. 165.

20   Thomas Aquinas, *Summa contra Gentiles* 4.11.19., tr. Charles J. O'Neil (Garden City, NY: Image Books, 1957), p. 90.

21   Joachim Jeremias, *New Testament Theology*, tr. John Bowden (New York: Charles Scribner's Sons, 1971), pp. 61–8.

22   This analysis, unfortunately, lies behind *A Brief Statement of Faith*, Presbyterian Church (USA). See William C. Placher and David Willis-Watkins, *Belonging to God: A Commentary on 'A Brief Statement of Faith'* (Louisville, KY: Westminster/John Knox Press, 1992), pp. 94–5.

23   See Pannenberg, *Systematic Theology*, vol. 1, p. 260.

24   See Joachim Jeremias, *The Prayers of Jesus*, tr. John Bowden (Naperville, IL: Allenson,

1967), pp. 57–65; and James Barr, '*Abba* Isn't Daddy', *Journal of Theological Studies* 39 (1988), pp. 28–47.

25 Mary Rose D'Angelo, 'Abba and "Father"', *Journal of Biblical Literature* 111 (1992), pp. 614–16. I am indebted to Amy Plantinga Pauw for first calling my attention to this important article.

26 Ibid.

27 Elisabeth Schüssler Fiorenza, *In Memory of Her: A Feminist Theological Reconstruction of Christian Origins* (New York: Crossroad, 1983), pp. 105–53.

28 See ibid., pp. 149–51; see also Diane Tennis, *Is God the Only Reliable Father?* (Philadelphia: Westminster Press, 1985).

29 Phyllis Trible, 'God the Father', *Theology Today* 37 (1980), p. 118.

30 Jürgen Moltmann, *The Crucified God* (New York: Harper and Row, 1974), p. 252.

31 Elizabeth A. Johnson, *She Who Is: The Mystery of God in Feminist Theological Discourse* (New York: Crossroad, 1992), p. 210.

32 There is also the medieval tradition of reference to Jesus as Mother.

33 Anne E. Carr, *Transforming Grace: Christian Tradition and Women's Experience* (San Francisco: Harper and Row, 1988), pp. 139–40.

34 Having praised diversity of usage, I am embarrassed that the rest of this chapter so consistently uses the language of 'Father' and 'Son'. As I traced complex historical arguments, it proved excessively confusing when my own commentary was using varied language different from that of the sources whose views I was tracing.

35 John Calvin, *Institutes of the Christian Religion*, 2.16.4, ed. John T. McNeill, tr. Ford Lewis Battles (Philadelphia: Westminster Press, 1960), p. 506. See the interesting discussion of Calvin on God's compassionate Fatherhood in Brian A. Gerrish, *Grace and Gratitude: The Eucharistic Theology of John Calvin* (Minneapolis: Fortress Press, 1993), pp. 28, 38–41.

36 See Pannenberg, *Systematic Theology*, vol. 1, p. 423. 'The being of the obedient man Jesus can be taken up into God's own being, as the confession of his lordship would have it, only if God's being is understood as love' (Regin Prenter, 'Der Gott, der Liebe ist', *Theologische Literaturzeitung* 96 (1971), p. 406).

37 Yves Congar, *I Believe in the Holy Spirit*, tr. David Smith, vol. 3 (New York: Seabury Press, 1983), p. 5. The Spirit is 'faceless' (Walter Kasper), 'shadowy' (John Macquarrie), 'ghostly' (Georgia Harkness), the 'poor relation' of the trinity (Norman Pittenger) (Johnson, *She Who Is*, p. 130).

38 Jerome, *Commentary on Isaiah 11* (on Isaiah 49:9–11), *Patrologia Latina* 24, 419b; cited in Congar, *I Believe in the Holy Spirit*, vol. 3, p. 157.

39 Rosemary Radford Ruether, *Sexism and God-Talk: Toward a Feminist Theology* (Boston: Beacon Press, 1983), p. 60.

40 Although on the other hand: 'In the divine economy it is not the feminine person who remains hidden and at home. She is God in the world, moving, stirring up, revealing, interceding. It is she who calls out, sanctifies, and animates the church' (Jay G. Williams, 'Yahweh, Women and the Trinity', *Theology Today* 32 [1975], p. 240).

41 Barth, *Church Dogmatics*, vol. 1/1, p. 535. That marvellous theologian Austin Farrer, for instance, writes, 'The revealed parable of the Godhead is a story about two characters, Father and Son. . . . The Trinity is not (in human terms) a society of three but a society of two' (Austin Farrer, *Saving Belief* [London: Hodder and Stoughton,

1964], pp. 128–9. Rowan Williams worries that even in Barth, 'the relative clarity of the treatment of Father and Son is itself put into question by the apparent failure of the same method to produce an adequate theology of the Spirit', and notes that Jüngel, following Barth on the trinity, almost never mentions the Spirit (Rowan Williams, 'Barth on the Triune God', in *Karl Barth: Essays on his Theological Method*, ed. Stephen Sykes [New York: Oxford University Press, 1979], p. 171).

42   I find intriguing but not finally persuasive Peter Hodgson's proposal to identify (with qualifications) 'One' with the Father, 'loves' with the Son, and 'freedom' with the Spirit. See Peter C. Hodgson, *God in History: Shapes of Freedom* (Nashville: Abingdon Press, 1989), p. 94.

43   Walter Kasper, *The God of Jesus Christ*, tr. Matthew O'Connell (New York: Crossroad, 1984), p. 202. 'The Spirit appears as resistance, rising above all hatred, hoping against all hope. The Spirit is that little flicker of fire burning at the bottom of the woodpile. More rubbish is piled on, rain puts out the flame, wind blows the smoke away. But underneath everything a brand still burns on, unquenchable. . . . The Spirit sustains the feeble breath of life in the empire of death' (Boff, *Trinity and Society*, p. 217).

44   'The Trinitarian event, then, means that the Father's "womb" is "empty" once he has generated the Son, that the Son who is God in receiving rather than taking is "poor" ... that the Holy Spirit as mere "breath" of the Father and Son is in some sense also "without being" – in other words the self-loving of the persons within the trinitarian life of love, which includes the way in which each person allows the other two to be, involves this kind of freedom of space, without any implication that God is less than God because of this' (Gerard O'Hanlon, *The Immutability of God in the Theology of Hans Urs von Balthasar* [Cambridge: Cambridge University Press, 1987], p. 55).

45   Augustine, *On the Trinity* 5.10, tr. Stephen McKenna (Washington, DC: Catholic University of America Press, 1963), p. 187. 'As a piece of trinitarian language, *hypostasis* is merely an item of linguistic debris knocked from Hellenistic philosophy by collision with Yahweh' (Jenson, *The Triune Identity*, p. 108).

46   Augustine, *On the Trinity* 9.5, p. 275.

47   Ibid., 9.15, p. 284.

48   Ibid., p. 285.

49   Ibid., 9.7, p. 276.

50   Ibid., 9.18, p. 289.

51   Richard of St-Victor, *The Trinity* 3.2, p. 375; I am using Grover A. Zinn's translation from the volume on Richard of St-Victor in the *Classics of Western Spirituality* series (New York: Paulist Press, 1979). So far as I can tell, this is the first English translation of Richard's work on the trinity.

52   Ibid., 3.3, p. 376.

53   Ibid., 3.11, pp. 384–5. Thus I think Moltmann is wrong to worry that in Richard the Spirit is merely a relation between two persons rather than a person. Augustine may be a more complicated case, but in Richard the analogy is to lover, beloved and third person with whom mutual love can be shared, not to lover, beloved and love. See Jürgen Moltmann, 'Antwort', in *Diskussion über Jürgen Moltmanns Buch 'Der gekreuzigte Gott'*, ed. Wolf-Dieter Marsch (Munich: Chr. Kaiser Verlag, 1967), p. 186.

54   I agree that there is a problem in Augustine's trinitarianism, but I do not think it lies in his rather careful use of the psychological analogy. Rather, it concerns the problem

that, as noted at the beginning of this chapter, LaCugna has argued afflicts the theological tradition since Athanasius: Trinitarian thought has gotten separated from the history of God's salvific activity in history. As Robert Jenson puts it in typically forceful fashion, Augustine's influence 'has blighted our trinitarianism, for Augustine experienced the triune character of God himself as one thing and the history of salvation as quite another. Thus the trinitarian formulas lost their original function' (Jenson, *The Triune Identity*, p. 116). To put the matter in more technical fashion, the result is that the 'missions' (the movements of God into the world) are completely separated from the 'processions' (the internal relations among the persons). See ibid., p. 125. '"Being sent" and "being given" are terms applying to God only in time; "generation" and "spiration", only in eternity' (Thomas Aquinas, *Summa Theologiae* 1.43.2., vol. 7, tr. T. C. O'Brien [London: Eyre and Spottiswoode, 1976], p. 213).

55 William J. Hill, *The Three-Personed God: The Trinity as a Mystery of Salvation* (Washington, DC: University Press of America, 1983), p. 61.

56 Moltmann, *The Trinity and the Kingdom*, p. 139. For a similar claim about both Barth and Rahner, see LaCugna, *God for Us*, p. 254. 'Augustine only gets beyond Modalism by the mere assertion that he does not wish to be a Modalist, and by the aid of ingenious distinctions between different ideas' (Adolf von Harnack, *History of Dogma*, tr. E. B. Speirs and James Millar, vol. 4 [London: Williams and Norgate, 1898], p. 131).

57 George Hunsinger, review of *The Trinity and the Kingdom*, *The Thomist* 47 (January 1983), p. 131. The 'danger of tritheism is even clearer' for Moltmann's theology in *The Trinity and the Kingdom* (Kasper, *The God of Jesus Christ*, p. 379, n. 183).

58 'The "imago Trinitatis" . . . can only be developed in two opposite lines of being and thought that point to each other. The one is the inner structure of the created spirit, which Augustine thoroughly explored. . . . But . . . [this] closes the created spirit in on itself and is unable to show how genuine objectification and genuine love – which is always directed toward the other – can come about. So the image of God must also lie in the opposite movement of the Spirit that compels it to go out from itself, that is, from the "I" to the "thou". . . . It is inappropriate, therefore, on the basis of the strictness of the first schema, where similarity to God lies primarily in the unity of the Spirit, to ban all use of the second schema, that is, to declare it impossible for the Persons within the Godhead to say "Thou". Conversely it is mistaken to make a naive construction of the divine mystery after the pattern of human relationships (as Richard of St-Victor attempted by way of a counterblast to Augustine) and make it absolute; for it fails to take into account the crude anthropomorphism involved in a plurality of beings. The creaturely image must be content to look in the direction of the mystery of God from its two starting points at the same time; the lines of perspective meet at an invisible point, in eternity' (Hans Urs von Balthasar, *Theo-Drama III*, tr. Graham Harrison [San Francisco: Ignatius Press, 1992], pp. 526–7).

59 George Herbert Mead, 'The Mechanism of Social Consciousness', *Selected Writings*, ed. Andrew J. Reck (Chicago: University of Chicago Press, 1964), pp. 131–41.

60 Martin Buber, *I and Thou*, tr. Ronald Gregor Smith (New York: Charles Scribner's Sons, 1958), p. 11. Having grown up on this translation of Buber, I cannot break myself of it. John D. Zizioulas talked about how 'person' means 'openness of being', *ekstasis*, so that to be a person is to be open toward communion and self-transcendence (John D. Zizioulas, 'Human Capacity and Human Incapacity: A Theological Exploration of

Personhood', *Scottish Journal of Theology* 2 [1975] p. 408).

61 Ovid, *Metamorphoses*, tr. Mary M. Innes (Harmondsworth: Penguin Books, 1955), p. 85. See also Julia Kristeva, *Tales of Love*, tr. Leon S. Roudiez (New York: Columbia University Press, 1987), pp. 103–21.

62 G. W. F. Hegel, *The Phenomenology of Mind*, tr. J. B. Baillie (New York: Harper and Row, 1967), p. 232.

63 Ibid., p. 237.

64 Ovid, *Metamorphoses*, p. 83.

65 Emmanuel Levinas, *Time and the Other*, tr. Richard A. Cohen (Pittsburgh: Duquesne University Press, 1987), p. 83. 'The face is, from the start, the demand. ... It is the frailty of the one who needs you, who is counting on you. ... It is not at all a question of a subject faced with an object' (Emmanuel Levinas, 'The Paradox of Morality', in *The Provocation of Levinas*, ed. Robert Bernasconi and David Wood [London: Routledge and Kegan Paul, 1988], p. 171).

66 Emmanuel Levinas, *Collected Philosophical Papers*, tr. Alphonso Lingis (Dordrecht: Martinus Nijhoff, 1987), p. 55.

67 Jean-François Lyotard, 'Levinas' Logic', tr. Ian McLeod, in *The Lyotard Reader*, ed. Andrew Benjamin (Oxford: Blackwell Publishers, 1989), p. 276.

68 Our body 'is the tragic instrument which leads to communion with others but at the same time it is the "mask" of hypocrisy, the fortress of individualism, the vehicle of the final separation, death' (Zizioulas, *Being as Communion*, p. 52). I think this mixes up embodiedness and sin.

69 See Harry A. Wolfson, *The Philosophy of the Church Fathers* (Cambridge, MA: Harvard University Press, 1956), p. 421. Wolfson's discussion (pp. 418–28) remains the best survey of the historical issues about perichoresis in English. For the passage from Gregory of Nazianzus, see 'Letter 101, to Cledonius the Priest against Apollinaris', tr. Charles Gordon Browne and James Edward Swallow, *The Nicene and Post-Nicene Fathers*, 2d ser., vol. 7 (New York: Christian Literature, 1893), pp. 439–43.

70 Daniel L. Migliore, *Faith Seeking Understanding: An Introduction to Christian Theology* (Grand Rapids, MI: Eerdmans, 1991), p. 70. 'Precisely through the personal characteristics that distinguish them from one another, the Father, the Son and the Spirit dwell in one another and communicate eternal life to one another. In the perichoresis, the very thing that divides them becomes that which binds them together. The "circulation" of the eternal divine life becomes perfect through the fellowship and unity of the three different Persons in the eternal love' (Moltmann, *The Trinity and the Kingdom*, p. 175).

71 'That which is common and one is considered in actuality by reason of the co-eternity and identity of substance, operation, and will and by reason of the agreement in judgment and the identity of power, virtue, and goodness – I did not say *similarity*, but *identity*. ... For there is one essence, one goodness, one virtue, one intent, one operation, one power – one and the same, not three similar one to another, but one and the same motion of the three Persons' (John of Damascus, *The Orthodox Faith* 1.8, tr. Frederic H. Chase, Jr [New York: Fathers of the Church, 1958], p. 186).

72 Ibid., p. 187.

73 Gregory of Nyssa, *To Ablabius: On 'Not Three Gods'*, tr. H. C. Ogle, *The Nicene and Post-Nicene Fathers*, 2d ser., vol. 5 (New York: Christian Literature, 1892), p. 334; I

have slightly revised the translation.

74 Gregory of Nazianzus, 'The Fifth Theological Oration: On the Holy Spirit', *Orations* 31.14, tr. Charles Gordon Browne and James Edward Swallow, *The Nicene and Post-Nicene Fathers*, 2d ser., vol. 7 (New York: Christian Literature, 1893), p. 322. See Jenson, *The Triune Identity*, p. 113. 'Through this reciprocal participation the three modes of being *become* concretely united. In this concrete unity they *are* God' (Jüngel, *The Doctrine of the Trinity*, p. 32).

75 Barth, *Church Dogmatics*, vol. I/1, p. 425; and Moltmann, *The Trinity and the Kingdom*, p. 157.

76 Gregory of Nazianzus, 'The Third Theological Oration: On the Son', *Orations* 29.2, *The Nicene and Post-Nicene Fathers*, 2d ser., 7, p. 301.

77 Quoted in Moltmann, *The Trinity and the Kingdom*, p. 195.

78 Ignatius, 'Letter to the Magnesians' 3, *Early Christian Fathers*, p. 95.

79 Patricia Wilson-Kastner, *Faith, Feminism, and the Christ* (Philadelphia: Fortress Press, 1983), pp. 122–3. 'The trinitarian God is eminently God for us, whereas the unitarian God is eminently God for himself alone' (Catherine Mowry LaCugna, 'The Baptismal Formula, Feminist Objections, and Trinitarian Theology', *Journal of Ecumenical Studies* 26 (1989), p. 243).

80 Kasper, *The God of Jesus Christ*, p. 307. 'God loves in freedom, lives in community, and wills creatures to live in community. God is self-sharing, other-regarding, community forming love. This is what might be called the "depth grammar" of the doctrine of the Trinity' (Migliore, *Faith Seeking Understanding*, p. 64).

81 Carr, *Transforming Grace*, pp. 156–7.

82 Jenson, *Triune Identity*, p. 33.

83 Johnson, *She Who Is*, p. 216.

84 Dante, *Paradiso* 33.116–20, tr. Charles S. Singleton (Princeton: Princeton University Press, 1975), p. 379.

5

The Atonement and the Triune God

Colin Gunton

This selection is taken from *The Actuality of Atonement,* a study of major themes in soteriology by one of the most significant constructive theologians writing in English today. Here Gunton argues for the coinherence of trinitarian, soteriological and ecclesiological doctrine. The excerpt is particularly notable for its resistance to the critical pressures exerted upon Christian accounts of salvation in modernity, and its sharp awareness of the need to correct potential distortions which such pressures can introduce.

> *Batter my heart, three-person'd God.*
>
> John Donne

Relation

The three metaphors of atonement take their meaning, when understood in depth, from relationships. On one level, the most important but by no means the sole, are the relationships we call personal. All the metaphors can be understood as expressing in human language the significance of the life of a man, born, crucified, risen and ascended, as at once coming from God and bearing upon the life of all humankind. But that is not the only level at which they are to be understood as bearing upon reality, for they also reveal that Jesus interacts with the whole world in which human life is set. When we speak of a victory over the demonic, we speak of an action performed both for the sake of human lives enslaved to a demonized creation and for the sake of the perfection of that creation. When we speak of the justice of God realized in the life and death of Jesus, we are reminded that our action takes form in a universe whose structures are not, despite our attempts to evade the matter, irrelevant to its outcome. When we speak of sacrifice, we speak of an action of God within and as part of a world polluted by human arrogance and cupidity. Human life is always to be treated in the context of its relationships to the whole of creation.

Alongside the concern for the relationship of God to the human and the whole created order, the argument has also been that metaphor, as representative of all our language, is a reality that relates: it relates speaker to word in such a way that the reciprocal openness of mind to word and word to mind comes into view. This is by no means an automatic matter, for language often fails in its attempt to be true to the word. It certainly never succeeds in saying all that we would wish. We are fallible and sinful mortals, and, in any case, the world has its own depth and, so to speak, privacy. We can look, question, probe, experiment, torture, but, nevertheless, may only speak of that which is opened to our minds. The wonder is that so much can be said. There is a rationality in things, which is reflected in the rationality of words. The wonder of theology is that it is by grace enabled to speak of the rationality of the divine action with the help of language which is also used of such disparate albeit important human activities. The particular glory of the doctrine of the atonement is that by metaphor we are able to speak not simply of some immanent rationality, but of the rationality of redemption. The adaptation of language to new realities comes as the world is made anew in Christ.

The time has come to enquire whether a consistent pattern can be discerned in the various relationships which have come to light. What, in general, is entailed for our understanding of God and the world, human and non-human alike? Who is the God who is claimed to relate himself, in the way our metaphors allow us to say, to the world in which we are set? What kind of world is it; what kind of beings are we, its most problematic inhabitants? If what the metaphors suggest is true, the relationship which determines all the others is that between God and everything else. But its historical and concrete centre takes shape in Jesus who is God's victory, justice and sacrifice. We shall, accordingly, begin there and work upwards and outwards into the various relationships involved. The discussion will provide an opportunity to survey in a new light some of the notorious difficulties of the theology of the atonement.

God: In the Beginning

If we use the word 'career', inadequate though it is, to serve as a summary of all the things that happened with and to Jesus, his birth, life, ministry, suffering, death, resurrection and ascension, in fact all that he did and suffered, it will form the basis of a theological development of the content of our three central metaphors. And the first thing that must be said in summary is that the whole career is to be understood as the victory, the justifying action and the sacrifice of God. That has already been said in the chapters devoted to the particular metaphors. But it has been said chiefly of the career as an event in past history, of something that has happened in time, in our past. In the Christian tradition great things have been claimed for this happening of God in our midst, and they must, despite contemporary scepticism, based as it is on the Enlightenment's alienated view of time, continue to be said. But on their own, they are not enough. The objection with which this chapter is in part designed to deal is that such a conception of the atonement is 'intentionist', that is, that it represents an abrupt breach in the fabric of nature and of history by an otherwise absent (or less present) deity. It appears to suppose, that is to say, that God once made the world and, now that it has shown itself to be in need of redemption, is compelled, so to speak, to interfere in its otherwise consistent course.

Against such an objection it must on the one hand be said that if it is true that the career of Jesus is decisive for the meaning of our life on earth, there is, in one sense of the word, an intervention. This event is once-for-all, unique and unparalleled, for it is the presence of the eternal Son in person to his world. Many theologies in our past and present do, however, suggest more than that, and the criticisms are not always of parodies. It is easy, particularly in our rather moralistic Western tradition, to hold the realms of nature and grace, of creation and redemption, so far apart that the incarnation is made to appear more 'interventionist' than it ought. On the other hand, however, the classic patristic theologies, particularly those of Irenaeus and Athanasius, stress a continuity in the action of God towards and in the world. For Irenaeus the incarnation is at once an initiative of redemption and the bringing to perfection of the creation. In Athanasius the incarnate one is the Word who is the means of God's continuing presence to the world. Therefore the 'intervention' of God for his world is not isolated from the rest of his action, because it is the mediator of creation who comes to ensure that the original purposes of God do not founder in futility.

The heart of the matter, accordingly, is the newness within continuity of the divine action in atonement. God cannot 'intervene' if he is present to the world already in a continuing dynamism of providence; his presence as incarnate is, indeed, once for all, but not, so to speak, out of character. In different ways our metaphors enable us to show how this matter of the particular action of the eternal God may be conceived as the centre of a history stretching from eternity to eternity. If, then, the career of Jesus is God's victory, justifying and sacrifice, what does it reveal in these terms of the ways of God *in general*?

'Was it not thou that didst cut Rahab in pieces, that didst pierce the dragon?' (Isaiah 51:9). In these words the 'second' Isaiah draws upon the language of near Eastern creation myth in order to express the lordship of God over the created order. In so far as the myths express a recalcitrance of the creation or any limitations on the action of God, they are banished from Old Testament usage, and their language used only to express the opposite: the utter freedom of God over against the cosmos. Westermann, indeed, denies the once common belief that there is an allusion to mythical language in Genesis 1:2.[1] In particular, 'There is no sign at all of any struggle between God and תהום corresponding to the struggle between Marduk and Tiamat.'[2] This means that we cannot speak of the creation of the world by God as a kind of victory if by that is meant a struggle to overcome some opposing and recalcitrant power. But there is a victory of a kind, over the darkness and chaos against the background of which Genesis shows the creation to take place. In the Bible's characterization of the very beginning of things we see the metaphor of victory employed to depict the creator's complete authority over that which is made by him. Where other myths had portrayed the world as the product of a battle between gods or as a process of giving birth, Israel came to conceive everything as subservient to the rule of the one God. That is why there is in the Old Testament no final divorce between history and cosmology. Some of the Psalms, for example, speak of the Exodus in such a way that the historic liberation is shared by the cosmos, while Psalm 104:5–9 interweaves the languages of creation and the covenant with Noah. Creation is all of a piece, because of the victorious rule of God over and in it. Leviathan, the great beast, is not now the defeated monster who becomes the world, but simply part of the furniture of the one creation (Psalm 104:26: 'Leviathan which thou didst form to sport in [the sea]'). For our purposes, the point is that the rule of God in creation, his conquest over such evil which afflicts history and the cosmos, is grounded in his 'victory' in the beginning.

If creation is a victory, it is also right to call it, in the broadest sense of the word, a justification.[3] It is the movement by which things, in the beginning, are placed in their due order. In no sense is creation a neutral act for the biblical writers. The affirmation of the work of God 'in the beginning' is well expressed in the refrain of Genesis 1, whose climax is in verse 31: 'And God saw everything that he had made, and, behold, it was very good.' A similar point is made by Psalm 104, whose celebration of the goodness of the creation is achieved by drawing pictures taken both from the history of salvation and from the everyday life of nature. It is not, however, a naively optimistic or static rendering, as if no further divine justification were required; and the writer is aware that death, too, is part of the just order: 'when thou takest away their breath, they die and return to their dust' (v. 29). To this can be added the witness of the Wisdom literature as a whole, which is misunderstood either if it is interpreted through moralistic eyes as an aberration from the true path of salvation history or is treated as primitive natural theology. It belongs, rather, in Israel's tradition of seeing all things as deriving from the gift of the one creator. The expression of creation as justification is therefore grounded in the kind of concept of God to which von Balthasar makes reference: 'In addition to other meanings relating to man's justification and derived from its primary sense, *justitia Dei* above all means the rightness (*Richtigkeit, justesse*) of everything pertaining to God.'[4] The only question to be asked of von Balthasar is whether the use of the concept in human justification is truly the primary sense. Perhaps the latter is the derived sense, and the primary reference the overall goodness of the way in which God is both in himself and towards what is not God: human justification is but an aspect of the justification of all things by their creator.

Thus our first two metaphors can be shown to throw light on the ways of God towards his creation in general. The purpose of such a development is to build a theological basis for a non-interventionist concept of the atonement which yet maintains the utter uniqueness and definitiveness of the career of Jesus. But the third? When Revelation 13:8 (cf. 1 Peter 1–20; John 17:24) speaks of 'the lamb slain from the foundation of the world' we should not take him to be fancifully projecting back into the past an event from recent history. If Jesus is the sacrificial self-giving of *God*, we must take it with every seriousness as an insight into the eternal being of the Godhead. The temporal sacrifice which is the 'giving-up' (Romans 8:32; John 3:16) or 'sending' (Romans 8:3) of the Son is not an act foreign to the deity, not an isolated intervention, because it springs from what God is in eternity. For this reason, it is not a mistake to conceive creation, too, as a function of the self-giving of God, in which out of the free, overflowing goodness of his life he gives reality and form to something that is other than he, simply for its own sake.

In these brief sorties into the doctrine of creation, one point is being made: that to interpret the career of Jesus as the historic victory, justice and sacrifice of God is not to speak of something uncharacteristic, something coming merely 'from outside'. Modern theology finds it difficult not to think deistically, and so tends to see the world either as externally related to God or as a self-sufficient entity, complete and self-enclosed. On such conceptions, the historic atonement appears to be a breach in the seamless cloth of creation. But if we learn, with the help of our metaphors, the Bible and the great theologians of every age, to realize the interrelatedness of redemption and creation, that both are the fruit of the way in which the world is what it is through the free self-relating of God to it, we shall not so easily be led astray. We shall be freed to conceive the redemptive action of God in Jesus as of a piece with his just and sacrificial ordering of all things.

God: In the End

If, however, we are to be true to the biblical accounts of creation, other forms of static thinking must also be eschewed. Creation may be very good and even, in its own way, complete, but it is only so if room is made to allow that it is directed to an end. That is particularly important when we are concerned with the doctrine of redemption. Some stress has been placed on the fact that sin, as it is understood as the other side of the atonement, is a form of disorder, disorder affecting both the person and the creation as a whole. On such an account, the atonement is a reordering, a setting right of that which has been disrupted. But if that reordering is understood as merely a restoring to origins, as no more than a restoration, there is a danger that it will be conceived as merely or mainly conservative in form (as, sad to relate, has often been the case). Against such a limitation it must be stressed that redemption is not merely a removal of disorder but a redirection and a liberation: it is a resurrection.

We take up the argument with the rehearsal of a central theme of the previous section, that things are what they are in virtue of the victory, justice and, as self-giving, sacrifice of God in the beginning. We are therefore bound to conclude that God created all things *through* his Son or Word, who is his victory, justification and sacrifice. In the apparent aside of 1 Corinthians 8:6, Paul speaks of 'one Lord, Jesus Christ, through whom are all things', and similar points are made in John 1:1ff. and Hebrews 1:2ff. Yet, without any inconsistency, it is also proclaimed that Christ is the end of creation, that to which it aims: 'to unite all things in him, things in heaven and things on earth' (Ephesians 1:10; cf. the 'for him' of Colossians 1:16). The past ordering, which is the victory of the just God over chaos, is not the making of a static and perfect whole, a deist machine, but the setting in motion of that whose being has a destiny in the freedom of the Spirit.

If the uniting of all things in Christ is purposed from the beginning, certain consequences follow. The first is that the basis of the atonement is what has been termed 'prelapsarian'. It is the purpose of God from eternity to bring his creation to perfection through his relation to it through his Son, independently of whether or not sin supervened. Here we meet a difficulty. All of the metaphors which have been the vehicles of the development so far appear to take their shape not from such a completion of the creation, but from the active overcoming of evil which is the meaning of Jesus's career. That would appear to imply that the cause of what happened with Jesus was not the love of God from eternity, but the *failure* of the original purpose or that there is no continuity between creation and atonement, because the incarnation appears to be an entirely different matter from creation. In either case, the continuity in the meaning of our metaphors is in danger of being lost.

What is the status of the sin and evil over which God in Christ triumphed? Irving argued that sin is the 'immediate' and 'also the formal cause of the incarnation; that is to say, what gave to the purpose of God its outward form and character'.[5] In other words, the incarnation took the form it did leading to a judicial execution and ritual sacrifice because the end of creation, given the way things had turned out, could be achieved only by one able so to enter the network of slavery, evil and corruption as to free the good creation from its meshes. Sin and evil on such an understanding are those corruptions which impede the creation's achievement of its promised perfection.

The second implication of the teaching that all things are to be reconciled in Christ is that the metaphors must be understood from the end as well as from the beginning, as has already been suggested in the chapters devoted to them. Indeed, it may be said that in the light of the resurrection of Jesus they should be understood primarily in that way. Such is undoubtedly the case with the concept of victory. As a victory, the cross is final in the sense that it is the decisive meeting, in the midst of fallen time, of the person of the Word incarnate and the powers holding the creation in thrall. It is as such the signal, pledge and first fruits of the final victory when God shall be all in all. God reigns now through Christ, and in anticipation of the 'time' when that victory shall be complete. That, without doubt, is at least part of the point made by the puzzling vv. 20–22 of Paul's extended discussion of the resurrection in 1 Corinthians 15. They imply that victory is achieved only where Christ, risen and so the first fruits of victory, exercises his rule. 'Then comes the end, when he delivers the kingdom to God the Father after destroying every rule and authority and power.' The Son is the agent of the Father's victory in the world, but when all is complete the economy – the historic presence of the triune God to the world in creation and redemption – will likewise be complete.

It is, in this context, to be noted that according to the passage from Paul 'the last enemy to be destroyed is death' (v. 26). We recall the words of Psalm 104:29, which appear to imply that death is part of the good order of the creation, and so can appreciate another facet of the distinction in continuity between the orders of creation and redemption. In the conditions of fallenness, death is no longer part of the good order of things, but meets us as judgement, destruction and defeat. It has been conquered by the saving resurrection of Jesus, but also has continually to be overcome in fact and as promise by the action of the creator Spirit. So it is that Paul can see evil and suffering, the ministers of death, as realities whose power is broken, but which have to be endured in hope (Romans 5:3ff.). That, also, is one of the chief themes of the Apocalypse, which depicts the suffering of the persecuted church both to result from the victory of the lamb and to be endured in hope until the final victory, when the sea, symbol of evil and death, will be no more (Revelation 21:1).

The other metaphors, similarly though not so obviously, give up their full meaning only eschatologically. Even if, with Forsyth, we conceive the justice of God as taking shape in the regeneration of the wicked, it is finally a concept which is filled out only from the end. That is why it is a mistake to picture human destiny in terms of a return to paradise. The Western tradition in particular has tended to fit the human story into the schema of a beginning in paradise, a fall into disgrace and a restoration to former glory. The concept of the justice of God makes better sense in a more Irenaean form, in terms that is of God's bringing to completion that which was begun with the creation. Here, despite the tendency of much modern theology to be over-influenced by the notion of evolution, there is no doubt that the concept of development is a useful one. So long as it is not supposed that evolution is an automatic process, or one which operates purely immanently, so that human destiny is built into the fabric of things, it is helpful in showing that nothing is complete in the beginning. Justification means that God in his freedom as Spirit will bring to perfection that which was begun, despite the worst efforts of the creation to resist. It means the completion of the creation, in spite of and beyond our 'injustice', not by compulsion but by means of the transformation of human possibilities in Christ.

Combining the metaphors, we can say that the sacrifice which the victorious and risen Son makes to the Father *is* the perfected creation. Hence, Colossians (1:22) speaks of the end of the reconciling death of Christ to be 'to present you holy and blameless and unreproachable before him': as, we might gloss, a perfect sacrifice. Moreover, according to the Letter to the Hebrews, it is as sacrifice that Christ is judge, the one who exercises the judgement of God. And what is the outcome of that judgement? 'Christ, having been offered once to bear the sins of many, will appear a second time . . . to save those who are eagerly waiting for him' (9:28). The end of all things inevitably involves judgement, the sifting of the good from the bad, just as it involves the final victory over evil. But the process is not, as traditional imagery of heaven and hell sometimes suggests, oriented equally to heaven on the one side and hell on the other. There is indeed a judgement, but it is an eschatology of promise through judgement, not of promise and threat in equal balance (see here 1 Corinthians 3:12–15). Victory, justification and sacrifice alike are oriented to the end, and they conceive the atonement in terms of the perfection of the creation, in the Son's bringing to the Father a renewed and completed world.

In such ways as these, then, the metaphors enable us to express something of the work of the triune God through, in and with his creation. The purpose of the Father achieved by the incarnation, cross and resurrection of the incarnate Son has its basis in the creation by which the world took shape, and will find its completion in the work of the Spirit who brings the Son's work to perfection. We can speak in this way because the metaphors enable us to conceive the career of Jesus as the victory, sacrifice and justice *of God*, and so to write that particular story into a determinative place in the narrative of the ways of God with the world. But to say that is only to begin to spell out its theological consequences.

Subjective and Objective

In the previous sections there were drawn out some of the implications of saying that the human career of Jesus is also the decisive action of God in and towards his world, and is therefore both the centre point of and clue to the way in which God is related to the world from beginning to end. When we turn to the human dimensions, we have to ask about the way in which that same career is not simply the victory, justification and sacrifice of a man but at the same time takes up into itself and realizes the life of the creation. In asking such a question, we come first of all face to face with a matter which has often been near the surface of the discussion, and has dominated the history of the doctrine of the atonement, certainly in the West. (One of the reasons for the way this book has been structured is a hope that the aridities of some previous debates could be avoided.) In relation to the rest of us, is Jesus a substitute, a representative, an example, or some combination of them all? At the outset, two preliminary points must be made. The first is that to ask the question in that way is misleading, because it may suggest that the three notions are fixed in meaning and clearly understandable simply as concepts. There lies the danger of abstraction, of bringing to the topic assumptions which obscure. If all or any of the three are to be found to be appropriate, it will be because they enable us to give some account of the meaning of Jesus, and so have their meaning controlled by him.

The second preliminary point is that the underlying systematic question, that of the universal or inclusive meaning of Jesus, meets us in a particular form at our place in the theological history of Western Christianity. We saw in chapter 1 how three seminal thinkers in our tradition made particular rational criticisms of the traditional way in which the atonement had been taught. Some years before them, Socinian theologians had voiced specific attacks on the notion of substitution. As Harnack shows in his account of Socinianism,[6] the movement's objection to substitutionary theologies of the atonement combined what he calls Scotist doctrines of God with Pelagian tendencies in anthropology. By Scotist doctrines of God he means in effect appeals to omnipotence: God, if he wants, is entirely free to remit sin without penalty. Why, then, is there any need for Jesus to suffer in our place?[7] The Pelagian arguments appeal to notions of the untransferability of guilt: guilt is individual and particular, and cannot therefore be taken by or transferred to another. They are Pelagian in the sense that an underlying assumption of the argument is that actions cannot be determined, given or enabled by another, even if that other be God, but must be produced

by the individual alone. The Enlightenment, especially with Kant's development of a strong if nuanced notion of individual autonomy, strengthened the
tendency to Pelagianism, with the result that God came to be conceived as a
competitor of, or threat to, human freedom rather than its source.

The allusion to the Pelagian tendencies of the Enlightenment has been
repeated here because it shows why 'subjective' or 'exemplarist' forms of the
theology of the atonement have become increasingly popular in recent times.
The terms *subjective* and *exemplarist* refer to different aspects of a single
approach to the topic. The former calls attention to the contention that the
central feature of a doctrine of the atonement is the effect the life and/or death
of Christ should have upon the believer. What matters, it is argued, is that there
should be repentance, a new moral seriousness, Christian love and the like.
Exemplarism, on the other hand, stresses the objective basis of the doctrine,
holding the love of God and the life of Jesus to be examples the believer must
follow rather than a substitutionary transaction – as the opposing view is often
parodied – changing the human status before God. (Clearly, there is no need
for substitution in the light of the 'Scotist' belief that God can do exactly what
he likes.)

We shall return to the matter of substitution. Our present concern, however,
is with the adequacy of an exemplarist doctrine of the atonement. And first it
must be accepted that both God and Jesus are used in the Bible as examples
for human imitation. Israel's calling is to be holy as God is holy (Leviticus 1:44;
cf. Matthew 5:48), or, more generally, to reflect in her life's orientation the
pattern of God's goodness in choosing them to be his people. Similarly, the
synoptic gospels present the cross as something to be 'taken up' in imitation
of Jesus's example. For Paul, the notion of following an example appears
frequently, but it is worth referring, once again, to Romans 12:1, where the
recipients of the letter are told to 'present your bodies as a living sacrifice', in
clear echo of the sacrifice of Jesus. Similarly in the Johannine tradition, in
another passage we have met before, faith is seen as victory which overcomes
the world, therefore, if we are to establish a case for an objective, past
atonement, it cannot be at the cost of denying the subjective and exemplary
implications. The story of Jesus, whatever else it tells, is presented as an
example, a supreme pattern to follow (Hebrews 12:2), the one example of a
genuine human life in the midst of a fallen world.

The reference to the Letter to the Hebrews, however, introduces the reasons
why a merely subjective or exemplarist theology is inadequate. The first is that
it takes passages from the Bible out of context and makes what is a part, and
a part consequent on the priority of divine initiative, into almost the whole.
Without prefacing, for example, the exhortations to follow Jesus with a
theological account, expounding his saving significance on the basis of which
imitation is *reasonable* (Romans 12:1 again), the imitation hangs in the air. That

consideration brings us to the second, dogmatic reason for the inadequacy of a purely or largely exemplarist doctrine. Jesus is an example because he and he alone is the incarnate Son who by the enabling of the Holy Spirit remained unfallen where we universally fall. His humanity is only what it is because it is that of the one sent by the Father through the Spirit. As the only human victory, the life of the one just man, the only true offering of free obedience to the Father, *this particular* humanity is what it is because it is his who is sent by the Father to save lost mankind. There is no treatment of the person of Christ in the New Testament which does not place it in the context of its end in the redemption of the creation, the reconciliation of all things in Christ.

Furthermore – and this brings us to the third reason for the inadequacy of a mainly exemplarist treatment of the atonement – there is no treatment which does not also make the death and resurrection of Jesus the pivot of the events in which the reconciling action takes place. The fact that the ministry and mission of Jesus led to his death dominates the narrative in all its forms, gospel and epistle alike, so completely that no treatment of the Christian theology of salvation which wishes to be true to scripture is possible apart from it. We have seen that the death and the way Jesus approached it is indeed set before the New Testament's readers as an example (and see here especially Philippians 2:5ff.). But what, to use a hackneyed illustration, distinguishes this death from that of Socrates? The latter's death is often presented as the paradigm of the true philosopher's welcoming of death as the casting off of the shackles of the flesh in order to return to timeless eternity (Plato, *Phaedo*). For Christian theology, by contrast, the death of Jesus has generally been represented as having to do first with the perfection and completeness of his life as human (so Hebrews 5:8: 'he learned obedience through what he suffered'); and second with its determination as an act of God (hence the appeal of Isaiah 53:10: 'it was the will of the Lord to bruise him'). That is not to say *tout court* that God punishes Jesus instead of us but that the death of Jesus is first of all to be understood as part of the divine purpose of redemption. In the language of sacrifice, God 'gives up', hands over his Son to death. Why?

In his 'Subjective and Objective Conceptions of Atonement',[8] Donald MacKinnon argues that the crucial weakness of subjective theologies of the atonement is that they trivialize evil. Anselm has a similar point with his 'Have you not considered how great is the weight of sin?' (*Cur Deus Homo* I, xxi). Although Anselm's may, as has been remarked already, appear to be a rather quantitative way of putting the matter, it draws attention to the fact that the human condition is too enmeshed in evil to be able to be restored by its own agency. Forgiveness is not, therefore, simply a matter of omnipotence: something God can do simply because he wants to. A mere declaration changes nothing. It is the proponents of subjective theories who are, for this reason, in danger of succumbing to an atonement of legal fiction, as they often accuse their opponents of doing. The point could be reinforced by a discussion of the concept of sin which is implied in any of the three metaphors of atonement, although it is done most easily by a reference to the discussion of the demonic. On such an account, sin is a slavery, and slavery is not abolished by appeals to follow a good example. What is required is a setting free, an act of recreation, of redemption, which yet respects the humanity of its object.

All three of our metaphors operate with a double focus, on both God and the world. They reveal that the problem which the atonement engages is primarily *theological*. It does not consist primarily in morally wrong acts whose effect is on human life alone and can therefore be rectified by merely human remedial action, but in a disrupted relationship with the creator. As a result of the disruption there is an *objective* bondage, pollution and disorder in personal and social life, encompassing all dimensions of human existence and its context. By virtue of both truths, that the problem is one we cannot solve and that our being clean and free and upright is the gift of the creator, there needs be a recreative, redemptive divine initiative in which the root of the problem, the disrupted personal relationship, is set to rights.

Representation and Substitution

The three metaphors, accordingly, form the basis and framework of an account of the divine initiative, in that they enable us to think systematically about the recreating action of God, without ever supposing that we have plumbed its depths in an exhaustive rational account. The victory theme tells that there is something intractable and demonic, the accumulated enslaving weight of idolatry and falsehood to be overcome. It shows that the liberation is achieved where the slavery was entered, on the field of human moral struggle. There is, however, no suggestion of recreation by fiat, by the mere exercise of omnipotence, because the means of victory is the humble Son of God's recapitulation of the human progress from birth, through death and beyond, in a conquest of the power of the demonic by faithfulness and truth. It is a victory that only God can win, but he wins it from within human reality, engaging personally with the radical depersonalization of the world.

Similarly, the metaphor of justice derives, as we have seen, from a broader conception of human life in the world than the merely legal or forensic. But it demonstrates that there can be no restoration of relationships unless the nature of the offence against universal justice is laid bare and attacked at its root. P. T. Forsyth's assault on those theologies which would trivialize the grossness of human evil was buttressed by an insistence on the *holy* love of God. Holiness is of purer eyes than to behold human iniquity; but it does. As man, the eternal Son of God, God's outgoing love, allows the consequences of human evil to fall upon his head. Evil is thus taken seriously: as seriously as it can be, for its destructive consequences are accepted and borne. Correspondingly, the metaphor of sacrifice calls attention to the manner in which the divine action in the world is effected: by the Father's sending of the Son who, by virtue of the Spirit's humanizing action, returns the first fruits of a true, recapitulated human life to the Father. By entering the sphere of our pollution, by touching tar and yet not being defiled, humanity pure and undefiled is brought to the Father as a concentrated offering of worship and praise.

There is too much in all this to be accounted for solely or mainly in terms of an example, example though it is. Jesus is indeed man before God, but only as he is also God among men in his conquering and holy love. The chains must first be broken, the pollution cleansed. The logic is inescapable: if Jesus is man before God, then he must be said either to *represent* or to be a *substitute* for the rest of us. It is sometimes suggested that the former is a preferable alternative to the latter, in that it avoids the objectionable notion that Jesus is, as a man, punished by God in our stead. *Representation* is certainly a very useful concept, as we shall see, but much hangs on what is made of it. If, with Sölle,[9] we understand Jesus as a temporary representative, one who stands in for us until we can, so to speak, stand upon our own feet, the outcome is again Pelagian and exemplarist. We do not really require Jesus for our salvation here and now. But there are other less immediately objectionable conceptions of representation, like that of Moberly.[10] He suggests that the penal aspects of the passion of Jesus be taken as a kind of representative penitence. Jesus is not punished in our place, but accepts on our behalf the requirement to repent before God. Moberly is here not far from the Kingdom, for he emphasizes the fact that because Jesus's humanity is the humanity of deity, it stands 'in the wide, inclusive consummating relation . . . to the humanity of all other men'.[11] What, then, he asks, does 2 Corinthians 5:21 mean when it says that Christ was 'made sin' for us? Moberly rightly opposes the dualistic idea, so deeply engrained in the minds of both its supporters and opponents in the main Western tradition, that Jesus as man is punished by God in place of others. But he also accepts that the human person is affected by an objective weight of transgression and guilt whose removal is the precondition of true obedience. 'There must be something in the direction of undoing of the past, without which indeed the present obedience would not be in its true sense really possible'[12] Because, then, a perfect obedience is not sufficient to achieve all that is required, Moberly argues that Jesus offers before God a vicarious penitence. 'In respect of this guilt of sin, consummated and inhering, human nature could only be purified by all that is involved in the impossible demand of a perfect penitence.'[13] The one who does not need to be penitent takes upon himself the burden of sharing our consciousness of sin. He therefore exercises the penitence which, precisely because of our sin, we are unable to do. Moberly asks: 'Is not consummation of penitence, that penitence whose consummation sin makes impossible, the real, though impossible, atonement for sin?'[14]

The answer to such a question can only be in the negative, despite the moments of truth in Moberly's account. It is undoubtedly true that the gospel story does depict Jesus as identifying himself with sinful Israel in penitence, as the story of his baptism by John indicates. But the reference to baptism indicates also the deficiencies of such an account. The first is that to be baptized along with penitent Israel is not simply to be penitent, but to place oneself under the judgement of God which John, the prophet, exercises. We cannot write out of the story the justice – judgement – of God which Jesus voluntarily undergoes: the cross is the baptism – death by water – and the cup of God's wrath (Mark 10:38; cf. Psalm 75:7ff.; Isaiah 51:17). In view of what, as a matter of objective fact, has happened, there must be a correspondingly objective demonstration of justice, or the world is a morally indifferent place. The second point follows, that vicarious penitence does not require death on the cross, which is the centre of the gospel accounts and not an unfortunate completion of the human story, as tends to be the case with exemplarist theologies The outcome of Moberly's account is a – admittedly somewhat beefed up – version of Schleiermacher's view that redemption consists in the transmission of Jesus's God-consciousness to later believers. It is an account in which the transformative and agonistic elements of the cross are lost. Something real had to be undergone.

The third weakness of Moberly's account is that its conception of sin is heavily psychological, centred chiefly upon the rather pietistic concern of the removal of a burden of sinful feelings from the individual. That is, indeed, important, but it is only a part of the deeper disorder which has been illuminated by our exploration of the metaphors. The matter of sin and its removal concern two realms of being which are not satisfactorily treated in an account which places the weight on vicarious penitence. The first is that acknowledged by Moberly, and it is the question of the undoing of the evil past. The unredeemed past is more than sins and feelings of guilt; it is the objective disruption of the life and fabric of the universe. What is at stake is the movement of all things from their good creation to their destiny in Christ. All the ways of expressing the meaning of the atonement which we have explored unfold the cosmic context of redemption. In such a theatre of war, vicarious or representative penitence is ontologically and conceptually puny. The second realm of being which receives only jejune treatment in Moberly's personalistic account is the matter of relationships. We return to the death of Jesus. That the network of relationships in which he was involved *necessitated* a death and not a good moral example alone is indicative of the fact that we are here concerned with a breach of relationships so serious that only God can refashion them. The metaphors of a universe out of joint, of an indelible stain, are ways of speaking of a world whose relationship to its creator is disrupted to such an extent that only the crucifixion of the incarnate Son is adequate to heal it.

It is in such a context that there is required a concept of substitution, albeit one controlled not by the necessity of punishment so much as by the gracious initiative of God in re-creation. To conceive Jesus as primarily the victim of divine punitive justice is to commit three sins: to treat one metaphor of atonement, the legal, in isolation from the others; to read that metaphor literally and merely personalistically; and to create a dualism between the action of God and that of Jesus. Yet to ignore the fact that Jesus is shown in scripture as bearing the consequences, according to the will of God, of our breaches of universal justice – to forget that he was bruised for our iniquities – is, again, to trivialize evil and to deny the need for an atonement, a restoration of relationships which pays due attention to the way things are with the world. At issue is the actuality of atonement: whether the real evil of the real world is faced and healed *ontologically* in the life, death and resurrection of Jesus.

To put it another way, we have to say that Jesus is our substitute because he does for us what we cannot do for ourselves. That includes undergoing the judgement of God, because were we to undergo it without him, it would mean our destruction. Therefore the 'for us' of the cross and resurrection must *include*, though it is not exhausted by, an 'instead of'. He fights and conquers where we are only defeated, and would continue to be without him; he lives a just life, where we disrupt the order and beauty of the universe, and where without him we should continue to do so; he is holy, as God is holy, where we are stained, and would continue to be but for him. And just because of all this he bears the consequences of the world's slavery and pollution; and he does it because as the Son he accepts the burden as his obedience to the Father.

Here we reach the heart of the offence against autonomy which was seen to be the chief reason for the modern revolt against the theology of the atonement. To speak of *substitution* carries with it the assumption that to be truly – autonomously – human is to have our being formed not by ourselves but by God. Moreover the centre of the doctrine of the atonement is that Christ is not only our substitute – 'instead of' – but that by the substitution he frees us to be ourselves. Substitution is *grace*. He goes, as man, where we cannot go, under the judgement, and so comes perfected into the presence of God. But it is grace because he does so as God and as our representative, so that he enables us to go there after him. That is what is meant by the ancient teaching that Christ is our mediator. He brings us to the Father as one of us, but does so as one who, because he is God incarnate, is able to do so.

It is for such reasons that substitution and representation are correlative, not opposed concepts. Because Jesus is our substitute, it is also right to call him our representative. The two concepts take their meaning from different aspects of the many sided personal interaction with which we are concerned. In the network of relationships which is the world in interaction with its creator, there are many salient features which can be expressed in language. We need both substitution and representation to begin to do justice to the implications of the decisive events with which we are concerned. In this context, it is also important to remember that we cannot simply read off the theological meaning of such terms like representation from some supposed paradigmatic use, as in representative democracy or the like. Just as the notion of substitution derives largely from metaphors of legality, and must be understood in the context of the justice of God as transformative rather than punitive, so that of representation takes its heart from the world of sacrifice. When the Letter to the Hebrews speaks of Jesus as the author and pioneer of our faith, it is saying that he represents us as man before God in order that we too may participate in a like relationship. Thus representation and substitution are two sides of the one relationship, with Jesus taking our place before God so that we ourselves may come, reconciled, before God.

Two Systematic Questions

Two important questions are raised by an argument of the kind that we have been pursuing. The first arises from the claim that substitution and representation are a matter of grace: of the mediator's lacing himself where we are so that we may be where he is. In what sense, then, does it follow that God in such a way causes us to be what and who we are? The question arises because to say that Jesus is our substitute (albeit as also our representative) is to say that through him God re-establishes our life in its orientation to its promised perfection. The directedness of our life is now determined not by slavery, lawlessness and pollution, but by grace: by the pull of the Spirit to completion rather than the pull of sin to dissolution. The pressure of the argument is leading to a conclusion that we are not faced with a choice between autonomy and heteronomy, between self-directedness and directedness by another, but between an enslaving or a gracious boundness (as Paul says, between being slaves to sin or slaves to God, Romans 6:15ff.). Here we must be wary of all dualistic and deistic thinking which conceives God's relation to the world logically or causally. Grace is a personal–relational concept, not a substantial or causal one, so that a sharp distinction must be made between grace and mechanical determination. If the matter is put in terms of the action of God the Spirit, the point can be made concretely. Jesus was free in the midst of the pressures towards enslavement to the demonic because his life was maintained in freedom by the action of the liberating Spirit. So it is in general: the Spirit is God enabling the world to be itself, to realize its eschatological perfection. That is a kind of constraint, but the constraint of love, as Paul knew (2 Corinthians 5:14).

The second systematic question is related to the first, in that it concerns the matters of constraint and freedom in a different dimension. In what sense may it be claimed that Jesus and his salvation are of universal significance? The question divides into two. Why, it should first be asked, is Jesus claimed not only to have lived victoriously, and the rest, but to have won a victory of universal significance, the promise and guarantee of the final reconciliation of all things to God? The second question is the other side of the first. What prevents the claim of universality from being mere empty rhetoric, unrelated to the way things actually are with the world? If the achievement is universal, where is the evidence? (That, of course, carries within itself the question of the kind of evidence we expect in such an enquiry.) If a satisfactory – which does not mean a final – answer is to be found for the first question, a dualist or deist conception of the relation between the world and God must again be avoided. Such a – deist – conception would assume that God and the world were essentially unrelated beings or realms of being. The world would have its own autonomous being and go its own way, except that God would intervene from time to time, and especially in Jesus to initiate a change of direction. By contrast, a trinitarian conception enables us to understand the matter relationally.

It has been argued above that the metaphors of atonement encourage us to think in terms of the continuity of creation and redemption. An adequate Christology will in such a context first of all direct attention to the fact that as the incarnate Son, Jesus is the one through whom the Father created and upholds all things. It is significant that many of the theologies of salvation in the New Testament, the Pauline (Colossians 1:1–3ff.), the Johannine (John 1:1ff.) and that of the Letter to the Hebrews (1:1ff.) all bracket their accounts of salvation in Jesus within a proclamation of his cosmic significance. It follows that the soteriologies presuppose that all creation is from the beginning and at all times in relation with God through the divine Word. Christ is the mediator of salvation because he is also the mediator of creation. The universality of the significance of the cross is therefore based in the universality of the activity of the Word, reaffirmed and realized by the Spirit in the resurrection of Jesus from the tomb.

One of the ways in which the universality of Jesus has been expressed in the dogmatic tradition is by means of the doctrine of the *enhypostasia*, which teaches that the humanity of Jesus takes its particular character from the fact that it is the humanity of the eternal Word. Because it is the Word's humanity, it is real and particular humanity, and yet carries with it significance for the rest of humankind. If the mediator of creation takes flesh, then Jesus is related, as a matter of fact, to all flesh, and, indeed, to the whole order of creation. The claim must be understood dynamically, and in terms of relations: 'the . . . Word of God comes to our realm, how be it he was not far from us before. For no part of creation is left void of him' (Athanasius, *de Inc.* 8). The Word therefore comes

129

in person to renew the face of the earth. Underlying such a conception of the relation to the world is the trinitarian bedrock: *to be part of the creation means to be related to the Father through the Son and in the Spirit*. But the creation, and particularly the human creation, has lived as if this relation were not real, and so has become subject to the slavery to sin and corruption. The fact that the Son takes flesh in the midst of time means that the relationship is reordered and renewed: redirected to its original and eschatological destiny.

But – and this brings us to the second side of the question of universality – the reordered relationship has to be realized, to take concrete form in time and space. The *ontological* relationship of creator and created, grounded in the Word and reordered in the enhypostatic humanity of Jesus, must become *ontic*. Christology universalizes: but the universal salvation must then take concrete shape in particular parts of the creation. We are accordingly concerned not with myth, with the mere repetition of an event imprisoned in the past, but with a process of recreation which respects the createdness and freedom of that which is reshaped. It is the function of God the Spirit, the Lord and giver of life, to *particularize* the universal redemption in anticipations of the eschatological redemption. All of the metaphors we have considered are in some way or other concerned with the creation of space in which the creation has room to breathe and expand, to move in freedom to its appointed end. They are specifications of the way in which the universal atoning work becomes real.

Is all this an evasion, a mere abstraction? It would be, but for the fact that there is a concrete place, a community whose sole purpose is the creation of a form of life in which the victory, sacrifice and justice are to be realized. Scholars have sometimes argued that Colossians 1:1–8a, 'He is the head of the body, the church . . .' is an intrusion into a hymn celebrating the cosmic significance of the person and work of Christ. But as its stands, its logic – its *theo*-logic – is impeccable. All the talk of the cosmic Christ, of his work in creation and redemption, must be realized in a community whose life takes place in time and space. The church is called to be that midpoint, the realization in time of the universal redemption and the place where the reconciliation of all things is from time to time anticipated. Notice that it is not being claimed that there is no salvation outside the church, that those outside the actual institution are lost for ever. It has frequently been claimed, for example by Anselm, that the salvation won by Christ is of such moment as to serve for those who are outside the temporal and spatial limits of the institution, and nothing prevents us from seeking and finding the work of the Spirit in other forms of life than the self-consciously Christian. The point about the Christian community is that it is in receipt of a particular call and mission: to orient itself to the place where the universal salvation of God takes place in time and to embody in community and for the world the forms of life which correspond to it.

Notes

1   Claus Westermann, *Genesis 1–11: A Commentary* (London: SPCK, 1984), pp. 103, 105ff.

2   Ibid., p. 106.

3   See K. Barth, *Church Dogmatics* III/1 (Edinburgh: T&T Clark, 1958), pp. 366ff., where Barth argues that part of the Yes of God to the creation is its justification. 'The reality which it has and is, is not just any reality. Its being is not neutral; it is not bad, but good' (p. 366).

4   Hans Urs von Balthasar, *The Glory of the Lord: A Theological Aesthetics*, vol. 1, *Seeing the Form* (Edinburgh: T&T Clark, 1982), p. 472.

5   Edward Irving, *The Collected Writings of Edward Irving in Five Volumes*, ed. G. Carlyle, vol. 5 (London: Alexander Strahan, 1862–5), p. 10.

6   Adolf Harnack, *History of Dogma*, vol. VII (London: Williams and Norgate, 1899), pp. 118–67.

7   Appeals to omnipotence are almost always unsatisfactory, being in effect abstract appeals to logical possibility rather than arguments from the way in which God is in his action.

8   D. M. MacKinnon, 'Subjective and Objective Conceptions of Atonement', *Prospect for Theology: Essays in Honour of H. H. Farmer*, ed. F. G. Healey (Welwyn: Nesbet, 1966).

9   Dorothee Sölle, *Christ the Representative: An Essay in Theology after the 'Death of God'* (London: SCM Press, 1967).

10 Ibid., p. 90.

11 Ibid., p. 116.

12 Ibid., p. 117.

13 Ibid., p. 129.

14 One of Moberly's aims was to adapt and defend part of the thesis of J. McLeod Campbell (1864), who appears to share Moberly's fatal weakness, a final collapse into exemplarism. See Robert S. Paul, *The Atonement and the Sacraments: The Relation of the Atonement to the Sacraments of Baptism and the Lord's Supper* (London: Hodder and Stoughton, 1961), p. 167.

6

Freedom and Reality

Oliver O'Donovan

This excerpt is taken from a widely praised outline of theological ethics, *Resurrection and Moral Order*. O'Donovan's work seeks to articulate a theologically derived account of morality as response to given reality, and in this section offers a treatment of some primary themes in moral anthropology, especially freedom, conversion and conscience – all, in important respects, counter-intuitive in terms of the anthropocentric orientation of a good deal of the modern theological tradition.

Christian moral thought must respond to objective reality – the reality, that is, of a world-order restored in Christ, the reality which the gospel declares. But a further task lies before us if we are to show that Christian ethics are evangelical ethics. For we cannot simply take it as read that the redemption of the world is in fact good news for us moral agents. Why should it not mean, after all, that our moral agency is now proved to be pointless and futile, since we are caught up in a restoration which has proceeded quite independently of us? Why should it not mean that God, having vindicated his new and perfect humanity in Jesus Christ, will be content to leave us old and unsatisfactory humans on one side? Or why should it not mean that such an act of kindness on God's part requires of us a superhuman effort in response, an effort in which we are thrown back entirely on our own resources, and to which it must be probable that our moral agency will not prove adequate? The answer to such doubts is the apostolic proclamation of the Holy Spirit. If ethics are to be evangelical, they must conform to this part of the apostles' message too. We have to speak of God at work within us, applying and confirming God's act in Christ for us. We have to show that the redeemed creation does not merely confront us moral agents, but includes us and enables us to participate in it. This is the point of the transition from the objective to the subjective mode.

The heart of that inadequate approach to moral teaching which has gained the name 'Pelagianism' in the church (although not every form of it corresponds exactly to what Pelagius himself thought) is a misunderstanding about divine initiative and human response. While wishing quite sincerely to emphasize the importance of the divine initiative, the reality of grace and the absolute dependence of man upon it, Pelagius supposed that the human response lay outside the sphere of that divine initiative, as an independently grounded reaction to it. The more emphatically the gracious deed of God was stressed, the more remarkable the initiative of grace was made to appear, so much the more awe-inspiring, in Pelagius's eyes, was the responsibility thrown upon man to respond appropriately. God does everything except infringe upon our freedom by taking over the response that we must make to him. The reply of Western Christianity to this view, a reply most influentially articulated by Augustine, is simple: there can never be a moment when the divine initiative pauses and waits, as it were in expectation, to see what man will do. Even man's 'response' is still God's initiative, and, so far from this undercutting the freedom of man, it is the only possible ground on which man can be free. 'God is at work in you', says Saint Paul (Philippians 2:13), 'both to will and to work for his good pleasure.'

In using the words 'objective' and 'subjective' in a trinitarian context to differentiate the proper works of the Son and the Spirit, we follow a lead given by Karl Barth, though well aware (as he was) of the mistaken impression which this pair of terms can convey. They may remind us all too easily of the Idealist polarization of 'subjectivity' and 'objectivity', in which object and subject lose their primary relational sense – their concern with the *vis-à-vis* – and become overweighted with psychological and ontological implications. To speak of God as 'subject' in this tradition is not simply to regard him as the agent of some action, but to place him in the realm of Mind, Spirit or Personality, which is to be valued above the merely objective realm of Things. If our words are read in that way, we can hardly prevent the suggestion of an affinity between the psychological and the divine, thus losing sight of the difference between the Spirit and simple human inwardness. It is important, then, to spell out at the beginning what we intend by this reference to the 'subjective mode', and this can be done by way of two complementary assertions: first, that the Spirit makes the reality of redemption, distant from us in time, both *present* and *authoritative*; secondly, that he evokes our *free* response to this reality as moral agents. We will attempt to give a schematic outline of these complementary assertions.

(1) The Spirit makes the reality of redemption *present* to us. The restoration of created order is an event which lies in the past; its universal manifestation

belongs to the future. Yet on these two points, the resurrection of Jesus Christ from the dead and his parousia, the whole of our life is made to depend even now, as each moment of it successively forms our present. We have not said that the Spirit makes the timeless and transcendent God present to us. A theologian can certainly say that with a good conscience, and we may rejoice that it is true. But such an assertion can follow only from the New Testament's assertion that we are crucified and raised with Christ and reign with him in glory. The nearness of God to our present existence is always nearness 'in Christ'. A doctrine of the Spirit which would avoid the perils of Montanism will turn first to this 'in Christ'. But the events of Christ's death, resurrection and parousia are past and future to us. Any sense in which they can be said to happen now (in the disciple's *imitatio Christi*, in conversion or in the sacraments) must be secondary to the fact that they happened, and will happen, then. We speak of the Spirit when we make the transition from 'then' to 'now', when the remembered past and the unthinkable future become realities which shape our present. The work of the Holy Spirit defines an age – the age in which all times are immediately present to that time, the time of Christ.

We say further: the Spirit makes the reality of redemption *authoritative* to us; for authority is the mode in which this past and future reality is also present. There are other ways, immanent and non-authoritative, by which past and future events enter into the present and affect it. Events have consequences which endure, sometimes in the form of lasting institutions or pervasive habits of thought. Events can be anticipated, and excite us to action in expectancy and hope. But the redemptive moment, or moments, of Christ's passion and triumph act upon our present in quite another way. They are God's final deed, the *eschaton* in which history is given its meaning; and as such they stand equidistant from all moments of time and determine what the reality of each moment is. 'Authority' and 'reality' are inseparable aspects of the presence of God.

Whatever our reservations about Kierkegaard's appeal to 'subjectivity', we can learn much from his concept of the believer's 'absolute contemporaneousness with Christ'. In the section entitled 'Come Hither!' in *Training in Christianity*, he begins with the reminder that the one who said 'Come unto me' lived eighteen hundred years ago in conditions of humiliation. Is he not now in glory? Yes, but heaven is not open to us. 'From the seat of his glory he has not spoken one word.' Therefore we encounter him, if at all, only through the conditions of his incarnation as an object of faith.[1] Can we learn anything about Christ from history? Kierkegaard's negative answer is easily misunderstood, when it is made the servant of a quite different problematic, that of historical scepticism. By 'history' he tells us that he means 'world-history', the total course of events; and by 'learning about Christ' he means learning about *Christ*, i.e. as an object of faith. Christ does not belong immanently to the course of events; he is a paradox. We cannot infer from any possible course of events that a certain man was God. The 'consequences of Christ's life', by which Kierkegaard means especially the history of Christendom, prove nothing relevant.[2] Hegel's world-historical individual is 'noteworthy' only because his life had 'noteworthy consequences', not in himself. 'But the fact that God lived here on earth as an individual man is infinitely noteworthy. . . . How could it be noteworthy that God's life had noteworthy consequences?'[3] The misfortune of a world-historical Christendom is that it has 'done away with Christianity',[4] i.e. with faith, as encounter with the absolute. 'In relation to the absolute there is only one tense: the present.' But it is the unique character of one past event – the eschatological event, as we would say – that it can be present, and so part of 'reality' (which Kierkegaard defines narrowly as present reality). 'Every man can be contemporary only with the age in which he lives and then with one thing more: with Christ's life on earth; for Christ's life on earth, sacred history, stands for itself alone outside history'.[5]

The term 'authority' warns us that when redemption is present to us it does not encounter a vacuum. It exercises its authority over an existing reality. It encounters an apparent structure of order which is presented within the world, criticizing it and transforming it. It brings true reality to bear upon the appearances of reality which our world (that segment of the whole which shares our moment in history with us) presents to us. The effect of this is twofold: our world is judged, and it is recreated. The unreality of its existing coherence and continuity is exposed; and there is introduced a new series of events which present a truer coherence and continuity. There are within Christian moral thought a large number of pairs of contrasts which reflect, in one way or another, this double aspect of moral authority. Among the general moral concepts we see it in the distinction between the reflexive and the directive conscience, in the contrast of deontic and teleological ethics, and, most fundamentally, in the opposition of reason and will. In the specifically theological concepts we see it in the contrasts between repentance and moral learning, between justification and sanctification, and between conversion and instruction. The Holy Spirit brings God's act in Christ into critical opposition to the falsely structured reality in which we live. At the same time and through the same act he calls into existence a new and truer structure for existence. He gives substance to the renewed creation in Christ, giving it a historical embodiment in present human decisions and actions, so that it becomes partly visible even before its final manifestation. We speak of two *aspects* of the Spirit's work, not of two works. It is perilous to draw too sharp a line in particular items of experience between repentance and moral learning, between justification and sanctification, between conversion and instruction. When did we ever not have to repent while we learnt? When did obedience not go hand in hand with the need for forgiveness? When did we not find worldliness at the heart of the church we thought to instruct, and belief surprising us in the world we thought to convert? Yet the distinction is fundamental to our understanding. When the opposition of death and resurrection is collapsed, neither death nor resurrection remains. A moral authority which does not both judge and recreate is not the authority of Christ, but a purely natural authority, to follow which is to be conformed to the world.

We sum up the first assertion by referring to the words of Jesus's farewell discourse in John 16:8–11: 'And when he [the Counsellor] comes, he will convince the world concerning sin and righteousness and judgement: concerning sin, because they do not believe in me; concerning righteousness, because I go to the Father, and you will see me no more; concerning judgement, because the ruler of this world is judged.'

The work of the Holy Spirit is presented here in three steps which correspond to three moments in the work of Christ: the crucifixion, the resurrection (with the ascension) and the parousia; these three are seen in turn as three judgements: the world's judgement on Christ (unbelief), the Father's judgement on Christ (exaltation), and Christ's judgement on the ruler of the world. Each of these three moments of judgement is included in the one act of God by which creation is redeemed and fulfilled. It is the Spirit's office to make them impinge immediately upon the reality which constitutes 'the world', to 'convince' it. The repudiation of Christ, as the Spirit performs his office, becomes *our* repudiation of him; his exaltation is the life that is offered to us; every decision that *we* make now takes on importance as a pre-echo of that final decision in which the false spirits reject, and are rejected by, God. Sin, righteousness and judgement become present and authoritative to us; they determine the meaning of the life that we are given to live, and we are made to participate in the redeeming work of God. This office the Holy Spirit performs 'when he comes'. Not in the age of Christ himself (that is, when the drama is still being played out), not in the course of sacred events which are enacted for us; but in *our* age, the age after Pentecost (as Saint Luke would present it), the age of Christ's exalted absence (in Saint John's conception), 'when he comes'. This age is the age of the secret presence of God, Father and Son, to the believer and the believing community (14:22–23), the age of the apostolic witness to Christ (15:27), of martyrdom (16:2), of eschatological expectation (16:13), of prayer (16:24). It is in this age that we need the divine ministry which makes a 'then' into a 'now'.

We have quoted the RSV translation of the Greek verb *elengxei*, 'he will convince'. The revisers of 1880 chose 'convict'; the NEB, with expansive prodigality, indulges itself in no fewer than four verbs, 'confute', 'convince', 'convict' and 'show'. What is meant is what used to be contained in the English verb 'convict', and is still, barely, contained in the noun 'conviction'. It means, to make someone recognize something in such a way that he is seen to have been at fault before. It is to bring about a discovery of truth which judges even as it enlightens. The Spirit's office of conviction, then, is a critical office, but is not an office of final judgement, or condemnation, but is set in a missiological context. The apostolic ministry, enabled by the Spirit, addresses the world, the world which God loved and sent his Son to save, and proclaims that its ruler is judged (i.e. finally), the spirit which has shaped its rebellion. But the world, in being 'convicted' of that judgement, is not judged finally, but has an opportunity to be the rebellious world no longer. Are we to contrast this missiological service of the Spirit with the ecclesiological service, of which we read a few sentences later (again, with special reference to the apostles' ministry), that 'he will guide you into all the truth' (16:13)? Only to the extent that the ministry to the world is typically critical, that to the church typically constructive. But it is always understood that criticism leads to reconstruction, conviction opens into guidance. Even at the moment of criticism, the moment of confrontation and illumination, it is not only sin, but also righteousness and judgement that are given as 'conviction'. There is already present in that moment the call to live life in a continuing sequence of decisions which will embody Christ's exalted life and anticipate his final triumph over this world's ruler.

(2) The Spirit evokes our *free* response as moral agents to the reality of redemption. This assertion makes it clear in what sense 'subject' and 'subjective', once the misleading Idealist implications have been set on one side, are the appropriate terms to use of the Holy Spirit's work. He confirms and restores us *as moral agents*, which is to say, *as the subjects of our actions*, not as divorced subjectivity which subsists in its own self-awareness. In confirming us as subjects, he teaches us how, within this age of eschatological judgement, we may act. To do this he does not take over our subjecthood; he enables us to realize it. In a sentence of critical importance for theological ethics Saint Paul wrote: 'God is at work in you, both to will and to work for his good pleasure' (Philippians 2:13). This sentence, too, may sometimes be misunderstood, as though the apostle were speaking of an absorption of man's work into God's by virtue of a qualitative inwardness. But the willing and the working (as the Greek syntax makes clearer than the English) are man's willing and working. Human willing and working are made possible by the divine work 'within', which brings the free human agency to expression. God is present to man-as-subject, God the Holy Spirit attesting God the Son and evoking human attestation of him in human will and deed.

Need we add, then, that the Holy Spirit's work is not restricted to individual human agents, and so goes beyond what is normally thought of as subjectivity? Communities, too, act as subjects; and if they are to act in such a way that the sin, righteousness and judgement manifest in Christ shape their acts and attitudes, it will be only by the Holy Spirit's work. This is what makes the life of the church possible, both as a catholic whole and in its many local manifestations, official and unofficial. The relationship of ecclesiology to the doctrine of the Holy Spirit is too well established to need any elaboration here. We need only voice a caution against a misunderstanding, analogous to those Idealist misunderstandings which we have rejected, which treats the Holy Spirit as a kind of global personality or communal subjectivity into which the several subjectivities of the members are taken up. It is no more acceptable to speak of the church as possessing a semi-divine subjectivity than it is to speak of an individual believer doing so. There are, as we know, conceptual difficulties in the idea of a communal agency; but the doctrine of the Holy Spirit is not to be regarded as a short cut to solving them. If communities can be agents and subjects (though without being persons, or possessing personality), then they are human agents, just as much as individual agents are. The Spirit enables this agency in the case of the church and its dependent communities just as he does in the case of believing individuals. He is not ambiguously 'I' and 'Thou' to the church, but always 'Thou' to it, as it is to him. He addresses it, 'Set aside for me Paul and Silas', and it addresses him, 'Come, Holy Ghost, our souls inspire!'

The effect of the Holy Spirit's presence to man-as-subject, individual or communal, is *freedom*. It is this freedom that makes Christian ethics meaningful, and indeed demands it. For freedom is the character of one who participates in the order of creation by knowledge and action. That man is free implies that he can know and act; thus moral enquiry is a meaningful undertaking for him. The proclamation that he is *set* free carries with it a further implication, that man's freedom has been, and so can be, alienated. Moral enquiry is therefore demanded in the face of this dangerous possibility.

In saying that someone is free, we are saying something about the person himself and not about his circumstances. Freedom is 'potency' rather than 'possibility'. External constraints may vastly limit our possibilities without touching our 'freedom' in this sense. Nothing could be more misleading than the popular philosophy that freedom is constituted by the absence of limits. There is, to be sure, a truth which it intends to recognize, which is that the 'potency' of freedom requires 'possibility' as its object. For freedom is exercised in the cancellation of all possibilities in a given situation by the decision to actualize one of them; if there were no possibilities, there could be no room for freedom. Nevertheless, there do not have to be many. Even in deciding whether we will accept an inevitable situation cheerfully or resentfully, we exercise our freedom in choosing between alternative possibilities of conduct. Where the popular philosophy becomes so misleading is in its suggestion that we can maximize freedom by multiplying the number of possibilities open to us. For if possibilities are to be meaningful for free choice, they must be well-defined by structures of limit. The indefinite multiplication of options can only have the effect of taking the determination of the future out of the competence of choice, and so out of the category of meaningful possibility for freedom. For example, a decision to marry depends upon marriage becoming possible within the limiting structure of one's existing relationships. If that limiting structure were withdrawn, and one had all the conceivable partners in the world immediately available, one could not freely choose to marry any of them. The empty space for freedom must be defined if one is to move into it. Furthermore, the decision to marry itself cancels out both marriage and singleness as *possibilities*, by actualizing marriage as a new limit to which one has bound oneself. The empty space must be cancelled when one does move into it. Decision depends upon existing limits and imposes new ones. Limit is the very material with which freedom works. When the Holy Spirit makes a person free, that freedom is immediately demonstrated in self-binding to the service of others: 'You were called to freedom. . . . In love be one another's slaves!' (Galatians 5:13).

But although any choice which cancels out possibilities by actualizing one of them is a 'free' choice, it is not a matter of indifference for the exercise of freedom which possibilities one will choose to actualize. Certain existentialist thinkers, following the ancient Stoics, have commended suicide as the action which most supremely vindicates man's inalienable freedom in the face of constraining circumstances. Indeed suicide may be a free act, but it is not an act that affirms freedom. For freedom as there exercised encompasses its own annihilation, not in the necessary cancellation of the empty space of possibility by the creation of new limit, but in the destructive and defiant attack upon the nature of the free agent himself, who is permitted thereafter to make no more free choices. For although human freedom operates by the cancellation of possibilities, it is ordered to its own continued exercise. It is not merely a means to an end, which can then disappear. The end of man itself, described from the point of view of man's functioning, can be called 'perfect liberty'. Freedom is a teleological structure, in which freedom-given serves freedom to-be-achieved. '*For* freedom Christ has set us free', says Saint Paul; 'stand fast therefore, and do not submit again to a yoke of slavery' (Galatians 5:1). This further submission to slavery would, of course, be the result of a false exercise of freedom: 'do not use your freedom as an opportunity for the flesh' (5:13). Freedom can alienate itself and produce unfreedom. This is why the gospel speaks of the 'bondage' of sin and of freedom 'restored' by the Holy Spirit's indwelling, bringing man into union with the free humanity of the risen Christ.

The alienation of human freedom does not mean that mankind can be subject to necessity in the same way that creatures not originally created for freedom are subject to necessity. Man does not become like a stone or a plant. We might

139

wish to say that fallen man is 'unfree' in a more radical sense than stones or plants which have never alienated a freedom that they once possessed; but we would have to say, too, that he can never be simply *without* freedom as they are without freedom. Created to exercise free choice, mankind is bound to the terms of creation and remains, even in a state of alienated freedom, a race of free agents. Nevertheless, fallen man does not live freely; for, as a free agent, he is bound to the choices he has made for unfreedom. His bondage, quite unlike the passivity of a tree or a stone, is brought upon him by his own free refusal of certain possibilities which would have allowed him the continued exercise of his freedom. Unfreedom, for him, is a galling and condemning state of affairs.

What, then, are these possibilities which he refused? They are the possibilities of recognizing and rejoicing in the objective reality of the good. The sin by which man has bound himself is the determination to live fantastically, in pursuit of unreality. But freedom can be exercised only in relation to real possibility. Fallen man remains, of course, a being who goes through the motions of free decision, but he lacks that relation to the realities of the universe which could make such decisions effective for 'perfect liberty'. Clearly the restoring of man's freedom must involve his awakening once again to the reality of God's creation as it is revealed in Christ. The work of the Spirit as 'witness' to the objective deed of God in Christ, and his work as 'life-giver' who restores freedom and power to mankind enthralled, are not two distinct works but one. For man's thrall is precisely that he has lost touch with reality.

Our two assertions, then, bring us to a common point. The *authority* of redemption lies in its power to determine the present reality of the world with which we have to do. Our freedom as agents depends upon our acting in accord with reality. Reality is the point on which both freedom and authority rest, and at which they complement each other. When we speak, then, of the 'subjective reality' from which Christian ethics proceed, we are speaking of this point: the bearing of reality upon the acting subject, its presence to him as authority and his fulfilment within it as a free agent. The 'subjective reality' is, as is by now obvious, no different reality from the 'objective reality'. It is the one reality, the reality of a world redeemed, which is both apart from us (in Christ once for all) and immediately engages us (through the Spirit here and now). Our present task is to explore this active engagement with reality, which we continue to do through its complementary aspects as freedom and authority; we continue with some further exploration of the alienation of freedom.

Alienation and Conversion

Free human engagement in the ordered reality which God has made and restored is described by Saint Paul in a single Greek word, *hypakoē* (Romans 1:5; 6:16).

It is difficult to find a satisfactory translation for it. It means 'obedience', which is a practical idea; but its derivation from the noun *akoē*, 'hearing', is still very much alive in Paul's mind, which requires that a cognitive sense also be understood. Perhaps the best we can manage is 'attentiveness'. Paul speaks of the 'attentiveness of faith', and in that phrase is contained the whole of our response to God, from hearing, understanding and assenting, to willing and acting. But James, in a well-known passage, raises an issue about this response which Paul's phrase does not envisage: 'Be doers of the word, and not hearers only, deceiving yourselves' (James 1:22). Here there arises the thought that *hypakoē* may be split into two distinct elements, 'hearing' and 'doing'. This thought arises out of the experience of sin, which is a failure of *hypakoē*; it fails precisely when its two elements are not co-ordinated, when hearing is not doing. What in the operation of divine grace is one, falls into two parts in human sin.

The celebrated controversy (which is now generally admitted to be no controversy at all) between Paul and James, on the question of whether man is saved by faith alone or by faith and works, resolves itself in this way. James is conscious of the possible fissuring of man's response to the gospel into a mere intellectual assent apart from existential commitment (2:14–26). Paul, on the other hand, never advocated a mere intellectual assent: his contrast between 'hearing with faith' and 'works of the law' was intended to make quite a different point (Galatians 3:2). The phrase *akoē pisteōs* (Galatians 3:2, 5) should be interpreted in the light of *hypakoē pisteōs* at Romans 1:15; 16:26.[6] Paul's 'faith' is always the unified response of mind and will, 'faith working through love' (Galatians 5:6). Correspondingly, the cognitive content of *hypakoē* should not be ignored: it appears clearly enough in the phrase 'obedience (or attentiveness) to the truth' (*hypakoē tēs alētheias*) at 1 Peter 1:22.

Saint Augustine's interpretation of the holy trinity, built on the analogy of the human mind in its relationship to truth, depends upon the point which is here being made. Knowing and willing must be entirely proportionate and coextensive, to establish the consubstantiality of the Son and the Spirit and the procession of the Spirit from the Son. Without passing judgement on the adequacy of this analogy for the doctrine of the trinity, nor upon the understanding of the *imago Dei* which it implies, we can learn from the psychology simply in its own right. The fallen and corrupted human mind, thinks Augustine, is the mind which knows something without loving it, or without loving it proportionately; which loves something without knowing it sufficiently to justify its love; which understands without willing, and wills without understanding; but such conditions only betray the fact of the mind's disorder. The mind in perfect possession of the truth loves as it understands and understands as it loves. Reason and will are at one. (See especially the ninth book of *De Trinitate*.)

We start at this point in order to emphasize that the problem of the relation of 'reason and will', as it has come to be thought of in Western moral philosophy, springs out of a malfunction of the moral life and does not belong within its normative morphology. The disjunction of hearing and doing, or of reason and will, is sin. It is the failure of man to make the response that is appropriate to him as a free rational agent. In such a failure man himself seems to disintegrate into dissociated powers, into a rational self on the one hand, which has a cognitive relation to reality, and a voluntative self on the other, which consists of affections, emotions and decisions. This is the psychological aspect of the alienation of freedom. In the effective operation of the Spirit, to know is once again to will, or, to speak more theologically, to believe is to love. That is why we can speak of the work of the Spirit as witness and life-giver, his ministry to the reason and to the affections, as complementary aspects of one work and not as two.

The possibility and the limits of this disintegration are represented for Western culture in Milton's portrayal of Satan in *Paradise Lost*. Satan's absolute and irreparable rejection of God becomes, in Milton's treatment, a representation of what man is ultimately capable of doing – not within the confines of time, of course, but eschatologically. As such Milton's portrayal interprets the ultimate significance of sin. The famous line which Milton puts on Satan's lips, 'Evil, be thou my good!' perfectly captures the double movement of the soul which is the essence of the Satanic gesture: in the first place, the convulsive turning of the will to evil in place of the good which is its natural orientation; in the second place the veiling of the reality of evil under the guise of good. The moment of brilliant light which enables Satan to address evil as evil, even while he embraces it, is replaced by the darkness in which the evil is addressed and embraced as good. In the will's convulsive embracing of evil the reason must find a point of rest. It cannot rest in the reality of the chaos which the will has embraced, but must create for itself a new order, a fantastic order without objective reality or substance, formed around the new orientation of the will, a parodistic imitation of reality which it calls 'my' good. Thus reason and will part company only for an instant of self-destroying freedom, in which Satan looks to evil and says, 'Be thou . . .!' From then on reason is enslaved to this new orientation of the subject, obligated to form representations which will justify it.

The movements of the soul which are seen in the myth in their eschatological finality are, of course, entirely familiar features of moral experience. There is, on the one hand, the experience of yielding to temptation: knowing some course of action to be right, the agent proceeds, conscious of guilt, freely to do the opposite. 'The man who knows the good he ought to do and does not do it is a sinner' (James 4:17: NEB). This is the movement which moral philosophy since Aristotle has analysed as 'incontinence' (*akrasia*), the paradoxical triumph of the appetite over reason. On the other hand there is what we call the 'rationalization' of our decisions, in which we revise our moral convictions to justify our past performance. There can be, of course, good reasons to refine and correct moral opinions in the light of experience; so that not every modification of an agent's moral principles is rationalization in the sense that we condemn it. But human beings do rationalize; the reason and the will, once they have been torn apart in the moment of yielding to temptation, demand to be reconciled. The consciousness of having acted irrationally must be assuaged, even at the cost of reason's grasp on reality. And so it is that, in the free exercise of the will to sin, man deprives himself of his freedom, for he cuts off his cognitive access to the created order. He cuts himself off from the earth on which he must have a purchase if his agency is to amount to more than a flailing of limbs.

The redemptive work of the Holy Spirit involves the restoration of our access to reality. But this restoration cannot be wrought upon the reason alone, in isolated separation from the will. That would be merely to recreate the dividedness of will and reason which accompanied the moment of temptation. In fact, since man does not, within the co-ordinates of time, effect the two movements of his rebellion with the eschatological completeness of Satan, dividedness continues to be part of his experience. He lives in guilt, which may, perhaps, be a reassuring sign that he has not yet entirely sold his soul to the devil, or may, alternatively, be a terrible anticipation of divine judgement, but is certainly not in itself a work of grace. That work must involve also a detachment of the will from its self-chosen orientation; man must be freed to cease willing his own past. But as willing his own past is, in itself, a natural thing to do, a guarantee of the coherence and integrity in our purpose that is indispensable to our fulfilment as moral beings, that 'freedom' is, in one sense, death. If we cease to reinforce the fundamental choices of our past with the continuing affirmation of our will, we abandon altogether that 'I' which we were in the way of realizing; it becomes to us the 'old man' who, as Saint Paul says, is crucified with Christ. Repentance cannot be the mere realignment of a will that retains a fundamental continuity with its past; it involves a moment of self-annihilation.

But neither can this self-annihilation of will take place in isolation from the cognitive realm. If it did, it would not be a repudiation of the arbitrariness of its own past convulsion. It would merely add a new convulsion, equally arbitrary, to the old. If the will merely turns in repudiation upon its own past, as earlier it turned against the objective order, it is no more than a continuation of the pattern of wanton self-assertiveness. Sin has its own vain regrets, its own self-hatred, every bit as wilful as self-confidence and pride. The systematic negation of reality can lead to a self-negation which has nothing to do with repentance as Christians know it. To repudiate arbitrariness, we must regain contact with that which is not arbitrary. Repentance must go hand in hand with faith, which is the proper stance of reason when it attends to an object which it cannot transcend or contain. It is a form of cognition, though a unique form as its object is unique. And as the knowledge of good, whether created or uncreated, cannot be had without commitment, it is a form of cognition which depends in its turn upon the reorientation of the will, as the reorientation of the will depends upon it. Conversion, then, is not something in which either the will or the reason has a leverage upon the other, by virtue of a residual connection which either can claim with objective good. It is an event in which reason and will together are turned from arbitrariness to reality, an event which is 'miraculous' in that there are no sufficient grounds for it, whether rational or voluntative, within the subject himself. Repentance and faith do not come in that order as a matter of logical necessity; neither is it a logically necessary sequence when we reverse the order and speak of 'faith working through love'.

Can there be repentance without faith? The question is put with extraordinary poignancy at the conclusion of Thomas Mann's great novel *Doctor Faustus*, as the first-person narrator draws together his reflections on the fate of the hero, the composer Leverkühn, and his anguish over the hell into which Nazi Germany has sold itself. Leverkühn's last work, the cantata 'Faustus' Lament', rejects, we are told, the thought of being saved, 'not only out of formal loyalty to the pact with the devil and because it is "too late", but because with his whole soul he despises the positivism of the world for which one would save him, the lie of its godliness'.[7] And yet 'he dies as a bad and as a good Christian: a good one by the power of his repentance, and because in his heart he hopes for mercy on his soul; a bad one in so far as ... the Devil will and must have his body'.[8] What this means for Germany appears in the last paragraph of the book.[9] 'Germany, the hectic on her cheek, was reeling then at the height of her dissolute triumphs, about to gain the whole world by virtue of the one pact she was minded to keep, which she had signed with her blood. Today, clung round by demons, a hand over one eye, with the other staring down into horrors, down she flings from despair to despair. When will she reach the bottom of the abyss? When out of uttermost hopelessness – a miracle beyond the power of belief – will the light of hope dawn?'

The question which Mann's novel poses for us can be understood in two ways. In the first place it can be taken as a problem arising entirely within unbelief: how is one to repent who has nothing to believe in? How can there be rebirth without a gospel? If Mann thought that any currently proclaimed gospel was adequate to deal with the self-invoked damnation of his people, he was not acknowledging the fact. His was the problem of religious man with nothing really certain to believe in but damnation; all else was 'the positivism of the world for which one would save him, the lie of its godliness'. From this point of view the hope for mercy was nothing but the self-evidently vain hope of the truly damned; the plight was nothing other than the plight of there being no divine mercy. But behind this problem arising within unbelief we can recognize a different problem, which is rather a question put to faith itself: how can true faith be characterized except as faith in miracle, absolutely beyond looking for or counting on, miracle that snatches man out of the very reality of hell itself? Faith that is faith indeed and not merely prudentially pious calculation cannot dare to think itself or propose itself or describe itself for fear of falsity. It can only be observed as the possibility of miracle reflected through the mirror of the impossibility of human self-redemption. 'No, this dark tone-poem permits up to the very end no consolation, appeasement, transfiguration. But take our artist paradox: grant that expressiveness – expression as lament – is the issue of the whole construction: then may we not parallel it with another, a religious one, and say too (though only in the lowest whisper) that out of the sheerly irremediable hope might germinate? It would be but a hope beyond hopelessness, the transcendence of despair – not betrayal to her, but the miracle that passes belief'.[10] Such hope in sheer miracle (which dares not call itself, in the stricken silence, faith in the resurrection) is nevertheless not hope that is quite apart from faith.

Conscience and Autonomy

The consciousness of guilt, in which our moral reason disapproves of what we are, nevertheless, freely willing to do, offers a paradigm of how reason and will can, in the absurdity of sin, be torn apart. This characterization, however, is only a schematic one. Guilt is also, as Saint Paul describes it in Romans 7, a dividedness of the will against itself, in which our true affections, as well as our judgement, are offended by the 'other law within [our] members'. Modern thinking about the guilty conscience has stressed its emotional component as self-repudiation, where the ancients stressed its rational component as self-criticism; both interpretations have some justice, such is the complexity of the phenomenon. The word 'conscience' comes from the Graeco-Roman world, where it meant 'self-consciousness', especially that uneasy awareness that one has of oneself when one knows one has done something wrong. Primarily with this meaning it was introduced into the New Testament, and so into Christian moral thinking, by Saint Paul. But in medieval and modern usage it has acquired a new sense, and has come to be used not only for the guilty moment of self-awareness but for the whole faculty of moral understanding and self-direction. This shift in meaning marks an important, and largely damaging, development in moral psychology, in which the separation of reason and will comes to be treated as normative. This in turn generates a conception of freedom as autonomy, the agent's independence of reality.

In the ancient world the words *syneidēsis* (in Greek) and *conscientia* (in Latin) meant 'consciousness', and especially a consciousness in which two or more people shared (cf. 1 Corinthians 10:29, which should perhaps be translated: 'I do not mean your own self-consciousness, but the consciousness which you share with the other man'). More narrowly they mean consciousness of oneself, usually in the experience of guilt, which the ancients liked to portray dramatically as having a secret witness to all one's actions. When the ancient world spoke (as in the much-quoted line attributed to Menander) of conscience as 'a god to all of us', it had in mind not a legislative deity but an avenging one, like the Furies in classical myth. From this point the meaning of the word broadened out, as moral self-consciousness became a general psychological category for the seat of moral agency in the soul. This last development is especially marked in Latin, where *conscientia* became a synonym for 'heart'. In the New Testament this complete range of meaning is represented, so that there is no one English word which can do duty for *syneidēsis* every time it appears there.[11]

But nowhere in the New Testament (nor indeed in the classical world as a whole until a later period) does *syneidēsis* mean a faculty of *moral direction*. Later moral theology (followed by some more recent biblical studies) was accustomed to read this idea back upon texts which did not contain it, and especially upon Paul's two discussions of the morality of eating meat sacrificed to pagan deities (1 Corinthians 8 and 10; Romans 14). These two discussions, we must note, are somewhat divergent in their emphasis. The later discussion (Romans 14), conducted without any use of the word *syneidēsis*, is altogether simpler, focusing clearly upon the need for faith in any doubtful or controversial action. 'He who has doubts is condemned, if he eats, because he does not act from faith' (Romans 14:23). It is a warning against what we might call 'inauthentic' action, done under community pressure. A sense of conviction is a necessary condition (though Paul would hardly have thought it a sufficient condition) for any action to be acceptable to God. The argument in 1 Corinthians is more complex, and is directed to a different point: the peril of the weak believer who, by 'habituation to the idol', is likely to eat sacrificed meats with actual idolatrous intent. 'If someone sees you, the enlightened one, present in an idol's temple, will not his *syneidēsis*, since he is weak, be fortified to eat of the sacrifice?' (1 Corinthians 8:10). It is wrong to read this as though it were simply an anticipation of the Romans argument, warning against inauthentic decisions accompanied by scrupulous doubts. Paul is rather concerned with the *consciousness* which is 'habituated to the idol'; that is to say, the weak brother is really superstitious, and cannot help taking such beings seriously, so that if he became involved in a pagan feast he would approach it 'as an idol-sacrifice', i.e. with an idolatrous mind.

The idea of a directive conscience emerges clearly only with the later Greek Fathers, where it is a development of speculations about natural law. Chrysostom[12] speaks of conscience as making knowledge of good and evil 'self-taught'; it 'rings in the ears, teaches and instructs'; it is the depository of the law, which is therefore already familiar to us when we hear Christ's teachings; it 'suggests what ought to be done'. This is to think about conscience in a new and very different way. Yet it is still left for medieval thinkers to take the decisive step which shapes the modern conception of conscience: to identify it with the power of moral reason as such.

When conscience becomes a category for all moral understanding, we may suspect that dividedness has come to be seen as the natural condition of moral knowledge. Why should this be? It arises on the one hand from the characteristic medieval concern to ensure the freedom of the moral agent. Freedom is associated with the will. The will, therefore, comes to be thought of as the ontological ground of personal agency, the 'real me' who is the subject of all my acts. For reason, it appears, is bound to objective reality, and therefore cannot be free as moral agents are free. It arises on the other hand from the classical interest in the forcefulness of conscience, its power to impose tortures upon the soul, which derives in fact from its emotional components but was widely interpreted as evidence of the natural authority of reason. Such an interpretation reinforces the tendency to see reason, together with the external world, as 'not-I', distinct from and set over against the will which is the seat of my personal agency. The perceptions of reason thus come to be placed among the *circumstances* of the subject's agency. From the concern to vindicate freedom, then, and the concern to exalt the inherent authority of reason, there flow the objectification of reason and its alienation from the acting subject. The psyche is fragmented. The subject is no longer a reasoning–willing subject, but a will which has at its disposal the services of a reason; while the reason exercises an authority over the subject's activity which should properly belong only to external reality. Thus arises in the West a moral psychology in constant oscillation between rationalism and voluntarism, all the time unable to establish a satisfactory relation between the agent and the real world.

This conception may already be detected behind an important discussion in Thomas Aquinas (who, anxious as always to qualify prevailing voluntarist conceptions, is unenthusiastic about it). When he asks himself two questions, 'whether an errant conscience creates an obligation' and 'whether an errant conscience constitutes an excuse', we can see that he is confronting an idea of moral agency in which the conscience (or reason) stands over against the moral subject, either as an external authority which imposes obligations upon him or as an unfortunate circumstance which excuses him from blame. The question of a mistaken conscience is understood by analogy with the misguided commands of a ruler or with the accidental weakness of a faculty such as sight or hearing. Thus the will alone is the true moral subject who is 'obliged' or 'excused'. In answering these questions Thomas does his best to undo the damage done by the way they have been put. He reminds us that the will is incapable of doing any thinking on its own apart from the reason; he insists that every act of will apart from reason is disruptive of moral agency; and he recalls that there is such a thing as culpable error of the reason. But the way the questions have been framed make it too hard for him. Once the issue has been conceived in terms of the conscience's 'obliging' or 'excusing', the objectification of reason is complete. The key questions of *Summa Theologiae* are II–I.19.5 and 6: *utrum ratio errans obliget* and *utrum voluntas concordans rationi erranti sit bona.* We may note that he immediately rephrases the questions in terms of conscience, treating *ratio* and *conscientia* as synonymous for the purposes of this discussion. The first question is answered positively, though not without a certain evasiveness. Rather than state outright that one is obliged to follow an errant reason, he converts the question into another form which is said to be equivalent: *utrum voluntas discordans a ratione errante sit mala,* 'whether an act of will is bad when it goes against a mistaken reason'. To this he can answer 'yes' directly. The theory that it is bad for the will to be at variance with an errant reason only in matters of indifference is answered by the wise observation that the will has no independent knowledge of right and wrong. It is absurd to think of the will as a subject which can weigh the dictates of the reason against other considerations and find them wanting: 'If one knew that the dictates of human reason ran contrary to God's precept ... one's reason would not be entirely in error'. The second question is phrased in the form 'whether an act of will is good when it follows a mistaken reason', and then converted back into the original form, 'whether an errant conscience constitutes an excuse'. To this Aquinas will not say 'yes'. Certainly, there is such a thing as ignorance which is in no respect voluntary, and a conscience affected by such ignorance must plainly be followed. But there is ignorance, as Aristotle taught, which is 'indirectly voluntary', such as 'ignorance of the law of God which one is bound to know' (cf. *Nicomachean Ethics* 1113b–1114a), and this does not serve to excuse a wrong act. 'It is possible to go back on the error, since the ignorance is vincible and voluntary.'

And so Thomas Aquinas implies that if you have a mistaken conscience, anything your will does will be sinful. It is possible to see in this paradoxical conclusion simply a cautious reluctance to draw the obvious conclusions from the way the question has been argued. Thus Eric D'Arcy[13] argues that Thomas's successive discussions of the issue show him edging nearer and nearer to the view that ignorance is culpable only if it is voluntary; yet he will not quite let go of the classical idea that ignorance of certain things is culpable in itself. Thus he is almost a modern, wanting only the courage to carry through the separation of reason and will to its necessary conclusion, which, for D'Arcy, is the rationalist rather than the voluntarist conclusion, namely the unquestionable authority of the subjective moral reason. And indeed Thomas has opened himself to this interpretation. He has said that 'the principle of good and evil in human acts derives from the act of the will . . . the end of the act is the object of the will and not of the other faculties' (19.2). He has identified the 'inner act' with an act of the will (18.6). Yet perhaps it may be truer, as well as more charitable, to suggest that Thomas understood his paradox as an indirect challenge to the separation of reason and will which was implicit in the form of the question. In his discussion of how acts are 'commanded', we may observe, he refused to separate the will and the reason as originators of action (17.1);

and he maintained that the object of any act of will must be presented to it by the reason (19.3). Furthermore, in his earlier discussion of conscience (I.79.12 and 13) he was most unready to reify the conscience (which he thought of, dividing it into two parts in the medieval way, as habit and act), and he well understood that to speak of conscience 'binding' was to use a metaphorical expression which actually referred to something that the agent himself does in applying his knowledge to his action.

Without any of the caution that Thomas displayed, moralists of the seventeenth and eighteenth centuries simply gloried in the absolute authority with which conscience, displaying, as they thought, its rational character as well as its divine institution, presided over the vacillations of the will and the ambiguities of judgement. It was, in Butler's famous words, that 'superior principle ... which distinguishes between the internal principles of [the] heart ... which, without being consulted, without being advised with, magisterially exerts itself ... and which, if not forcibly stopped, naturally and always of course goes on to anticipate a higher and more effectual sentence'.[14] If anyone was tempted to chafe under the rule of this guide which had been assigned him by the author of his nature, he was told simply: 'That your conscience approves of and attests to such a course of action is itself an obligation' (3). Moralists of this tradition were, in effect, setting up conscience as an arbitrary tyrant, as was evidenced by the copious observations on conscientious disorder which interested pastoral writers such as Jeremy Taylor. The tribute that had too often to be paid to the categorical authority of subjective moral reason was the paralysis of indecision or the frenzy of exaggerated scruple.

The eighteenth-century reaction to this, anticipating the emergence of voluntarism as the dominant force in modern moral philosophy, was to deny the competence of reason to pass moral judgements and to attribute them instead to 'affection' or 'sentiment'. 'Morality', as Hume said, 'is more properly felt than judg'd of'.[15] Here first arose the modern presumption that strong conscientious conviction is emotional rather than rational in its source. For to suppose any one feeling rather than another uniquely authorized by reason was, this school of thought maintained, to fall victim to an illusion. Moral judgements could not be 'reasonable' or 'unreasonable' in the ordinary sense, since they did not deal in claims of truth and falsehood. By appealing to the affections in this way these thinkers hoped to reassert freedom of moral agency against a conception of moral reason which had become oppressive. In so doing they opened up the 'fact–value distinction' which was to be of such weighty importance for modern thought. With no chain of reason (by which was meant _deductive_ reason) to connect factual judgement with practical decision, the agent was left to value things on his own responsibility, without the world to help him.

But that meant that he was thrown back on a sheer act of will. Modern voluntarism, with its ponderous talk of responsibility and of making the world by our decisions, has a very different sound from the early attempts to free moral agency from the constraints of reason, but it is their natural outcome. For if it were left simply in the sphere of feeling, morality would appear to be nothing more than a spontaneity of mood and emotion. What distinguishes moral attitudes from mere impulse, and gives them a higher claim to our respect, is precisely that they are not spontaneous but deliberated. Yet how can there be deliberation without a train of reason? The modern substitute for moral deliberation in the traditional sense (i.e. the attempt to bring action into conformity with the good) is a kind of extended and meditative foresight which accompanies decision and transforms it into a solemn act of will. The 'responsible' agent is the one who, while still taking his decision for no objective reason, has nevertheless peered anxiously into its likely consequences and implications and, as we say, 'knows what he is doing' – which, after all, is the only thing that there is left for him to know!

It is the most curious feature about the separation of reason and will in Western thought that each, as it is cut off from the other, takes on the characteristics of the other. The rationalists' conscience 'commands', while the voluntarists' moral sentiment is forced to learn to think. In Kant's profound distillation of the modern ethos we see how voluntarism and rationalism can become, in effect, indistinguishable, while the Western programme of agent-autonomy is carried to its height. Kant's 'rational will' derives from reason its ability to think generically and to respect universal moral laws, and from will its independence from all laws that it has not legislated for itself. It binds itself to universal principles, but without acknowledging any indebtedness to external reality. Its rationality lies in its adherence to a purely formal order. In satisfying the champions of conscience and the champions of freedom simultaneously, it shows the extent to which the aspirations of both parties were the same. Each had it in mind to vindicate freedom as autonomy, that is to say, in terms of an authority for action which belonged entirely to the moral agent himself and was not derived from external reality.

It was exactly this project which lay behind the elaboration of the consciousness of guilt to become an all-embracing principle of moral understanding. Conscience, it seemed, was a power within the soul which could generate its own forceful moral judgements without any dependence upon the world outside. This otherworldly self-sufficiency was in truth never more than an illusion created by the memory of past perceptions of moral order; the forcefulness, while not an illusion, was due to emotional rather than rational factors. The project was misconceived from the beginning. Moral freedom can never be established on a basis of self-sufficiency and independence of the world. Freedom, if it is freedom to act *within* the world, must itself be *of* the world. Man's status as agent is part and parcel of his created being in the world, and his acts depend for their significance on their context in the world's history. Man has, therefore, nothing to fear from the world-order within which and into which he acts. He has only to fear being cut off from it. For God has given him his freedom at the same time as he has given him a world in which to be free.

We return, then, to the presence of external reality as the essential condition for the exercise of freedom. Reason has its importance only as the agent's means of purchase upon reality, and not in itself: the authority attributed to reason is more properly understood to belong to reality. We speak of 'authority'. The real world *authorizes* man's agency in general by being the context of its exercise, and his particular acts by being the context in which they have a point.

Notes

1 Søren Kierkegaard, *Training in Christianity*, tr. W. Lowrie (Princeton: Princeton University Press, 1941), pp. 26ff.
2 Ibid., pp. 28–34.
3 Ibid., p. 34.
4 Ibid., p. 39.
5 Ibid., pp. 67ff.
6 Contra W. F. Arndt and F. W. Gingrich, *A Greek–English Lexicon of the New Testament*, 4th edn (Chicago: University of Chicago Press, 1952), *s.v. akoē* 2b.
7 Thomas Mann, *Doctor Faustus*, tr. H. T. Lowe-Porter (New York: Vintage Books, 1971), p. 490.
8 Ibid., p. 487.
9 Ibid., p. 510.
10 Ibid., p. 491.
11 See C. A. Pierce, *Conscience in the New Testament* (London: SCM, 1955), whose general conclusions are secure, though his detailed exegesis of texts is not always satisfactory.
12 John Chrysostom, *Homilies on the Statues (De statuis 12:13)*, tr. W. R. W. Stephens, *The Nicene and Post-Nicene Fathers*, 1st ser., vol. 9 (New York: Christian Literature, 1889), p. 423.
13 Eric D'Arcy, *Conscience and its Right to Freedom* (London: Sheed & Ward, 1961).
14 Joseph Butler, *Sermons*, ed. W. E. Gladstone (Oxford: Clarendon Press, 1896). See Sermon 2.
15 David Hume, *A Treatise of Human Nature*, ed. L. A. Selby-Biggs (Oxford: Clarendon Press, 1888). See III.1.2.

Theology in Dialogue

J. Augustine DiNoia

This is the fourth chapter of a book dedicated to discovering a way beyond the impasse of the 'inclusivist', 'exclusivist', 'relativist' debate about theological principles grounding interreligious dialogue. The first three chapters offer conceptual clarity about what religions are, how to speak of them in Christian theological discourse, and what doctrinal convictions are needed for such discourse. The present selection reflects upon what the resulting conversation with other religions might look like.

The nineteenth-century Japanese Buddhist scholar Enryo Inoue remarked once: 'It is neither because I favor Sakyamuni [Gautama the Buddha] nor because I am prejudiced against Jesus that I uphold Buddhism and reject Christianity. It is simply because I love truth and hate untruth.'[1] Similar statements could be culled from the writings of other scholars of Buddhist as well as non-Buddhist communities. This concern for truth exhibits itself particularly when one community seeks to define its own positions over against those of other communities. Inoue implies that his adherence to Buddhism represents, not an arbitrary allegiance, but a reflective conviction about the truth of Buddhist teachings.

At the same time, it is not unusual for a religious community to acknowledge that the truth about important matters can occur outside its own teachings. As K. Dhammananda remarked: 'The Buddha stressed that no one religious teacher can reveal all the important manifestations of the truth for mankind. Most of the world's religious leaders have revealed certain aspects of the truth according to the circumstances that prevailed at that time. The Buddha explained that he had pointed out only the most important aspects of religion and the truth.'[2] How it happens that truth can be found outside its authentic doctrines is the kind of issue addressed by a community's doctrines about other communities. Thus, without prejudice to the 'historical uniqueness' of the Buddha's role in the 'rediscovery' of the Dharma, Sangharakshita none the less insists that since 'the Dharma states with a precision and clarity . . . those universal laws in accordance with which the attainment of Enlightenment by a human being takes place, and . . . the conditions upon which it depends and the means by which it must be achieved', knowledge about it is in principle accessible to any well-disposed inquirer.[3]

Among other things, these remarks express the conviction that Buddhist teachings have a universal relevance. These teachings are addressed to the widest possible audience and offer all human beings the opportunity to seek and attain the true aim of life. A further conviction is implied. The truth of Buddhist teachings can be supported at least in part by appeal to considerations drawn from commonly shared experiences of the world and of human existence within it. If Buddhist teachings possess a universal relevance, then it follows that they must interpret or at least speak to certain commonly recognizable features of human existence. Thus, in explanation of the wide acceptance that Buddhism and Christianity have enjoyed, the Buddhist scholar and philosopher Hajime Nakamura remarked that the beliefs and practices of these communities address 'what may be described as universal problems, or questions raised and needs and aspirations expressed by men everywhere, irrespective of country, race or cultural differences; problems arising from our common experience of life itself with reference to man's condition, environment and destiny'.[4]

Many Christian communities approach current circumstances of religious interaction with a renewed esteem for other traditions and a readiness to engage in dialogue with their adherents. This seems to entail that the Christian theologian of religions should notice and take seriously the distinctive doctrines of other religious communities. When the soterio-centric principle is set aside, even if only experimentally, traditional Christian doctrines about other religions can be formulated in ways that acknowledge the varieties of aims pursued and commended by other communities. The Christian community's confidence in the availability of truth and salvation beyond its ambit can be expressed in terms of affirmations of the providential diversity of religions and of the prospective salvation of their adherents.

With this account of a theology *for* dialogue in place, we turn to a consideration of theology *in* dialogue. This topic is, of course, as broad as Christian theology itself and as wide ranging as are the doctrines of our potential dialogue partners in Buddhist, Hindu, Muslim and Judaic communities. The comments of the Buddhist scholars Inoue, Dhammananda, Sangharakshita and

Nakamura will help us to focus our discussion here on a topic of considerable significance for Christian theology in dialogue.

The remarks quoted above tell us something about how a religious community might go about securing its claim to the truth and rightness of its doctrines. In addition to resources afforded by its canon of scriptures and influential authors, a community is normally prepared to link its teachings with accepted or well warranted knowledge about the world at large. There are variations from one community to the next about the extent to which their schemes of doctrines permit such connections. But the doctrinal schemes of the world's major religious communities generally do not seem to rule them out. Indeed, highly ramified doctrinal schemes normally comprise extensive interpretations of features of human existence and possess the capacity continually to incorporate new relevant knowledge. Such connections play an important role in interreligious dialogue and similar situations when a community needs to define its doctrines over against those of other communities. The presumption that their doctrinal schemes are not epistemically isolated allows the members of one community to propose and defend their teachings in ways that are cogent and understandable, even if not persuasive, to the members of other religious communities.

Like the Buddhist and other religious communities, the Christian community approaches dialogue with well-established convictions about the truth and rightness of its doctrines and about their bearing on the full range of human life, knowledge and experience. We shall observe that, considered in this light, philosophical theology assumes a prominent role in Christian theology in dialogue.

A New Conversation

In the Christian community, the whole meaning of human life can be expressed by saying that human beings are directed to union with God or, in more explicitly scriptural imagery, to the vision of God: we shall see him as he is (1 John 3:2). But the Christian belief that the true end of life is the beatific vision or union with God is affirmed today in a climate in which knowledge and appreciation of rival claims about the meaning and aim of human life may be expected to be widespread. According to sociologist Peter Berger's analysis, today's social and cultural climate is characterized by a wholesale and seemingly irreversible 'pluralization of both institutions and plausibility structures', and thus by an immeasurable expansion of the realm of choice and decision in religious and other areas of life. Alternative views of the meaning of human life compete for attention with Christian beliefs in an enlarged market-place of ethical and religious wisdom.[5] The teaching functions of the Christian community at every level (catechetical, theological and magisterial) are today inevitably exercised in dialogue with alternative positions, not the least important of which are those associated with the teachings of other religious communities.

As we have seen, different teachings about the focus of life as a whole appear to distinguish the overall patterns of life and belief that Christian, Buddhist, Hindu, Muslim and Judaic communities foster in their members and commend to outsiders. With the increased religious interaction typical of our times has come a heightened awareness of these differences. In earlier chapters it was noted that genuine tolerance of other religious people presupposes an acknowledgement of the significance of these differences. It seems clear that the Christian community will need to take other communities' teachings into account as it engages in conversation with their members and as it develops its own doctrines about the focus of life as a whole.

The new conversation is different from another one that has preoccupied the Christian community in recent centuries. Modernity brought with it a pressing need for Christian communities to engage in dialogue with thinkers who built religious proposals into their philosophical positions. The intentions of some of these philosophers were friendly: they meant to offer support for Christian claims perceived to be under attack for one reason or another. Other philosophers were markedly unsympathetic to Christian claims. Increasingly the dialogue turned into a conversation with thinkers seeking to challenge central Christian claims about God, about revelation, about the course of history, about the reliability of the Bible, and the possibility of natural theology, about the meaningfulness of religious (that is, 'Christian') discourse, and so on.

Such thinkers might adopt a religiously sceptical or atheistic point of view, or they might propose an independent religious philosophy, partially congruent and partially contrasting with the pattern of life and doctrines proposed by particular Christian communities. Very much at issue in these discussions were 'religious' matters as these had come to be defined since the Enlightenment. It was during that period that the idea first seriously occurred to people on a large scale that one could be religious (by holding to some fundamental religious beliefs about God, human destiny and the moral order) without being an adherent of any particular religious tradition (that is, without being Christian, Jewish or Muslim). Furthermore, other thinkers seem to challenge the very scope of religious knowledge and explanation itself, which was seen to be in constant retreat before the inexorable advance of knowledge in the human and natural sciences. John Updike furnishes a graphic description of Christian theology's flight into ever-narrowing contexts of explanation: 'In the sixteenth century astronomy, in the seventeenth microbiology, in the eighteenth geology and palaeontology, in the nineteenth Darwin's biology all grotesquely extended the world-frame and sent churchmen scurrying for cover in ever smaller, shadowy nooks, little gloomy ambiguous caves in the psyche where even now neurology is cruelly harrying them, gouging them out of the multi-folded brain like wood lice from under the lumber pile'.[6]

This situation is in marked contrast to the one posed by religious interaction. Here, Christian communities confront, not merely personal religious philosophies, but massive and enduring bodies of religious wisdom and highly ramified systems of doctrines derived from sources as ancient and rich as any of their own. Furthermore, the challenges that arise from this encounter come not from religiously sceptical individuals but from religious communities advancing well-developed alternative conceptions of the ultimate aim of life and the pattern life ought to take in view of this aim.

Topics that fall under traditional natural or philosophical theology have a central, though perhaps unexpected, role to play in this new conversation. Arguments about the existence and nature of the ultimate object of worship or quest in a religious community are fundamental to the overall strategy by which its particularistic claim to universality is secured. This is true for the Christian no less than for other religious communities.

Religious References and Predications

To gain some perspective on this topic, imagine a conversation between a Muslim and a Buddhist about religious matters. After listening for a while, the Buddhist asks the Muslim to identify the term 'Allah', which has come up several times in the conversation. The Muslim replies that Allah is the one who spoke to Muhammad, as recounted in the Qu'ran. Although the Buddhist is not yet familiar with the Qu'ran and knows little about Muhammad, he begins to catch the drift. He asks whether Allah is like one of the gods of the Hindu pantheon who appear occasionally to human beings. No, replies the Muslim: Allah is God, the only one God, who rewards the just and punishes the wicked, and who can never be seen by human eyes. The Buddhist continues to be puzzled. So the Muslim invites him to observe the beauty and orderliness of the natural world. Allah is the one who made and preserves all this. The whole meaning of life is to live in submission to him ('Islam'). And so the conversation might proceed.

Suppose that during the course of the conversation the Buddhist should refer to 'Nirvana'. Since the Buddhist seems to attach such great importance to the reality designated by this term, the Muslim begins to assume that the Buddhist might be talking about God. Is Nirvana a name for God? No, Nirvana is not any kind of God. Indeed, it is not a presently existing entity at all. It is a state of being. The Muslim needs help in grasping this. So the Buddhist might now invite him to think of intense experiences he has had that have been so absorbing that he has felt transported outside of himself. Nirvana is something like this, only ineffably more so. The chief aim of life is to attain this blissful state by following the Excellent Eightfold Path.

In each of these cases, some fact or state of affairs within experience serves as a starting point for a reference to the focus of life in the Muslim and Buddhist communities respectively. The Muslim points to the observable pattern of things and attributes this to the agency of Allah. The Buddhist invokes a certain range of intense states of experience in order to identify Nirvana.

This hypothetical conversation throws light on a certain group of arguments that seem to be logically required if a religious community is to support its claims about the focus of life as a whole.[7] Referential arguments of this kind function logically to introduce a logical subject – the focus of life – into the discourse of a religious community. The style of such arguments varies widely with the range of distinctive beliefs about the focus of life among religions. What are usually called 'arguments for the existence of God' in the Christian and other theistic communities thus have formal parallels in non-theistic doctrinal schemes.

A word about the logic of references in general discourse will throw light on special problems posed for religious references. When I speak about the 'tulips in the cloister garden', an ostensive reference is enough for you to know what I am talking about: all I have to do is point to them. If I say that I have vacationed on Barbados, however, simple ostension won't do: you will need an atlas if you are unfamiliar with the island and its location. If I start speaking about protons and neutrons, ostension will fail completely: something more is needed to establish a reference for sub-atomic or theoretical particles. In order to get along in most conversations about particular subjects, of course, we rely on broad general knowledge for supplying the required references. It is rare that something utterly unheard of and unfamiliar comes up for discussion.

Religious references are more complex. In most religious communities, even those with relatively undeveloped doctrinal schemes, the focus of life and worship is normally not thought to be identical with any sense-perceptible object within ordinary experience. We saw above that talk about 'Allah' and 'Nirvana' requires starting points in experience, which orient us in the right 'direction' to see what is being referred to. But it turns out that more extended arguments will be needed to bridge the gap between ordinary experience and the focal objects and states at the centre of religious affirmations.

Let's proceed directly to the contexts defined by theistic religious affirmations as in the Christian community. Two modes of reference play a central role in referential arguments for religious doctrines whose focus is a transcendent agent. These are references that construe certain observable facts or patterns in experience as (1) regular or (2) extraordinary effects caused by the transcendent agent.

The first type of reference appeals to regular or persistent features of the natural order like perishability, or design, or finality, and so on. Arguments are framed to show that the whole natural order exhibiting such features is brought into and preserved in existence by the transcendent agent. Jewish, Muslim and Christian theologians have developed many versions of such arguments, usually in connection with some metaphysical schemes, employing broadly Platonic or Aristotelian conceptualities, or hybrids of these. The second type of reference appeals to extraordinary or unusual facts or events – whether straightforwardly miraculous or simply non-regular. Normally such events have been recounted in the sacred literature of the community or the testimony of its leaders and saints.

As a kind of shorthand, we can say that these two types of reference are distinguished by their appeal to nature on the one hand, or to history on the other. References and arguments of the first type have a broader sweep, logically speaking, than those of the second type, for two reasons. First, particular events with a religious import belong to the larger class of historical events and are thus subject to the principles of observation and explanation applicable to events generally. Secondly, the extraordinary events that function as the starting point for religious references are reported in confessional narratives and are in principle subject to non-confessional explanations.

A third type of reference should be mentioned here. It takes as its starting point certain features of the subjective states of human beings. In so far as some of these states have the character of regular or extraordinary effects caused by a transcendent agent, this mode of reference is not clearly distinct from the first two. But their designation as a third type is justified by the logical peculiarity they exhibit: references of this type are largely self-certifying. They depend for their force, not on observation and publicly shared experiences, but on testimony about private or interior experiences of God, or on necessary entailments of concepts about God, or on recognition of the pervasive law-abidingness of human beings, or on the widespread conviction of many people that there is a God, and so on.

Another group of arguments can be identified in the hypothetical conversation we have been considering. These are arguments that serve to keep the discourse moving, once a successful reference has gotten the conversation off to a good start. When the participants have some idea of the objects or states of existence to which terms like 'Allah' and 'Nirvana' refer, then the way is open for descriptions of them. Thus, the Muslims will go on to assert that Allah is holy, and the Buddhist that Nirvana is the fullness of bliss and the absence of bliss. To advance and develop these kinds of assertions, arguments in support of predications would be needed. How can these and other attributes be ascribed to entities or states that transcend sense perception? Do such predications have properly assertive or only evocative force? Why are some primary ranking predicates appropriate and others excluded? Arguments in support of a religious community's descriptions of that upon which its pattern of life is focused would be needed to address these and related questions. In the Christian community, talk about the divine attributes falls into this category of argument.

In one respect, the hypothetical conversation sketched above is misleading, in that it suggests that such arguments have mainly apologetical uses in discussions between the members of a religious community and non-members. In fact, however, the primary logical setting of both referential and predicational religious arguments is internal to the religious scheme itself. Such arguments serve to locate the central affirmations of a religious community with reference to the widest possible conceptual map. In effect, they show that a doctrinal scheme has redrawn the map of human existence in the world. Highly ramified doctrinal schemes are field-comprehensive – to switch metaphors – and, although they do not generate everything, they do normally interpret and encompass wide ranges of knowledge and experience. The doctrinal schemes of the world's major religious communities seem to be field-comprehensive in this sense.

Referential and predicational arguments function chiefly to signal and explicate this field comprehensiveness of a community's doctrines, their universal scope and relevance. Although important, their apologetical or dialogical uses are subsidiary to their internal uses. Arguments of these types serve complex purposes in understanding the whole of a doctrinal scheme, since they show how a community's doctrines connect with all sorts of human concerns, experiences and knowledge.

These two forms of arguments – referential arguments and arguments to support predications – are familiarly known in the Christian community under the tags 'natural theology' or 'philosophical theology'. But these forms of arguments are not peculiar to the Christian scheme. As the hypothetical conversation above suggests, Christian forms of these arguments seem to have analogues or parallels in other communities as well. Such arguments seem to be required by the logical structure of the discourse of religious communities: they help to secure the particularistic claims to universality that all communities appear to make for their doctrines.

It is hard to see how the new interreligious conversation could keep up its momentum if the participating religious communities were unwilling to mount any referential and predicational arguments in support of their doctrines. This is an important lesson for Christian theology in dialogue. It is also a refreshing one. After having undergone relentless critique in the course of the Christian community's conversation with modern philosophers since the Enlightenment, Christian forms of these arguments turn out to have an extended viability in Christianity's new and more challenging conversations with Buddhist, Hindu, Muslim and Judaic communities in the present day.

Philosophical Theology in Historical Perspective

Generally speaking, debate between the Christian community and its philosophical critics has centred on the validity of referential patterns of argument. There is no possibility here of charting in detail the complex history of this debate, except in so far as it bears on the prospects for continued use of these forms of arguments in the new interreligious conversation now gathering momentum.

We have seen that referential arguments normally involve appeals of three types: to the natural course of things in the world (e.g. the design of the universe), to particular events in history (e.g. miracles), or to subjective states or experiences (e.g. the human sense of ultimacy). In classical Christian theology, references of all three types, whether well developed or implicit, were interwoven and mutually reinforcing. Arguments of the first type played an increasingly prominent role in the medieval period, with the growth of interest in and knowledge about the physical world. But with the coming of modernity, arguments of the first type were subjected to a devastating critique from which they have never fully recovered. In the wake of this critique, arguments of the second and third types – appealing to history and the self – have gradually taken over the field.

This development has posed considerable difficulties for Christian theology as it strives to secure the universal scope and relevance of the Christian confession. For it has long been recognized that logical rigour and objectivity decrease as one moves from the first to the third type of referential argument. While appeals to subjective experiences and states possess a great psychological interest and intensity, they are largely self-certifying. Appeals to history rest on the reliability of confessional documents or on speculative philosophies of history. Without the reinforcement of arguments of the first type, referential arguments warranted exclusively by historical or subjective data are peculiarly vulnerable logically speaking. A few remarks about the history of modern theology will serve to confirm this judgement.

Two developments in particular had decisive consequences for the internal or doctrinal uses of arguments of the first type. In the first place, the connection of these arguments with the doctrinal schemes of Christian and other theistic communities was severed. This separation developed on two fronts. First, with the Enlightenment such arguments were pried from their doctrinal settings in order to specify the kernel of natural religion within (and eventually opposed to) revealed or positive religion. In effect such arguments were turned against the doctrinal schemes they were developed to support. Secondly, their apologetic virtualities were increasingly exploited: they served to demonstrate to sceptical outsiders the 'reasonableness' of Christianity. As a result, such arguments came to be viewed as establishing part of the subject matter of distinct fields of inquiry – 'natural theology' or 'philosophical theology' – largely independent of the doctrinal contexts of particular theistic traditions.

A second development had a more serious and wide-ranging impact on the viability of the first type of reference. This came with Immanuel Kant's critique of what he took to be all versions of such arguments. The widespread acceptance of this critique set the stage for the historical and subjective turns executed in much nineteenth-century Protestant and twentieth-century Catholic theology.

Kant (1724–1804) contended that such arguments fail to deliver the results they promise. They suppose the possibility of moving from metaphysical assertions about the structures of things in themselves conceived as a single effect to God as the First Cause. In fact, such cosmological and teleological arguments (as Kant tagged them) are covertly versions of the ontological argument. Tied to the rationalist conception of metaphysics in which he was reared, Kant contended that such arguments traffic in concepts (causality, contingency, design, being, world, God) that derive not from experience but from the mental apparatus used to structure incoming perceptions. Such arguments achieve no more than the ontological argument: they unpack the content of the concept of God rather than showing that he exists.[8]

Kant's combined critique of metaphysics and classical natural theology was understood by many philosophers and theologians to have permanently undermined the plausibility of arguments of the first type. In so far as theologians accepted this critique as definitive, they turned to arguments of the second and third types to support Christian affirmation. G. W. F. Hegel (1775–1834) in effect transformed the whole of the philosophy of history into an all-encompassing dialectical argument of the second type. Friedrich Schleiermacher (1768–1834) welcomed the Kantian critique of metaphysics and natural theology as a liberation of theology from metaphysical categories. He substituted appeal to the God-relation given in the very structure of the self for appeal to nature or history. Subsequently, even when they did not adopt the details of Hegel's or Schleiermacher's programmes, theologians were deeply influenced by the turns to history and the self that these programmes commended. This influence was felt differently in Reformation, Orthodox and Roman Catholic communities.

In large measure, the subsequent history of theology in Reformation communities has seen the erosion of theological positions that took these turns. Without the massive reinforcement provided by the Hegelian system, the appeal to history has proved to be extraordinarily vulnerable as a support for theological affirmation in the face of the combined challenge of Feuerbach, Marx, Freud, Darwin and the historical–critical study of the Bible. Despite its continued appeal, the turn to the structures of self-consciousness is widely regarded as having received a deathblow from Ludwig Feuerbach (1804–75) and (somewhat derivatively) Karl Marx (1818–83) and Sigmund Freud (1856–1939). Feuerbach's critique of Christian affirmation seems an inevitable response to the retreat of theologians from the field of natural theology classically conceived as an enterprise involving appeal to some accounts of a non-subjective order. A 'natural theology' rooted exclusively in some account of the transcendent dynamism or structure of human subjectivity relies on self-certifying propositions about internal experiences. Feuerbach can be construed as having fixed on this weakness in contending that theological concepts of God objectify human traits, aspirations, ideals and perfections and project them onto a transcendent realm. The profoundly influential polemic against natural theology associated with the theology of Karl Barth (1886–1968) may be construed as an acknowledgement of the force of Feuerbach's critique of the subjective turn. Barth secures the divine identity, as essentially independent of the human reality, by basing it radically in the divine act of revelation and the narrative it engenders. Theology either begins with this revelation and its overarching narrative or falls prey to human hypostatization masquerading as God.

The move toward postmodern positions among American Protestant theologians received a powerful stimulus from Barth's reading of the history of nineteenth-century theology. Acceptance of the Kantian critique of referential arguments of the first type and acknowledgement of the failure of arguments of the second and third types has done much to shape theology in contemporary Reformation communities. Theologians who have been influenced by Barth are forging an ingenious combination of resolutely anti-Cartesian Anglo-American analytical philosophy and Continental hermeneutics, to fill the role of discredited referential arguments. Postliberal theologians can be distinguished from revisionists not with respect to background assumptions about these matters (which they largely share) but with respect to the role in theological affirmation they accord to specifically Christian language and narrative.

The response to modernity has been somewhat delayed in the theology of the Roman Catholic and Orthodox communities. This is especially clear in Roman Catholic theology, in which the more markedly defensive reaction of the nineteenth century gradually gave way to the welcoming response of the forty or so years spanning the pre- and post-conciliar periods in this century. The short-lived (at least among Catholic theologians) neo-scholastic revival is perceived by many to have provided only a temporary bulwark against the tides of modernity pressing against it. As might be expected, Catholic strategies for dealing with modernity's challenge to classical natural theology have matched earlier Protestant moves. The twentieth-century transcendental turn in Catholic theology, associated especially with the work of Karl Rahner, roughly parallels the nineteenth-century turn to the subject in Protestant theology. The prevailing Rahnerian (if not Rahner's) theology in the Catholic community exhibits remarkable formal and material similarities to modern Protestant theological positions. But transcendental styles are giving way to aesthetic, critical and hermeneutical styles as Catholic theology yields to the pressures of anti-Cartesian developments in Protestant theology and in contemporary philosophy.

The ongoing conversation between Christian theology and modern Western philosophy has not favoured referential arguments of any of the traditional types. In effect, nature, history and the self have yielded to language and narrative as the context for theological affirmation. In the perspective of the history of theology in the Christian community and of the new conversation with the other religious communities, this context seems a sharply narrowed one.

The encounter with other religious communities invites Christian theology to develop its agenda with a view to the internal requirements of Christian discourse as a form of discourse exhibiting certain structural features – among them a fairly straightforward claim to the existential force (in the logical sense) and truth of primary doctrines that convey beliefs. Certain patterns of argument arise in response to this logical requirement for forms of reasoning that will secure the community's particularistic claim to universality for its doctrines. Philosophical theology in the Christian and other theistic traditions, and its cognates in non-theistic religions, comprise important sets of arguments developed to support claims of this sort. It is not clear that a religious community could maintain such a claim if it refrained from developing any arguments for it. It has been an unfortunate outcome of the conversation with sceptical modern philosophers that Christian confidence in the possibility and importance of such arguments has been gradually undermined.

One of the more challenging tasks for Christian theology in dialogue is to recover the broadest possible context in which to secure the fundamental claims of the Christian community. It can be expected that the claims of other communities will be advanced in the same logical space. As we have seen, claims to a universal relevance are typical of the doctrinal schemes of the world's major religious communities. Respect for other communities and recognition of the distinctiveness of their doctrines provide some of the impetus for developments of new forms of referential and predicational arguments for primary Christian doctrines.

Traditional theology furnishes perhaps unexpected resources for postmodern Christian theology as it seeks to develop arguments of this sort. The work of Thomas Aquinas can be of some help here. For one thing, Aquinas is innocent of the key moves that have been the subject of such vigorous attack in postmodern philosophy and theology: the quest for a unitary method for all knowledge and inquiry ('foundationalism'), the conflation of epistemology with metaphysics, and the separation of consciousness from bodiliness. Further-more, Aquinas's theology furnishes a rich resource for exhibiting the logic of referential and predicational patterns of argument, as they function both in the Christian scheme itself and in interreligious dialogue.

Naturally it is neither possible nor desirable to repristinate Aquinas as if the intervening centuries had evaporated. As Bernard Williams recently remarked in another context: 'There is certainly more to be said for [traditional understandings of ethics] than much progressive thought has allowed; indeed there is more to be said for them than there is for much progressive thought. But even if one grants value to traditional knowledge, to try to suppress reflection in that interest can only lead to disaster, rather as someone who finds that having children has disrupted her life cannot regain her earlier state by killing them.'[9] Christian philosophical theology has been permanently trans-formed by the past two centuries of debate. None the less, as will become clear, Aquinas's treatment of these issues retains much of its cogency when considered in the light of the new interreligious conversation.

In addition to aiding our understanding of the logic of references and predications, study of Aquinas helps to expose certain deficiencies in some current accounts of these patterns of argument as they bear on interreligious conversations. We shall observe, to put it briefly, that in their current influential versions, inclusivists say too much and pluralists say too little: inclusivists tend to exaggerate the probative force of Christian references, while pluralists seem to attenuate the potential range of religious predications. In these ways, prominent pluralist and inclusivist positions tend to minimize the significance of religious differences. Christian theology in dialogue needs an account of Christian references and predications that reflects the seriousness of these differences and hence the import of the interreligious conversation whose challenge it embraces.

Referring to the Triune God

Monastic communities from the Buddhist and Christian traditions have been in the forefront of the newly blossoming conversation among the world's major religions. Recently, a delegation of Buddhist bhikkhus and bhikkhunis (monks and nuns) visited several Christian monasteries across the United States. Imagine what such a visit would be like, say in a monastic community of contemplative Dominican nuns.

As they followed the daily monastic routine, the Buddhist visitors would find many practices and attitudes familiar to them from their own communities. Despite the striking contrast of their saffron robes with the black and white of the Dominicans, they would see in the common garb of the nuns the same singleness of religious purpose and commitment to simplicity of life that they have learned from the Buddha. The silence, the discipline, the early rising, the unpretentious fare, the manual labour, the chanting of prayer, the care and attention bestowed on the small details of life, indeed the sheer regularity of the daily schedule – all would make the Buddhist travellers feel at home.

A sufficiently leisurely visit would surely provide opportunities for conversation about their respective forms of life. Perhaps such conversation between the Buddhist visitors and their Dominican hosts would disclose similarities in the very rationale for their characteristic practices and comportment. The nuns would tell some of their favourite stories, particularly the one about how St Dominic founded a community of nuns before ever getting around to organizing the friars. In addition, given the large measure of daily public prayer and liturgy in the Dominican monastic schedule, conversation would undoubtedly turn to the style and content of these activities.

At this point, the Dominican hosts would surely have to mention God. For they would not get too far along in discussing their worship without mentioning the one who is invoked continually in its psalms, antiphons, hymns and prayers. Indeed, they might report to their Buddhist visitors, God is at the very centre of the Dominican contemplative life. From their worship and love of God radiates the inner meaning of all the activities of their daily life. They are supposed to live, as the Dominican rule expresses it, 'free for God alone'. The God whom we love, they would say, has loved us first. He is the God of Abraham, Isaac and Jacob, the God who saved us in Christ and who abides with us in his Spirit. Moreover, he is the God who inspired and sustained St Dominic, the selfsame God to whom Dominican nuns like Catherine de Ricci, Margaret of Hungary and countless others have been praying throughout the ages, the God who is present to us now even as we speak. And so the conversation would proceed.

A conversation about God among a group of Buddhist and Dominican monastic people would presumably make for some fairly stimulating talk indeed. But we must take our leave of it for the time being. For our purposes, the point of imagining this hypothetical encounter is that it helps us to see that Christian references to God in such a setting would take, at least initially, a markedly scheme-specific form. To express this point somewhat technically, we could say that the triune God would appear as the principal character in an overarching narrative, as it were, which stretches over the whole length and breadth of his engagement with humankind, and extends to embrace present and future experience and events. References to him normally would take the form of narrations of his activities as reported in the scriptures, celebrated in the round of the liturgical hours, days and seasons, recounted in the lives of holy people, and so on.

Implicit in these scheme- or narrative-specific references is a broader one.

The triune God who is worshipped in the Christian community is none other than the cause of the world. Some expressions of this conviction would eventually emerge in some form during the course of the hypothetical conversation between Buddhists and Christians described above. To the question, 'Who is it that you worship in your prayer?' the Christian would first respond, the God of Abraham, Isaac and Jacob, the God made known to us in Christ. To the further question, 'But who is he?' an apt Christian response would be, the God whom we worship is the cause of the world. Still, the conviction itself does not depend for its logical force on occasions of interreligious (or apologetic) conversations when it might come to be expressed explicitly. Christian confession and worship of God imply the belief that the scope of divine activity and engagement is as wide as the universe itself, and wider. Indeed, the God who is worshipped is, absolutely speaking, unlimited in his range of interest and power.

These considerations help to illumine the theological role of arguments for the existence of God. Their presence in early pages of Aquinas's *Summa theologiae* does not signal a methodological doubt such that Christian theology cannot go about its business until it has 'proven' the existence of its subject.[10] This possibility is ruled out from the start by Aquinas's prior description of the nature of theological inquiry. To assert that theology gets its subject matter from revelation implies that faith in God constitutes one of the principles of the inquiry. The triune God is already 'in place', so to speak, in his full, scheme-specific characterization. The one confessed as Father, Son and Holy Spirit is the cause of the world. Referential patterns of argument in theology serve not so much to establish God's existence as to secure the particularistic claim to universality that the Christian community makes for its doctrines.

Arguments for the existence of God function to secure this universal claim. Beginning with observable or generalized features of the world like causality, finality and design, such arguments affirm the divine agency as the source of such features and of the world order as a whole. Whatever their logical merits or probative force, their position at the beginning of the theological inquiry (according to Aquinas's procedure) signals the logical space that Christian claims are understood to occupy. The arguments for the existence of God in the second question of Aquinas's *Summa theologiae* (the celebrated 'Five Ways') thus function to locate Christian worship, nurture, practice and belief on the widest possible conceptual map. The triune God who is adored, proclaimed and confessed in the Christian community has not only a local, narrative or contextual reference within the usage of a particular cultural and linguistic community; even more, he is none other than the cause of the world.

Since such arguments are developed in connection with scientific and metaphysical claims, it has sometimes been objected that they mark the intrusion of alien conceptual categories and claims into a properly theological (and hence scripturally based) inquiry. But, according to the construal of Aquinas being suggested here, such a complaint misses the mark. These arguments do not displace but rather presuppose the reading of scripture as a 'canonically and narrationally unified and internally glossed ... whole centred on Jesus Christ, and telling the story of the dealings of the triune God with his people and his world in ways that are typologically ... applicable to the present'.[11] In effect, Aquinas can be construed as addressing the question (here and in subsequent discussions of the divine nature and agency, of angelic and human natures, and, finally and decisively, of Jesus Christ as divine–human agent): what must be true of the main characters of the Christian narrative for it to have the features Christians claim for it, truth and 'followability'? Natural science, metaphysics, psychology and other 'secular' inquiries contribute as needed or well suited to filling out these complex characterizations. A literary analogy may help at this juncture. In a critical study of Melville's *Moby Dick*, for example, the complex narrative need not be continually retold in the course of literary analysis of the motivations and structure of the main characters. In somewhat the same way, in the *Summa theologiae* Aquinas presumes his readership's detailed familiarity with the Christian narrative in order to show or, more correctly, to remove obstacles to seeing that its central claims are true and its chief injunctions are followable.

The initial referential arguments are harnessed to this larger theological purpose. They serve primarily internal theological purposes in sustaining the broadest possible context for Christian affirmation, in connection not only with the doctrine of God but also with the doctrines of grace, Christology, sacraments and so on throughout the Christian scheme. They serve subsequently as the warrant or legitimation (logically speaking) for locating such affirmations, case by case, with reference to a variety of objective states of affairs.

Precisely because of their logical function in securing the universal scope of Christian claims, such arguments naturally come to serve purposes beyond the internal ones. Thus, because they press the truth and rightness of Christian claims by appealing to commonly shared experiences and knowledge, they may have a role in persuading outsiders to adopt the Christian pattern of life. But of more immediate concern here is the function of such arguments in the setting of interreligious conversations, where the claims of other communities are advanced in the same logical space.

Thus, for example, some version of arguments for the existence of God would be needed in conversations between Buddhists and Christians. Segments of the Buddhist community seem to be non-theistic in their doctrines, and their canonical and commentatorial literatures possess highly subtle explanations for the prevalence of the theistic beliefs in other religious traditions. Presumably, in conversation with members of such Buddhist communities, Christians would need to invoke patterns of referential argument analogous to those sketched by

Aquinas in the Five Ways. A readiness to advance such arguments would be a way of taking Buddhist objections to theistic beliefs seriously. The notion of causation that is intrinsic to these arguments would presumably offer wide scope for debate. Theories of causation play a crucial role in the Buddhist account of the conditions of human existence that need to be transcended if the round of rebirths is to be escaped and Nirvana attained. In addition, given the markedly empirical orientation of Buddhist patterns of reflection and argument, there is considerable scope here for empirically based discussions such as those merely adumbrated in the Five Ways and similar arguments. Current scientific knowledge of the origins and structure of the universe would presumably be admitted as relevant by both Christian and Buddhist participants in such a conversation. Hence, the Five Ways could not be invoked without appropriate revisions reflecting the considerable advances in scientific knowledge of the relevant issues since Aquinas's time.

It is clear, then, that referential patterns of argument of the first type, appealing to objective states of affairs in the world, would have an important place in interreligious conversations. This kind of argument presupposes a field broad enough to sustain such conversations. The issues would be joined in a common logical field, so to speak, where rival particularistic claims to universality are taken seriously and debated. The participants' readiness to advance such arguments would make it possible for a true meeting of minds, though not necessarily agreement, to occur. Naturally, other starting points for references would have their place in such conversations. But it seems clear that, in order to rise to the occasion (logically speaking), appeals to history, narratives, texts, personal experiences and the like would need to be combined with referential arguments having features of the natural order of things as their starting point.

We need to consider at this juncture an influential inclusivist version of a referential argument that appeals, not to regular features of the world, but to the structure of human knowledge of the world. In his philosophical theology, Karl Rahner developed a referential argument in connection with his analysis of the conditions for the possibility of human knowledge of God's existence and, in addition, for the possibility of human recognition of a divine revelation. In its original setting the argument was not developed for service in theology of religions. But given the theory of religion it implied, the argument had important ramifications for Rahner's broadly inclusivist construal of traditional Christian doctrines about other religions.[12]

According to this argument, the capacities to exercise concepts and beliefs and to desire actual or possible existents presuppose the possession and exercise of the concept of being. But the concept of being, because it always eludes full conceptualization, points beyond itself to Absolute Being. Further, since Absolute Being is Absolute Mystery – or that which unconditionally engages human beings – and Absolute Mystery is identified in the primary doctrines of the Christian community as the triune God, then it follows that every exercise of intellectual and affective capacities necessarily engages human beings with the triune God. Thus, the Christian reference to God is secured by means of a transcendental argument showing that God is none other than that entity beyond all entities, who unconditionally engages human beings in all knowing and willing.

In Rahner's theology of religions, the Christian community's particularistic claim to universality and an ascription of a salvific value to other religions are supported by a further argument that develops certain consequences of the transcendental argument sketched above. It follows from the main argument that all religious experience, expression and conduct have for their object the Absolute Mystery who is identified in Christian doctrines with the triune God. This complex argument combines premises from the philosophy of mind, metaphysics and the philosophy of religion in order to extend the Christian doctrine of uncreated grace (construed in terms of Rahner's concept of divine self-communication) to an account of the presence and quasi-sacramental operations of grace in non-Christian religions. According to this account the doctrines and patterns of life of other religions – as externalizations of a supernaturally elevated experience of a universally accessible divine self-communication in grace – can be viewed as affording their adherents a real contact with the triune God on whom the Christian pattern of life is centred. Hence it is possible to develop in a single overall argument both an assertion of the universal relevance of Christian doctrines and an ascription of salvific value to their doctrines, institutions and other forms of religious expression.

The basic valuation of a religious community's scheme of doctrines ascribes to the object (e.g. the triune God) or state of being (e.g. Nirvana) on which its pattern of life is centred some unrestricted primary-ranking predicates (e.g. most holy, perfect in being, supreme goal of life). Thus the basic valuation of the Christian scheme can be conveyed in a statement like this: the blessed trinity is most holy. The basic valuation of Buddhism can be expressed in this way among others: Nirvana is the supreme goal of life.

A general theory of religion would, among other things, strive to give an account of basic valuations in religious communities by developing some broadly applicable value for the predicate terms in doctrines that propose basic valuations. Since there is a great variety of possible predicates in the characteristic discourse of particular religious communities and in the religious domain generally, a general theory of religion would be expected to propose some value for as many such predicates as could be adduced.

Basic valuations are different from general theories in a notable way. Religious doctrines that convey basic valuations always assign values both to the subjects and to the predicates in expressions of the form 'm is P', where *m* stands for that existent or state of being on which a religious community's pattern of life is centred and *P* stands for predicates ascribed to *m*. But general theories of religion propose values only for predicates. A theory of religion would fail to be a general theory if it assigned some value to *m* in such expressions. It would be more like a religious doctrine that conveyed a basic valuation to which alternative valuations could be proposed, rather than like a general theory that sought to explain something of the diversity of basic religious valuations among existing religious communities.

Rahner's argument, as outlined above, appeals in part to what appears to be a general theory of religion. If we rephrase the term 'Absolute Mystery' as it is used in Rahner's theology of religions, we will have an expression that could serve as a value for *P* in a general theory of religion. Thus, let us say that 'Absolute Mystery' is equivalent to 'that which ought unconditionally to engage human beings'.

Employing this predicate value in a general theory of religion, we could say that it would be a sign that some utterance in the discourse of a particular religious community expressed its basic valuation if the phrase 'that which ought unconditionally to engage human beings' could plausibly be substituted for predicate terms like 'holy' or 'perfect in being', and so on, which appeared in this utterance. Thus, in terms of such a general theory of religion, it would be possible to restate the basic valuations of the Christian and Buddhist communities in the following ways: the triune God is that which ought unconditionally to engage human beings; Nirvana is that which ought unconditionally to engage human beings. Thus, a general theory of religion would help persons engaged in religious inquiries or arguments to formulate common terms by means of which basic religious valuations could be compared and contrasted, or simply studied as samples of the rich variety of discourse in the religious domain.

But we can notice a difficulty in the way the predicate value 'that which ought unconditionally to engage human beings' is employed in the argument laid out above. Although this predicate value appears to be used as the basis for a general theory of religion, the argument itself seems not to envisage (logically speaking) the application of this predicate value to the referents of any basic valuations other than the Christian one. Although it would be possible to employ this predicate value in a general theory of religion (in saying: predicates in basic religious valuations assert of some referent that it is the object or state of being that ought unconditionally to engage human beings), in the argument above it would be used (as 'Absolute Mystery' is in fact used) to define the referent of the Christian basic valuation. According to this argument the existent with which all human beings are unconditionally engaged in all religious communities is the triune God. There are in effect no self-consistent alternative basic religious valuations; there are only more or less inadequate versions of the single basic version which is given fullest expression in the Christian scheme and pattern of life.

We are now in a better position to grasp the difficulty posed by this inclusivist version of a referential argument in the setting of interreligious conversations: by importing a basic religious valuation into an apparently general theory of religion (developed in the context of philosophy of religion), the argument presupposes what it must in fact show. It sets out to show that the Christian community expresses more adequately what is partially embodied in other religions. But instead of showing this it presupposes it. Although, in terms of a general theory derived from the philosophical premises of this argument, the basic valuation of Buddhism could be construed as asserting 'Nirvana is that with which human beings ought unconditionally to be engaged', the argument itself assumes that 'Nirvana' (and related terms in other communities) either stands for or deflects attention from that which ought unconditionally to engage human beings, that is, the triune God. This assumption is made not on the basis of comparison and contrast between Christian doctrines and Buddhist doctrines but *a priori* and with reference to all possible basic religious valuations at the centre of other schemes of doctrines. In effect, the Christian community proposes the only self-consistent basic religious valuation.

The difficulty here is not simply that religious doctrines always elude full explication (something that would be true of Christian as well as of non-Christian doctrines, as we shall observe in the next section). Nor is a judgement being asserted according to which many non-Christian religious doctrines are appraised as erroneous in what they teach or misguided in what they value or recommend. One could judge this to be the case and still take those doctrines as self-consistent, serious alternatives of which their adherents could give a full account (relatively speaking). No difficulties are posed by these points. Nor is there a difficulty in asserting that Christian doctrines express better what other religious doctrines express only partially. If judgements of this sort proceed case by case, there is nothing inappropriate about dialectical arguments that compare and contrast particular religions with Christianity in order to show the latter's superiority to them in the areas in question.

To put the matter briefly, the difficulty posed by the inclusivist argument we have been considering is that it tries to prove too much. In effect, the theory of religion on which it relies suggests that other religious communities could never give an adequate and self-consistent account of their doctrines. In order to be complete (logically speaking), such an account would always have to include an appeal to the basic valuation of the Christian community. The distinctive basic valuations of non-Christian communities, especially non-theistic ones, could not be consistently acknowledged and debated. In effect, prior to dialogue, the universal claims of Buddhist, Hindu, Muslim and Judaic communities would be absorbed into the embrace of Christian doctrines.

Interreligious conversations would in effect serve the purpose of disclosing Christian-like virtualities in the doctrines of these other communities rather than of entertaining such doctrines as self-consistent alternative teachings about that upon which human life should be focused.

Pluralist patterns of referential argument have the more curious result of introducing a new basic religious valuation into the conversation alongside those advanced by Christian, Judaic, Muslim, Buddhist and Hindu communities. While inclusivists argue that a Christianly construed 'Absolute Mystery' is that upon which all religious patterns of life are focused, some pluralists substitute more religiously indeterminate concepts like 'Reality' or 'Ultimacy' to interpret otherwise distinctive religious objects. Some pluralists argue that the various foci of worship and quest in the major, soteriologically oriented religious communities represent a focus that transcends them all. In effect, this 'interpretation' of what religious communities are about constitutes, logically speaking, an independent religious proposal.

Consider the following remarks of Stanley Samartha. He is concerned to avoid exclusivism. In Samartha's view, 'Mystery provides the ontological basis for tolerance, which would otherwise run the risk of becoming uncritical friendliness'. What Professor Samartha means by 'Mystery' is clear when he states that it is the 'transcendent Center that remains always beyond and greater than apprehensions of it or even the sum total of those apprehensions'. So much is this the case that 'Mystery lies beyond the theistic–non-theistic debate'. For Professor Samartha, the concept provides the basis for understanding the focal objects of religious worship and quest in religious communities. Thus, in Hinduism and Christianity, respectively, 'the terms "Brahman" and "God" are culture-conditioned. One could as well use the term Mystery, which may be more acceptable'. Distinctive Hindu and Christian doctrines about Brahman and God can be understood as diverse 'responses to the same Mystery in two cultural settings'. This is true, according to Professor Samartha, of 'the two statements . . . that "Brahman is *sat-cit-ananda* [truth–consciousness–bliss]" and "God is triune, Father, Son, and Holy Spirit"'. At best, the two formulations can only be symbolic, pointing to the Mystery, affirming the meaning disclosed, but retaining residual depth.[13]

The presumption here is that the list of doctrinally specific religious terms pointing to Mystery could be extended beyond Brahman and the triune God to include the Muslim's Allah, the Jew's Lord God, and the Buddhist's Nirvana. It is a common feature of theological proposals in the pluralist vein to construe the focal objects of communities in this fashion. Terms like 'Mystery', 'Reality' or 'Ultimacy' appear to function as logical equivalents in what seems to be a general theory of religions underlying the pluralist account of distinctive basic valuations. But we can notice in Professor Samartha's remarks that the term 'Mystery' functions chiefly not as an equivalent for a predicate value like 'that which ought unconditionally to engage human beings' but as a substitute for terms in the place of *m* in basic religious valuations. In effect, on the basis of Professor Samartha's and similar accounts, one could say that 'Mystery' or 'Reality' is that which ought unconditionally to engage human beings. 'Mystery' is that to which basic religious valuations refer when they speak of the focal objects of worship and quest upon which life ought to be centred. Beyond those existents or states lies something that finally eludes reference. Terms like 'Mystery', or 'Reality', favoured by pluralist theologians of religions, function as the actual underlying subject of the various unrestricted primacy-ranking predications assigned by religious communities to God, Brahman, Nirvana and so on.

In terms of the foregoing analysis, pluralist theology of religions thus seems in effect to import a basic religious valuation under the guise of a general theory of religion. In a general theory, the basic valuation of the Buddhist scheme could be construed as asserting that Nirvana is that with which human beings ought unconditionally to be engaged. But, by implying that there is something beyond Nirvana that engages human beings unconditionally, pluralist theology of religions advances a broadly theistic account of the Buddhist doctrine of Nirvana. This account posits the existence of some entity, 'Mystery', with which some engagement, even the vaguest experience, is possible. Yet, according to the logic of Buddhist doctrines, Nirvana refers not to a presently existing object – no matter how impersonally or non-theistically conceived – but to a state of being yet to be realized. The concept of 'Mystery' seems to retain inexpungibly presential or existential features that run counter to Buddhist descriptions of Nirvana. By suggesting that 'Mystery' lies beyond or behind Nirvana, God, Brahman and the like, pluralist theology of religions unwittingly gets itself into the position of seeming to advance the only self-consistent basic religious valuation.

This presumably unintended outcome arises because pluralist theology of religions introduces a new basic religious valuation into the conversation alongside those advanced by Christian, Judaic, Muslim, Buddhist and Hindu communities. Pluralists substitute religiously indeterminate concepts like 'Reality' or 'Mystery' for otherwise distinctively conceived religious objects (whether they be presently existing entities or yet to be realized states). Pluralists argue that the various foci of worship and quest in the major, soteriologically oriented religious communities represent a focus that finally transcends them all. In effect, this 'interpretation' of what religious communities are about constitutes, logically speaking, an independent religious proposal.

Taken as a reading of the particular referential arguments advanced by existing religious communities, the pluralist account construes religious differences about the nature of the objects of worship and quest as ultimately resolvable into a higher synthesis that transcends the reach of the doctrines of all existing religious communities. On this view, interreligious conversations would chiefly occasion, not debate about serious religious alternatives, but disclosure of the cognate soteriological structures of the participating religious communities.

In fact, pluralist accounts of these issues are in part warranted by theories about the nature of religious predications that significantly underrate their assertive force. Let us turn now to a consideration of the logic of arguments in support of predications.

Expressing the Inexpressible

The triune God whom we worship, Christians say, is holy, good, eternal, all-powerful, merciful, loving and so on. Indeed, all perfections in their highest degree can be ascribed to him. Such ascriptions are warranted by arguments that combine complex appeals to the scriptures, to liturgical and doctrinal sources, to common Christian usage in prayer, teaching and nurture with philosophically framed appeals to objective states of affairs in the world. Once a reference to the triune God as cause of the world has launched Christian discourse – in theological exposition, in interreligious conversations, or in other settings – then there is room for arguments that support the range of things that Christians believe to be true about him. Patterns of argument that support such predications can be understood to address the question, what kind of life does the cause of the world enjoy?

Aquinas neatly expresses the difficulty such arguments pose for Christian theologians when he frankly states at the start of his own discussion of these matters that 'we cannot know what God is, but rather what he is not'.[14] It follows that the burden of arguments warranting Christian ascriptions of various primacy-ranking predicates to the triune God – the so-called divine attributes – consists largely in excluding imperfections from him. In addition, it must be shown that such predications, despite their limitations, do indeed advance truth claims about the triune God.

Both of these functions of such arguments are relevant to their serviceability in interreligious conversations. Rival and possibly conflicting claims about the reality that ultimately engages human beings are central to the exchange for which such conversations afford the opportunity. Such conversations would lack intellectual seriousness and religious urgency if the predications expressed by the doctrines of participating communities were thought not to bear directly on the nature of this reality. Granted the fundamental ineffability of this reality, major religious communities have concurred in holding that their respective doctrines express the truth about this reality and about humankind's relation to it. Indeed, disagreements among these communities about what this truth is and what its implications are for the shape of human life drew their point from this basic conviction about the force of their doctrines.

In the Christian community, an influential defence of this conviction has been developed by Aquinas in connection with a theory of the analogical character of religious doctrines that express propositions. This theory serves to support predicational patterns of argument in Christian theology. In combination with the referential patterns of argument examined earlier, such arguments have an important role to play in interreligious conversations. Study of Aquinas's account of these arguments helps us to see what is at stake for Christian theology as it embraces such conversations.

Fundamental to Aquinas's account of the logic of predicational patterns of argument is his construal of the divine simplicity in terms of the notion of sheer existence.[15] Enjoying the life of the cause of the world entails being sheerly existent (a concept expressed by Aquinas in the phrase, *ipsum esse per se subsistens*), as opposed to everything else that, as caused, enjoys a life that is only derivatively existent. Only that which is sheerly existent can be the cause of what is derivatively existent. Discussion of the divine simplicity provides Aquinas with the opportunity to make this point because, in ruling out composition in God, the attribute of simplicity rules out any potentiality in him, including the most basic potentiality to the actuality of existence. In contrast with all derivatively existent entities – that is, things that receive, and are therefore in potentiality to, existence – only the triune God is simply and fully actual. Derivatively existent things are not simple: they are composed, most basically by the actuality of existence and the potentiality for existence. If the triune God were composed in this way, then something else would be cause of the world or source of the existence of all derivatively existent entities.

It is because the triune God is sheerly existent in the sense stipulated that our predications fail to encompass him. The difficulty we face in our discourse about God emerges clearly when we notice the grammatical structure of all our predications. They are precisely that, ascriptions of predicates to subjects. The very grammar of our talk about things reflects their 'composed' nature as derivatively existent entities. Hence, as Aquinas notes, the mode of signification matches the nature of what is signified. The ascription of various predicates ('smart', 'a New Yorker', 'skilled at tennis' and so on) to a particular subject ('Jack') reflects the fact that these and many other traits and dispositions come together to constitute this subject. Our predications about God possess the same grammatical structure as our predications about Jack: we say that God is holy, merciful, sheerly existent and so on. We have no other linguistic forms at our disposal but these. Yet, in our use of such forms of utterance to speak about God, the mode of signification fails completely to match the nature of what is signified. God just isn't composed in the way that our talk about him suggests. Being holy, being merciful, being sheerly existent and so on – these are nothing else than being God. Our talk about God draws distinctions where in him no distinctions exist. God is holy, merciful, sheerly existent and so on, in a way that utterly surpasses our capacities to understand or describe. These capacities are fit for talk about the only things of which we can have direct experience, viz. what is derivatively existent.

Christian theology needs some account of our predications about the triune God to show that, despite their serious limitations, they none the less entail claims to truth. When Christians assert that God is holy, or merciful, or sheerly existent, and acknowledge that they do not know what it is like for God to be these things, they still mean to assert that these predications are true of him. On the face of things, many of the utterances Christians employ in talking about God, in praying to him, in invoking his power, in teaching about him, and in other settings imply an affirmative propositional force.

For this reason, some semantic characterizations of the force of such predications do not adequately account for what Christians seem to mean by them. Aquinas proposes his own theory of analogy as an alternative to three such characterizations.[16] The first suggests that all such predications can be reformulated as paradoxical or apophatic utterances that deny limitations to God (thus: 'God is good' would be equivalent to 'God is not evil'). Another semantic theory of religious predications reconstrues them as assertions about the divine causal activity as experienced by us. What appear on the surface as ascriptions of attributes to the triune God are in fact construable as descriptions of our experience of him, or of our relation to him (thus: 'God is good' is equivalent to 'God is the cause of goodness'). Neither of these theories denies the propositional force of Christian doctrines that express predications. Rather, according to the first view, the propositional force is always negative, while according to the second, it is always relative to human states. There is a third view that seems to exclude the propositional force of predications about the triune God. According to this view, such predications must be construed as metaphorical, as evocations (non-discursive symbols) that afford, occasion or express certain experiences of the transcendent realm without being directly descriptive of it (thus 'God is good' is symbolic).

These accounts of the force of religious doctrines are correct as far as they go: the nature of the triune God transcends the reach of our terms and concepts in their ordinary uses and meanings. But these accounts are partial in that they require an implausible reconstrual of all the straightforwardly affirmative predications that occur throughout the range of Christian usage. Some non-reductive account of such predications is needed, and Aquinas advances the theory of analogy as such an account. There is a conviction that many ordinary concepts are already employed in analogous senses and that, given the proper qualifications, they can be employed in religious and theological discourse.

The theory of analogy thus provides the basis for predicational patterns of argument that both acknowledge their peculiar logical form and allow for their propositional force. The theory of analogy functions as a theory of predication, framed to account for Christian discourse in use, and providing a straightforward reading of utterances that have the form of affirmative predications. Aquinas supports the theory by appealing to philosophical and theological premises. The use of well-developed concepts of being, causality and participation (the so-called '*analogia entis*') links Christian predications about the triune God with objective states of affairs and thus reinforces the universal scope that is signalled for such doctrines by referential patterns of argument. Theological premises, particularly concerning creation and the created order, yield the basic context for applying concepts and terms honed in talk about the derivatively existent to talk about that which is sheerly existent.

Aquinas's discussion of human knowledge of God confirms the foregoing reading of the logic of predications about God. In question 12 of the first part of the *Summa theologiae* the bulk of the articles (eleven to be exact) are devoted to the beatific knowledge of God, and only one article each to faith and natural knowledge of God. This disproportionate treatment might be construed as follows. Any adequate description of the range of human knowledge of God in the present life must begin with some account of what our knowledge of him will be like in the life to come. To put this another way: we will grasp the full scope of our capacity to know God now only by considering the consummation toward which our present knowledge is directed by grace. What is possible to us now can be appreciated only in the light of what our knowledge shall become. We are invited to see human knowledge of God from above, as it were, down to its lower levels. It is not so much a matter of independent bodies of knowledge, natural and then revealed, which develop independently and then come to be related to one another. All that is true knowledge is taken up into the knowledge of faith, and that in turn into the knowledge of vision. Everything that is part of human knowing and willing as natural capacities is taken up to function at a higher level, that is, successfully knowing and loving God.

Thus the chief strength of Aquinas's account of the nature and grace of religious knowledge and the logic of religious predications lies in its capacity to relate Christian affirmations to a wide variety of explanatory contexts beyond their linguistic, narrative, historical and subjective settings. Such an account breaks through the constraints imposed on Christian theology in the course of its long dialogue with the modern Western philosophical tradition. The internal logic of the discourse of religious traditions entails at least the possibility that primary doctrines can be supported by arguments to establish a reference to the entity or state at the centre of the community's pattern of life and arguments to explicate the force of its predications.

An account of Christian predications that admits their propositional force would equip Christian theology in dialogue to engage in conversations with other major religious communities. Generally speaking, these communities concur with the Christian community (though accounting for it differently) in claiming objective states of affairs as the context for their teachings about God (if they have any), the true aim of life and the conditions of human existence in the world. Equipped with an account of the logic of religious predications, such as that inspired by a reading of Aquinas, a Christian theologian would be prepared to take disagreements about these matters seriously. In particular, there are significant disagreements between Muslim and Christian communities about whether the unity of God excludes or permits relations in him, and between Buddhist and Christian communities about whether the ultimate state entails or negates personal identity and interrelationships. These differences are not vacuous, though whether they represent true oppositions is a matter for dialogue and debate among the communities concerned. In effect, an account of the logic of religious predications that admits their propositional force, such as the one provided here, can be read as a defence of the possibility and seriousness of interreligious disagreements and conversation about them.

It is a weakness of pluralist accounts of religious predications that they seem to underrate the fundamental seriousness of such disagreements. We noted above that one warrant for Professor Samartha's introduction of the concept 'Mystery' was that the 'transcendent Center . . . remains always beyond and greater than apprehensions of it or even the sum total of such apprehensions'.[17] It is typical of pluralist accounts of religious predications to stress the ineffability of the transcendent realm and furthermore to argue that differing doctrines about the foci of religious quest or worship in the major traditions diversely designate something that is itself absolutely indescribable. Behind and beyond the Christian's triune God, the Jew's Lord God, the Muslim's Allah, the Hindu's Brahman and the Buddhist's Nirvana, there lies an ineffable 'X' – variously identified by pluralist accounts as 'Ultimacy', 'Reality' or 'Mystery' – that itself never appears except in these scheme-specific manifestations. John Hick calls these manifestations 'personae'.[18]

Ascriptions of ineffability of religious communities to the objects of worship or quest upon which their patterns of life are centred have a variety of functions. Naturally, they have the obvious function of stating that no concepts or expressions can succeed in comprehending that which completely surpasses ordinary experience, sense-perception and knowledge. But such ascriptions also function as unrestricted primacy-ranking predicates. What is describable and comprehensible is also accessible and therefore similar to other entities within our experience. But the object of worship or quest is normally not thought to be one more item within our experience but either the transcendent source of all there is (as in most theistic traditions) or the goal beyond all there is (as in some non-theistic traditions). An indication of this function is that in the literatures of the Buddhist and Christian communities respectively, for example, affirmations of the utter ineffability of Nirvana or the triune God are juxtaposed to extensive descriptions of what Nirvana entails and what the nature of God is like. To combine ineffability with other unrestricted primacy-ranking predicates like most holy, or perfectly good, or supreme goal of life, is to acknowledge the limitations of all discourse that seeks to speak about that which transcends human knowledge and speech. But from the ineffability of the transcendent realm it does not follow for either Buddhists or Christians that certain forms of predications about it are not more appropriate than others, or that particular forms of predications are not ruled out, or that in some way these communities' authorized ways of speaking about Nirvana and God do not bear on the truth of the matter. In other words, predicate-expressing doctrines do possess some propositional force.

For this reason, the members of these communities generally believe that some real disagreements obtain between them. Buddhists, for example, have developed highly sophisticated accounts for the prevalence of theistic beliefs. An account of religious predications that admits their propositional force, though it does not deny their limitations, is basic to interreligious dialogue. Generally speaking, as we have noted, the major religious communities of the world agree in identifying objective states of affairs as the context for their teachings about God, the true aim of life, the conditions of human existence in the world and so on. This conviction gives rise to arguments that seek to secure each community's particularistic claim to universality. An account of religious predications that admits their propositional force (without denying their negative, rulish, symbolic or metaphorical functions) is presupposed if disagreements among religious communities are to be taken seriously. There are significant disagreements between Muslim, Jewish and Christian communities about the nature of divine unity, and between Buddhist and Christian communities about whether personal identity and personal interrelationships are ultimately enduring. These differences are significant, although to what extent they constitute real oppositions is a matter of reflection, dialogue and debate. In effect, an account of the logic of religious predications that admits their propositional force takes the possibility of interreligious disagreements seriously.

In its familiar versions, pluralist theology of religions seems to hold a view of religious predications that sharply qualifies their propositional force. The logic of pluralist accounts seems to entail that no predicate expressing doctrines of one religious community could ever be said to embody descriptions bearing on the true nature of the ineffable 'X' such as to conflict with or rule out predications expressed in the doctrines of other religious communities. Furthermore, the chief function (logically speaking) of doctrinally specific arguments for the primary predications by which religious communities identify their objects of worship or quest would be to converge upon and point to the 'Mystery' or 'Reality' that eludes them all.

Pluralist accounts of religious predications are reminiscent of modalistic explanations of the Christian doctrine of the trinity. It will be recalled that the modalism that spurred doctrinal controversy in the early church involved some version of the view that 'Father, Son and Holy Spirit' designate roles or 'personae' adopted by God in executing various stages of the economy of salvation. The historic mainstream repudiated this view by affirming the reality of the distinct relations in God as warranted by the scriptural witness to the real processions of the Son and the Spirit. In effect, in rejecting modalistic explanations of the doctrine of the trinity, the Christian community took 'Father, Son and Holy Spirit' to constitute the substance of a divine self-identification. Anything less was understood to amount to a retrogression to the sophisticated philosophical interpretations of pagan polytheism according to which the gods were viewed as so many diverse manifestations of a single transcendent divine spirit. If 'Father, Son and Holy Spirit' represent only modes of God's engagement with humankind, then it would follow that God in himself remains unknown. His true identity is hidden from human view behind the 'personae' he displays for soteriological or other purposes. For modalism, 'Father, Son and Holy Spirit' finally constitute a practised concealment rather than, as the gospel was understood to proclaim, a full disclosure of God's identity and purposes.

Pluralist positions are equivalently modalistic in their account of the logic of religious predications. In the current 'neo-modalism' of pluralist theology of religions, the diverse doctrines by which each religious community designates the otherwise ineffable 'X' (Nirvana, the blessed trinity, Allah, etc.) embody only partial and possibly complementary descriptions of something that finally eludes them all.

Suppose that a well-informed but non-affiliated inquirer is welcomed as an observer into a dialogue with members of Judaic, Christian, Muslim and Buddhist communities. He is permitted an intervention, and in the course of speaking announces that either Christianity is true, or Buddhism is true, or no religion is true. His argument for this ferociously contentious claim is not without interest. It takes its starting point from the importance of personal identity and interpersonal relationships among human beings. Christian doctrines, as he understands them, affirm the centrality of these relationships to the extent that person and relation are ascribed even to God himself. That which is most important to human beings, their self-fulfilment in the context of intimate relations with other persons, turns out to be most important in the transcendent realm as well. As he construes it, the doctrine of the trinity allows for the possibility that human beings can be intimately related to God in a truly interpersonal way. He understands this possibility to be excluded by non-trinitarian theistic faiths, which allow only for worship of or submission to God. Buddhist doctrines, on the other hand, seem to him to assert the illusoriness of personal identity and the impermanence of interpersonal relationships. Thus he concludes that since Christian and Buddhist doctrines both take into account observably central features of the objective states of human existence in the world, and advance predications about what is ultimate that reflect these features, they have a greater truth potential than religious doctrines failing to do so.

On the pluralist account of religious predications, it is hard to see how responses from the religious participants in such a conversation could amount to anything for or against this complex interpretation of their doctrines. If religious doctrines expressing predications are in principle construed as failing to assert anything definitive about that which is transcendent, then there is no point in debating the truth of religious doctrines expressing contradictory or even just different accounts of it. Moreover, there are no reasonable grounds, all things being equal, upon which to prefer one community's pattern of life to another's. The very inquiry about such matters loses urgency, and interreligious conversations are rendered finally otiose. Such an outcome runs counter to the deepest convictions with which religious communities commend their doctrines and the patterns of life they foster. Generally speaking, pluralist accounts of religious predications appear to attenuate the significance of religious differences in the course of trying to account for them.

I have argued that traditional philosophical theology equips Christian theology in dialogue with a conception of the logic of religious references and predications that is well suited to the challenge of the encounter with other religions. There is wide scope for referential and predicational arguments in interreligious conversations. Christian theology in dialogue is in effect invited by its new conversation partners in the great world religions to recover and reconstruct arguments of this kind. Such arguments stake a claim, logically speaking, in the large territory of human knowledge about the world. There are no internal restrictions that prevent the appeal of such arguments to relevant scientific findings or to metaphysical and conceptual analysis. The Kantian critique of metaphysics and natural theology continues mistakenly to be invoked in support of such constraints. The mistake here is the failure to recognize that the pervasive rationalism of Kant's conceptions of epistemology and metaphysics is itself susceptible of counter-argument and revision. In effect, whatever their other weaknesses, non-rationalist metaphysical positions (Aristotle's for example) escape unscathed. As accounts of the discourse of religious traditions, philosophical theories that rule out in principle a broadly realist construal of religious predications will seem implausible and counter-intuitive. As far as the logic of the discourse of religious communities is concerned, the burden of proof lies with these theories themselves.

In addition, the recovery of a philosophical theology such as that sketched here avoids some of the pitfalls associated with projects labelled 'fundamental theology' or 'foundational theology'. Attention to the logic of arguments that support references and predications and thus secure the universal scope claimed by the Christian community for its doctrines does not commit Christian theology in dialogue to the discredited Cartesian project of grounding the certitude of all knowledge in unassailably true, simple, lapidary propositions or conceptions. 'Foundational theology' has come to be linked with neo-scholastic apologetics of a rationalist cast or with the more recent transcendental project of explicating the truth of Christian doctrines in terms of the conditions for the possibility of our knowledge of them. The proposal of a role for arguments in support of the references and predications embedded in Christian affirmations is a much more modest one. Philosophical theology, according to this account, does not seek to ground the truth of these affirmations, but locates the widest possible context for our understanding and explication of them. It resists the suggestion that these affirmations apply only in the narrow contexts defined by subjectivity, historical consciousness or language. Staking this claim is not equivalent to establishing a foundation for the truth of all Christian doctrines once and for all. That 'foundation' exists only in the truth who is God himself and can never be a human construction. Rather, the readiness to develop and employ arguments of the sort described here characterizes a conception of the theological enterprise in which – case by case, doctrine by doctrine – the force of Christian affirmations is expounded in connection with the full range of human knowledge of the world. The label 'foundational theology' is taken to designate, rightly or wrongly, a project far more grand than the one in view here.

Arguments that support references and predications function to locate Christian affirmations about the nature and existence of God, his inner-trinitarian life, creation, revelation and grace, human nature, sin and evil, incarnation and redemption, justification and sanctification, morality and spirituality, church and sacraments, resurrection and glory, eschatology and the last things in the widest possible context of reality, thought and experience. In this way, such arguments have an important role to play in interreligious conversations, where Christians encounter in the doctrines of other communities the challenge of similarly particularistic claims to universality. Philosophical theology helps Christian theology in dialogue to rise to this challenge.

Notes

1 Quoted in Masao Abe, 'Buddhism and Christianity as a Problem of Today', *Japanese Religion* 3 (1963), no. 2, p. 21.

2 Sri K. Dhammananda, *Why Religious Tolerance?* (Kuala Lumpur: Buddhist Missionary Society, 1974), p. 8.

3 Sanarakshita, *A Survey of Buddhism*, 5th edn (Boulder, CO: Shambhala Publications, 1980), p. 3.

4   Hajime Nakamura, *Buddhism in Comparative Light* (New Delhi: Islam and the Modern Age Society, 1975), pp. 10–11.
5   Peter Berger, *The Heretical Imperative* (Garden City: Doubleday, 1979), p. 17.
6   John Updike, *Roger's Version* (New York: Knopf, 1986), p. 32.
7   This account of arguments in religious discourse is dependent upon William A. Christian, Sr, *Meaning and Truth in Religion* (Princeton: Princeton University Press, 1964), pp. 185–237.
8   Immanuel Kant, *Critique of Pure Reason*, trans. Norman Kemp Smith (New York: Macmillan, 1929), I, Second Division, ch. 3, sects 3–7, pp. 495–531.
9   Bernard Williams, *Ethics and the Limits of Philosophy* (Cambridge, MA: Harvard University Press, 1985), p. 168. On the absence of 'Cartesianism' in Aquinas see, for example, Anthony Kenny, *Aquinas* (New York: Hill and Wang, 1979), pp. 27–31.
10 Thomas Aquinas, *Summa theologiae*, Ia. 2,1–2.
11 George A. Lindbeck, 'Scripture, Consensus and Community', in *Biblical Interpretation in Crisis*, ed. Richard John Neuhaus (Grand Rapids, MI: Eerdmans, 1989), p. 75.
12 Karl Rahner presents an extended argument in philosophical theology in his works *Spirit in the World*, trans. William Dych (New York: Herder and Herder, 1968), especially pp. 132–236, and *Hörer des Wortes*, ed. J. B. Metz (Munich: Kosel-Verlag, 1963).
13 Stanley J. Samartha, 'The Cross and the Rainbow', in *The Myth of Christian Uniqueness*, ed. J. Hick and P. Knitter (Maryknoll: Orbis Books), pp. 75–6.
14 Thomas Aquinas, *Summa theologiae*, Ia. 3, prologue.
15 Thomas Aquinas, *Summa theologiae*, Ia. 3, 4.
16 Thomas Aquinas, *Summa theologiae*, Ia. 13.
17 Stanley J. Samartha, 'The Cross and the Rainbow', p. 75.
18 John Hick, *An Interpretation of Religion: Human Responses to the Transcendent* (New Haven, CT: Yale University Press, 1989), pp. 233–96.

PART

Methods

Beyond the Hermeneutical Deadlock

James J. Buckley

This revision of an earlier article attempts a reconceptualization of the standard categories of the debate in hermeneutics between 'revelationist', 'functionalist' and 'textualist' views of the problem of how to interpret the scriptures. It proposes that prior convictions about what 'scripture' is must be investigated to discover that all three views are part of a single problem, rather than essentially competing positions. Chapter 3 of Buckley's book *Seeking the Humanity of God: Practices, Doctrines and Catholic Theology* (Collegeville, MN: Liturgical Press, 1992), entitled 'Quests for Jesus Christ', could usefully be read in conjunction with this essay.

If asked to define hermeneutics, I am tempted to say that there are two kinds of people: those who think reading is easy, and those who think it is hard. People in the second group engage in 'hermeneutics', mystifying or angering or entertaining those in the first group. The point might be academized by considering Jeffrey Stout's two descriptions of hermeneutics. Hermeneutics in its 'bad sense' (Stout says) is 'epistemology . . . imported by the humanities; the first science of the human sciences; the quest for the method . . . of interpretation'.[2] We might call this the 'bad sense' of hermeneutics if we are sceptical that there is anything significant to be said about the method of interpreting (say) scripture, no matter what scripture is about, what kind of literature in scripture we are reading, or what circumstances we are in. In other words, we might call this the 'bad sense' if we think that hermeneutics is a quest for a method of making it easy to read – and that it is rarely easy to read anything worth reading.

On the other hand, hermeneutics in its good sense (Stout says) is the 'art of enriching our language in conversation with others; also, reflection designed to raise this art to consciousness without reducing it to a set of rules'. Stout calls this a 'good sense' of hermeneutics because it does not presume there is a single method for interpreting (in our case) scripture. Instead, we interpret scriptures in 'conversation' with each other. The first sort of hermeneutician might wonder how helpful this second sense of hermeneutics is. Is it not another name for relativism, perhaps a solipsistic conversation in the 'consciousness' of middle-class academics? No wonder that, faced with the deconstruction of this consciousness, some have recommended we conceive of our circumstances as 'post-hermeneutical'.[3]

My own preference would be for a very modest use of the term. Hermeneutics would be a quest for 'what is said (asserted or recommended or commanded or otherwise expressed) in some source or in some part of a source or in the sources of a community as a whole. How are the sources to be interpreted?'[4] We ask such questions when we wish to know, for example, whether these sources are internally consistent as well as how they are consistent with what is said in other religious and secular communities.

However, I am less concerned with whether or how we ought to use technical terms such as 'hermeneutics' than how we might describe a problem or deadlock in language we can all understand. A deadlock, as the reader may know, is a lock so constructed that it must be opened on one side by a handle and on the other by a key. A deadlock, then, has three components: a lock in a door, a handle on one side of the door, and a keyhole on the other side. Similarly, I will propose that our current hermeneutical deadlock has three components. More often than not, one part of the deadlock is worked upon and the other parts ignored, combated or mocked. I will propose a way such debates constitute a single lock. I will not, be it noted, propose a single key to unlock the door. In fact, I think that no such single key exists. In this and other respects, there are limits to the analogy. But let us see how far it can take us in three steps. First, I will sketch the *status questionis* of our current deadlock as outlined by Edward Farley and Peter Hodgson; they are worthy representatives of a position we might dub 'liberal', or 'revisionist'.[5] Second, I will argue that the deadlock is more severe than Farley and Hodgson imply. Finally, I will propose how this deadlock is indeed a common lock rather than a set of different sorts of locks for incommensurable doors.

Some Options

In an astute overview of the *status questionis*, Edward Farley and Peter C. Hodgson distinguish two senses of 'scripture'. In one sense, '"scripture" refers to the existence of a normative collection of writings and their function in the origin and perpetuation of a religious faith'; scripture (they say) is 'necessary to the Christian faith' in this sense.[6] In another sense, 'scripture' is a collection of writings containing 'a unique deposit of divine revelation'. Farley and Hodgson dissent from this second sense of scripture, not least because it generates two 'extreme' positions on the use of and claims about the Bible. On the one extreme are those who regard the Bible as 'obscurantist, provincial, no longer authoritative for life in the modern world'. On the other extreme are 'antiquarians or renovators', bent on affirming the Bible as 'a written deposit of the complete and definitive revelation of Yahweh to the people, functioning as the primary source of cultic and moral regulation for the community'.

The real argument, Farley and Hodgson propose, is among those who occupy 'the middle ground'. The problem is that here (as elsewhere) there is no single middle ground. Thus, Farley and Hodgson call 'revelationalists' those who locate scripture in relation to 'its revelatory substratum'. Some 'specific events, figures, concepts, or subsets of texts' (something like a 'canon within a canon') is selected, and the rest of scripture is read in relation to those events, figures, concepts or texts. For example, some appeal to the doctrines (Warfield), some to the concepts (Kittel) and others to acts of God (Wright) behind or beyond the biblical text.[7] The key challenge to revelationalists is whether and how they can warrant their appeal to this extra-textual, revelatory substratum. Indeed, those who claim the Bible no longer fits into our world might find it difficult to distinguish revelationalists from 'antiquarians and renovators'.

On the other hand, Farley and Hodgson call 'functionalists' those who focus on the uses of scripture, claiming that certain texts are scripture to the extent that they pass certain 'pragmatic and functional' tests. For example, some appeal to biblical symbols expressive of the depths of our being (Tillich), some to myths expressive of my authenticity (Bultmann), and others to the way scripture functions to shape new human identities (Kelsey) – Jew and Greek, men and women, rich and poor. From the point of view of revelationalists, a central problem with functionalists is whether solely pragmatic and functional tests can identify what scripture is and is about. For example, functionalists like Farley and Hodgson propose that the concept of a 'canon' of scripture 'should be abandoned', and admit that this leaves them with the problem of identifying the constitutive writings of Israel and the church.

This conclusion is odd. Recall that Farley and Hodgson began by stipulating a sense in which 'scripture' is necessary to the Christian faith, i.e. 'the existence of a normative collection of writings and their function'. And yet their conclusion leaves them with no way to identify any such writings. Farley and Hodgson leave us with questions about the identity of these texts – questions (we might say) of 'textuality'. However, before pursuing this issue, I would like to suggest that there is a reason why Farley and Hodgson leave us with this problem. Simply put, despite their endeavour to be fair to revelationalists and functionalists and others, Farley and Hodgson underestimate the problem of formulating a doctrine of scripture and its uses.

Reconstructing the Deadlock: From Revelation to God to Religions

To make this case, let us begin with the so-called revelationalist position. Presume that to ask about the 'revelatory substratum' of scripture involves asking what scripture is 'about'. What, we might ask, is 'the subject matter' of scripture? Scripture is obviously about lots of things: God and Christ, history and the cosmos, cities and individuals, and so forth. But what (if anything) is it centrally or ultimately about? What is its central subject matter? On this view, the 'revelationalist' position is that scripture is ultimately about God. Or, as David Kelsey has suggested, part of what goes into 'theologians' decisions about scripture' is a way 'to construe the *mode* in which *God* is present'.[8]

However, despite the common ground Farley and Hodgson claim with Kelsey on most issues, Kelsey's account is distinct from theirs in taking seriously the simple fact that we disagree about this issue. For example, for some God is taken to be present in and through the doctrines or concepts proposed by scripture; on this view, God is present 'in the *ideational* mode'. For others, God is taken to be present 'in the mode of *concrete actuality*' – as an agent (Barth, G. Ernest Wright) or cosmic process (Thornton, Gustafson). For still others, God is taken to be present 'in the mode of *ideal possibility*' – the possibility of authentic individuality (Bultmann), the more social power of the new being (Tillich), or 'a certain limit-mode-of being-in-the-world' (Tracy).[9] Here is the first respect in which Farley and Hodgson underplay the deadlock between revelationalists and functionalists: the argument is not only or primarily over some revelatory substratum or the functions of scripture; their argument is a deadlock over 'the mode of *God's* presence'.

However, we need to go even further than Kelsey. It is not accurate to characterize these as different 'construals of the mode of God's presence' – if this implies that there is something called 'God's presence' on which we agree and a 'mode' on which we disagree. In reality, these are not different ways of describing or imagining God. They are, as far as I can see, different gods. Indeed, I think it would be even more accurate to say that these are not only different gods but different religions, i.e. different ways of living, focusing on objects or subjects which are of ultimate and unrestricted importance.[10]

This does not mean that conversation among these different religions (or, less radically, different construals of the mode of God's presence) is impossible. The issue at this point is not whether there can be such conversation but what it will be about. What I propose is that, instead of taking the argument over subject matter to be an argument over opposed predicates ('modes') attributed to the same subject ('God'), we take the argument to be over different subjects (e.g God's teachings, the power of Being, God's acts, or being-in-act) for an identical predicate (e.g. x is of unrestricted importance). Far from inhibiting conversation, this makes discussion possible, for we are now clearer on what we disagree about.

But my aim here is not to adjudicate this argument over God, gods and different religions. The main point is that, if the 'revelationalist' position has to do with what scripture is ultimately about (or with the subject matter of scripture), the first part of our deadlock is that we disagree over what scripture is ultimately 'about'. If so, it is unfair to pit revelationalists against functionalists. Farley and Hodgson, for example, call themselves 'functionalists'. In this respect, they agree with Tillich, Bultmann and Kelsey. They also reject a God 'represented mythically as thinking, willing, reflecting and accomplishing in the mode of an in-the-world-being who intervenes selectively in world process', and yet they propose that we take scriptures as 'normative vehicles of [an] ecclesial process' which is 'the salvific work of God in history'.[11] But, unlike (on one reading) Tillich they do not choose to *replace* divine agency in favour of an ideal possibility – or (like Gordan Kaufmann) to construct a God who is the ground of cosmic process. Instead, they seem to wish to *reconstruct* traditional claims about divine agency so that God 'works in history' without 'intervening selectively'.[12] In this respect, they are as much 'revelationalists' as Karl Barth or G. Ernest Wright.

Another implication of this deadlock is that we ought to be wary of the label 'revelationalist'. I agree with Kelsey, Farley and Hodgson that locating a doctrine of scripture solely in relation to a doctrine of revelation was and is a large mistake. But this is not because 'revelation' can be (as Farley and Hodgson put it) 'obscurantist' or 'antiquarian'. Rather, appeals to 'revelation' cloud appeals to different and opposed ways of construing the mode of God's presence (ideational, concrete actuality or ideal possibility) – or, better, different religious referents'.[13] To this extent, the label 'revelationalist' is deceptive. If this part of the deadlock concerns what scripture is ultimately about, we might preferably and more simply say that it is a debate about the ultimate subject matter of scripture. With this proviso, in what follows, I will use 'revelationalist' as a code word for the complex claims (sometimes opposed, sometimes similar, sometimes difficult to compare) made on behalf of this subject matter.

Reconstructing the Deadlock: From Function to Functions and Contexts

Next, take functionalists, i.e. the position which focuses on the uses of scripture, claiming that certain texts are scripture to the extent that they pass certain 'pragmatic and functional' tests. The key problem with Farley and Hodgson on this score is that they underestimate the degree of conflict among such functionalists. For example, recall that some functionalists appeal to biblical symbols expressive of the depths of our being (Tillich), some to myths expressive of my and your authenticity (Bultmann), and others to the way scripture functions to shape new human identities (Kelsey). In all these cases scripture is pragmatically and functionally tested over against diverse views of human persons (as individual subjects or agents in a physical, social and/or historical world). But there are clearly people who might be taken as functionalists for whom the pragmatic tests are different and opposed. For example, functionalists like the Roman Catholic Nicholas Lash insist that it is not the script that is holy but the people; scriptures are 'performed', and 'the quality of our *humanity* will be the criterion of the adequacy of the performance'. Functionalists like the Eastern Orthodox Anthony Ugolnik insist that the pragmatic and functional test is liturgical, i.e. how these scriptures are used in, shaped by, and shape the baptismal and eucharistic practices of the Christian community'.[14] This is not to say that appeals to 'the quality of our humanity' and appeals to liturgical practices are incompatible; in fact, Lash and Ugolnik would, in different ways, argue that they are compatible. The point is that Lash and Ugolnik could not disagree more on the central pragmatic test for our uses of scripture (our humanity or our liturgical performance), and yet they are both aptly characterized as 'functionalists'.

Indeed, we might go a step further. Functionalists of all sorts have taught us that to test our own or others' understanding of scripture is not simply to test whether we know what the Bible is about. Instead, 'understanding the Bible' is having the ability to use scripture in a variety of ordinary circumstances.[15] For example, we use the Bible as individuals for prayer and study. We learn to listen to the Bible read and preached as well as read and preach and sing the scriptures throughout the liturgical year. We learn to use the Bible to make moral decisions as a community – for example, how we are to stand in solidarity with the poor and afflicted. We also display our understanding of the Bible as we use it in the presence of strangers – estranged Christians, Christians in alien Christian communities, and non-Christians. As a final example, we enact an understanding of the Bible as we probe its uses not only in various contexts today but also throughout the tradition of its uses and misuses, from the formulation of the biblical canon through its pre-critical and critical uses.[16] On this expanded functionalist view, we 'understand scriptures' differently in different contexts and circumstances. It takes different skills to use the Bible for prayer than for study, to listen to the readings at the Lord's Supper and to sing them, to use the Bible with adults and children, with Catholics and Christians and non-Christians. It takes yet different skills – e.g. the virtues of faith and hope and love – to seek and find in these texts the Word of God.

Not all of us have all these skills, and it takes a lifetime to hold them all together – to become (to use St Paul's metaphor) 'a letter from Christ' (2 Corinthians 3:1–3) or to become a text legible to all. But a key lesson of functionalism is that we can have orthodox understandings of what scripture is about and yet use these texts in the most perverse and sinful ways. It is functionalists who have forced us to see the importance of the distinction between 'using scripture' and 'holding a doctrine about scripture'; who have shown us that the former has a kind of priority over the latter, and who have encouraged us not to identify a theologian's or a church's *uses of* scripture with her or his or their *claims about* scripture, who have encouraged us to tell the historical tale of scripture not primarily as a set of arguments about scripture but as a set of diverse uses of scripture in diverse historical and cultural circumstances.

In any case, the second part of our deadlock is that we disagree over the nature and ordering of the diverse functions of scripture. Whether we wish to say that 'the ultimate test is pragmatic and functional' or (as I prefer) that one test is pragmatic and functional, we must also say that this solves very little, for we hold opposed and often incommensurable positions on what functional test scriptures must pass. Is the function existential or political, liturgical or ecclesial, all of these or something else? If there is more than one function of scripture, how are they related? If these functions include the shaping of our identities as individuals, do our individual acts of understanding and interpretation stand outside of or within other contexts, or both? That is, do they form a special (perhaps even transcendental) perspective on these contexts or do we understand and interpret only that with which we can do something else besides understand or interpret?[17] In any case, from this point of view, it is once again unfair to pit functionalists against revelationalists. Just as most theologians have a position on the ultimate subject matter of scripture (and so are, in some sense, revelationalist), so most theologians have a position on the nature and scope of the functions of scripture (and so are, in some sense, functionalists).

Finally, as the first deadlock ought to make us wary of the label 'revelationalist', so this second deadlock ought to make us wary of the label 'functionalist'. The Bible is a book, or a library of books. It does not *do* anything; the texts are not self-authoring, self-using or self-interpreting. Texts do not 'function' either. Instead, human beings do things with these texts – use them, author them, interpret them. To this extent, the label 'functionalist' (like the label 'revelationalist') might lead us astray. One preferred label (I believe) would be 'contextualists', for what functionalists share in common is an insistence that texts not only have subject matters but also contexts. They disagree on the particularities and scope of those contexts but not on the central importance of contexts.

Reconstructing the Deadlock: From Simple to Complex Textuality

Finally, Farley and Hodgson have underestimated the deadlock not only in underestimating conflicts within revelationalism (arguments over the mode of God's presence as the ultimate subject matter of scripture) and functionalism (arguments over the contexts within which scripture functions). They have also underestimated the degree to which arguments over texts are a set of arguments distinct from those over subject matter or contexts.[18] The argument of (what we might call) textualists is against those who make some objective or subjective fact or possibility foundational for explicating a text. Instead, textualists argue, the focus of our claims about and uses of the Bible ought be 'intratextual', showing how the world of the Bible embraces our world.[19]

But, once again, there are diverse and opposed ways of describing what these texts are. They have been taken to be systems of doctrines and collections of concepts, recitals of acts of God and realistic narratives of Jesus, symbols and myths, letters and poems and prayers. In fact, I dare say that most Christians would today say that the scriptures are a variety of kinds of texts (literary genres) appropriate for use in different contexts in relation to diverse subject matters. In this sense, just as all of us are revelationalists and functionalists (in the senses described above), so all of us are textualists. What, then, is at stake in arguments over textuality?

Terrence Tilley has recently contributed to answering this question by distinguishing 'pure intratextualism' and 'dirty intratextuality'.[20] The former position (Tilley claims) is represented by George Lindbeck and Hans Frei. Tilley does not agree with the standard liberal Catholic or liberal Protestant charge against Frei and Lindbeck that 'pure intratextualism' is a 'fideism' *simpliciter*.[21] Instead, his central charge is the more modest one that 'they do not clarify the relationship of intratextual to "extratextual" meanings'. In claiming that the scriptural world 'absorbs the universe', pure intratextualists separate the text from its context (e.g. its readers and audience). We ought to prefer (Tilley argues) a 'dirty intratextualism' in which texts are shaped by 'ongoing conversation' in worship and tradition and in the way our whole lives are lived.

Tilley's distinction between 'pure' and 'dirty' textualism is useful, although I think distinguishing 'simple' and 'complex' textualism is a better way to help us understand what is at stake. Consider Tilley's stand on the subject matter and contexts of scripture. Tilley claims that, rather than 'construing a scriptural text as constituting a single world into which all others are absorbed, unity and fidelity can be found in the practice of bringing Jesus Christ to life in every world'.[22] Such claims seem to presume (rightly, I think) that the contexts of scripture are practical, from hearing scripture preached and read in worship to the whole life of Christian discipleship in the world. But, on what grounds do we make such claims, given the diverse contexts mentioned above – from existential self-understanding through solidarity with the oppressed? I do not see how Tilley's 'dirty intratextualism' settles the question of what the contexts of scripture are and ought to be. In fact, what Tilley also calls his 'radical contextualism' risks ceasing to be a textualism at all and becoming a 'pure [or, as I prefer to say, simple] contextualism'. Pushed to an extreme which Tilley avoids, simple contextualism would claim that we appeal only to 'patterns' in the text rather than 'the text', or 'the text construed-as-a-certain-kind-of-whole' *rather than* 'the text as such'.[23] Now textualists do not have to argue that there is such a thing as a 'text-in-itself' unrelated to context and subject matter. They simply have to argue that inquiry into texts is distinct from inquiry into subject matters and contexts. However, as our textualism ought to be complex rather than simple (i.e. as we ought to refuse to reduce questions about scripture's subject matter and context to questions about the scriptural texts), so our contextualism ought be complex rather than simple (i.e. we ought to refuse to reduce questions about scriptural texts and subject matters to questions about contexts for using scripture). In other words, textualists insist that texts are used in and function in contexts, although they might disagree over what those contexts are. What textualists insist upon is that asking what scripture is about and how scripture is used are not the only hermeneutical questions.

Parenthetically, I do not find Lindbeck to be consistently a 'pure intratextualist' rather than a 'contextualist'. Lindbeck (like most of us) aims to hold together subject matter, context and text. If there is an anomaly to Lindbeck's position on hermeneutical issues, it is that he does not seek a full-blown theory of subject matters and contexts and texts but a set of rules 'essential to Christian identity' on such issues.[24] Tilley, like many other critics of Lindbeck, has overlooked the key distinction Lindbeck makes between 'doctrine' (teachings which are essential to Christian communal identity) and 'theology'. Read from this point of view, the *primary* issue is not whether we are simple or complex, pure or dirty on these issues. The primary issue is whether we 'Christians' from diverse churches and communities are *Christians*, e.g. whether our use of and teachings about scripture enable us to engage in *common* prayer and worship and service to God's world, or whether they are so diverse and opposed that we cannot truthfully pray and worship, work and think together. In short, I do not know if Tilley is criticizing Lindbeck for not holding authentic Christian teaching about scripture – or for not being consistently cultural–linguistic; the former is heresy, the latter mere bad anthropology. I suspect that Tilley would say the latter. But, to speak on Lindbeck's terms, we must be clear about the difference.

Second, Tilley's claim that the unity of scripture is constituted by 'the practice of *bringing Jesus Christ to life in every world*' presumes (rightly, I think) that Jesus Christ is the ultimate subject matter of scripture – the Jesus Christ who must ultimately be followed and described (for reasons we shall see shortly) in the context of a trinitarian vision of God. But on what grounds do we make such claims given the diverse construals of the modes of God's (or the gods') presence mentioned above? Just as his radical contextualism does not deal with the diverse and conflicting contexts of scripture, so I do not see how it yields his view of the subject matter of scripture. In fact, for those of us persuaded by Hans Frei's use of (if not always his claims about) scripture, we do not 'bring Jesus Christ to life'. Jesus Christ, as an 'agent in a narrative plot, in his particular narratable plot', lives and brings *us* to life.[25] Whether Tilley's contextualism permits this sort of christological realism I am not sure. It is true, I think, that Frei focuses on the relationships between subject matter (Jesus Christ) and texts (narratives), wary of confusing this subject matter and text with any anthropological or ecclesiological context. In other words, he sometimes leaves a gap between how Jesus Christ lives and how we live in relationship to Jesus Christ, a gap which can be filled by no text or context but only the miraculous free love of God. But he is not a 'purist' on such issues, for he insists that questions of subject matter and text (and context) are interrelated.[26] Here, once again, our contextualism ought to be dirty rather than pure or radical – complex rather than simple. Questions of subject matter cannot be reduced to questions of context. In still other words, textualism is not a position on what scripture is ultimately about. Complex textualists, then, do not claim that scripture is ultimately about itself, although they may not agree on what the central subject matter of scripture is. 'Book religion' for them would not merely be the ancient practice of venerating the scriptures.[27] Instead, book religion (including stories of a book-writing God) would be idolatrously confusing this book and its subject matter – God.

In sum, there are also questions about what these texts *are* which are irreducible to questions about subject matter or context. What we might call 'simple textualists' might insist that questions about subject matter and context reduce to questions about texts – just as 'simple revelationalists' reduce questions about texts and contexts to questions about subject matter and 'simple contextualists' reduce questions about subject matter and texts to questions about context. But, just as I know of no concrete examples of 'simple revelationalism' or 'simple contextualism', so I know of no examples of 'simple textualists'. What we might, then, call 'complex textualists' insist that questions about texts are distinct but inseparable from questions about subject matter and context.

Thus, the third part of our deadlock is that we disagree over what these texts are. Even *if* we wish to say that our uses of scripture ought to be 'intratextual' (whether simple or complex), we must also say that this solves very little, for we hold opposed and often incommensurable positions on what these texts are. What we disagree on is most often not whether questions about these texts are important but whether and how to order and rank them.[28] Once again, from this point of view, it is unfair to pit textualists against functionalists and revelationalists. Except for those bibliolatrists who make the text its own subject matter or those deconstructionists who make all texts self-referring contexts, all of us are textualists in some way or another.

Reconstructing the Deadlock: Subject Matter, Contexts and Biblical Narrative

What conclusions can we draw? Contrary to appearances, the severity of the conflict between revelationalists, functionalists and textualists makes it easier rather than more difficult to describe the current hermeneutical deadlock. The deadlock is not a debate over three relatively isolated positions *between* which we must *choose* – between, say, revelationalists, functionalists and textualists. Instead, it is an argument over the *relationships between* the subject matter, the contexts and the texts of scripture. We ought not to *choose between* subject matter, contexts and texts but seek for ways to relate these three to each other. If we choose to stick with labels like revelationalism and functionalism and textualism, we ought to say that such positions are not working on three different doors to different houses but are each part of a single deadlock. The hermeneutical deadlock will be opened when we have reasoned answers to three questions: what is the ultimate subject matter of scripture? What are the diverse contexts for using scripture? What is scripture?

Finally, I initially promised that I would not supply a single key for unlocking this deadlock. The reason is now (I hope) clear: like all deadlocks, all three parts must somehow work together to open the hermeneutical door. However, if pressed to suggest a (not *the*) key, I would suggest that one reason for the recent popularity of discussions of narrative is because narratives are the sorts of texts which felicitously raise questions about the relationship between the subject matters, contexts and texts. That is, I think that Stanley Hauerwas and Gregory Jones are right that discussions of narrative are currently stalemated over the very simple question 'Why narrative?'[29] In this sense, 'narrative' has driven itself onto the same rocks that have shipwrecked most discussions of scripture: the temptation to think that the hermeneutical deadlock has a single part – that, if we could discover the handle or the lock or the key, we could open the hermeneutical door. And yet, as Hauerwas and Jones also suggest, the category of narrative does fruitfully raise a number of questions in domains ranging from metaphysics and epistemology to preaching and reading scripture.

Applying such lessons to our hermeneutical deadlock, we might say that, *if* we take the central subject matter of scripture to be Jesus Christ, the gospel narratives are particularly apt ways of relating this subject matter to these texts, for the central aim of these narratives is to depict the identity of Jesus Christ, including this particular character's relationship to the triune God and the world. This is not to say that we *only* use these narratives to find out about this subject matter or that *all* narratives have this role; in fact, it seems clear that we use these narratives for a number of reasons (historical, literary, etc.), that most narratives are not about the God of Jesus Christ, and that no narratives are about Jesus Christ in the way these gospel narratives are. In any case, on this view, God engages the world 'in the mode of concrete actuality' creating and redeeming us for life everlasting.

What more can be said about the relationships between this subject matter and these texts? Various doctrines of scripture as the inspired Word of God have been, until recently, a main way of binding the scriptural texts to their subject matter (God) – whether inspiration was a predicate of the words, the message behind the words, the authors behind the message, the community behind the authors, and/or the readers of the text.[30] We now know that such doctrines of inspiration were only too frequently tied to a construal of the mode of God's presence as 'ideational', an intellectualist view of the contexts of scripture, and a constriction of the texts to their doctrinal or propositional force. However, if the subject matter of scripture is God as a concrete actuality, we can see the logic of the classic description of these texts as 'the Word of God', without pretending to address all the issues involved in inspiration. In these texts, we might say, we have the necessary depictions of Jesus Christ in relationship to the triune God. To confess these scriptures as 'Word of God' is to confess that these texts faithfully depict who God is on our behalf.[31]

I have said that these texts are 'necessary', not sufficient, for these texts depict this God in relationship to a world of many joys and griefs calling us to unpack the patterns of relationships between the storied Christ and the world which is the context of these texts – the worlds of synagogue and church, of our public as well as private joys and griefs. In fact, the way that these texts belong in particular contexts helps us understand the logic of the classic claim that these texts are 'the body of Christ',[32] shaped by the Pentecostal Spirit. That is, these texts are not the isolated Word of God but the Word spoken to and by a eucharistic community, empowered by the Spirit. Scripture and Eucharist and church, we might even say, are different aspects of the same thing in the sense that these texts are bound to eucharistic and ecclesial contexts. These are not only contexts in which we live but also contexts we enact and produce as we read and pray and debate these texts over the course of our lives. However, we do not need to claim (with Hans Urs von Balthasar) that scripture and Eucharist and church are so closely related that they 'can *only* be different aspects of the same thing',[33] for scripture has its distinctive joys and griefs distinct (although not separate) from church and sacrament. The Catholic claim that scriptures are 'the body of Christ' is not opposed to the Reformation claim that scriptures are 'the Word of God'; the former has to do with the relationships between subject matter and context, while the latter has to do with the relationships between subject matter and the texts. As Word of God and body of Christ, scriptures are (as David Yeago has put it) 'the Spirit's witness to the Father and the Son' in the church for the world.[34]

Indeed, construed in this trinitarian fashion, the central issue sublates the Catholic–Protestant debate, for the metaphor 'the body of Christ' includes not only our sinful yet holy pilgrim church but all of God's world on a journey toward the time when God will be all in all, the eschatological *totus Christus.* Here 'narrative' is not only a genre for rendering the identity of God and Christ but also a genre for displaying who we are, i.e. characters in an ongoing story. In fact, one of the central theological debates with regard to the contexts of scripture is whether these contexts form a narrative unity or whether any such unity is undercut by the 'vulnerability and loss and wasted opportunities' that constitute so much of our lives.[35] But the main point here is not to settle this debate over how evil, sin and suffering threaten to undercut any putative contexts for these texts. The main point is that *scriptures* remain *Word of God* (by virtue of the relationship between their ultimate subject matter and these texts) even while they are also *body of Christ* (by virtue of the relationship between this subject matter and these contexts) – held in communion by the Holy Spirit.

Finally, it is not simply that subject matter is related to text (so that these texts are *Word of God*), and as well as to contexts (so that these texts are *body of Christ*). It is also that these texts are related to myriad contexts, making them subject to the full range of human inquiries: historical and philological, literary and philosophical, and so forth. The results of such inquiries are not always directly relevant to theology, any more than theological inquiry is always directly relevant to these inquiries. The hope for a day when we have a perfectly consistent vision of scripture-in-relationship-to-everything-else (from archeology to philosophy) is as apocalyptic as the hope (suggested in the Jewish Kabbala) that there will be a day when these texts will be annulled to make room for God's immediate presence unmediated by the materiality of things like these texts.[36] It is crucial to remember that *scriptures* are not only *Word of God* and *body of Christ* but also simply texts, writings, books. When descriptions of them as *Word of God* and *body of Christ* become ideological reification of these texts, we need to remember our ordinary description of them is more material, i.e. they are writings, 'scriptures', of no single literary genre. Their style is, overall, 'mixed', for they mingle the sublime and the ordinary, calling us to treat them with the obedience and freedom with which we treat any text which speaks to us about 'God's incarnation in a human being of the humblest social station, through his existence on earth amid humble everyday people and conditions, and through his Passion which, judged by earthly standards, was ignominious' – and vindicated in the resurrection.[37] Humble, everyday people will go on using these texts to find out about God, their neighbours and themselves *sans* the complexities of any sophisticated hermeneutics. But theological hermeneutics can simply remind such people of who they are before God and their neighbours and these texts. From within the midst of such a people, we learn to repent of our hermeneutical diseases as well as call others to repentance for not relating subject matter, context and text in ways faithful to what we all ought to teach, do and be.

Notes

1 This is a slightly revised version of 'The Hermeneutical Deadlock between Revelationalists, Textualists, and Functionalists', *Modern Theology*, 6 (1990), pp. 325–39.

2 Jeffrey Stout, *Ethics After Babel: The Languages of Morals and Their Discontents* (Boston: Beacon Press, 1988), p. 298. Subsequent quotes from Stout are also from this page.

3 Hans W. Frei, 'The "Literal Reading" of Biblical Narrative in the Christian Tradition: Does it Stretch or Will it Break?', *The Bible and the Narrative Tradition*, ed. Frank McConnell (Oxford: Oxford University Press, 1986), p. 60. For a critique of interpretation as 'our basic way of being in the world' from the point of view of one political theory, see James Tully, 'Wittgenstein and Political Philosophy: Understanding Practices of Critical Reflection', *Political Theory*, 17 (1989), pp.172–204 (especially pp. 192ff.).

4 William A. Christian, *Doctrines of Religious Communities: A Philosophical Study* (New Haven, CT: Yale University Press, 1987), p. 91.

5 For further analysis of these labels, see James J. Buckley, 'Revisionists and Liberals', in *The Modern Theologians: An Introduction to Christian Theology in the Twentieth Century*, ed. David F. Ford, 2nd edn (Oxford: Blackwell Publishers, 1997), chapter 17.

6 'Scripture and Tradition', in *Christian Theology: An Introduction to Its Traditions and Tasks*, ed. Peter C. Hodgson and Robert H. King, 1st edn (Philadelphia: Fortress Press, 1982). Quotations in the following paragraph are from pp. 36, 37, 50, 51, 52, 54, 55.

7 For detailed analysis of the theologians cited as examples, Farley and Hodgson presume familiarity with David H. Kelsey, *The Uses of Scripture in Recent Theology* (Philadelphia: Fortress Press, 1975).

8 David H. Kelsey, *The Uses of Scripture in Recent Theology*, pp. 161ff.

9 See Tracy's *Blessed Rage for Order: The New Pluralism in Theology* (New York: Seabury Press, 1975), p. 221. Hans Frei has proposed that Tracy's *The Analogical Imagination: Christian Theology and the Culture of Pluralism* (New York: Crossroad, 1981) reflects

a change on this issue which yields 'two simultaneous [and unstable] referents'; see 'The "Literal Reading" of Biblical Narrative', pp. 75–6 (note 16). For discussion of 'the range of subject matter proposals' in the nineteenth century, see Hans Frei, *The Eclipse of Biblical Narrative: A Study in Eighteenth and Nineteenth Century Hermeneutics* (New Haven, CT, and London: Yale University Press, 1974), pp. 255–66.

10 For religions as ways of life and thought centred on something or other of 'unrestricted importance', see William A. Christian, *Oppositions of Religious Doctrines: A Study in the Logic of Dialogue Among Religions* (New York: Herder and Herder, 1972), pp. 62–74. For an analogous discussion (in terms of debates over competing 'goods' and 'hypergoods'), see Charles Taylor, *Sources of the Self: The Making of the Modern Identity* (Cambridge, MA: Harvard University Press, 1989), especially pp. 63–73.

11 'Scripture and Tradition', pp. 50, 60. We find the same tension in Kelsey. Kelsey proposes that 'instead of taking "God saying" as the overarching image for all the various things Christians are inclined to say God "does" with the Bible', we ought say God '"uses" the church's various uses of scripture' for various ends (p. 214). But, *sans* the scare quotes, this will not satisfy those for whom God is present in the mode of ideal possibility; for them, it is difficult to talk about God *doing* anything (whether 'saying' or 'using'), except as metaphors which have no 'cognitive' value.

12 For Farley's reinterpretation of 'revelation', see Edward Farley, *Divine Empathy: A Theology of God* (Minneapolis: Fortress Press, 1996).

13 For further comment on this issue, see my reviews of Ronald Thiemann's *Revelation and Theology* (Notre Dame: University of Notre Dame Press, 1985) and Avery Dulles' *Models of Revelation* (Garden City, NY: Doubleday, 1983) in (respectively) *Horizons*, 14 (1987), pp. 390–1 and *Horizons*, 10 (1983), pp. 379–80.

14 Nicholas Lash, 'Performing the Scripture', *Theology on the Way to Emmaus* (London: SCM Press, 1986), pp. 37–46; Anthony Ugolnik, 'An Orthodox Hermeneutic in the West', *St. Vladimir's Theological Quarterly*, 27 (1983), pp. 93–118. Note also that Lash and Ugolnik seem to agree on the subject matter (in contrast to the function) of scripture: the God of Jesus Christ, construed in trinitarian fashion.

15 See Charles M. Wood, *The Formation of Christian Understanding: An Essay in Theological Hermeneutics* (Philadelphia: Westminster Press, 1981). See also Nicholas Wolterstorff's criticisms of 'performance interpretation' in *Divine Discourse: Philosophical Reflections on the Claim that God Speaks* (Cambridge: Cambridge University Press, 1995), chapter 10.

16 For a collection of articles and astute commentary, see Stephen E. Fowl, *The Theological Interpretation of Scripture: Classic and Contemporary Readings* (Oxford: Blackwell Publishers, 1997). The primary theological usefulness of 'historical criticism' is its contribution to deconstructing and reconstructing the narrative of the origins and uses of scripture – a narrative (it could be argued) inseparable from a narrative of the origins of the church and its episcopal office; as George Lindbeck puts it, 'It is to [the] episcopally unified church ... that all the major Christian traditions owe their creeds, their liturgies, and above all the scriptural canon. If these later are inexpungible, why not also the episcopate?' ('The Church' in *Keeping the Faith: Essays to Mark the Centenary of Lux Mundi*, ed. Geoffrey Wainwright [Philadelphia: Fortress Press, 1988], p. 199.)

17 See Charles Wood's contrast between those who seek 'to understand a text, apart from

any specific employment of it' and those who argue that what 'constitutes understanding depends a great deal on the use one wants to make of the text, as well as on the character of the text itself' – as well (I would say) as the subject matter of the text. (*Formation of Christian Understanding*, pp. 16, 19.)

18 Farley and Hodgson do admit that a complete doctrine of scripture must take account of new studies of 'how language functions, especially in texts of religious, poetic, and narrative character' ('Scripture and Tradition', p. 57). But to leave this issue unresolved is to leave unresolved what is, on their own terms, a key claim: scriptures are 'normative texts'.

19 See especially George Lindbeck, *The Nature of Doctrine: Religion and Theology in a Post-liberal Age* (Philadelphia: Westminster Press, 1984), chapter 6; 'Barth and Textuality', *Theology Today*, XLIII (1986), pp. 361–76; 'Scripture, Consensus, and Community', *This World* (1988), pp. 5–24.

20 Terrence W. Tilley, 'Incommensurability, Intratextuality, and Fideism', *Modern Theology*, 5 (1989), pp. 87–111. The following quotes are from pp. 95, 105 and 107. For a criticism of Lindbeck for opposite reasons (i.e. for possibly reducing intratextuality to 'performance' [or what I am calling function] and downplaying issues of 'reference' [or what I call subject matter]), see George Hunsinger, 'Beyond Literalism and Expressivism: Karl Barth's Hermeneutical Realism', *Modern Theology*, 3 (1987), pp. 209–23. Hunsinger (like, I think, Barth) is wary of granting what Barth calls *applicatio* ('performance' or 'function') any sort of priority.

21 See David Tracy, 'Lindbeck's New Program for Theology', *The Thomist*, 49 (1985), pp. 460–72; James Gustafson, 'The Sectarian Temptation: Reflections on Theology, the Church, and the University', *Proceedings of the Catholic Theological Society*, 40 (1985), pp. 83–94.

22 'Incommensurability, Intratextuality, and Fideism', p. 104.

23 *The Uses of Scripture in Recent Theology*, pp. 14, 101, 103. Kelsey's 'functionalism' is clear less in his claims about the importance of uses of (in contrast to claims about) scripture than in these claims about texts, as well as his claim that a (or the) 'decisive and fatal way in which the doctrine of creation from nothing could fail: that it should simply cease in fact to express the most basic way a community of persons is set in the world' ('The Doctrine of Creation from Nothing' in *Evolution and Creation*, ed. Ernan McMullin (Notre Dame: University of Notre Dame, 1985), p. 192.

24 See *The Nature of Doctrine: Religion and Theology in a Post-liberal Age* (Philadelphia: Westminster Press, 1984), p. 74. Note how Lindbeck's discussion of 'intratextuality' is 'an addendum to the main argument of the book' stressing the theological (in contrast to doctrinal) uses of his theory of religion (p. 112). I do not aim to defend Lindbeck here, although I think such a defence could be mounted by showing how there are Catholic (Anglo, Roman or other) ways of taking the *sola scriptura* which rule out *solitaria scriptura*.

25 Hans Frei, 'Barth and Schleiermacher: Divergence and Convergence', in *Barth and Schleiermacher: Beyond the Impasse?*, ed. James O. Duke and Robert F. Streetman (Philadelphia: Fortress Press, 1988), p. 72.

26 With regard to Frei, shall we say (with Ron Thiemann) that Frei's position shifts from textualism to contextualism – or (with Stanley Hauerwas) that even Frei's earlier proposals always situated the text in liturgical and ecclesial context? See Ronald Thiemann, 'Radiance and Obscurity in Biblical Narrative' and Stanley Hauerwas, 'The Church as God's New Language', in *Scriptural Authority and Narrative Interpretation*,

ed. Garrett Green (Philadelphia: Fortress Press, 1987), especially p. 41 (note 18) and p. 192. This may be the place to say that the unfinished nature of Frei's (as well as Lindbeck's and Kelsey's and others') theology is warning against premature construction of a 'Yale school', as Tilley and others have done. If forced to summarize the differences, I would say that Frei focuses on issues of subject matter, Kelsey on context and Lindbeck on textuality. Once we probe the surface similarities of their positions, I find that the Yale school has no more unity on the relationships between subject matter, context and text than any other single school. This, we might say, is part of what makes it a (good) school rather than (say) a church.

27 It is unclear why Farley and Hodgson reject the ancient practice of 'veneration' of the Bible ('Scripture and Tradition', p. 35) – if veneration is distinguished (as Christians have traditionally done) from worship. I fear that they (like so many functionalists) presume an alienation between 'things' (e.g. texts and writings) and 'persons' (e.g. us).

28 These are not arguments over a 'canon within the canon' but arguments over how to order canonical texts in different historical, liturgical, political and other contexts. The problem is not peculiar to Christian (or even theistic) religions; see William A. Christian, Sr, *Doctrines of Religious Communities*, pp. 38–41.

29 *Why Narrative?* (Grand Rapids, MI: Eerdmans, 1989).

30 For a review of the literature on inspiration, see Robert Gnuse, *The Authority of the Bible: Theories of Inspiration, Revelation, and the Canon of Scripture* (New York: Paulist Press, 1985), especially pp. 20–1, although Gnuse focuses on issues of the function of scripture without taking up issues of subject matter (p. 3).

31 For a philosophically acute and theologically sensitive treatment of scripture as *Word of God*, see Nicholas Wolterstorff, *Divine Discourse: Philosophical Reflections on the Claim that God Speaks* (Cambridge: Cambridge University Press, 1995) – although a focus on 'divine discourse' risks eclipsing the Spirit's shaping of scripture in the body of Christ.

32 On the patristic view of scripture as *body of Christ*, see the literature cited in Hans Urs von Balthasar, *The Glory of the Lord: A Theological Aesthetics, vol. I: Seeing the Form* (San Francisco: Ignatius Press, 1982), pp. 527–56. In medieval theology, see Henri du Lubac, *Corpus Mysticum. L'eucharistie et l'église au moyen-age* (Paris: Aubier Montaigne, 1949).

33 *Seeing the Form*, p. 529. My emphasis.

34 See David Yeago, 'The Spirit, the Scriptures, and the Church: Biblical Inspiration Revisited', *The Spirit, Church, and the Knowledge of God*, eds. James Buckley and David Yeago, forthcoming.

35 See Gene Outka, 'Following at a Distance: Ethics and the Identity of Jesus' in *Scriptural Authority and Narrative Interpretation*, ed. Garrett Green (Philadelphia: Fortress Press, 1987), p. 158. If Outka's position has analogies to Barth's, Alasdair Macintyre's has analogies to the Augustinian–Thomist insistence on narrative unity – the unity of a tradition beyond the bypass of Enlightenment history and Nietzschean genealogy; see his *Three Forms of Moral Inquiry: Encyclopedia, Genealogy, and Tradition* (Notre Dame: University of Notre Dame Press, 1990).

36 On such apocalypticism, see the remarks on Jewish Kabbala in Terry Eagleton, *Walter Benjamin or Towards a Revolutionary Criticism* (London: Verso Editions and NLB, 1981), pp. 115–17.

37 Erich Auerbach, *Mimesis: The Representation of Reality in Western Literature* (Princeton: Princeton University Press, 1953), p. 41.

Tradition and the Tacit

Andrew Louth

Not directly influenced by the predominantly American sources of postliberal theology, this excerpt from Andrew Louth's essay on the nature of theology, *Discerning the Mystery*, shows that the search for a theology beyond the paradigm of the Enlightenment has deep roots in the Catholic traditions of Christian thought. The retrieval of a positive understanding of tradition as a source of truth rather than an obstacle to critical activity is an important aspect of postliberal theological work.

Since the Reformation, at least, tradition has been a matter of dispute in theology: on the one hand, Catholics have been seen as using the notion of tradition to supplement scripture, finding in it a source for those theological positions that cannot be proved from scripture; Protestants, on the other hand, have dismissed such an idea of tradition, and have wished to keep close to the original revelation of God in Christ as witnessed to in the scriptures. Recent scholarship, however, has shown that this simple opposition is something that developed in the course of controversy between Catholic and Protestant, and that from this point of view both those who defended it, and those who rejected it, misunderstood its nature.

One way of bringing out this misunderstanding is to notice how both sides in the Reformation and post-Reformation controversies seemed to conceive of tradition as something comparable with scripture, either complementing it or a rival to it. Both scripture and tradition are objectified: they are *that* which we seek to understand, there is a distance between them and us who seek to understand them. There are a good many hidden assumptions behind all this:

the idea, for instance, that what is revealed is a collection of truths, so that if tradition supplements scripture, what we mean is that in addition to the apostolic witness that was written down in the scriptures, there are other truths which have, as it were, been whispered down the ages, and not written down. These truths are objective, independent truths, which we who seek them will, if we go about it the right way, come across and recognize. The problem of how we know at all, what it is that is taken for granted when we seek to understand God's revelation, has not been broached with any very searching intensity.

George Tavard argues[1] that this opposition of scripture and tradition was something that arose in the later Middle Ages, and that it is not at all characteristic of the understanding of tradition in the Fathers or in the theology of the High Middle Ages. What I shall seek to do in this chapter is to explore some of the dimensions and implications of the understanding of tradition found in the Fathers (an understanding that continued into the Middle Ages, and was at least occasionally glimpsed by some of the writers of the Reformation period): my exploration will not be primarily historical (though I hope it will not be thought unhistorical) – such historical work has been well done by Congar[2] and others – rather I shall be concerned with the pattern of theological understanding that emerges from their attitude to tradition.

'Words, both because they are common, and do not so strongly move the fancy of man, are for the most part but slightly heard: and therefore with singular wisdom it hath been provided, that the deeds of men which are made in the presence of witnesses should pass not only with words, but also with certain sensible actions, the memory whereof is far more easy and durable than the memory of speech can be.'[3] This principle, enunciated by Hooker, of the distinction between words and deeds or actions, a distinction he uses to lay emphasis on the deeper power and significance of deeds, is a principle which not only underlies many of the crucial points of Hooker's theology (the importance of the Incarnation, and, in dependence on that, the importance of the sacraments, and indeed of liturgical worship which is a matter not just of words but of actions in general), but also points the way to the significance of tradition. For the central truth, or mystery, of the Christian faith is primarily not a matter of words, and therefore ultimately of ideas or concepts, but a matter of fact, or reality. The heart of the Christian mystery is the fact of God made man, God with us, in Christ; words, even his words, are secondary to the reality of what he accomplished. To be a Christian is not simply to believe something, to learn something, but to *be* something, to experience something. The role of the church, then, is not simply as the contingent vehicle – in history – of the Christian message, but as the community, through belonging to which we come into touch with the Christian mystery. This emphasis on reality, rather than on a message or ideology, comes out in one of the passages in the scriptures which is central to any understanding of the Christian notion of tradition:

> That which was from the beginning, which we have heard, which we have seen
> with our eyes, which we have looked upon, and our hands have handled, of the
> Word of Life; (for the life was manifested and we have seen it, and bear witness,
> and show unto you that eternal life, which was with the Father, and was
> manifested into us;) that which we have seen and heard declare we unto you, that
> ye also may have fellowship with us: and truly our fellowship is with the Father
> and with his Son Jesus Christ. (1 John 1:1–3).

Here the reality that John proclaims is not simply a message, but something
seen and heard and handled, a genuine physical reality, and what John asks for
from his readers is not belief, intellectual assent, but fellowship, a fellowship
which is ultimately fellowship with the Father and the Son, fellowship with the
trinity itself. Joining a fellowship, commitment to a community, involves more
than assent to its beliefs, but rather a sharing in its way of life, in its ceremonies,
and customs and practices.

Now this broader understanding of what is involved in engagement with the
truth, is something that has already been adumbrated in the earlier chapters of
this book – in Polanyi's idea of the importance of a community and of a tradition,
within which one learns to perceive and know, or in Gadamer's concept of
tradition as bearing the preconceptions necessary for us to know anything at
all, and of initiation into this tradition as *Bildung* or what the Greeks called
paideia.

Werner Jaeger, in his great work *Paideia: The Ideals of Greek Culture*,[4] has
drawn attention to the central importance within Greek culture of the notion
of *paideia*, in its dual meaning of education and culture, the process by which
one is initiated into a culture. The two poles of this notion are a continuing
tradition, borne by a society, and the individual who seeks to become a member
of that society. Hence the importance within Greek culture of the civic virtues,
justice, prudence, fortitude and temperance. Plato's *Republic* shows how the
individual is to fit himself for this society, and combines this with the idea both
that life in society prepares the individual to come to knowledge of the Good,
and also that such contemplation of the Good on the part of the rulers of the
city-state enables them to direct the life of that society. This Greek
understanding of *paideia* was taken up in the theology of the Fathers: both
Irenaeus and Origen, to mention but two early examples, develop approaches
to theology that revolve around the notion of *paideia*. The most fundamental
reason for this, it seems to me, is that the notion of *paideia* involves taking
seriously the nature of man as a social being. For the Greeks this seems to have
been a kind of basic *aperçu*, for the Christians it was a consequence of their belief
in God as creator: for both it could be expressed as a belief in divine providence,
fundamental for Christians, and in Plato's later philosophy, for instance, one
of the basic beliefs required of those who wish to be citizens of the society he

depicts in his *Laws*. Christians were driven to see the significance of all this by the challenge of Gnosticism in the second century. For Gnosticism, with its belief in the fundamentally evil character of the world and its consequent rejection of any belief in divine providence, hit at the basis of both Christianity and Hellenic culture. Such late representatives of the classical ideal as Plotinus see the heart of the error of the Gnostics in their rejection of *paideia* – a natural consequence of their belief in man as an individual divine spark trapped in a hostile world. So we find Plotinus opposing, with some vehemence, the Gnostics in such terms as these:

> We are not told what virtue is or under what different kinds it appears . . . we do not learn what constitutes it or how it is acquired, how the soul is tended, how it is cleansed. For to say 'Look to God' is not helpful without some instruction as to what this looking imports: it might very well be said that one can 'look' and still sacrifice no pleasure, still be the slave of impulse, repeating the word 'God' but held in the grip of every passion and making no effort to master any. . . . 'God' on the lips without a good conduct of life, is but a word.[5]

Christians, in opposing the Gnostics, used the Greek notion of *paideia* as a way of articulating their understanding of the goodness of creation, and their understanding, consequent on this, of redemption not as something opposed to creation, as with the Gnostics, but as the restoration of creation – a re-creation, which restored the original coherence between man and man, and man and the cosmos.

The consequence of all this was that Christians very quickly came to see that their understanding of God and his dealings with men entailed a positive evaluation of human tradition. Though there was much in the current pagan tradition that they felt they had to reject, and though such opponents of Christianity as Celsus were right when they saw in the Christians' intolerant rejection of pagan religion something that would mean the end of ancient society (hence his fundamental charge against the Christians was one of sedition), the Christian rejection of paganism was often presented (classically in Justin Martyr) as an appeal to a pristine human tradition, untainted by demonic deceit. And this involved a positive appreciation of what Jaeger, at least, presents as fundamental to Greek culture – Plato's great metaphysical vision. How such a positive concern for human tradition, an appreciation of what one might broadly call humane tradition, could be articulated within Christianity can be seen in a very significant way in Augustine's treatise *On Christian Doctrine*.

There is much dispute as to what Augustine means in this work by 'Christian doctrine' (*doctrina christiana*), but it seems to me that Marrou was right – or at least saw more deeply than others into what was involved in Augustine's enterprise when he insisted that *doctrina* cannot be narrowly interpreted as 'doctrine' or 'teaching' (what the church, or her accredited ministers, teaches), but means 'culture', in short what we have been calling *paideia*.[6] For the work is concerned, as Augustine himself makes clear, with the whole enterprise of teaching and learning within the Christian community, the Catholic Church, and with all that is presupposed by this activity. This is a Christian *paideia*, and so distinct from simply pagan education, but not (as we shall see) from human culture: indeed it restores a truly human culture. This culture is learnt within the community of faith: that already distinguishes Christian *doctrina* from pagan education, for faith is faith in the unseen God, and trust in his help. And this immediately raises a question that is not raised where faith is not presupposed: if what is needed is faith, which is a gift of God, why does anyone need to teach anyone anything; and further, what is the point of such teaching, since what is taught will not be understood if the divine gift of faith is withheld? The latter objection is met by comparing faith with light, the light in which the truths of the Christian faith are seen. The Christian teacher points, as it were, to these truths, but, says Augustine, 'although I can lift my finger to point something out, I cannot supply the vision by means of which either this gesture or what it indicates can be seen.'[7] To the former objection, that if faith is required then there is no need of precepts and teaching, Augustine replies that those who say that 'should remember that they have learned at least the alphabet from men': the Christian faith presupposes human culture, a theme that Augustine is to develop. But further, if we are not ready to learn, because we have received the gift of faith, there is at least the danger of pride in such a refusal to submit to learning – pride in the fundamental sense of isolation of the individual – for 'charity itself, which holds men together in a knot of unity, would not have a means of infusing souls and almost mixing them together if men could teach nothing to men'.[8] Augustine makes two points here in clearing a space in which he can talk about teaching and learning within the Christian community: first, the way in which learning demands of us humility, and secondly, the fact that the Christian community is essentially a community of love, love which presupposes and perfects the togetherness of human society. Both these points will be developed later, both in relation to human tradition and also in relation to the tradition of the church.

Augustine begins Book I of *On Christian Doctrine* by making a distinction between things and signs, *res* and *signa*: signs point beyond themselves to things, but things are what they are, though only discerned and understood through signs. The word *res* has, in fact, a resonance in Latin which is obscured by the English word 'thing' or 'reality'. In his work on Virgil (from which we have already quoted) Theodor Haecker, in commenting on the words from the *Aeneid*, 'sunt lacrimae rerum', draws attention to the way in which the word *res* is used in Latin to designate reality in a way both comprehensive and concrete. So the State is called *res publica*; history is just *res* and a historian a 'writer of things', *rerum scriptor*; the greatest philosophical poem in Latin is significantly entitled *De rerum natura*; Rome as the capital of the Empire is *caput rerum, domina rerum*. Haecker illuminates the significance of the word *res* in Latin by introducing the idea of a heart-word (*Herzwort*) of a language:

> The invisible, individual spirit of a people is finally revealed in all its external, visible business, but most clearly in the living body of its language. And from each such body of a language we hear words which sound from the heart, which betray to us where this individual heart is most inclined, what is its greatest care, what its grief, its longing, its passion, its joy and its pleasure is. Because they are the most inward to the body of a language, such heart-words are understandably the most difficult to translate. At best they are to be left, as and where they are, at any rate if there is to be any complete understanding. In order to understand these words, one must already have gained access to the whole language.[9]

He suggests that we can find such 'heart-words' in *logos* in Greek, in *raison* in French, in 'sense' in English, in *Wesen* in German: and in Latin *res* is such a heart-word. So it is the word Augustine uses in his *On Christian Doctrine* to designate things, the reality disclosed to us by signs. To treat of things is to treat of what is fundamental, and this Augustine proposes to do for the rest of Book I.

Book I turns out to be a treatise on love. When we are dealing with things as they are, we are at the level of *love*: the moral primacy of love reflects an ontological primacy. Augustine develops his doctrine of love by using the distinction between *frui* and *uti*, enjoying and using. To enjoy something is to cleave to it for its own sake; to use something is to love it for the sake of something else. God alone is to be loved for his own sake; people are to be loved in him because with them we can share our delight in God; things are to be used. Here we have a doctrine of *ordered love*, and for Augustine our love can only be properly ordered when we submit in humility to learn from the Incarnate Word of God. To imagine that we can order our love and cleave to God alone in our own strength would be pride: and it is such pride that Augustine found in the endeavours after self-culture (a merely humanly administered *paideia*) among the Neoplatonists.

The heart of the matter, then, is love, and it is this love that the scriptures are to teach us. How scripture teaches us this, is what Augustine goes on to discuss in Books II and III. Scripture teaches us through signs, and just as Book I was about things, so Books II and III are about signs, *signa*, and how they are to be interpreted. First Augustine distinguishes between natural signs (*signa naturalia*) and conventional signs (*signa data*). He does this to dispose of *signa naturalia* (smoke as a sign of fire, a contorted expression on the face of a man as a sign of pain), for though they are an important way of communicating, they provide no basis for any developed form of human communication. It is by means of *signa data* that we communicate with one another, and the most important form of such signs is words (for though anything that can be understood can be explained through words, words themselves cannot be explained exhaustively in terms of any other conventional signs). Words can be made permanent through letters and writing. Augustine then makes the important point that *signa data* depend for their efficacy on consent among human beings, and that it is just such consent among human beings that makes possible human society. Words cannot be regarded as natural signs (which would not require such human consent), for even though we often try to make words correspond with what they signify (Augustine knows as well as more recent investigators into the origins of language about the part played by onomatopoeia in the formation of words), 'since one thing may resemble another in a great variety of ways, signs are not valid among men except by common consent'. Augustine's whole discussion of language and signs, with the important place it gives to the notion of consent, emphasizes the way in which the whole enterprise of human understanding is something that cannot be understood in a purely individualistic manner, but on the contrary depends upon and grows out of a shared tradition, a common sense. And in fact for the most part Augustine means by this shared tradition, this common sense, a shared *human* tradition, a common *human* sense. Only occasionally does he tighten this sense of shared tradition to mean the shared tradition of the church: rather he emphasizes how the human enterprise of knowing and coming to understanding involves the common human tradition of those who speak the same language and interpret their experiences in the same way.

Chapter 7 of Book II gives a summary account of how we are to approach and use scripture so as to come to the knowledge of God. Augustine presents this approach as a ladder with seven steps. We begin with the fear of God, and quickly pass to the next step, which is piety, *pietas*. In this way our pride is cut down and piety enables us to approach scripture in a receptive spirit: we are approaching scripture willing to learn, we are accepting its claim to have something to teach us. The third step is *scientia*, knowledge. This comprises all the knowledge we need in order to *understand* the scriptures: it involves knowledge of languages, knowledge of various kinds presupposed by the scriptures (natural history, a certain amount of history, logic, numbers, music and so on), the knowledge required to establish accurate texts. It also comprises a knowledge of the scriptures themselves: we are to read the scriptures, and commit a great deal of them to memory, for it is in the scriptures as a whole that we find the voice of God speaking to us. What Augustine has in mind here is not any sort of method, but rather a deep familiarity with the language and content of the scriptures. Such a reading of the scriptures, as Congar has said of the patristic approach to the reading of the scriptures as a whole, 'is sapiential in form and founded on a double conviction: first, everything is the work of the Word or Wisdom of God; second, God does not manifest and communicate himself in words alone, and so ultimately in ideas, but in realities.'[10] As a result of all this, the student discerns from scripture that he is enmeshed in the love of this world, a love very remote from the kind of love of God and of our neighbour that the scriptures commend. The next step is fortitude, by which the student avoids falling into despair and turns to a love of the eternal. The fifth step is the counsel of mercy, which urges us on to love of our neighbour and thereby leads to a purging of the mind. On the sixth step the soul is filled with love of his enemy, and here 'he cleanses that eye through which God can be seen'. The top step is *sapientia*, wisdom. 'The fear of the Lord is the beginning of wisdom': that sentence from Proverbs is drawn out by Augustine into a ladder by means of which we ascend through scripture to wisdom, knowledge of God not in the sense of knowledge about God, but rather of communion with him.

What Augustine offers us here is reminiscent of similar ladders of ascent to God which we can find elsewhere in Augustine, and in the Christian tradition both before and after him, and indeed more widely. They are ways in which the soul prepares itself for knowledge of, union with, God; they consist of purification of the soul by the practice of the virtues. In the Christian tradition such 'ladders' reach back to Plato and the platonic tradition where the virtues are seen as restoring a man to harmony with himself, and thus enabling him to accomplish that for which he was made: the vision of God. We can then join together – or rather see the deeper connection between – Augustine's emphasis on human tradition, as underlying any human enterprise of knowing and coming to understanding, and his adumbration of an approach to the scriptures as a way of spiritual ascent to the knowledge of God; for they both spring out of an understanding of Christian *paideia* that is continuous with, and a development of, the understanding of *paideia* developed among the Greeks, and in particular given classical expression in the works of Plato.

But the specifically Christian understanding of tradition goes a great deal further than this, though we shall see that something of the pattern that has emerged already remains, but is deepened and developed. Let us begin by quoting a few significant passages from the writings of the early Fathers. First a passage from Clement of Rome: 'The apostles were taught the Gospel for our sake by the Lord Jesus Christ, and Jesus the Christ was sent from God. Christ therefore was from God, and the apostles from Christ; in both ways then things were brought about in an ordered way by the will of God.'[11] This recalls the passage quoted earlier from the first epistle of St John, and recalls two such passages from St John's Gospel as 'As my Father hath sent me, even so send I you' (20:21), 'As thou hast sent me into the world, even so have I sent them into the world' (17:18), 'And the glory which thou gavest me I have given them; that they may be one, even as we are one: I in them, and thou in me, that they may be made perfect in one; and that the world may know that thou hast sent me, and hast loved them, as thou hast loved me' (17:22–23). Jesus is the One sent from God the Father; the apostles are those whom he has sent into the world. Whereas tradition understood in a human sense is perhaps the continuity of man's search for the truth, and whatever progress there is in such a search, tradition in the sense of the tradition of the church is the continuity of the divine sending, the divine mission, which the church has received from her Lord and which she pursues in the world. The scriptural passages we have quoted, and the passage from *1 Clement*, speak of the church's sending as echoing the Father's sending of his Son into the world, but to understand its full significance we need to recall other passages from St John's Gospel: 'Receive ye the Holy Ghost' (20:22) (the very next verse after the first one we quoted), 'But when the Comforter is come, whom I will send unto you from the Father, even the Spirit of truth, which proceedeth from the Father, he shall testify of me: and ye also shall bear witness, because ye have been with me from the beginning' (15:26–27), 'But the Comforter, which is the Holy Ghost, whom the Father will send in my name, he shall teach you all things, and bring all things to your remembrance, whatsoever I have said unto you' (14:26). The church's sending is in the power of the Spirit: the heart of the church's tradition, Holy Tradition, is the life of the Holy Trinity, in which the church participates through the Holy Spirit, the fellowship which is 'with the Father, and with his Son Jesus Christ'.

A passage from St Irenaeus takes us somewhat further:

> The true knowledge is the teaching of the apostles; and the ancient order of the Church found throughout the world; and the character of the Body of Christ according to the succession of bishops, to whom the Apostles committed [*tradiderunt*] that Church which is in each place, and which has come even to us, preserved without any writings by the fullest exposition [i.e. the rule of truth] which admits of neither increase nor diminution; and reading of the scriptures without any falsification and their legitimate and careful exposition, avoiding danger and blasphemy; and the special gift of love, which is more precious than knowledge, and more glorious than prophecy, surpassing all other charisms.[12]

Here we have more detail as to how the tradition is passed on throughout the history of the church. Irenaeus speaks of the character of the church which is preserved through the succession of bishops: by this he means not just the articles of faith handed down by the apostolic succession of bishops, but the whole character of the Christian community, its rites, its ceremonies, its practices and its life. The final point he makes about the 'special gift of love' underlines the fact that for Irenaeus the tradition of the church is not, like the traditions to which the Gnostics appealed, simply some message, truth or ideology, but a life, something lived.

In the passage quoted Irenaeus alludes to the rule of truth (as he usually calls it; others call it the rule of faith, *regula fidei*, which is how it is usually known). Early on in his *Adversus Haereses*, he says that 'one who possesses undeviatingly the rule of truth, which he received in baptism, and knows the names of the scriptures, and the sayings, and the parables, will not recognize the blasphemous suggestions that they [the Gnostics] put forward',[13] and goes on in the next chapter to explain the rule of truth thus:

> For the Church which is disseminated throughout the whole world, right to the ends of the earth, received from the apostles and their disciples the faith in one God the Father Almighty, maker of heaven and earth, the seas and all that is in them; and in one Christ Jesus, the Son of God, who was incarnate for our salvation; and in the Holy Spirit who prophesied through the prophets about the economies, and the comings, and the birth from the Virgin, and the passion, and the resurrection from the dead, and the ascension into heaven of the body of the beloved Christ Jesus our Lord, and his coming from heaven in glory of the Father to sum up all things.[14]

The rule of truth, then, is the faith, the fundamentals of Christian belief. It is the basis of the creed, which developed later on in the history of the church.[15] This is the tradition which has been handed down from the apostles and is received in baptism: the fact that it is *received* almost as important as what is received – tradition is not something we make up, but something we accept. So Congar remarks illuminatingly at the beginning of the systematic section of his book on tradition:

> Tradition, taken here in its broadest meaning, is an example, the chief example, of the quite general law of man's dependence on, and obligation towards, his fellows. Elementary analysis of the concept of tradition, as a matter of transmission or delivery, shows moreover that *two* persons are implied, one to transmit and one to receive. This structure of human interdependence or brotherly mediation is a very important feature, of the human condition in the first place, and so also of the Christian condition. We belong to, and are part of, a world. Fecundation by another, recourse to another in order to fulfil oneself – this is a general law of life, at least in corporeal beings. We can bring about our own death, but we cannot give ourselves life. In the closed world of living creatures, species even live on one another, and the balance of the whole system is assured by the cooperation of the individual parts – 'it is a vast web, a seamless garment.' In the normal course of events we receive our faith from another; we cannot baptize ourselves. Thus, it is normal for persons to depend on one another in order to achieve their supernatural destiny. In our sharing in the divine life through another's mediation we may see a reflection of the divine life itself, which is the self-giving of one Person to another.[16]

Further dimensions of the notion of ecclesiastical tradition come out in the remarks St Basil makes in the course of his work *On the Holy Spirit*. Here he makes a distinction between *kerygma* and *dogma*: 'We have both dogmas and proclamations [*kerygmata*] preserved in the Church, proclamations in the written teaching, and dogmas which we have received from the tradition of the apostles and given to us in secret.'[17] But Basil is not appealing to some secret, 'whispered' tradition that has come down from the apostles: the sort of thing of which Irenaeus denied the very existence a couple of centuries earlier. The examples Basil gives of such unwritten traditions are all liturgical practices: the sign of the cross, prayer towards the East, the epiclesis at the eucharist, and indeed most of the rest of the eucharistic prayer, the blessing of water in baptism, of oil and so on. The secret tradition is not a message, but a practice, and the significance of such practice. We come back to the fact that Christianity is not a body of doctrine that can be specified in advance, but a way of life and all that this implies. Tradition is, as it were, the tacit dimension of the life of the Christian: what is proclaimed (for Basil, the *kerygmata*) is only part of it, and not really the most important part. This comes out if we realize the significance of Basil's appeal to tradition here. For Basil's appeal to tradition is his ultimate defence of the divinity of the Holy Spirit: a defence which, significantly, he cannot express wholly in words. He never in this work says explicitly that the Spirit is of one substance – *homoousios* – with the Father and the Son, for to write it down would be to make it public, make it a *kerygma* (and his reticence here is shared by the Creed accepted at the Second Ecumenical Council of Constantinople in 381). But the truths of *theologia* – in the strict Cappadocian sense, the doctrine of God as he is in himself; the doctrine of the trinity, therefore, which we attain when we recognize the divinity of the Holy Spirit – these truths are *dogmata*.[18] That means they are not truths that can be proclaimed, they are not 'objective' truths which could be appraised and understood outside the bosom of the church: rather they are part of the church's reflection on the mystery of her life with God.

This becomes clearer, perhaps, when we look at the arguments Basil uses in *On the Holy Spirit* to prove that the Spirit is God. These arguments all revolve around the Christian's experience of the life of grace, or as Basil would more naturally put it, *Life in the Spirit*. The life of the Christian is a participation in the life of God, and this cannot take place without the Spirit. The work of sanctification is the work of the Spirit:

> As for the union of the Spirit with the soul, he manifests his presence not by spatial approach (for how can one speak of space when thinking of the corporeal and the incorporeal?), but by the exclusion of passions which assail the soul from the love of the flesh and separate it from intimacy with God. To be cleansed therefore from this shame contracted by wickedness, and return to the beauty

of one's nature, and receive through purity one's pristine form in the royal image, thus is the only way one can approach the Paraclete. And he, like the sun reflected in a clear eye, shows you in himself the image of the Invisible; in the blessed contemplation of the Image, you will see the ineffable beauty of the Archetype.[19]

Basil then goes on to say that as a result souls become spiritual – diaphanous to the Spirit – and become themselves sources of spiritual illumination for other souls. What this means Basil sums up as 'prevision of the future, understanding of mysteries, comprehension of hidden things, the distribution of spiritual gifts, a heavenly life, fellowship with the angels in their praise, unceasing joy, rest in God, likeness to God, and the summit of their desires: they become God.'[20] For Basil all this is only possible in the Spirit. One of his ways of expressing this is to speak of the Spirit as intelligible light (*phos noeton*) in which the soul becomes mind or *nous*. As *nous* the soul can contemplate: in the Holy Spirit, intelligible light, it is enabled to contemplate the image of the Archetype, the Son of the Father. Even the angels can see nothing apart from the Holy Spirit, the light of the intelligible realm: for 'as in the night, if you remove the light from your house, your eyes will be blind, their powers inert, all you value indistinct, so that, through ignorance, gold and iron appear alike. So in the intelligible order it is impossible, apart from the Spirit, to lead a life conformed to the law.'[21] The same idea is being expressed when he says:

> Since through an illuminating power we reach forth to the beauty of the Image of the Invisible God, and through that come to the surpassing vision of the Archetype, this cannot take place apart from the presence of the Spirit of knowledge, who gives in himself to those who love the vision of truth the power to behold the Image, not doing this as an external act, but receiving us into Himself for this knowledge . . . as it is written, 'In thy light shall we see light', that is, in the illumination of the Spirit we shall see the true light, that lightens every man coming into the world.[22]

As the Spirit makes possible our participation in the divine life, so he himself must be divine. But this can hardly be stated, for the premise is only available to those who participate in the divine life. For others there is nothing to appeal to. And even for those who do know this participation in the divine life, it is difficult to state anything objectively and clearly about the Spirit, for he is not what we perceive, but that in virtue of which we perceive anything at all. We might put it like this: that it is difficult to say anything about the Spirit, for we are only in a position to say anything at all, when we are in that very place where the Spirit is. Here 'Truth is Subjectivity'.

What this seems to suggest is that ultimately the tradition of the church is the Spirit, that what is passed on from age to age in the bosom of the church is the Spirit, making us sons in the Son enabling us to call on the Father, and thus share in the communion of the trinity. Modern commentators have seen this implied in the words St John uses to record the death of Jesus: 'and gave up the ghost' (*paredoken to pneuma* – and passed on, or handed over, the Spirit: 19:30). Hoskyns comments:

> But it is very strange language. If it be assumed that the author intends his readers to suppose that the Beloved Disciple and Mary the Mother of Jesus remain standing beneath the cross, the words *He bowed his head* suggest that *He bowed His Head* towards them, and the words *He handed over the Spirit* are also directed to the faithful believers who stand below. This is no fantastic exegesis, since vv. 28–30 record the solemn fulfilment of vii. 37–9. The thirst of the believers is assuaged by the rivers of living water which flow from the belly of the Lord, the author having already noted that this referred to the giving of the Spirit.[23]

This exegesis is supported by Lightfoot[24] and is sympathetically considered by Barrett,[25] though it is interesting to note that it appears to be quite unknown in the Fathers.[26]

Understood like this, tradition is not another source of doctrine, or whatever, alongside scripture, but another way of speaking of the inner life of the church, that life in which the individual Christian is perfected in the image of God in which he was created. Speaking of it as tradition brings out the fact that it is received, that it is participated in, that it is more than the grasp that the individual has of his faith. To quote Congar again: 'Tradition involves not merely a recollection, but also a deepening of insight; it is preserved, not merely in the mind, but also in the "heart", which meditates lovingly on what it holds fast (cf. Luke 2:19, 57); it involves not merely a fidelity of memory, but also a fidelity of living, vital adherence.'[27]

Here we see the importance of liturgy for the realization, and continuity, of tradition, and thus why it is that when Basil appeals to a tradition that goes beyond scripture, he appeals to the liturgy. For it is, most fundamentally, in the celebration of the liturgy, and especially in the celebration of the eucharist that we realize and celebrate the mystery of Christ, that we share in and come to know the Son's offering himself to the Father in love and obedience. For the heart of the Christian faith is not something simply conceptual: it is a fact, or even better, an action – the action, the movement, of the Son sent into the world for our sakes to draw us back to the Father. And it is this movement that the liturgy, with its dramatic structure, echoes and repeats. As Dom Gregory Dix has finely said:

> There is but *one* coming, in the incarnation, in the Spirit, in the eucharist and in the judgement. And that is the 'coming' of 'One like unto the Son of Man' (who is 'the people of the saints of the Most High', i.e. Christ and the church)

to the Father. This is the end and meaning of human history, the bringing of man, the creature of time, to the Ancient of Days, in eternity. The same eternal fact can touch the process of history at more than one point.[28]

Liturgy is not something we 'make up', nor is it something that can be simply 'understood': it is something we participate in, not just as minds, but with all that we are – body and soul. Hence the importance in the liturgy of gestures and movement, of the sequence of the seasons, through which time itself is sanctified. The liturgy unfolds the varied significance of the mystery of Christ, and the fact that it cannot all be explained, the fact that much that we do, we do simply because we have always done it, conveys a rich sense of the unfathomableness of the Christian mystery. Basil undertakes to explain, or give a provisional explanation of, some of the ceremonies he has cited as belonging to the unwritten, the secret, tacit tradition of the church. 'It is for this reason that we all look to the East at the time of prayer, though few of us know that we thus look to our ancient homeland, Paradise, which God planted in Eden towards the East.' He gives several other explanations of the various practices of the church, but concludes, 'Even a whole day would not suffice for an explanation of the unwritten mysteries of the Church'.

The danger of attempting to reduce the liturgy to what can be understood in simple conceptual terms is one that has beset the West since at least the time of the Reformation, and it is a marked feature of much modern liturgical reform. It is a danger it has been one of the purposes of this chapter to warn against. What can be articulated, what can be understood, is only a part, if an important part. The life in which we share as we commit ourselves to the tradition of the church goes much deeper. At the Reformation the English church preserved a liturgy, preserved a sense of continuity with the past, and it is worthwhile in this context to recall Hooker's defence of the principle of the liturgy:

The end which is aimed at in setting down the outward form of all religious actions is the edification of the Church. Now men are edified, when either their understanding is taught somewhat whereof in such actions it behoveth all men to consider, or when their hearts are moved with any affection suitable thereunto; when their minds are in any sort stirred up unto that reverence, devotion, attention, and due regard, which in those cases seemeth requisite. Because therefore unto this purpose not only speech but sundry sensible means besides have always been thought necessary, and especially those means which being object to the eye, the liveliest and most apprehensive sense of all other have in that respect seemed the fittest to make a deep and a strong impression: for hence have risen not only a number of prayers, readings, questionings, exhortings, but even of visible signs also; which being used in performance of holy actions, are undoubtedly most effectual to open such matter, as men when they know and remember carefully, must needs be a great deal the better informed to what effect such duties serve. We must not think but that there is some ground of reason even in nature, whereby it cometh to pass that no nation under heaven either doth or ever did suffer public actions which are of weight, whether they be civil and temporal or else spiritual and sacred, to pass without some visible solemnity: the very strangeness whereof and difference from that which is common, doth cause popular eyes to observe and mark the same.

The things which so long experience of all ages hath confirmed and made profitable, let not us presume to condemn as follies and toys, because we sometimes know not the cause and reason of them. A wit disposed to scorn whatsoever it doth not conceive, might ask wherefore Abraham should say to his servant, 'Put thy hand under my thigh and swear:' was it not sufficient for his servant to shew the religion of an oath by naming the Lord God of heaven and earth, unless that strange ceremony were added?[29]

Hooker gives several other examples and concludes by quoting from Denys the Areopagite's *Ecclesiastical Hierarchy*: 'the sensible things which religion hath hallowed, are resemblances framed according to things spiritually understood, whereunto they serve as a hand to lead, and a way to direct.'

The importance of liturgy, then, for tradition is that by the very fact of its being performed, of its being the doing of something that others have done before us, of its being a matter of significant actions that suggest meaning rather than define it, it introduces us into a context, a realm of values, in which the significance of tradition can be seen. By the fact that it goes beyond speech, it impresses on us the importance of the inarticulate: and it is not without significance that inarticulateness about what is deeply important is characteristic of the child, whom we have to be like if we are to enter the kingdom of heaven.

This stress on inarticulateness can be developed in another way. In an essay called 'Tradition and Traditions', Vladimir Lossky suggested that one fruitful way of considering tradition is to think of it as silence. If scripture is the word, the voice, the utterance, then tradition is, in contrast, silence. Lossky quotes from St Ignatius of Antioch: 'He who possesses in truth the word of Jesus can hear even its silence', and remarks that the significance of this passage for the patristic understanding of tradition has not apparently been previously noted. Lossky develops this idea by speaking of a 'margin of silence' which belongs to the words of scripture and which cannot be picked up by the ears of those who are outside. He links this up with something Basil says in his *On the Holy Spirit*: 'There is also a form of silence, namely the obscurity used by the scriptures, which is intended in order to make it difficult to gain understanding of teachings, for the profit of readers.' This idea of an obscurity inherent in the scriptures, an obscurity that is penetrated only within the church, within the tradition of the church, is something we shall explore in more detail in the next chapter when we consider the notion of allegory.

218 ◈

Lossky also develops this idea from Ignatius by speaking of tradition as the *unique mode* of receiving the truth of revelation:

> We say specifically *unique mode* and not *uniform mode*, for to Tradition in its pure notion there belongs nothing formal. It does not impose on human consciousness formal guarantees of the truths of faith, but gives access to the discovery of their inner evidence. It is not the content of Revelation, but the light that reveals it; it is not the word, but the living breath which makes the words heard at the same time as the silence from which it came (cf. Ignatius of Antioch, *Magnesians* 8:2); it is not the Truth, but a communication of the Spirit of Truth, outside which the Truth cannot be received. 'No one can say "Jesus is Lord" except by the Holy Spirit' (1 Corinthians 12:3). The pure notion of Tradition can then be defined by saying that it is the life of the Holy Spirit in the Church, communicating to each member of the body of Christ the faculty of hearing, of receiving, of knowing the truth in the Light which belongs to it, and not according to the natural light of human reason.[30]

This recalls ideas I have already developed from Basil's consideration of tradition and the Holy Spirit. But Ignatius's words point us further in a slightly different direction. 'He who possesses in truth the word of Jesus can hear even its silence': the word for 'silence' here is *hesychia*, which is silence or *stillness*. Ignatius is talking about the stillness necessary for us to hear the words of Jesus: a stillness which implies both receptiveness and presence. We come back to a point I have repeatedly emphasized: that Jesus did not simply communicate a message. The apostles were those who had been *with* him, not simply those who knew what he said. Indeed there is something about the words of Jesus, even in the fourth gospel, that makes us feel that what is being communicated is deeper than mere words, deeper than any mere message. Hort puts it well: 'The power of the Life that dwelt in Christ comes forth in His words. There are hardly any precepts among them, nothing could be less like the edicts of a law-giver. Almost all are calm affirmations of truth, often sounding like repetition and like vagueness. Yet while the terms elude all efforts at definition the sense of each as a whole is seen to be unutterably precise as we study it.'[31] To hear Jesus, and not just his words, we have to stand within the tradition of the church; we have to put our trust in those to whom our Lord entrusted his mission, his sending. Part of the stillness that is needed for us to hear the words of Jesus is a sense of presence, and it is this that tradition conveys. We become Christians by becoming members of the church, by *trusting* our forefathers in the faith. If we cannot trust the church to have understood Jesus, then we have lost Jesus: and the resources of modern scholarship will not help us to find him.

Stillness, silence: which I suggested means both presence and receptiveness. Receptiveness, and attentiveness: and these are qualities deepened and realized in prayer. When Ignatius lays emphasis on the importance of 'hearing its silence', at least part of what he means is the importance of a kind of docile receptiveness, in contrast with the spirit which listens in order to put what is heard to its own uses. And this is something we need to cultivate, we need to learn. Again the liturgy provides an important context for this, as the words are repeated and brought again and again to our consciousness, and thus enabled to penetrate beneath our surface minds to our very heart. 'The Gospel in the heart': this is one of the ways in which Congar sums up the notion of tradition. 'The Gospel written in men's hearts goes far beyond the written text, despite the fact that what is written is itself, in a sense, inexhaustible. The Fathers were well aware of this.'[32] 'Written in the heart' meaning dwelt on, pondered on – of which Mary's 'pondering in her heart' is the profoundest example – and expressed not just in the attaining of some conceptual enlightenment, but in what we do. 'Not to *hear* the word', as St Gregory the Great puts it, 'is not to put it into practice in one's life.' Or one could simply continue our quotation from St Ignatius: 'He who possesses in truth the word of Jesus can hear even its silence, that he may be perfect, that he may do through what he speaks and know through that of which he is silent.'

The notion of tradition as silence is so witnessed to in another way in the church's life. If we think of Jesus's communicating by his presence and by his words, what we are pointing to is expressed by the importance and power of the *living voice*. Within the church we learn the Christian faith from particular individuals, it is not something we can learn from books. Similarly we learn how to pray from others. Here we meet the notion of the spiritual director as an organ of the tradition: Clement of Alexandria's *gnostic*, the spiritual fathers of the Eastern tradition, and especially of the desert tradition, the *startsi* of the Russian tradition. Here what is important is the relation of the disciple to his master, to the voice of his master. Men visited a Desert Father to 'ask for a word'. These words can be, and were, collected: but the heart of the experience was the word of a holy man spoken to a particular person in a particular context. It is interesting to note that this tradition is primarily concerned with love, and prayer, what one might call 'undogmatic' matters, and yet it was representatives of this tradition of seemingly undogmatic piety who played an important role in the defence of the church dogmatic tradition in the fourth century and thereafter. The living voice of the master, the one who through prayer and self-discipline has come to know, that is, come to communion with the heart of the faith, has immediacy and directness, and incarnates the fundamental experience of encounter with the living Lord. Jerome remarked that 'the effect of the living voice has some strange and hidden power; it has greater resonance when coming direct from the mouth of the master to the ear of the disciple.'[33]

If we see tradition as the life of the Holy Spirit in the church, then we must also see it as something that brings us into the freedom that the Spirit confers, the 'boldness' (*parresia*) that enables us to stand in the divine presence and speak with simplicity of what is there made known. It is in some such way that we should see the Fathers: as those who spoke with such *parresia* that their words have the immediacy of direct witness. From such a point of view the age of the Fathers is not past, though certainly the archetypal 'patristic' voice is something we recognize in those who formed the fundamental dogmatic tradition of the church.

Congar puts it thus: 'When we see the Fathers in this way, as those who have formed the milieu of the Church's historical growth ... we find that they are unanimous, we are at the heart of the real consensus. We have seen that Tradition is for a Christian almost what the educational milieu is for man in general; the child needs to form its own conclusions in a milieu which provides him with security; it is fundamentally the role of the consensus of the Fathers to provide such an element in the Church.'[34] Such openness to the Spirit, issuing in freedom and *parresia*, is not won without effort: the Fathers were saints, they were men of prayer. Again to quote Congar: 'Their work was blended with prayer, fasting, penitential exercises and the life of divine union. This gives to many of their writings a tone which puts them among "the writings of an eye-witness about the country of his birth"'.[35] And so we find Hort saying: 'the moment we study the greater theologians who have done more than reflect or even systematize current beliefs, we find the harmony of contemporary assumptions broken, and we often find also these isolated but not isolating voices to reflect the inarticulate feelings of the simply devout who are not theologians.'[36]

We make contact again with an inarticulate living of the mystery, the tacit dimension, which is the heart of tradition, and from which theology must spring if it is to be faithful to the truth it is seeking to express. For the truth that lies at the heart of theology is not something there to be discovered, but something, or rather someone, to whom we must surrender. The mystery of faith is not ultimately something that invites our questioning, but something that questions us.

Notes

1 In his *Holy Writ* or *Holy Church* (London: Burns and Oates, 1959).
2 Yves M.-J. Congar, *Tradition and Traditions* (London: Burns and Oates, 1966), part 1.
3 Richard Hooker, *Of the Laws of Ecclesiastical Polity*, IV.i.3, ed. J. Keble, 3rd edn (Oxford: Clarendon Press, 1845), p. 419.
4 W. Jaeger, *Paideia: The Ideals of Greek Culture* (Oxford: Blackwell, 1954).
5 *Enneads*, II.ix.15, tr. S. MacKenna, revd edn (London: Faber, 1969), pp. 147–8.
6 H.-I. Marrou, *Saint Augustin et la fin de la culture antique* (Paris: E. de Broccard, 4th edn, 1958), section III, especially p. 332, and note A, pp. 549–60.

7   *On Christian Doctrine: Prologue* 3, tr. D. W. Robertson (New York: Bobbs-Merrill, 1958), p. 4.

8   Ibid., *Prologue*, 6 (Robertson, p. 6).

9   T. Haecker, *Vergil, Vater des Abendlandes* (Munich: Hegner, 5th edn, 1947), p. 110.

10   *Tradition and Traditions*, p. 67.

11   *I Clement*, 42, pp. 1–2.

12   *Adversus Haereses*, IV.xxxiii.8, ed. W. W. Harvey, vol. II (Cambridge: Cambridge University Press, 1857), pp. 262–3.

13   Ibid., I.x.4 (Harvey, I, pp. 87–8).

14   Ibid., I.x.1 (Harvey, I, pp. 90–1).

15   See J. N. D. Kelly, *Early Christian Creeds* (London: Longman, 3rd edn, 1972) and R. P. C. Hanson, *Tradition in the Early Church* (London: SCM Press, 1962).

16   *Tradition and Traditions*, pp. 240–1.

17   *On the Holy Spirit*, XXVII.66, ed. C. F. H. Johnston (Oxford: Clarendon Press, 1892), pp. 127–8.

18   Ibid., XX.51 (Johnston, p. 102).

19   Ibid., IX.23 (Johnston, p. 53).

20   Ibid. (Johnston, pp. 53–4).

21   Ibid., XVI.38 (Johnston, p. 82).

22   Ibid., XVIII.47 (Johnston, pp. 94–5).

23   E. C. Hoskyns and F. N. Davey, *The Fourth Gospel* (London: Faber, 1940), p. 633.

24   R. H. Lightfoot, *St. John's Gospel* (Oxford: Clarendon Press, 1956), p. 319.

25   C. K. Barrett, *The Gospel According to St. John* (London: SPCK, 2nd revd edn, 1978), p. 554.

26   M. F. Wiles, *The Spiritual Gospel* (Cambridge: Cambridge University Press, 1960), p. 67.

27   *Tradition and Traditions*, p. 15.

28   *The Shape of Liturgy* (Westminster: Dacre, 1945), pp. 262–3.

29   *Ecclesiastical Polity*, IV.i.3 (Keble, pp. 418–19).

30   *In the Image and Likeness of God* (London: Mowbray, 1975), pp. 151–2.

31   F. J. A. Hort, *The Way, The Truth, The Life* (London: Macmillan, 1897), p. 205.

32   *Tradition and Traditions*, p. 348.

33   *Epistle* 53, quoted in Congar, *Tradition and Traditions*, p. 368.

34   Ibid., p. 400.

35   Ibid., p. 449, quoting Ivan Kireevsky.

36   *The Way, The Truth, The Life*, p. 186.

10

Self-Critical Cultures and Divine Transcendence

Kathryn Tanner

This selection is a chapter from *The Politics of God: Christian Theologies and Social Justice*. In the course of an argument on the relation of politics and Christian belief, the purpose of this chapter is to argue for the reality of divine transcendence as an intrasystematic key to self-critical religious belief.

I approach the question of Christian beliefs most supportive of critique of the status quo by using the socio–cultural perspective on belief that I introduced earlier. This question takes a particular form when expressed in terms of that perspective. I ask here whether, and if so how, Christian beliefs are productive of what I call self–critical cultures.

As I have said, Christians are participants in socio–cultural practices as the holders of Christian beliefs. They are inevitably involved in institutionalized forms of social interactions and the circulation of beliefs within them. I now ask whether those social and cultural practices in which Christians participate are likely to take a self-critical shape, to turn a critical eye against themselves, to the extent they are influenced by Christian beliefs. Fundamentally, I am trying to determine whether and in what manner Christian beliefs are able to play a role in socio–cultural practices in which established beliefs and social relations are habitually objects of possible criticism. In short, are Christian beliefs able to foster self-critical cultures? If they are, which Christian beliefs might play a crucial part?

These questions about Christian belief presuppose a positive answer to a more general question: is it possible for the beliefs of any culture to encourage critical reflection on that culture itself and the social relations of which those beliefs are a part? I argue on general socio-cultural grounds in the first section of this chapter that self-critical cultures are indeed possible. Although some understandings of the way culture works may discourage recognition of the fact, critical reflection on its own practices is difficult for any society to rule out entirely. Cultures may differ, however, in the resources they present for positively encouraging critical reflection. To make this point, I envision in the second section of this chapter two possible extremes: cultures where established practices are altered almost entirely by purposeful and deliberative means, and cultures where established practices are almost never altered in that way. In the former type of culture, established practices are not merely changed and contested; a society institutionalizes its own means for the purposeful criticism of such practices. In this type of culture, I argue in the third section, a capacity for critical self-reflection is created by a structure of belief that encourages a 'view from a distance' on a society's own forms of life. I suggest in the fourth section that this structure of belief may be found in a form of religious culture in which a belief in divine transcendence figures centrally. By this rather circuitous route I establish a resource in religious belief for a culture critical of its own beliefs and of the institutionalized social relations in which it is implicated. The ambiguities of belief in divine transcendence as a resource for self-critical cultures, which I develop in the closing section of the chapter, point to chapter 3. There I discuss what belief in divine transcendence means and how it may be developed *vis-à-vis* other beliefs in a Christian religious context, if such ambiguities are to be resolved.

The Possibility of Self-Critical Cultures

Two understandings of culture exclude the possibility of self-critical cultures. According to one, cultures form homogeneous, monolithic and organically interconnected wholes. They do not allow therefore for any diversity of opinion or contest over the fundamental terms according to which social interactions proceed. Nor do they allow any breathing room for radically innovative ideas. According to the second, commonly held beliefs, values and attitudes support established social practices in some fixed and static way. When beliefs support established social practices, they perform only that function, never a critical one. The support offered is never a focus for contest. Finally, practices that gain such support must be monotonously reproduced thereby.

These two understandings of culture are often, indeed, found together.[1] Both take at face value an ideology legitimating the status quo in the cultures they study: 'this is the only way to do things, given the way the world is, and there is no other way of thinking about it'. Both tend to justify such claims by an inflated notion of the cultural uniformity required for social order: social order is not possible without a consensus in beliefs, norms and values; social order is not possible unless uncontestable interconnections exist between social practices and commonly held beliefs, values and norms. Both ignore, therefore, the importance of other modes of social control that are not mediated by beliefs or norms – for example, coercion and the threat of force, a lack of other options, the lure of monetary and status benefits for compliance, isolation from others in similar circumstances, sheer physical exhaustion among an exploited work force. Both of these views fail to look for the cultural diversity and political contest surrounding beliefs, norms and social practices that might otherwise be obvious to historical investigation unbiased by prior expectations of cultural uniformity. They occlude the way in which patterns of social relations and beliefs are constantly susceptible to construction and reconstruction in ongoing processes of social and cultural interaction.

I am not denying here that social order requires shared background beliefs that are taken for granted by all parties involved, background beliefs that are not, therefore, subject to persistent renegotiation. No co-ordinated action of any sort among human beings is possible without some commonality of belief establishing what one can expect from others. Institutionalized social relations cannot operate without being interwoven with some pattern of belief distinguishing the true from the false, the credible from the incredible, the real from the unreal. The constituents of such background beliefs may, however, vary from interaction to interaction. The requirement of some background of beliefs does not require the same body of them to reappear each time. Any belief might be subject to renegotiation or contest (given the right circumstances) since all of them are the potentially temporary precipitates of interactions that are ongoing. A background of taken-for-granted beliefs is a presupposition for any conflict to take place regarding others, but in such conflicts it is possible for parts of an existing background of beliefs to be taken down bit by bit. Indeed, such a background was initially constructed piece by piece in negotiations over good sense and meaningful, credible belief. Background beliefs, which are the fallout, the settling out, of processes of interaction in the past, can be shaken up again, so to speak, since the processes that produced them continue. In this way the patterns of social relations that bank on a particular background of taken-for-granted beliefs can themselves be renegotiated and contested.[2]

If this is the way background beliefs are constructed and reconstructed, they are liable to provide quite a bit of room for discursive manoeuvre. As the precipitates of contestation, beliefs with a prima facie plausibility are likely, first of all, to be shadowed by disqualified and illegitimate ones. They do not have the cultural field all to themselves. Alternative beliefs, which have been defeated and contained by some sort of charge of illegitimacy, are rarely forced entirely out of circulation in a way that would prevent their resurgence as dangerous memories informing present possibilities or future hopes. Moreover, every belief with a prima facie plausibility inevitably produces a vision of what it logically excludes – a photographic negative of itself on the level of belief. Thus even if the losers of every cultural contest are driven from the field, every taken-for-granted belief is still susceptible to logical reversal. A platform for contesting the status quo can be formed by simply denying the beliefs at issue or reversing the way they assign value to things.[3]

Second, because they are the result of contestation, beliefs with a prima facie plausibility are unlikely to be entirely compatible with one another or with established social practices. Gaps in the coherence of background beliefs prevent them from exercising an all-determining influence over discourse. Ill-defined longings that run contrary to socially approved forms of interrelations can come to the surface in such gaps. Moreover, background beliefs in such a situation can simply be played off against one another. For example, a view of women as wives and mothers might conflict with a view of women as autonomous individuals. The one view can be used to criticize the other and the practices it informs. Or background beliefs can come into conflict directly with taken-for-granted social practices. Thus beliefs about liberty, which were established in contests between American colonialists and England, might come to sit uneasily next to US institutions based upon slavery and provide grounds thereby for their ultimate criticism.[4]

Finally, for all the reasons adduced in the last chapter, beliefs that support certain social practices can be uncoupled from them – given new twists of meaning, aligned differently with others, granted a new practical force when employed in different circumstances.

At all these different junctures taken-for-granted beliefs and social practices can become objects of critical reflection. Rather than being presuppositions for disputes about other matters, taken-for-granted beliefs or social relations become at all these different sites the focus themselves of explicit contention. They become matters requiring the support of reasons, and matters susceptible of criticism.

I have not yet established the possibility of genuinely self-critical cultures by these means, however. The ongoing construction and reconstruction of accepted beliefs and social practices, and the kind of socio-cultural disorder that is likely to be their result, make possible sites where the sort of critical reflection I seek can occur. Avenues for critical reflection on established beliefs and social practices are available at those points. But what actually prompts critical reflection to be pursued there? What, if anything, positively encourages critical reflection at such junctures? I have not yet shown that established beliefs themselves do any work of that sort. On the basis of what I have said so far, it appears instead that critical reflection on taken-for-granted beliefs and practices is the result of different beliefs (and practices) working at cross-purposes with each other. This sort of process with this sort of outcome does not appear to be one that any established belief (or body of beliefs) itself directs. If that appearance is correct, then established beliefs do not turn a critical eye on themselves and the social practices in which they are implicated. One belief (or body of beliefs), and the form of social relations with which it is associated, is being criticized by others.

One might try to argue that the sort of reflexivity I am after is impossible. A culture cannot turn back against itself and the social relations it informs by raising fundamental critical questions. The taken-for-granted beliefs of a culture are presumed in any arguments about truth, meaningfulness and propriety. Those beliefs are the prerequisites for such arguments, the basis or standard against which such arguments proceed. As such, they cannot make themselves the objects of the same sort of critical scrutiny. The same beliefs cannot be the background beliefs establishing the lines along which critical reflection proceeds and be objects of that critical reflection at the same time. One can argue on similar grounds that when established beliefs support the plausibility of established practices those beliefs cannot also encourage criticism of them.

I say these arguments have similar grounds because they both pass off a form argument for a substantive one. They argue from circumstances that have to hold everywhere – reflective criticism must always have background beliefs, established social relations must always seek intelligibility in terms of established beliefs – in order to beg the question about the specific shapes that beliefs and social relations can assume. Such inferences are fallacious because from the start everything depends on the particular beliefs or social relations at issue. Thus the ubiquitous circumstance of taken-for-granted beliefs gives one no reason to think that such background beliefs cannot be of a sort to encourage critical reflection on the beliefs that a society takes for granted. For example, beliefs that were taken for granted in the Enlightenment were of that sort. Similarly, the ubiquitous fact that established social practices tend to be informed by taken-for-granted beliefs gives one no reason to think that particular beliefs of that sort cannot promote social practices that are to be constructed and reconstructed as much as possible by public wrangling. Democratically run governments are supposed to be something like that; and they are quite obviously informed, for example, in a US context, by all sorts of taken-for-granted beliefs.

I assume, then, that genuinely self-critical cultures are possible. Socially accepted beliefs can inform patterns of inquiry and social relation that proceed along self-critical lines. They can promote a form of society with established channels for criticizing what a society takes for granted. Whether socially accepted beliefs do so depends on the particular shape they take. The kind of pattern of socio-cultural interactions that established beliefs promote depends on the nature of the established beliefs at issue. Cultures made up of different sorts of belief are likely to differ, then, in the capacities that they exhibit for self-criticism.

The idea of culture-specific resources for promoting self-criticism can be contested, however, on two grounds. First, one can claim that criticism of the status quo is not propelled by cultural resources at all. The impulse for such criticism comes from outside culture. It has its source in bodily based desires or in a capacity to transcend any given situation in one's imagination that is everyone's simply as a human being. The sort of socio-cultural disorder mentioned previously simply gives such desires and imaginative longings a place to enter. Criticism of the status quo occurs in places where established forms of socio-cultural relation suffer the intrusion of desires and longings out of keeping with them.

Claims of this sort make an indefensibly strong separation, however, between the cultural and the natural (or the culturally unformed). All sorts of supposedly natural endowments turn out in fact to be culturally shaped.[5] The very distinction between the natural and the cultural is the product of particular times and places.[6] How the line is drawn between the natural and the cultural also varies in the same way; cultures differ in what they believe to be susceptible of human influence.[7]

Second, one could claim that such resources are constitutive features of *all* cultures.[8] Though this does not appear to be empirically the case, one could insist none the less that it is so. One could argue that the most basic features of cultural life (e.g. the proposing of beliefs about what is the case) bring along the necessary cultural resources, even if they remain implicit and underdeveloped. One could also argue that all cultures are on the way toward making such resources explicit if they are not so now. This first line of argument can be convicted, however, of simply reading into the analysis the particular cultural assumptions of the interpreter. The second line of argument is susceptible to the charge of a question-begging teleology: an 'all roads lead to Rome' argument like this does not prove the universality of resources for critical reflection; it gets off the ground only by assuming it.[9]

With these objections out of the way, the crucial task that remains is to delineate the cultural differences at issue. What do cultures look like when they foster critical reflection on their own practices? What do they look like when they do not? How are the belief structures in the two cases different? Only with this information in hand can one talk about how religious beliefs might figure in the process.

Two Types of Culture

I begin by imagining cultures at two extremes: customary cultures at the one end; reflective cultures at the other. At one extreme the transformations that a society undergoes happen by way of unreflective habits. At the other, transformations are promoted by reflection on principles or standards of procedure, and in that way produce a self-critical culture.[10]

What such a contrast means will become clear as I proceed, but to avoid misunderstandings at the start I should say that in distinguishing between types of cultures on these grounds I am not suggesting that a reflective culture changes while a customary culture does not. I am not suggesting that the former is innovative while the latter is not. Change and innovation in cultural formations are inevitable.[11] All that I have said so far about the messy and unruly features of culture points to that fact. But even if one considers distinct cultures as fairly homogeneous and well-defined bodies of more or less logically coherent beliefs, cultural understandings are still always liable to transformation. In order for a cultural formation to sustain itself over time, it must be reproduced in ongoing interactions that put it at risk.[12]

Engaging the background beliefs of a culture in new physical circumstances presents one sort of risk. Circumstances may fail to meet culturally conditioned expectations by providing cases of beings that are anomalous with respect to taken-for-granted categories (e.g. androgynes when categories of sexual difference are limited to male and female) or happenings that are unintelligible on existing cosmological schemes (e.g. as Clifford Geertz reports, the enormous, fast-growing mushrooms that prompted the cultural consternation of the Javanese).[13]

The human parties in the interpersonal relations that are necessary if cultural understandings are to be sustained present another inevitable source of risk. Even if a society moves from one cultural consensus to another, differences in the understanding of a society's cultural reserves by participants in such interactions are liable to lead to the renegotiation of those reserves. For example, different understandings of loyalty to country on the part of doves and hawks during the Vietnam War effected a renegotiation of the meaning of patriotism in contemporary American culture: loyalty to country does not mean now quite what it did before. The possibility of cultural revision on the basis of such clashes is at its height when the cultural understandings of the people involved have been shaped in different circumstances and in relative isolation from one another – cases that verge therefore on actual interchange between distinct cultures.

This extreme case of intercultural differences makes a general point about the essential revivability of any distinct culture. In the same way that knowing one language provides the basis for an ever-expanding linguistic horizon in interchanges with foreign-language speakers, any distinct culture forms an essentially expandable horizon of basic categories and assumptions. Cultures are essentially scenes of mediation in which the relatively different may be made intelligible by assimilation to prior cultural understandings but not without some alteration of those very understandings themselves.[14] For instance, the extended kinship structures of so-called traditional societies can be assimilated to the contemporary Western notion of a nuclear family but not without altering the Western notion of what family is all about.

To sum up: the reproduction or maintenance of any culture is liable to be a matter of its transformation, and transformations of culture are the means by which cultures may be extended and therefore sustained. The same cultural processes may be called, then, ones of transformative reproduction or, with little difference, reproductive transformation. It is important for my present purposes to see that this reproduction can occur in either of two ways: in a customary fashion, by way of unreflective habit, or via reflective deliberation.

When culture is reproduced in a customary fashion, its transmission is a matter of spontaneous flexibility and automatic adaptation to circumstances. Habits always exist in the flux of adjustment to immediate practical needs. 'Custom', as Michael Oakeshott observes, 'is always adaptable and susceptible to the *nuance* of the situation', making it 'capable of change as well as local variation'. 'Nothing is more continuously invaded by change' than habit or custom.[15]

When culture is reproduced by deliberate application of some principle or standard of procedure, one would expect transmission of it to hold greater prospects for restraint on invention. An objectified rule or norm has some sort of general status; it is not embedded in specific contexts. One might expect a single norm of that sort to be applicable therefore to many different contexts, and to enforce thereby a fairly rigid conformity to a single way of thinking and acting. One would think that, at the minimum, reproduction of culture via principles or standards would vary little with circumstance.

These anticipations are not wholly warranted, however. No matter how rule governed a course of action and belief, the application of those rules, their interpretation and use in particular circumstances, cannot be similarly rule bound. The reproduction of culture via deliberation requires invention to meet the needs of varying circumstances.[16] As Thomas McCarthy makes the point: following social rules calls for 'not mere conformity but competent practical reasoning to deal with ... contingencies. ... There is always an element of the discretionary, elaborative and ad hoc about how we apply rules and schemes, for they do not define their own applications'.[17] Without such judgemental leeway, rules are too rigid and oversimplified to deal effectively with the complexity of actual social interactions.

This inventiveness in the deliberative reproduction of culture may not match in degree the flexibility of habitual or customary reproduction. But the most significant difference with customary reproduction is that deliberative reproduction makes possible a different attitude toward the inevitable transformation of culture and a different sort of change. Elaborating upon such differences in the character and understanding of change enables one to distinguish two types of culture – deliberative and customary – in the matter of their respective capacities for socio-cultural critique. Cultures marked by deliberative reproduction are not simply self-transformative; they are self-critical.

It is obviously a caricature to draw in this way a topological contrast between sorts of culture on the basis of their respective modes of reproduction. Any culture must include both, for two reasons. First, no culture could sustain itself over time entirely or even mainly by the conscious application of rule or principle. Established courses of action and belief must be primarily habitual; and action and belief become habitual through processes of primary socialization in which training figures prominently. Explicit rules, generalized standards or principles, must be employed for the most part in a regulative rather than a constitutive capacity. That is, rather than being the primary mode of *generating* conduct of a certain sort, they alter, direct or otherwise shape forms of action and belief that are already habitual. They enter on the scene of reproduction as secondary means of control, particularly in times of crisis, when the risks of cultural reproduction discussed become a reality. Second, it is hard to imagine a society without the reflective capacities at least to formulate norms or standards that sum up and render explicit the forms of action and belief a society judges best. There is a point, nevertheless, to working out the case of unmixed extremes. The clarity of the contrast is a useful heuristic tool in the evaluation of particulars – in the present case, ultimately, the evaluation of the function of Christian beliefs in supporting or undermining established socio-political practices.

What are these differences in the character and understanding of cultural change that distinguish deliberative from customary cultures? First one would expect changes of culture in customarily reproduced cultural contexts to be relatively imperceptible. Customary cultures may have greater flexibility, but the more extreme such flexibility becomes the less likely it is to be recognized by participants. There is nothing fixed against which change might be noted.[18] For example, the past is retained in customary forms of cultural reproduction only in the shape of the present exercise of the same habits. As a result, it is very difficult to see that what happens in the present is different from what occurred in the past.

Second, because change is imperceptible, there is the presumption of continuity, even of stasis, for socio-cultural formations: 'we believe what we have always believed'; 'we do what we have always done'. Present performance is authorized by this presumption of past performance: if something happens, that is grounds enough for assuming that it has happened before, and if it has happened before it must be proper now.[19] What is right is what is done, and what is done varies with the occasion in the course of the enforced sort of improvisation found in habitually reproduced forms of culture.[20]

Proper behaviours may be objectified and standardized in the form of stories about ancestors or heroes or gods. In that case, present behaviour is authorized not merely, or not at all, as a simple transmission of the past but as its veritable re-creation or reinstitution. The present is not just the continuation of what has gone before, but its identical reproduction.[21] The past is not lost in an immemorial process of transmission so that the present can be justified only by the fact of that transmission. A tradition of inheritance has instead a specifiable origin.

But this objectification of a standard for otherwise unreflective habits merely serves as an ideology of stasis. No more than an unspecifiable past does it foster a recognition of change, of distance. Why not? It is true that rules of conduct are no longer merely embedded in a context as unreflective habits; they have been objectified in the sense that they have been raised out of a course of conduct in the form of stories that may be told apart from that conduct. Rules for conduct are not, however, generalized or made more abstract when they take the form of stories. Stories remain as particular as the course of conduct from which they arise. Abstracted from these contexts, they nevertheless continue therefore to mirror them. If storied cultures are themselves reproduced customarily – that is, if the stories exist only as they are transmitted by unreflective habit – they do not have the fixity in any case to ensure a difference between present practice and what they recount. Stories and conduct tend to adjust together to situations, as any customarily reproduced form of belief or conduct is wont to do.

Third, therefore, cultures that are customarily reproduced tend to be characterized in the main by adjustment to, rather than criticism of present practices. If the past exists only in its retelling in the present, it can provide no critical edge on present practice. Thus any norm or standard abstracted from the context of conduct – be it in the form of a specified past or a reputedly timeless origin – will lack the capacity to do more than reproduce the shape of present practice. It will retain the particularity and concreteness of those contexts and vary with them as a result of its own customary form of transmission.

Direct opposition to customarily reproduced cultures on the part of individuals is also difficult for a number of reasons. First, it is easy for genuinely subversive or grossly non-standard behaviour to be erased in customarily reproduced cultures. These behaviours are simply swallowed up by the continued practice of the group and forgotten. Subversion has no platform with any degree of permanence.[22] Second, it is hard for any form of conduct or belief to be deviant in a way that would jeopardize the character of a culture that is customarily reproduced. The boundaries of customarily reproduced cultures are so fluid that it would be relatively difficult even to come up with forms of behaviour and belief that definitely cross over the line of normalcy. Therefore, it is not just that subversion lacks a platform with any permanence. It is hard to be an outsider and so take the stance of a cultural critic. Customarily reproduced cultures are radically assimilative and incorporative. Even the beliefs and behaviours of another culture – beliefs and behaviours established and maintained in a hitherto separate sphere of co-ordinated action – are not immune. Habitually grounded behaviours and beliefs are marked by an eclectic syncretism. They have the apparent capacity to invent variations appropriate to any occasion, including those of encounter with the culturally strange.[23]

Encounters with what is genuinely strange or deviant may involve, however, the alteration of a cultural formation – something more like actual change than the mere development of situational variants (more like the case of Native Americans adopting European dress than their changing the sort of plumage used in traditional costumes with the near extinction of American eagles). But such change will be circumscribed. It is unlikely to signal drastic or system-wide revision. It is unlikely to prompt any re-evaluation, therefore, of cultural practices as a whole or the fundamental principles of their performance. What revision there is will tend to be ad hoc and situation-specific in keeping with the ad hoc, situation-specific character of habitually grounded cultural reproduction. Adjustments of an established belief or practice in order to cope with new circumstances will be favoured over wholesale rejection of a belief or practice. When a belief or practice is scrapped, it is unlikely that it will take many others with it. Cultures of this sort are highly tolerant of theoretical inconsistency, since they are sustained through habits or unreflective dispositions. Consistency is not a requirement for cultural maintenance. Moreover, when beliefs are embedded in context and habitually sustained, it is difficult for participants to set them side by side in a way that would make contradictions among them apparent. If beliefs and behaviours are maintained primarily by habit, it is hard for participants to recognize them as any kind of system; it is hard to consider them all together as a whole, and therefore partial alterations of beliefs or actions are unlikely to spread to others.[24]

Even though change in such cultures will tend therefore to be gradual rather than dramatic, a matter of partial adjustments rather than radical revolutions, customarily reproduced cultures are nevertheless susceptible to a certain kind of extreme change: change in the form of an overall degeneration. Because they proceed in a quasi-automatic or spontaneous fashion and case by case, simply as circumstances might dictate, alterations of customarily reproduced cultures are inclined to be thoroughly undirected. The result may not just be theoretical inconsistency; it may be practical incoherence. Differences in habitual response may eventually prohibit co-ordinated action altogether. Furthermore, the lack of clear boundaries permits the fluidity of syncretistic assimilation on the part of customarily reproduced cultures and allows for their eventual demise via a loss of identity. It may be by progressive increments, but sooner or later, especially in encounters with other cultures, a habitually reproduced culture is liable to lose its distinctiveness as a particular cultural formation.[25]

The attitude toward cultural transformation and the form change takes in deliberately reproduced cultures are the obverse of those in customarily produced ones. First, transformations in belief and action tend to be perceptible since there is something relatively unchanging against which to measure them – a norm for belief and action referenced apart from the changing circumstances of habitual belief and action. For example, the character of the action at a particular time can be formulated in a relatively fixed way that saves it from the oblivion of the past. Past action in that way becomes a standard or bench-mark against which present change can be charted.

Second, along with a perception of change comes a possible criticism of it. Standards in a more strictly normative sense, standards of propriety, whether they be identified with the past or with generalized rules for proceeding or with temporal ideals, may have their origin in the flux of habitual performance, but once abstracted from it, they gain a certain distance on it. What is proper will not tend to vary in sync with what is done, since standards of proper practice will not exist merely in the form of customary behaviours. Moreover, such standards are not likely simply to mirror the particulars of established practice since they are in some way more general or abstract than those particulars.

Third, because of the existence of relatively fixed, generalized standards, change does not proceed automatically, apart from conscious reflection upon it. Cultural changes are more likely to be deliberately instituted or to require, after the fact, some sort of justification. Changes in culturally acceptable practices are liable to require either the deliberate reform of existing standards for behaviour (i.e. change in their formulation or interpretation) or some principled reason for their inapplicability in present circumstances.

It is because changes in practice require principled reflection on established standards that deliberately reproduced cultures are more resistant to change than customarily reproduced ones. This resistance does not spell, however, any kind of cultural entrapment. Unlike customarily reproduced ones, deliberately reproduced cultures are not encased within the ongoing flux of cultural formations since they do not automatically validate the changes that inevitably mark all efforts to sustain cultures over time. Moreover, when cultural change is deliberately instituted change is likely to be both fairly radical and contagious for the following reasons.

First, since cultural reproduction proceeds by way of reflection rather than by habit, response to changing circumstances will naturally tend to be less exclusively ad hoc or situation specific. Mere adjustments in established beliefs or practices to meet the needs of new circumstances are liable to be replaced, therefore, by substantive revisions or outright rejections of those beliefs and practices. Second, deliberately reproduced cultures do not have the fluidity of customarily reproduced cultures with which to tolerate situational variants by mere addition, by syncretistic incorporation. Inclusion of the different is more likely to require amendments or deletions of beliefs in the interest of consistency. Theoretical consistency becomes a requirement of co-ordinated action, of socio-cultural maintenance, when individuals determine what to do and evaluate what they have done by reflective means. Inconsistency can be perceived because principles of action and belief can be set side by side once they have been abstracted from the particular contexts they inform. In general, reflection upon habitual practices in the attempt to formulate the principles by which they abide is a step-by-step process of objectifying one's own culture. A culture of taken-for-granted beliefs becomes in this way an object of deliberation and possible change. Spontaneous flexibility is sacrificed for the potential of principled self-criticism. The gradual transformations of habitual practices make way for possible revolution. The background beliefs these practical routines presuppose become questionable.

Structural Features of the Two Types

These differences in the character and understanding of change on the part of deliberative and customary cultures can be correlated with basic differences in the structural organization of their respective belief systems. These different structural properties are the prerequisites, the supportive cultural tissue for self-reflective or customary forms of change respectively.[26] The crucial discrimination here – what distinguishes the structural properties of the one from the other – is the resources they represent for distancing a culture from its own established socio-cultural practices, from the routinized or habitual beliefs and forms of social relation with which it is involved. The self-criticism of deliberative cultures requires such distance. The self-transformative character of customary ones does without it.

I do not suppose that differences in such resources of distantiation are merely cultural. They also tend to presuppose certain differences of socio-economic circumstance. I cannot make much of a case for it here, but the structural distinctions in the organization of belief that I will mention can be tied to what social scientists call social differentiation and to the cultural differentiation attendant upon it. The structural distinctions in the organization of belief systems that I examine are a response to the relative cultural chaos that follows upon social differentiation.

Social differentiation means that (1) different aspects of social activities (e.g. familial, economic, military, governmental) are localized in different networks of social interaction; (2) a society is stratified into economic classes or prestige groups; and (3) occupations are specialized according to a highly refined division of labour. When these forms of social differentiation occur, the distribution of socially constructed and maintained knowledge is markedly uneven. That is, people in different social locations do not believe the same things or hold the same beliefs in the same way – the cultural reserves of a society are differentiated. The structural distinctions within belief systems that I discuss work to make this sort of cultural differentiation intelligible and restore intellectual order.[27]

The first structural feature of belief systems that provides a resource of distantiation involves a discrimination among three world concepts – external reality, the social order and personal subjectivity – and a separation of their respective validity spheres.[28] Cultures that are simply self-transformative tend to mix natural and social categories, in keeping with the taken-for-granted self-evidence of habitual practices. The unquestioned inevitability of social proceedings are to be accepted as one accepts the givens of the natural environment. The human order is naturalized; nature is anthropomorphized. Nature and society are more or less undifferentiated orders within a single ontological sphere. When natural and social worlds are distinguished, the latter loses its self-evidence as a natural given. The social order is de-reified, to use Peter Berger's term.[29] Social arrangements can be viewed as specifically human constructions that are not ingrained in the very nature of things. The alteration and manipulation of these arrangements become thereby a theoretically possible aim of action.

Similarly, in order for rebellious eccentricity not to be ruled out, as it is in customary cultures, a sphere of individual experience must be distinguished from the social world. Persons cannot be identified with their social roles, their feelings equated with socially stereotyped expressions. In order for individuals to be the source of critical possibilities, their wishes must not be swallowed up in the relentless tide of habitually reproduced group practices. They must be able to withdraw themselves from their place within established social practices and view such practices from the outside. Self-critical cultures make the requisite distinctions between individual and social spheres: they institutionalize individuality. Individuality is institutionalized culturally in the sense that the background of taken-for-granted communal convictions in such cultures is neither extensive enough nor concrete enough in its particulars to cover the life experiences of its membership. Thus these cultures force the recognition of a specifically individual sphere of experience and decision.[30]

Once these world-concepts have been distinguished, it is possible to segregate their distinct validity claims – the sincerity or authenticity of personal expression, the rightness of social behaviour, the truth of claims about the world. The difference between the last two sorts of validity claim is particularly crucial for the formation of self-critical cultures. It spells an ideal of objectivity in which facts and a domain of true descriptions concerning them can be distinguished from values and the human order in which they have a place.

Truth has its own criteria of assessment that are, ideally, not to be mixed with those of socially oriented values or concerns for utility. Something is not more likely to be true simply because it is espoused by a powerful or prestigious member of the community, because it occupies a long-standing or hallowed place in a society's tradition of belief, because it helps to maintain the social order, or because it boosts morale. Truths need not be socially serviceable. They may provide instead a platform for social criticism.

An interest in social order, conversely, need not hamper criticism of what is believed to be true. When beliefs are formed according to unmixed criteria, criteria formed, that is, without reference to social concerns, the number of beliefs that are socially entrenched tends to decrease. In other words, fewer beliefs are part and parcel of a society's orderly functioning. Social order will not be jeopardized, therefore, should such beliefs be radically emended or dropped.[31]

A second group of cultural distinctions that provide a resource for distantiation are those that construct notions of something outside or beyond established beliefs or normative arrangements. First, a sphere of reality is distinguished from that of ideas about it. Distinct orders of fact, on the one hand, and interpretation, on the other, take the place of a relatively undifferentiated cosmological–ideational order inclusive of words, thoughts and things.[32] Second, a notion of the *de facto* norms – of what is acceptable behaviour in a particular social group at a particular time – is distinguished from that of *de jure* norms – from what by rights should occur. The *fact* of social arrangements, in other words, is distinguished from what *ought* to be. Socially valid norms become distinguishable from ones that are ideally valid.[33]

The existence of such distinctions blocks the automatic self-validation of established beliefs or social arrangements. One cannot assume that one's words and ideas are bound up with the way things are. A linguistically formed worldview cannot be identified with the world order itself in any way that would prevent the former from being recognized as a particular interpretation of the latter, and consequently as something open to critical revision.[34] A concept of reality is available with which to perceive variations in worldview as different interpretations of natural and social orders that are subject to reflective assessment. One can ask whether what one takes to be true is *really* so. Similarly, once social and ideal normative validity are uncoupled as distinct categories, the mores of a particular society are not validated simply by virtue of being established. One can ask whether what is commonly perceived to be proper is really so. Socially valid norms as well as worldviews become subject to argumentative assessment. In both cases, what is, the setup or the given, is kept from forming a limit on the possible. A difference between appearance and reality – between the really true and the apparently true, the really proper and the apparently proper – becomes a potential measure of discontent.

Once distinctions are made between reality and interpretations of it and between ideal and socially valid norms, notions of reality and an ideal norm can be used in either of two ways: in a transcendent and regulative way, or in an immanent and constitutive way. In the latter case, the notion of reality or an ideal norm is substantively tilled, so that it may function as a criterion or *discrimen* in the process of evaluating a particular belief or normative claim. For instance, when reality is defined for such a purpose, the distinction between reality and one's idea of it amounts to a distinction between differently evaluated interpretations. That is, in the process of re-evaluating a particular account of reality – 'we believed that this was the way things are but now we know better' – one account of reality is set against another. One version is identified with the way things really are, the other with a mere idea about reality. Similarly, in the case where a distinction between ideal and socially valid norms is used to reflect critically upon a particular normative claim, the distinction is a way of making a point about the relative value of different socially valid norms. That is, in arguments that conclude 'we thought that was the best way for people to treat each other but now we know better', the distinction between ideal and socially valid norms simply serves to privilege the presently agreed-upon socially valid norm.

In a transcendent and regulative use of notions of reality or an ideal norm, their content remains unspecified. Such notions are zero semantic categories or surds, placeholders for a reality or ideal independent of our conceptions of it.[35] They mark a reference to a reality or norm beyond our ideas of either, by repelling differentiating descriptions, by eschewing the adequacy of any proposed account of what they are. As a result, notions of reality or the ideal cannot function as criteria in the evaluation of particular beliefs or norms. Nothing can be done with them for particular purposes. Because they have no content, they cannot be implemented as standards in the process of evaluating particular beliefs or norms. They may work, however, to ground a general ethic of cognition or normative judgement. They have a general procedural or regulative use in preventing claims of dogmatic finality for any belief or normative claim. That is, they prevent an immanent and constitutive use of such distinctions from permanently privileging any one account of reality or any one account of an ideal norm. A distinction between reality and one's idea of it or between the ideal and a socially valid norm is used in such cases, not to make relative discriminations among ideas of reality or among socially valid norms, but to discriminate between *all* ideas or socially valid norms and some reality or ideal beyond them. The general point is simply that ideas and norms at any particular time are subject to revision.

The transcendent use of these notions for regulative purposes extends, moreover, beyond this mere indiscriminate reminder of the ultimate inadequacy of every cognitive or normative proposal. The notions provide a general direction for forming judgements among proposed truths or norms. As I have suggested above, reality and an ideal norm cannot constitute criteria for judging proposed truths and norms apart from some conception of what they are like; apart from ideas about them, reality and an ideal norm have no standing that would enable them to be used themselves as such criteria. In other words, one cannot assess the relative adequacy of different accounts of reality by comparing them to reality itself or the relative adequacy of different normative proposals by comparing them with the ideal good itself. But the notion of a reality or an ideal norm beyond one's conception does set guidelines for the sort of criteria that should be brought to bear in making such judgements. If belief systems cannot be judged with reference to a reality absolutely independent of human conception, they can at least be judged according to a best approximation for particular purposes, that is, according to evidence or criteria that are relatively independent of human conception in the sense that they are independent of any of the particular belief systems under investigation. (For example, even if description of empirical data is never theory-neutral but always influenced by some understanding of the nature of reality, such description should not be informed by any one of the competing scientific theories to be assessed with reference to the data.) Similarly, if social norms cannot be judged with reference to an absolutely ideal norm, they can at least be judged according to criteria that are relatively unprejudiced by the social interests of the particular parties in disagreement. In sum, the transcendent use of notions of reality or an ideal norm translates into a procedural recommendation of openness to criticism by what is independent relative to the particular socially valid norms or interpretations of reality under consideration.[36]

Religion and the Two Types of Culture

What place might religion have in either of the sorts of culture just sketched? It is not uncommon to associate religious belief systems simply with what I have been calling customary culture. I need to address the reasons for such an association. If valid, they would make it unnecessary to investigate further whether Christian belief in particular can inform a culture of self-criticism. Like all other religions, Christianity would simply be allied with ideologies of stasis.

One might hold, with Jürgen Habermas, an evolutionary view, in which the structure of religious belief systems is said to be progressively replaced by more reflective relations to culture. One assumes thereby that religious beliefs are proposed and maintained in a way that discourages their argumentative assessment. One cannot get behind what is proclaimed to be sacred. The questioning of religious belief is a form of sacrilege. Religious belief is a classic instance of normatively ascribed consensus whereby established beliefs are simply presumed true.[37]

On this evolutionary view, it is then that the structure of religious belief systems might itself be altered in the progress toward argumentatively based belief. The authority of the sacred is no longer in that case a taken-for-granted given, but something for which one argues on the grounds supplied by a religious worldview. This represents a 'communicative thawing of traditionally solid institutions based on sacred authority'.[38] 'Convictions owe their authority less and less to the spellbinding power and aura of the holy, and more and more to a consensus that is not merely reproduced but achieved, that is, brought about communicatively . . . by way of inter-subjective recognition of validity claims raised in speech acts.'[39]

One might argue, however, that the basic structure of religious belief systems remains unchanged in this process, and hence such belief retains its alignment with customarily reproduced cultures. A religious worldview puts systematic restrictions on the argumentative assessment of action and belief by failing to distinguish among expressive, cognitive and normative spheres of validity.[40] The highest principle of such systems – God, in theistic ones – fuses notions of the true, the good and the perfect.[41] Religions refuse a discrimination between cognitive and normative spheres of validity in their demands for a world order that is ethically meaningful.[42]

One could also dispute that religious beliefs can be part of self-critical cultures, on the basis of historical evidence. The authoritarian and dogmatic character of religious forms of justification, in the West at least, was proved historically in the internecine religious conflicts of sixteenth- and seventeenth-century Europe. In this context, the way that religion informed competing political agendas made it impossible to resolve conflicts by rational means. Such resolution required the formation of a distinctively political vocabulary of natural rights, social contracts and public welfare. Rational assessment had to be set against religiously backed convictions. Proponents of a strictly political form of argument might have been wrong to think of their project as one that proceeded above history and independent of cultural inheritance: what they succeeded in doing was to institute a rational *tradition* for settling public disputes. They were not wrong, however, about the need for their project if a rational tradition of argument was to be set up. Reworking available cultural resources, the proponents of political argument arranged for the first time a cultural context, of a fundamentally non-religious sort, that permitted self-correction.[43]

None of these arguments, however, produces strong enough *a priori* reasons for thinking that an investigation of possible religious forms of self-critical culture is a waste of time. Aside from the problematic character of any evolutionary view of cultural development, the particular one I mentioned that distinguishes religious cultures from those that are reproduced and maintained by communicative acts appears to be based on an overly simplistic and narrow account of religious appeals to sacrality. The argument is a grossly general one that takes a particular sort of religious belief system for the whole.

One might respond to this rejoinder by claiming that an unquestionable sacrality for at least some beliefs or actions is the baseline of a religious worldview, however religions may differ in the extent and fervour of such attributions. But the burden of proof remains on the respondent to show that this unquestioned status exceeds in extent or character what any deliberative culture assumes. Even the most deliberative of cultures poses beliefs and actions for argumentative assessment against a background of what is not in question. It is true that in reflective cultures the background can be put into the foreground in a piecemeal fashion, but in all cultures at least some of these background beliefs are so basic that a culture lacks criteria for their meaningful assessment.[44]

The argument that the basic structure of religious belief systems puts systematic constraints on reflective assessment seems fallacious for a number of reasons. First, religious demands for the co-ordination or integration of norms and worldview do not necessarily indicate any failure to distinguish between types of claims or their criteria of assessment. Only the latter failure would conflict with structural prerequisites for a self-critical culture. A distinction between the natural world and social values is presumed whether one's theory of their relation detaches one from the other – on the assumption, perhaps, that the natural world runs contrary to an interest in human good – or brings them together in the belief, for instance, that the natural order is under the rule of a divine moral agent. In other words, a *distinction* between the orders of value and fact does not require their *detachment*. To assume so is to overlook the logical relation between these two orders explicated in the first chapter: normative claims are reasonable and motivated with reference ultimately to theoretical claims about what is the case. This does not involve a failure to distinguish between theoretical and normative claims; it merely presupposes a co-ordination of the two rather than their disjunction. To conflate such a distinction with separation is to demand a peculiarly quixotic character for normative proposals in reflective cultures – an existentialist nobility in extremis where people grit their teeth and carry on in a world that makes a mockery of their own desires and best intentions to further a human good. It should be clear that the mere differentiation of world-concepts or validity spheres does not involve such a demand. Furthermore, a simple co-ordination between normative proposals and claims about the world of the sort found in religious belief systems does not all by itself prejudice the issue of cultural self-criticism or self-validation. Everything depends on what one believes the world is like. A norm of self-criticism might be confirmed by the claims at issue. How can one know in advance that religious beliefs about what is the case rule out normative recommendations of critical reflection?

Finally, historical grounds for denying that religious systems have the resources to form rational traditions are just that – historical grounds, without the logical force to preclude such a possibility. Historical evidence can perhaps demonstrate that religious belief systems have never *yet* formed a rational tradition of reflection, but it cannot rule out such a possibility in the future or absolutely. In singling out religion for special opprobrium, historical arguments of this sort also overlook evidence of irreconcilable contests of opinion among purely politically motivated parties who produce reasoned defence of their convictions. Indeed, post-Enlightenment forms of public discourse are commonly indicted for the same sort of impasse of which religion is accused.[45] Were one to decide the question on historical grounds alone, one might be able to conclude that religiously backed convictions are no worse off than any other sort. There is a dogmatic potential, at least, in appeals to reason and in purely political arguments, just as there is in religious conviction. While a religious authoritarianism that prevents the application of critical intelligence may be properly faulted for dogmatism, appeals to reason may be equally dogmatic. Such appeals may claim a spurious universality for reasonable notions and presume a commonality of criteria for determining what is or is not reasonable in ways that invalidate from the start the possible rationality of conclusions differing from one's own. If one assumes, despite historical confirmation of this sort of dogmatic potential, that reasoned reflection has the capacity to undercut dogmatism, why categorically deny the same of religious forms of justification? Why, more specifically, cannot religious beliefs support rather than deflect the exercise of critical intelligence?

One should not beg the question, therefore, of religion's association with customary cultures by overlooking the possible complexity of religious systems and the diversity of the historical evidence. Instead, one should try to determine the particular sort of religious belief that can be correlated with the features of customarily reproduced cultures discussed previously.

Able to be so correlated is a mythological sort of religious belief that concretely articulates a sacred cosmos or divine sphere so that nature and society are fused as homologous orders. Two aspects of mythological religious constructions are important here. First, a storied depiction of gods or sacred forces permits an overall structure of repetition linking the natural, the social and the divine. Second, contemporary natural and social events are not merely correlated with such a storied world by way of symbolic representation, but enter within it as the actual reinstitution of events depicted.[46]

The ideology of stasis identified with customary cultures is one consequence. Continuity is understood in terms of repetition, reactualization and return. People do now what totemic ancestors or heroes or divinities in alliance with cosmic forces did before. They do more than merely repeat the same sort of acts. They make those very acts present again in their own acts, or by so acting enter within an ahistorical cycle of eternally recurrent, exactly repeated 'events'.[47]

The reification and presumed inviolability of social constructions, which occur when the world-concepts of nature, society and individual experience are not distinguishable, are another consequence. The natural, the social and the sacred are fused in mythological religious constructions in so far as human actions (e.g. institutionalized or co-ordinated action systems of building, founding, healing, marrying, ruling) and the corresponding social roles are thought to embody a cosmic and sacred order. For example, kinship structures are not merely representative of human social organization. The whole of being – from animals to personalized gods – is organized in a structurally similar manner. Participation in a human institutional order *means* therefore participation in a sacred cosmos.[48] A particular institution like marriage may be a re-enactment on a smaller scale of the union of heaven and earth that myth represents as the origin of a sacred cosmos.[49] Rites of building or founding may repeat those acts of the gods through which the world was constructed from the body of a sea dragon or giant. The first act of building may be, therefore, to drive a peg into the exact spot where 'lies the serpent that supports the world'. In this way the cosmogonic act by which a god 'smote a serpent' is repeated.[50] Those with political power may simply be gods, or just participate as human beings in a sacred order to the extent that they literally re-enact the gestures of the gods or mythological heroes.[51]

The human world is in this way embedded in a cosmic order that is itself sacred or that exists on a single plane of reality with gods or divine forces. In either case, human orders are grounded by way of participation in a trans-human realm so as to be spared, by definition, the contingency and variability of mere human constructions. Human orders are bound up with the very nature of things – a nature of things that is, moreover, imbued with the ultimacy and inviolability of sacrality. The way human beings do things is the way of the world; to deny the former is to deny the very being of the cosmos. The sacred character of such a cosmos bestows a further ultimacy of reality, value and validity upon it and the human orders it comprehends. Consequently, the human order is taken for granted as an inevitable aspect of an atemporally repeated or eternally reproduced sacred order. From mythological constructions it derives an aura of overpowering permanence and stability. In other words, the mythological process of locating a social world within a cosmic and sacred frame promotes the reification of those social arrangements as non-human, potentially coercive and unchangeable givens, for which human beings are not responsible and about which they can do nothing.

By reifying it, mythological religious constructions legitimate a social order.

Because a structure of repetition blends a particular social arrangement with cosmic and sacred orders, a religious worldview in such a mythological mode can do nothing but support institutionalized social norms. The stories of the gods, heroes, and cosmic forces may supply paradigms for proper action on the part of human beings – human actions may fall out of, and therefore need to be brought back into line with, what is recounted there, but the concrete articulation of such a sacred cosmos allows for a one-to-one match between established social practices and these normative accounts. The participation scheme that links a microcosm of human events with the macrocosm of a sacred universe does not force any distance between ideal model and realized social fact.

Mythological religious constructions have no capacity to challenge the ultimate validity of the norms, values and practices of the society they inform, since they do not establish any reference point for critique beyond such structures.[52] Particular forms of conduct may fail to meet the social standards for behaviour that mimetically reinstantiate a sacred cosmos. Such conduct is indeed susceptible to religious critique. But this religious criticism will assume the overall validity of the group's social standards. It will criticize a particular act with reference to the taken-for-granted normative system of the society whose overall order conforms to a sacred paradigm.

A human world of both socially acceptable beliefs and behaviours becomes uncriticizable, by religious means or otherwise, in the degree to which it is thought along mythological lines to be pervaded or suffused by divine or sacred forces. The social order also seems to be uncriticizable because mythological religious constructions block the distinction between spheres of social order and individual experience necessary if an individual is to withdraw from his or her place within established social conventions and institutional arrangements, and gain some critical leverage on them. The inexorability of the social world on a mythological worldview extends to the socialized identities of individuals within it. Social roles have the inviolable inevitability of cosmic facts and sacred realities. It would make no sense therefore to try to alter or rail against them. Moreover, the individual tends to a strong self-identification with social roles since one's socialized identity is not merely a social fact but a cosmic truth and a sacred trust.[53]

If this way of correlating mythological religious constructions with the features of customarily reproduced cultures makes sense, one would expect the general form of religion that plays a part in self-critical cultures to differ from the mythological sort in two important respects. First, one would expect the account of divinity or a sacred sphere to remain relatively unarticulated. At the extreme of what one might expect, no concrete story about the character of a divine or sacred realm is found. Without such a story, any structure of repetition linking the natural or social worlds with the sacred is precluded from the start.

A divine order will not be able to mirror, therefore, any particular social arrangement or buttress thereby assumptions of the latter's self-evidence. Moreover, an ideology of stasis will be much harder to ground in such circumstances with reference to a sacred origin or a temporal paradigm.

Countering the construction of concrete stories about a divine or sacred realm is a second feature one would expect of religions that inform self-critical cultures: a belief in a non-participatory relation between divinity, on the one hand, and natural and social orders, on the other. In short, divinity is believed to be transcendent. No natural force or human role can be identified as divine or sacred. Divinity is something 'other'. Natural forces and human beings have a distinct, specifically non-divine ontological status.

The terms that properly characterize human beings and natural forces should not therefore be applied to a divine or sacred realm. A gap in being between the divine and the this-worldly justifies a gap in expression. The ontological transcendence of divinity justifies its cognitive transcendence. At the minimum, concrete terms appropriate for the description of natural forces and human actions are devalued and, more often than not, replaced by less colourful, abstract characterizations. Talk of differentiated, multiple or changing forms, which is appropriate language for discussing human beings or natural forces, is inappropriate for a transcendent God. Abstract terms (e.g. of unity and simplicity) are to be preferred to concrete stories if the divine is not what human beings and natural forces are. At the maximum, one might have a simple prohibition on expression. No language is appropriate since all language is human language designed for discussion of human beings that are not God. This second feature and the first one are closely connected in this way: divine transcendence is a reason why accounts of divinity remain relatively unarticulated.

A belief in God's transcendence does not absolutely prohibit talk about a divine or sacred realm in the terms used to discuss the natural and social worlds. It does prevent, however, their fusion as homologous orders. Thus, if divinity is understood in the categories of human relation, a belief in God's transcendence might block the seriousness with which the same terms are applied to both divine and human realms. Though used for both, the categories properly apply only to one. For example, if God is a king then no human being is; or, if kingship is a term that properly describes a form of human power, then God is not really a king in the ordinary sense. Either way, a concrete story about divine kingship need not valorize human orders of power as they stand.

Divine transcendence is therefore the crucial factor blocking a homologous fusion of social, cosmic and sacred orders and this fusion's conservative social effects. A failure to articulate a sacred or divine order will prevent this fusion, but divine transcendence will also, whether or not, or in whatever manner, a story about divinity is told. I turn, then, to the exact way in which such a belief might figure in self-critical cultures as I have described them.

In all the ways I will mention, belief in divine transcendence is a force for distantiation and for distinction among social, natural and personal worlds. First, natural and social orders become objects of reflection in themselves from a platform supplied by that belief. In other words, the cultural construction of a divinity that lies beyond them permits a view from a distance. Natural and social orders can be considered as wholes with respect to a divine reference point existing over and against them.

Second, this reflection upon natural and social orders potentially involves their criticism. Divine transcendence fosters a critical distance. Once evacuated of sacrality by the claim of divine transcendence, natural and social orders cannot claim an unquestionable inevitability. Because the transcendence of divinity desacralizes natural and social orders, neither has the prima facie ultimacy to block critical questioning.

Extant social organizations are not themselves sacred, and therefore inviolable, if the true locus of sacrality is a transcendent God. Nor are they bound tightly with any sacred cosmic order. Beliefs, social norms and institutional arrangements may still be located within a cosmic framework so as to be taken for granted as natural givens. But that cosmic order itself no longer has any inevitability or ultimacy. The only ultimate and supremely real confronts it in the form of a transcendent divinity or sacred realm. An ontological realm different from the cosmic order relativizes the cosmic order. The cosmos does not exhaust the real, nor can it claim to be even the highest form of reality.

A belief in divine transcendence generally fosters the structural features of self-critical cultures I have mentioned. First, the notion of divine transcendence makes possible a distinction between moral and natural orders so as to de-reify the former. If social orders are not part of a sacred cosmos, it is at least possible for one to see them as mere human constructions, the historical products of human working and not inexorable aspects of the nature of things. The notion of divine transcendence opens up in this way the possibility for a distinction between what is naturally given and what is socially required. The natural and the social are also likely to come uncoupled as a result of the fact that any relation of a non-participatory sort between social and divine realms can bypass the natural world. A non-participatory relation between social orders and divinity does not take place via a sacralized cosmos. Indeed, it need not take place via the cosmos at all. Relations of a non-participatory sort between the natural order and divinity, and between the social world and divinity, may proceed independently of each other.

Second, for a similar reason the notion of divine transcendence permits a distinction between a social world and a world of individual experience. The non-participatory relations that individuals might have with divinity are not forced to proceed by way of a sacralized social order. In other words, an individual need not gain a relation to divinity by virtue of the sacred or divine character of her or his own social identity. An assured, unquestioned self-identification with a social role gives way, because the individual has now a distinct, potentially quite different identity in relation to the divine.

Third, the notion of the divine or the sacred as a fundamentally transcendent locus of ultimate reality, truth and value provides a paradigmatic centre for distinctions between what is taken for real and what is genuinely so, between the purportedly true and the actually true, between socially valid norms and ideal values. This notion forces a generally applicable distinction between appearance and reality. If divinity is the locus of what is ultimately true or good, and the human cannot be identified with the divine, appeals to a transcendent God are a possible focus for criticizing rather than reinforcing what passes for right belief and action in a particular society. Religion supplies an alternative locus for the true and the good with which to undermine social canons of good sense and proper behaviour. Socially entrenched beliefs, norms or institutional arrangements need not be ultimately legitimate. The transcendence of divinity suggests that human notions and norms might be judged and found wanting, inadequate and in need of change. A divine or sacred realm exists whose ways need harmonize with neither human opinion nor social expectation.

Human understandings of the real, the true and the good are also wanting to the extent they presume an ultimate validity for themselves. Because ultimate truth, value and reality reside in a transcendent realm, pretensions to ultimate finality for human understandings of what is real, true or good are destroyed. The notion of divine transcendence tends to compel in this way a recognition of (1) the limited and finite nature of human ideas, proposals and norms; (2) their historical and socially circumscribed bases; and (3) their essentially fallible and defeasible character. The transcendence of God functions as a protest against all absolute and unconditioned claims.

Belief in a transcendent divinity might have the sort of constitutive and immanent use to which I have referred. Religious forms of culture can specify what a divine standard of truth, reality and goodness is. That standard then becomes available for a religious critique of the norms and beliefs of a wider or foreign social order. Thus within the same society the values and affirmations of religious sub-groups may run up against those of non-religious ones. Conflict of this sort becomes possible when religious aspects of life are concentrated in distinct institutions with personnel and operations that are relatively independent of others – especially those of government and enforcement agencies. Without involving conflict between distinct social sub-groups, religious beliefs may simply run contrary to what is taken for granted as good sense in the society from which a religion draws its membership. Conflict of this sort is most likely to happen when a religious worldview is a response to intellectual and social crisis within a socially established outlook, or among such outlooks. Cultural disintegration and intra- or intercultural contention prompt religious solutions to problems of meaning or suffering that go beyond the common sense and common values of the social groups concerned.

The critical potential of a belief in God's transcendence is arbitrarily restricted, however, when only non-religious spheres fall under the awning of such critique. A religion maintaining a belief in a transcendent God is potentially critical of all human interpretations of reality, truth and goodness, including religious ones. Indeed, complaints against religious claims are the most direct implication of a notion of divine transcendence as a critical principle. If divinity is transcendent, then descriptions of divinity are most obviously inadequate; descriptions of divinity are brought first and foremost under a relativizing knife. Religious claims are the first human claims that must be recognized to be conditioned, limited and fallible. The kind of critique that a religion with a belief in divine transcendence directs against non-religious values and affirmations is therefore properly self-referential. Belief in a transcendent God turns back against itself and forms thereby a self-critical cultural tradition.

The Ambiguities of Divine Transcendence

I have specified, then, an intra-religious resource for socio-cultural critical-belief in divine transcendence. In forming the final conclusions in this chapter, I cannot overlook, however, the ambiguities of this resource. The notion of divine transcendence has a genuine but ambiguous potential for purposes of socio-cultural critique. Whether the belief functions for purposes of socio-cultural critique, whether it is drawn upon for such purposes, remains an open question for two general reasons.

First, the critical force of belief in divine transcendence is historically conditioned. Only certain historical circumstances favour the actualization of that belief's critical potentials. The social circumstance that social scientists term socio-cultural differentiation is most propitious.

The simple existence of societies holding beliefs and values different from one's own is not enough to shake their taken-for-granted certainty. Several strategies for maintaining the sacrosanct character of one's own beliefs and practices are readily available in such circumstances. A society can take measures to exterminate those groups with which it disagrees; it can try to ignore them, discount their beliefs and practices as those of barbarians or social deviants, or explain their positions as simple errors from within its own taken-for-granted worldview. None of these strategies is possible, however, where differences of belief and practice are the result of an internally differentiated socio-cultural order, where, that is, such differences do not occur between relatively isolated, independently operating groups, but are based upon differences in class affiliation, institutional membership, or occupation within a single, complex socio-cultural order. The beliefs and practices of others cannot be discounted by attributing them to deviants or strangers, since the beliefs and practices at issue are maintained by productive members of one's own society. Exterminating groups of people with beliefs and values different from one's own becomes self-destructive when such groups constitute, along with one's own, the functionally interdependent sub-groups of a single society. Ignorance via segregation or exile of offending parties is impractical for the same reason. Finally, claims of simple error, prejudice or partiality become less plausible against sub-groups of one's own society since such groups are often of similar prestige and commonly share or rotate their memberships.

By cutting off in these ways the usual strategies of response to differences in beliefs and practices, circumstances may open one to the suspicion that one's own beliefs and practices are wrong or improper. This suspicion affects one's religious views. The kind of religious fallibility that the notion of divine transcendence implies will therefore make sense in such circumstances. A general critique of socially established beliefs and norms on grounds supplied by a belief in divine transcendence will also find ready soil in this sort of social context. Because of socio-cultural differentiation, such a society's beliefs and values are prone of themselves to a crisis of plausibility and legitimation.

Second, apart from any consideration of historical context, belief in divine transcendence has a number of ambiguities of its own. If we make the rather uncontroversial assumption that socio-cultural differentiation is a feature of most modern societies in which Christianity is an influence, this second set of ambiguities becomes the more pressing focus for discussion in this book.[54] I need to adumbrate these further ambiguities with some care.

First, the fact that positing an ideal norm or truth allows human beings to claim it as their own renders the critical potential of a belief in divine transcendence ambiguous. The human tendency to pretend a universal, absolute or unconditional character for one's own beliefs and values may be undercut by the notion of a transcendent locus of ultimate truth and goodness; but the presumed existence of such an ideal locus serves as a constant temptation for the same inclinations. Specifically religious forms of fanaticism or dogmatism may result. One claims to speak for or as divinity. Surreptitiously or otherwise, one fails to feel the critical force of a belief in divine transcendence when it comes to some particular sphere of human claim.

Second, the transcendence of divinity, especially if it is understood in terms of distance or absence *vis-à-vis* the human order, can undercut its own critical potential for socio-cultural critique by suggesting that the norms and truths that divinity represents are irrelevant to human concerns. If divinity is transcendent, divinity has its own truths and norms; humans have theirs. The transcendence of divinity leaves the human order alone in that case to abide by its own standards of what is true and good; the norms or standards applicable to human concerns are specifically human ones and not divine. While the ideal truths and values of a divine sphere are clearly different from what passes for true or right in the social world, they lose in this way any critical leverage over that world.

This is an irrelevance of complacency in the human, which presumes a fairly positive evaluation of human spheres on their own terms. An irrelevance with more negative grounds is also possible, however. Human orders may be so completely devalued, in comparison with the transcendent ideals of truth and goodness that God represents, that applying divine standards to such orders is more hopeless than ungermane. Divine standards are pointless in a world that has fallen so far. This is an irrelevance of despair in the human.

Indeed, the more radical the transcendence of divine norms or standards *vis-à-vis* human orders, the more likely is despair over whether such standards can do human orders any good. The critical potential that is gained for a belief in divine transcendence on one front seems ironically in this way to be lost on another. The greater the distance between human truths and values and divine ones, the greater the critical potential of an appeal to a divine standard: a more extensive revision of human beliefs and values would be necessary to bring the human into line with the divine. The greater the distance, however, the harder it is to see how divine standards might apply to human circumstances, the harder it is to perceive the means with which the social world could be altered to conform to those standards – in sum the more likely a belief in the irrelevance of divine standards for human society out of despair over the possibility of ever implementing them there.

Third, belief in the transcendence of divinity might renege on its critical potential by feeding into standard sceptical arguments for abiding by convention.[55] If the transcendence of divinity means that no one can claim to know what is right or true with any confidence, then it might be best simply to conform to the customs and traditions of belief of one's social group. The transcendence of divinity would in this way support a sceptical equipoise of arguments pro and con a particular ethos or worldview, leaving one holding the same beliefs and values but non-dogmatically, without any assurance of their probity. Since one cannot know what truth, goodness or reality look like to God, one is forced to make do with how they appear to one. Scepticism about human capacities to know the true and the good, scepticism brought on by belief in divine transcendence, would prohibit in such circumstances any serious explication of divine ideals or standards for critique. No account of divine truths or norms could be proposed for use in criticizing socially entrenched beliefs and values.

Assimilating the results of a belief in God's transcendence to the effects of classical sceptical arguments in this way is probably inappropriate, however.

The claim of divine transcendence is not reducible to a simple agnosticism concerning the reliability of all human claims; it is the assertion of their imperfection and susceptibility to critique, *vis-à-vis* a realm of ultimate truth and goodness that exists whether human beings can articulate it or not. The claim of divine transcendence does not leave one, therefore, with a simple equipoise of arguments pro and con human conventions, but with a positive knowledge of their fallible, correctible character. Criticism of human conventions is therefore not a matter of illegitimate arrogance or dogmatism, as it is for classical scepticism. Judgement of, and possible dissatisfaction with, those conventions is just what an appeal to a transcendent divine focus of truth or goodness requires.[56]

But what sort of appeal to a transcendent locus of truth and goodness is available for purposes of critique? Do not the sceptical consequences of belief in divine transcendence prohibit, as has just been charged, any commitment to a particular concrete explication of divine standards for such purposes?

Even if that were the case, it is not clear that critical reflection and revision of human conventions require such a commitment. Like the regulative use of an appeal to reality or truth or goodness *per se*, a regulative use of a belief in divine transcendence can propel the hard task of arguments pro and con between ultimately provisional human claims without any specification of what truth, reality or goodness look like from God's point of view. It is that sort of argument among provisional human claims that should be directed against human convention. An account of a divine truth or goodness can indeed be proffered, but it must enter within such arguments as one human and therefore fallible account of truth or goodness in competition with others.

One might suggest, however, that under such conditions arguments will remain without direction. Where should one start, how should one proceed, without the material guidance of some privileged account of a divine standard of truth and goodness? Without some clear sense of direction, criticism of human conventions cannot get off the ground, even if one believes such criticism is appropriate. Another sort of despair of irrelevance sets in: a despair over the point of argument if no clear indications of divine standards exist.

At the end of the description of the structural features of a self-critical culture, I did try to show how a regulative use of an appeal to the true and the good could provide a general direction for such arguments. I have not developed that claim, however, for belief in God's transcendence and worries might remain in any case.

In fact, none of these ambiguities and worries regarding the critical potential of a belief in God's transcendence is resolvable without attention to a particular religion. To resolve them, one would need more information about what divine transcendence implies, and one would need to know about the rest of the religious beliefs with which a belief in divine transcendence is conjoined. In the next chapter, therefore, I turn to a belief in God's transcendence as a possible resource for socio-cultural critique within a specifically Christian religious context. The additional Christian beliefs under consideration are limited, as suggested in the first chapter, to basic ones concerning God's relation to the world as creator, governor and redeemer. By specifying the meaning of divine transcendence and considering these other beliefs, I try to determine whether and to what extent the critical potential of a belief in divine transcendence may be realized in Christianity.

Notes

1 They are dangers of functionalist forms of cultural analysis.
2 I am not saying that in virtue of such processes of formation the renegotiation of established social relations and taken-for-granted beliefs is always a real possibility in any society. I am merely saying that it is a possibility for any society unless a society takes steps to block it. (Most societies indeed make efforts to do so by ideological and institutional means.) My ideas here are not based on any one social theory. They have been informed directly, however, by the following disparate works of social theory: Raymond Williams, *Marxism and Literature* (Oxford: Oxford University Press, 1977); Roberto Unger, *Social Theory* (Cambridge: Cambridge University Press, 1987); Thomas McCarthy, *Ideals and Illusions* (Cambridge, MA: MIT Press, 1991); Joan Cocks, *The Oppositional Imagination* (London: Routledge, 1989), pt 1; James Scott, *Domination and the Arts of Resistance* (New Haven, CT: Yale University Press, 1990); Chris Weedon, *Feminist Practice and Poststructuralist Theory* (Oxford: Blackwell Publishers, 1987); Jürgen Habermas, *The Theory of Communicative Action*, trans. Thomas McCarthy, 2 vols. (Boston: Beacon Press, 1984); Michel Foucault, *Discipline and Punish*, trans. Alan Sheridan (New York: Vintage, 1979); Michel Foucault, *The History of Sexuality*, trans. Robert Hurley (New York: Vintage 1980).
3 'The world upside down' of Renaissance carnivals is a conspicuous case of the latter tactic. See James Scott, *Domination and the Arts of Resistance*, pp. 166–72.
4 For a sophisticated argument in support of such claims, see David Brion Davis, *The Problem of Slavery in the Age of Revolution* (Ithaca, NY: Cornell University Press, 1975).
5 See Clifford Geertz, *The Interpretation of Cultures* (New York: Harper Colophon Books, 1973), ch. 2, for a nice expression of the way in which culture might 'go all the way down'.
6 See Raymond Williams, *Culture and Society 1780–1950* (New York: Columbia University Press, 1958).
7 See Roy Wagner, *The Invention of Culture* (Chicago: University of Chicago Press, 1980).
8 Jürgen Habermas is the most sophisticated proponent of such a view. See his *Theory of Communicative Action*.
9 See Thomas McCarthy, 'Rationality and Relativism' in *Habermas: Critical Debates*, ed. John Thompson and David Held (Cambridge, MA: MIT Press, 1982), pp. 57–78, for decisive criticism of Habermas on these sorts of grounds.

10 Anthropological material, distinguishing traditional from modern Western cultures, and oral from literate ones, has helped me form this contrast. See, for example, Ernest Gellner, *The Legitimation of Belief* (Cambridge: Cambridge University Press, 1974); Jack Goody, *The Logic of Writing and the Organization of Society* (Cambridge: Cambridge University Press, 1988); Robin Horton, 'African Traditional Thought and Western Science', in *Rationality*, ed. Bryan Wilson (Oxford: Blackwell Publishers, 1977), pp. 131–71; Robin Horton, 'Tradition and Modernity Revisited', in *Rationality and Relativism*, ed. Martin Hollis and Steven Lukes (Oxford: Blackwell Publishers, 1982), pp. 201–60. I have no intention, however, of suggesting any evolutionary progression of cultural forms. Nor do I identify customary cultures exclusively with traditional or oral ones. In some respects late capitalist consumer culture fits the type more easily. See, for example, Herbert Marcuse, *One-Dimensional Man* (Boston: Beacon Press, 1964) and Ernest Gellner, *Words and Things* (London: Routledge and Kegan Paul, 1979), for a critique along these lines of technocratic societies where standards of all sorts have merely an operational sense (i.e. standards are simply what is done). For purposes of my argument here I will be sticking with a rather traditionalist version of customary cultures.

11 See, for example, Robin Horton's somewhat belated recognition of this fact in 'Tradition and Modernity Revisited', pp. 218–22.

12 See Marshall Sahlins, *Islands of History* (Chicago: University of Chicago Press, 1985); Marshall Sahlins, *Historical Metaphors and Mythical Realities* (Ann Arbor: University of Michigan Press, 1981).

13 Geertz, *Interpretation of Cultures*, p. 101.

14 See the interpretation of Hans-Georg Gadamer's notion of open horizons made by David Linge in his introduction to Gadamer's *Philosophical Hermeneutics* (Berkeley: University of California Press, 1976), pp. xxxiii–xxxxl.

15 Michael Oakeshott, *Rationalism in Politics* (London: Methuen, 1962), pp. 64–5.

16 See Stuart Hampshire, *Morality and Conflict* (Cambridge, MA: Harvard University Press, 1983); and Basil Mitchell, *The Justification of Religious Belief* (New York: Seabury Press, 1973).

17 McCarthy, *Ideals and Illusions*, p. 30.

18 See Goody, *Logic of Writing*, p. 137.

19 See James Pocock, *Politics, Language and Time* (New York: Atheneum, 1971), p. 237.

20 See Goody, *Logic of Writing*, p. 38.

21 See Pocock, *Politics, Language and Time*, ch. 7.

22 Goody, *Logic of Writing*, pp. 31, 136, 147.

23 See James Clifford's account of the cultural inventiveness of Native Americans in Mashpee, Cape Cod, in *The Predicament of Culture* (Cambridge, MA: Harvard University Press, 1988), ch. 12. See also critiques of the eclecticism of postmodern cultures by, for example, Gerald Graff, *Literature against Itself* (Chicago: University of Chicago Press, 1979).

24 Oakeshott, *Rationalism in Politics*, p. 64.

25 See, for example, Marshall Sahlin's account of the demise of the Hawaiian tabu system through encounters with European traders in his *Historical Metaphors and Mythical Realities*, pp. 33–66.

26 Here I am appealing to much the same sociological and anthropological material as

Jürgen Habermas and making many of the same basic points, but without any claims for ontogenetic or phylogenetic advance, or cross-cultural normativity for the structural organization of (what I call) deliberative cultures. See his *Theory of Communicative Action*.

27 For example, the epistemological use of a distinction between appearance and reality, which I will discuss, helps make sense of a lack of unified belief by suggesting the possibility of different perspectives on the same reality. The last two paragraphs are my more technical formulation of Ernest Gellner's sociology of modern intellectual history. See his *Legitimation of Belief*.

28 The term 'world-concepts' and the three different forms of world-concept I cite come from Jürgen Habermas. See again his *Theory of Communicative Action*.

29 See Peter Berger, *The Social Construction of Reality* (New York: Doubleday, 1966), pp. 89–92.

30 See Emile Durkheim, *The Division of Labor in Society* (New York: Free Press, 1933), for the beginnings of such an account. See also Steven Lukes, *Individualism* (New York: Harper and Row, 1973).

31 Notice that from my methodological point of view, the distinction between truth and social value is a particular cultural formation that permits a relative distinction among criteria of validity. I am not assuming that truth is ever finally separate from power relations or that it needs to be in order to be a resource of social criticism. Furthermore, although the distinction between truth and social value *permits* criticism of socio-cultural orders, it does not require such criticism. The claim for truth separate from norms of social validity can clearly be used to hide the fact that what is proposed as true serves particular interests. This is just another way of saying that the distinction itself between truth and social validity is implicated in struggles for power. It has therefore an ambiguous function, making possible both the criticism and the support of social orders.

32 See Michel Foucault, *The Order of Things* (New York: Vintage, 1973), ch. 2.

33 See Habermas, *Theory of Communicative Action*, vol. 1: pp. 88–9; vol. 2: p. 73.

34 Ibid., vol. 1: p. 50.

35 See Thomas Nagel, *The View from Nowhere* (Oxford: Oxford University Press, 1986), ch. 6; and Wayne Proudfoot, *Religious Experience* (Berkeley: University of California Press, 1985), pp. 124–36, for suggestions of how transcendent notions can be rule-governed cultural constructions of this sort.

36 See Gellner, *Legitimation of Belief*, esp. pp. 19–23, on this last aspect of a regulative use of notions of the transcendent. In this paragraph and the previous one I have been splitting the difference between those, on the one hand, who make an acultural and rather flat appeal to transcendent truths or norms as prerequisites for social criticism (e.g. Habermas, Christopher Norris, Peter Dews), and those, on the other, who deny altogether the legitimacy, sense or usefulness of transcendent notions as cultural constructions (e.g. Richard Rorty in some moods; Wittgensteinians who decide in advance, on general philosophical grounds, the limitations of cultural good sense instead of really leaving 'everything as it is'). See Habermas, *Theory of Communicative Action*; Christopher Norris, *Contest of Faculties* (London: Methuen, 1985); Peter Dews, *Logics of Disintegration* (London: Verso, 1987). For Rorty's vacillations (or change of heart) regarding the transcendent force of notions like truth, compare his 'Solidarity or

Objectivity' in *Post-Analytic Philosophy*, ed. John Rajchman and Cornel West (New York: Columbia University Press, 1984), p. 6 ('There is nothing to be said about truth save that each of us will commend as true those beliefs which he or she finds good to believe') and 'Pragmatics, Davidson, and Truth' in *Truth and Interpretation*, ed. Ernest Lepore (Oxford: Blackwell Publishers, 1984), pp. 334–5, where he notes a 'cautionary' use of appeals to the truth in which one reminds oneself that the world may not be as one's justified beliefs say it is. For Ludwig Wittgenstein's claim that philosophy should leave 'everything as it is', see his *Philosophical Investigations*, trans. G. E. M. Anscombe (New York: Macmillan, 1953), paragraph 124.

37 See Habermas, *Theory of Communicative Action*, vol. 2: pp. 77–111, on the 'linguistification of the sacred', for a recent, highly sophisticated version of this view.

38 Ibid., vol. 2: p. 91.

39 Ibid., vol. 2: p. 89.

40 Ibid., vol. 2: pp. 189, 194.

41 Ibid., vol. 1: pp. 246, 248, 348.

42 Ibid., vol. 1: pp. 160–3, 202–3.

43 See Jeffrey Stout, *The Flight from Authority* (Notre Dame: University of Notre Dame Press, 1982), pp. 235–42, on the historical significance of religious wars. He is following here Quentin Skinner, *The Foundations of Modern Political Thought*, 2 vols (Cambridge: Cambridge University Press, 1978). See also Stout, *Flight from Authority*, pp. 44–6, 74–6, on the notion of a rational tradition. With characteristic caution Stout does not flatly proclaim the bankruptcy of religious resources in the setting up of self-critical traditions. He merely strongly suggests it, and awaits, as he should, a sustained argument to the contrary.

44 See Habermas's own assimilation of these Wittgensteinian points in *Theory of Communicative Action*, vol. 1: pp. 335–7; vol. 2: pp. 109, 219–22. See Alvin Plantinga, 'Is Belief in God Rational?' in *Rationality and Religious Belief*, ed. C. F. Delaney (Notre Dame: University of Notre Dame Press, 1979), pp. 7–27, for an argument that certain beliefs are foundational in a Wittgensteinian sense. I do not believe that this argument is successful for reasons that are not germane to the present discussion. It is enough for my purposes here simply to throw doubt on *a priori* arguments for religious dogmatism, so as not to preclude further investigation into possible religious resources for self-critical traditions.

45 See Alasdair MacIntyre, *After Virtue* (Notre Dame: University of Notre Dame Press, 1981).

46 I am interested here in a type of religious belief that can be associated in an unambiguous way with the structural features of customary cultures described above. Of course, other forms of religious belief short of this have at least an obvious potential for such an association (e.g. the myriad forms of immanentism in Christian theism), but an argument of the sort I am making here for any one of them would be much more complicated and difficult.

47 See Mircea Eliade, *The Myth of the Eternal Return* (Princeton: Princeton University Press, 1954).

48 Peter Berger, *The Sacred Canopy* (New York: Doubleday, 1969), p. 34.

49 See Eliade, *The Sacred and the Profane* (New York: Harcourt, Brace and World, 1959), pp. 145–6, on the Upanishads.

50 Ibid., p. 52; idem, *Myth of the Eternal Return*, p. 19.
51 See Talcott Parsons, *The Evolution of Societies* (Englewood Cliffs, NJ: Prentice-Hall, 1977), p. 54 on Egyptian kings.
52 Mythological religious constructions that undergird a particular ethos and form of social organization can obviously challenge the propriety of *another* society's practices and values. The reader should remember that the issue here is a culture's capacities for *self-*criticism.
53 Berger, *Sacred Canopy*, pp. 37–8, 95.
54 For a discussion of the contemporary US context as one of socio–cultural differentiation, see ibid., chs 5–7.
55 See Richard Popkin, *The History of Skepticism* (Berkeley: University of California Press, 1979); Terence Penelhum, *God and Skepticism* (Dordrecht: D. Reidel, 1983); Pocock, *Politics, Language and Time*.
56 See Penelhum, *God and Skepticism*, p. 34.

Depth of Self-Awareness and Breadth of Vision: Joining Reflection and Interpretation

Frans Jozef van Beeck

This selection is a condensed version of two chapters in the first volume of a multi-volume work of systematic theology, *God Encountered*. After an initial four chapters limning the contours of catholic systematic theology, Van Beeck investigates the important asymmetrical relation of revealed to natural religion, through a study of both ancient and modern construals of the problem. There follows a third part of the book which lays out the foundational character of worship for theology, and its equiprimordial elements of cult, conduct and creed.

1 Interpreting Positive Religion

1 Friedrich Schleiermacher on positive religion

(i)   In the fifth of his *Speeches on Religion*, written – at the urging of his friends – in 1797–9, and published in Berlin in the year in which they were finished, the young Friedrich Schleiermacher wrote, with the fervour of an evangelist:

> Go back then, if you are in earnest about observing religion in its definite patterns, from this enlightened [natural religion] to those despised positive religions. There everything proves to be real, vigorous and definite; there every single intuition has its definite consistency, and a connection, all its own, with the rest; there every feeling has its own sphere and its particular reference. There you will find every modification of religiosity somewhere, as well as every state of feeling to which only religion can transport a person; there you will find every part of religion cultivated somewhere, and each of its effects somewhere achieved; there all

common institutions and every individual expression are proof of the high value that is placed on religion, even to the point of forgetting everything else. There the holy zeal with which religion is observed, shared, enjoyed, and the childlike desire with which new revelations of heavenly powers are anticipated, are your warranty that not a single one of religion's elements, which it was possible in any way to perceive from this standpoint, has been overlooked, and that not a single one of its moments has vanished without leaving a monument behind.[1]

This is unexpected advice to flow from the pen of the man who has been held responsible, more than any other modern theologian, for some of the most distinctive *universalist* developments in Western Christianity. Understandably, those developments have received mixed reviews – which is reflected in Schleiermacher's mixed reputation, down to our own day.

On the one hand, neo–Protestants and other liberal Christians have hailed him as the genius who availed himself of the freedom of the gospel to put an end to the long divorce between faith and human reasonableness. They have even credited him with the recovery of Christianity's catholicity, in the form of a new, enlightened universalism – one that has freed Christians from unnecessary bondage to sectarian doctrine and moral precept.[2]

The reaction of the orthodox has gone in the opposite direction. In their eyes, especially in the eyes of those who, in this century, have followed Karl Barth in his conclusions (without, however, always appreciating all his arguments),[3] Schleiermacher is the symbol of an historic mistake. By identifying religion as an integral part of enlightened human self-awareness, Schleiermacher was successful, they will admit, in starting afresh Christianity's dialogue with culture and rationality. By the same token, however, he also contributed decisively to the widespread loss of doctrinal and moral determinateness in modern Christianity, not to mention the abandonment of the *sola gratia*. Numerous orthodox (in the sense of doctrinally conservative) Christians, therefore, have concluded that Schleiermacher, for all his piety, was but the pioneer of modernism.

These contrary evaluations are both one-sided, and both are narrower than the person who prompted them. To confound, or at least surprise, his orthodox detractors as well as his liberal admirers, there is a striking interpretation of the *Speeches* from Schleiermacher's own pen. In a letter to his close friend Henrietta Herz, written on 12 April 1799, three days before the completion of the manuscript, Schleiermacher referred to his first book as his 'polemic against natural religion'.[4] Contrary to later reputation, therefore, the young Schleiermacher was *not* on a crusade to reduce the Christian religion to an unspecified, universally available and thus generally acceptable, 'natural' religiosity.

In fact, throughout his life he was to keep a high esteem for the concrete and the particular in religion – the same esteem that he commended when he was thirty years old, as he was finishing the *Speeches*. And if he also continued to insist, all his life, on 'piety' – that is, reverential, affective consciousness of absolute dependence – as the universal *proprium* of all religion, he did so on the basis of his interpretation of the Christian faith as he knew it in its concrete particularity.[5]

(ii) It is to be carefully noted that Schleiermacher's text treats particular, 'positive' religions as *structures*.

The passage from the *Speeches* quite naturally describes definiteness as occurring in a coherent way, resulting in patterns. The definiteness is due to the particularity of intuitions, feelings, modifications of religiosity, states of feeling, parts, effects, institutions, expressions, elements and moments. Far from being discredited, this definiteness is evaluated in strikingly positive terms: it is a matter of reality, vigour, consistency, culture, achievement, value, zeal, desire, attentiveness and remembrance. Furthermore, Schleiermacher emphasizes that the variety and multiplicity of positive religion is not a weakness but a strength; for all the profusion of elements, the organic coherence of the whole is never in doubt. Each 'intuition' (*Anschauung*) is firmly connected with other intuitions. All feelings are reliably set in a larger whole, and have stable objective correlatives. All modifications of human religiosity and all the feeling states to which religion can give rise are found somewhere in that larger whole. In Schleiermacher's opinion, whoever is prepared to examine a positive religion attentively and appreciatively, as a multifarious yet coherent structure, will also notice how all the virtualities of religion as such are actualized in it.

In all of this, Schleiermacher is not being naive. Immediately after the passage quoted above, he admits that not everything is sound and constructive about positive religions. They often appear in the form of the slave; they bear the marks of the poverty of their adherents, as well as the vestiges of their limitations in time and space. Positive religions, Schleiermacher implies, are not above criticism. Still, in order to criticize them correctly, thoughtful people must make an effort to interpret them as they deserve to be interpreted, namely, in the light of the *proprium* of all religion – the reverential feeling of absolute dependence on the deity. Once this basis is securely recognized, Schleiermacher has no qualms about particularity in religion – rather the opposite.

(iii) According to Schleiermacher, therefore, the only truly interesting religions are religions *as they actually exist* – that is to say, particular, 'positive' religions. However, positive religion is always *determinate* religion, and determinate religion is made up of *elements*; these elements, in turn, exist in coherent patterns, that is to say, in *structures*. Now what ultimately accounts for the coherence of any particular religion is an inner quality that characterizes all religions as such. This underlying quality, according to Schleiermacher, is accessible, but only by way of a self-authenticating, interior experience.

This experience cannot be reduced to any definite acts of knowledge, to any particular moral actions, or to any specific states of feeling. Rather, it consists in a person's awareness, at once affective and luminous, of self-identity as well as absolute dependence, in such a way as to make these two inseparable. This experience can be brought to explicit awareness by reflection, and it can be adequately thematized by saying that the person is originally and absolutely related to God – a relatedness whose actuality is experientially available in the person's very experience of self-identity or self-consciousness.[6]

(iv) Let us sum up our discussion so far. Schleiermacher's point in commending the study of particular, positive religions is that they alone are actual religions. It is a mistake, therefore, to despise them. It is true, they are soulless without the core-experience which alone is capable of authenticating them, but that does not mean that they can simply be reduced to that core-experience. They should, therefore, be appreciated and understood as they are, in their concrete actuality as positive religions.

(v)   Now what Schleiermacher suggests is that this appreciation and under-standing of positive religions *precisely as religions* is accomplished by appreci-ating and understanding them, along with all their parts and elements, as *coherent structures*. He seems to be implying that the interpretation of positive religions must be practised by focusing on their structural elements. He suggests that interpretation by elements, in turn, is tantamount to interpreting a positive religion precisely *as a religion*, that is to say, as a concrete actualization of that fundamental religious experience which accounts for its being a positive religion in the first place.

2   Natural religion and positive religion in Christianity

(i)   Schleiermacher's commendation of positive religion may serve as a first introduction to any phenomenology of the Christian faith. Such phenomenologies, however, should not be an exercise in *naiveté*. They would be just that if they were to consist merely in a cumulative, descriptive account of those elements of worship, conduct and teaching which catholic Christianity generally accepts as authentic, supported by the principal arguments from the authoritative, historic tradition. Such presentations of Christianity as a positive religion, no matter how authoritative or even attractive, would be inadequate. Any phenomenology of Christianity should be properly theological. Theology does well indeed to recognize and appreciate mature docility and acceptance, both of which are proper to faith; precisely as theology, however, it is concerned, not with enumeration or acceptance but with understanding. Understanding, however, is a matter, not only of doing justice to the *object* (i.e. the matter to be understood), but also of recognizing the demands of intellectual integrity on the part of the *subject*. Hence, we must show how a phenomenology of the Christian faith as a positive religion is compatible with the demands of human understanding and integrity in believing.

To make this case, let us begin by stating and elaborating as a formal thesis what is little more than a suggestion in Schleiermacher's *Speeches*. The thesis is the following. *There are mutually complementary ways of gaining intellectual access to the quintessence of human religiosity: transcendental reflection on fundamental human experience, and phenomenological study of positive religion.*

(ii)   The first – transcendental reflection – is the way principally practised by Schleiermacher in his *Speeches*. By reflection we come to realize explicitly and thematically what is implicitly and unthematically given in all our particular experiences, as the precondition for their possibility and meaningfulness. That realization consists in the awareness that our fundamental human integrity is ontologically related to the creative transcendence of God. From the point of view of transcendental reflection, therefore, there is a basic religious dimension to all particular, concrete human experiences.

A caution. The development of a theological anthropology, by means of careful 'transcendental' reflection on the depth of human self-awareness, is not simply a concession to the spirit of the Enlightenment. Put differently, it is not an exercise in liberal, agnostic modernism. On the contrary, it is a fundamental requirement of the need for human integrity in believing – an integrity created and cherished by God. Taking human self-awareness seriously guarantees that the positive elements of the Christian faith are appreciated as they should be, namely, as historic instances of true divine self-communication to humanity and the world – a self-communication that prompts true faith-responses.

In our own day, Karl Rahner (whose systematic theology shares some striking family features with Schleiermacher's) has forcefully argued this point, and in fact, made it into the heart of his theology. In Rahner's system, this leads to a whole range of conclusions; at this point one telling example must suffice.

Positive (or, to use Rahner's own terms, 'categorical' or '*a posteriori*') revelation simply cannot be heard or received *as* divine revelation, unless it finds, in the believer, a 'transcendental' (*a priori*) aptitude to hear and accept it – an aptitude that coincides with the divine immanence in the human person's subjectivity. In Rahner's own words:

> Consequently, there corresponds to the objective supernaturality of a revealed proposition a divine and subjective principle for hearing this proposition in the subject who is able to hear it. Only when God is the subjective principle of the speaking and of man's hearing in faith can God in his own self express himself.

> ... [I]f the objective proposition ... produced by God ... enters into a merely human subjectivity without this subjectivity itself being borne by God's self-communication, then the supposed word of God has turned into a human word before we know it. The *a posteriori* proposition of verbal revelation which comes in history can be heard only within the horizon of a divinizing and divinized *a priori* subjectivity. Only then can it be heard in the way that it must be heard if what is heard is seriously to be called the 'word of God'.[7]

(iii)   The second – attentive phenomenology – is the way commended by Schleiermacher in the fifth of his *Speeches*. As, in an attitude of careful attentiveness, we seek to understand the given, positive elements of a religion, we are also in a position to gain intellectual access to its true religious meaning. This is not accomplished by a mere enumeration of elements; mere inventories, no matter how authoritatively proposed, never convey understanding. Complex realities like religions require *interpretation*; but true interpretation occurs only when, in the process of discovering the coherence of a religion's elements, we gain an increasing appreciation of its *structures*. Most importantly, in doing so, we also attain its intelligibility. Far from being an exercise in theological sectarianism, therefore, the attentive phenomenological study of Christianity as a positive religion is capable of opening our eyes, in an indirect fashion, to its intelligibility, and hence also to the depth and universality of its significance as a religion.

It follows that the phenomenological study of positive religion is liable, indirectly, to lead to appreciation of natural religion as essential to *human integrity in its depth*, just as reflection on natural religiosity will, again indirectly, lead to an appreciation of positive religion as vital to *human culture in its breadth*. It also follows that what Schleiermacher calls 'natural religion' must never be brought into play against positive religion, to discredit it, nor must positive religion be summoned as a witness for the prosecution in order to mount a case against natural religion. The former is the modernist's temptation, the latter the integralist's.

Natural religion and positive religion, therefore, may never be *separated*, let alone placed in an adversarial relationship. They are mutually interdependent. Karl Rahner makes the same point when, in the context of Christology, he insists on

> the relationship of mutual conditioning and mediation in human existence between what is transcendentally necessary and what is concretely and contingently historical. It is a relationship of such a kind that both elements in man's historical existence can only appear together and mutually condition each other: the transcendental element is always an intrinsic condition of the historical element in the historical itself, and, in spite of its being freely posited, the historical element co-determines existence in an absolute sense. In spite of their

unity and their relationship of mutual conditioning, neither of the two elements can be reduced to each other.[8]

For all his spontaneous preference for transcendental reflection, Karl Rahner never tires of emphasizing that it is only by virtue of positive, 'categorical', historical experience that we have access to the 'transcendental' dimensions of existence.[9]

(iv) If, however, the two are mutually interdependent, this entails that they are legitimately used in the service of mutual critique. This must be elaborated.

Cut loose from the fundamental relationship between God and the human person, any religion's positive elements have an unfortunate tendency to become opaque and inert, and to degenerate into a multiplicity of beliefs and practices connected with 'objects of worship' (*sebasmata*: Acts 17, 23). When this happens, positive religion begins to equate *naiveté* with faith, and starts to foster, and even glorify, authoritarian fideism and traditionalism. It may end up commending sectarian intolerance, and even idolatrous slavery of the spirit. Positive religion, in other words, harbours the risk of idolatry.

To counteract this risk, and to anchor positive religion in the native religiosity of the human person, transcendental reflection is required, based on the conviction that fundamental human freedom and consciousness are natively equipped to tell the difference between true faith and naive forms of belief. Insisting on transcendental reflection in theology, therefore, serves to uphold intellectual integrity and freedom in believing as the birthright of all persons. Upholding that right is not only to the glory of humanity, but also to the glory of God, who created humanity in the divine image – that is, as natively oriented to God.

Positive religion must respect this basic privilege of humanity. In fact, it is an impressive achievement of the great apologetic tradition of the Christian church to have recognized the rights of the human spirit. This tradition has found eloquent expression in the order of treatment followed by the classic theological systems. From Aquinas's *Summa contra Gentiles* on, systematic theology has habitually started with a theology of creation, an epistemology of religious language, a philosophical theology, a theological anthropology, or another of the many forms natural theology can take.

On the other hand, advocates of natural religion do not always appreciate the extent to which positive religion contributes to the constructive exercise of human consciousness and freedom, in shaping forms of religious community, and even in building a common religious culture. They often fail to see that the contribution made to civilization by positive religions far exceeds the damage done by their sectarianisms.

Moreover, they tend to be blind to the principal inherent weakness of natural religion itself. This weakness lies, not in its plea for an enlightened humanism, but in the limitations that flow from the theoretical, abstract nature of its claims. These limitations are best appreciated when measured by the standard of practice; natural religion does not normally generate vigorous forms of community or generous commitments to values.[10] This can be briefly illustrated by recalling two historic forms which the advocacy of natural religion at the expense of positive religion has taken: anti-ecclesial Deism and heroic Romanticism.

Anti-clericalism has always been a feature of Deism,[11] especially, in recent times, in circles beholden to the militant anti-clericalism of nineteenth-century Europe. Consistent with this, there is in the Deist tradition a tendency to treat positive, ecclesial religion as, at best, a concession to the feeble-mindedness of the unenlightened, and at worst, sectarian obscurantism and degeneracy fostered by priests. The tendency is not infrequently accompanied by sentiments of shallow condescension parading as profound Enlightenment; of this, Benjamin Franklin's *Autobiography*[12] is a good example.

Unlike this militant laicism, however, the United States tradition of erecting a wall of separation between church and state (a tradition that is gaining worldwide recognition) does not necessarily involve any sort of secularist prejudice.[13] In fact, historically speaking, the opposite is true, witness, to mention just one example, Thomas Jefferson's fairly high regard for confessional religion. Still, Franklin's polite contempt has found followers, too, and some recent political and social developments in the United States would seem to indicate that the First Amendment is increasingly being construed in an adversarial, anti-religious sense.[14]

From a political and cultural point of view, the principal strength of Deist civil religion is that it allows and creates freedom for all forms of worship. In the United States, this is often demonstrated by the presence of a variety of ministers of religion praying at public functions where the unity of the nation under God is cultivated. Theologically speaking, however, Deism suffers from a fundamental weakness: an almost purely theoretical conception of God. In practice, this tends to take the bite out of the very thing Deist civil religion respects and wishes to make possible: common worship – that most characteristic feature of positive religion.

Given the tenuousness of the worship it inspires, it is not surprising that Deism tends to reduce, both theoretically and in practice, the possible meaning of any religion to *ethics*, and in particular, to a purely universalist ethic based on rationality and individual autonomy. This, however, frequently leads, again in practice, to misgivings about the kind of motivational morality in virtue of which members of churches (and other positive religions) typically make very particular moral choices. In this way, curiously, a public ethic divorced from worship harbours a tendency towards intolerance. In the name of universality, it ends up recognizing as respectable, or indeed acceptable, only an almost purely legal sort of social-contract ethic. Such an ethic, however, may eventually end up publicly discouraging individuals and particular groups from voluntarily making vigorous commitments and commending them – commitments which they consider both objectively good and beneficial, yet which they also recognize as principally binding on themselves and their co-religionists. Seen in this light, the common worship and the shared community values characteristic of positive religions turn out to be rather less sectarian and prejudiced than this brand of intolerant Deism would hold them to be.

There is another tendency in natural religion, and a deep-seated one. It consists in the simple identification of human self-consciousness with immanent divinity. This frequently takes the shape of an uncritical canonization of individual conscience; sometimes, however, it takes the shape of a heroic cult of human vitality or of human spirit, in which the very conception of God comes to coincide with inner pride.

There is a distinctively Romantic-heroic version of this, well exemplified by the thought of Johann Gottlieb Fichte. For Fichte, any true concept of God is both impossible and superfluous, because assurance about divinity simply coincides with self-consciousness. Fully self-identified by this radical immanence, the completely self-conscious person simply transcends the contingencies of historical existence. 'I am a God in the depth of my thoughts, enthroned, in my innermost soul, over myself and the universe', as a late Romantic Dutch poet was to convey the Fichtean stance.[15] In this way, human self-identity lays claim to a truly meta-physical sovereignty. In Fichte's own words: 'Only the Metaphysical, and in no way the Historical, makes blessed.'[16]

Rudolf Otto has rightly pointed out that Schleiermacher was very much aware of this issue. In treating the question as to whom Schleiermacher had in mind when he addressed his *Speeches* to the 'cultured among religion's despisers', Otto explains:

> Those 'imbued by the culture of the times' ... are those who, touched by literature and philosophy, have been grasped and imbued by the great Idealist movement of the day. The readers he has in mind are not the tired skeptics, those who know too much, those defeated in the battle between 'knowledge' and 'faith,' those for whom world, mind and ideas have become a source of discouragement; rather, he is thinking of the disciples of Herder, Goethe, Kant, and especially Fichte. He wants to overcome, not doubts or petty atheisms, but a conflict of mood. While vigorously sharing and endorsing the Idealism of his time, he confronts its high-mindedness and its proud self-awareness, and especially Fichte's grand heroic conception of the 'I' as lord of world and things, as gloriously self-sufficient and free. He wants to safeguard gentle humility and abandon, in opposition to all that captivates and carries away, not only the world and things, but also the 'I' and ourselves. Without that humility, the mood and the culture of the day, for all their vitality, are nothing but 'hubris,' nothing but 'promethean insolence'

– an insolence that steals, with a coward heart, what it could have claimed and awaited in quiet assurance.[17]

Theologically speaking, therefore, it is important to identify the *agenda* behind the tendency to present the human religious *a priori* as unrelated to positive religion. In and of itself, we must emphasize, the human religious *a priori* is the intrinsic, integral, 'natural' element within positive religion as it exists in the concrete. Those who, by a process of rational involution, raise it to the power of independent existence tend to overlook that the resulting conception of God is almost completely theoretical.

What is more significant in this move, however, is that those who thus canonize native human religiosity are interested in the affirmation of the human self, not so much as religious, but as autonomous, or in cases even as divine in its own right. This may sound noble, but it really amounts to the end of all religion. The human interiority laid bare by transcendental reflection can be safely understood as inherently religious, but only on condition that it is not conceived in terms of sovereignty over everything, including sovereignty over positive (or 'organized') religion.

Both Friedrich Schleiermacher and Karl Rahner have understood this. The former conceived of the fundamental religiosity that characterizes the human person as such in terms of absolute dependence on God (in the second of the *Speeches* and in §§32–5 of *The Christian Faith*); the latter stressed the total openness and receptiveness to God and to all of creation that lies at the root of human integrity (in *Foundations of Christian Faith*[18] and elsewhere).

Dietrich Bonhoeffer saw all of this with uncommon clarity, when he argued that the real issue is not natural religion, but the human demand for total autonomy, which has taken, in the course of history, a variety of forms. There are recurrent demands that the Christian faith justify itself before a superior tribunal, whether it be Reason (in the eighteenth century), or Culture (in the nineteenth), or *Volkstum* (in Nazi Germany). All those demands amount to one and the same irreligious demand: that the Christian faith justify itself before the tribunal of human autonomy.[19]

(v) Flannery O'Connor, too, was acutely aware, as well as savagely critical, of one typically North American shape which this identification of inner, autonomous self-assertion with religion tends to take. In one of her letters she writes:

> One of the effects of modern liberal Protestantism has been gradually to turn religion into poetry and therapy, to make truth vaguer and vaguer and more and more relative, to banish intellectual distinctions, to depend on feeling instead of thought, and gradually to come to believe that God has no power, that he cannot communicate with us, cannot reveal himself to us, indeed has not done so, and that religion is our own sweet invention.

And in a letter to a close friend she explains, savagely:

> This girl . . . who shows up here from time to time, was a seminarian at Union
> in New York and quite snarled up in the emotions, etc. When the psychiatrist
> got through with her, her emotions flowed magnificently and she believes nothing
> and she herself is her God, and everything for her depends on her success in the
> theatre – which I doubt she'll ever have.[20]

(vi) *Natural religion and positive religion, therefore, are real only in mutual
interdependence.* Appreciating the relationship between humanity's transcendental orientation to God and the Christian faith's historic structures means:
understanding it in terms of a mutual critique – one not rarely filled with
tension. On the one hand, the historic, authoritative structures of Christian cult,
conduct and creed are to be tested by the requirements of human integrity. If
this were not done, Christians would be forced into commitments unworthy
of human dignity, but indirectly also unworthy of the God who creates
humanity as inherently attuned to the divine majesty and mystery. On the other
hand, natural, universal human religiosity must be tested by the standard of the
positive, concrete structures of worship, life and doctrine. If this were not done,
natural human religiosity would arrogate to itself an unbecoming autonomy in
relation to God as well as in relation to human community. Such an autonomy
will also place humanity in an ultimately irreligious (and inhumane!) position
of sovereignty over the world.

2   Christianity and Natural Religion

1   *The asymmetry between natural and positive religion*

Natural religion and positive religion, we have argued, do not exist except in
a relationship of mutual dependence. Consequently, both are legitimately used
in the service of mutual critique, lest both cease to be religion, and lest both
end up distorting true humanity. These conclusions, it would appear, could
conveniently end our argument at this point. There is, however, an important
question left – one that will take us far afield. Do natural religion and positive
religion have equal standing in the relationship? In other words, is the
relationship between the two symmetrical? Or are they related asymmetrically
– that is to say, by way of a hierarchical relationship?

In the present context, we will answer this question only in a very incomplete
manner. For now, we must limit ourselves to the Christian faith, without
dealing with the claims that can be rightly made in behalf of other positive
religions.

However, the decision not to argue the thesis fully at this point does not mean that we must content ourselves with simply stating it. We will, therefore, state the thesis, and then immediately proceed to explore, at some length, some of its principal dimensions and consequences, both historical and systematic. The main reason for this procedure at this time is that the discussion of the relationship between natural human religiosity and the Christian faith has left profound marks on the Christian faith and on Christian theology as they have come down to us.

Our thesis, then, is that, at least in the case of the Christian faith, *the relationship between natural religion and positive religion is asymmetrical*, since the Christian faith as a positive religion must be recognized as the concrete shape of grace, and hence, accorded theological superiority over natural religion.

The thesis is a restatement of two fundamental insights of Thomas Aquinas. The first is that grace, far from 'cancelling' nature, both 'presupposes' and 'perfects' it. The second is that 'the gift of grace exceeds every power of created nature'.[21]

In the following exploration, it is of the utmost importance to keep in mind our previous argument that natural religion and positive religion do not actually exist except in a relationship of mutual dependence. Hence, any hierarchy occurs, not between two separable elements, but between two distinguishable 'moments',[22] which are related to each other by way of mutual, dynamic interpenetration (*perichōrésis*). The attribution of hierarchical superiority to one 'moment', therefore, does not entail the attribution of a separate existence to it.

The catholic tradition has always understood this rather well. It has always insisted that regard for humanity's transcendental orientation to God is an integral part of the theological task of understanding the Christian faith as a positive religion. The advocates of natural religion have not always demonstrated the same understanding; they have often treated natural religiosity as if it were capable of an independent existence. Against this, it is our contention that natural religion cannot but take the shape of a positive religion, and hence, that advocacy of natural religion can never simply claim to be universalist, noncommittal, unprejudiced, or even tolerant. The explorations of the next section are to be understood in light of this basic understanding.

2   The classic case for the superiority of natural religion

(i)   The position just adopted is likely to be unattractive to those who do accept an asymmetry between natural religion and positive religion, but construe it, whether by design or in practice, in the direction of a hierarchical superiority of natural religion over positive religion. The tendency to do so has an influential tradition, which has manifested itself in several shapes. While it has been especially prominent since the Enlightenment, it was far from unknown to the ancient church.

Contemporary Christian theology, especially in North America, must obviously concern itself with the contemporary version of the problem. However, it will come to this task better equipped if it lets itself be instructed by the great tradition. Against that classic background, modern theology will also be able to gain a clearer, and very necessary, understanding of the special features that characterize the modern version of the problem. We will, therefore, begin by briefly discussing the issue as the ancient church knew it. This will lay the groundwork for the treatment, in the later part of this essay, of the modern, post-Enlightenment shape of the problem.

In any case, we are dealing here with a crucial theological issue, to be treated with great care. The thesis that Christianity as a positive religion is hierarchically superior to natural religion must not be lightly asserted. Here if anywhere in theology today, 'zeal for God' must not be 'unenlightened' (cf. Romans 10:2). Precisely because it is an essential thesis, it must be very responsibly proposed. It can be so proposed only on condition that it is clearly recognized that the thesis has faced, is facing, and will continue to have to face, serious challenges.

(a) These challenges are more obvious in some periods than in others. One telling way to characterize the period between, roughly, the mid-fifth century and the late seventeenth century is to note that there were no serious systematic challenges to the thesis that Christianity as a positive religion is superior to natural religion. This is tantamount to stating that orthodox Christianity provided the culture with its normative intellectual climate. This became especially true in the medieval Christian West. There the pursuit of secular learning, logic, philosophical reflection, and eventually, natural theology came to be too solidly set in the context of Christian orthodoxy and ecclesiastical sponsorship to be able to direct themselves roundly against the faith. Moreover, the penalties meted out to heretics by the secular arm were too harsh to make a public critique of Christianity an attractive option. Heresies did occur, of course. But the many popular, charismatic uprisings[23] were not so much directed against the Christian faith as against the ecclesiastical establishment. Faith did coexist with heresy and residual paganism in places,[24] but this never amounted to a full-blown naturalist critique of Christianity as a positive religion, except in the eyes of those modern observers who see manifestations of such a critique everywhere.

While the instances where the authority of the Christian faith was really contested, therefore, were few and far between, they were none the less real. In the case of the extravagant, brilliant thirteenth-century Emperor Frederick II, the claim that he had transcended Christianity (which earned him a reputation for atheism, among other things) may have been mainly a matter of swagger. But there are good reasons to think that the medieval church had to deal with undercurrents of sophisticated critique, in a variety of quarters. The philosophical daring at the universities, the creative independence found in literary circles, and the increasing claims to secular authority voiced among the merchant class stimulated free thought not always compatible with Christian orthodoxy. In philosophy, there were tendencies toward Averroism and rationalism, sometimes feebly defended by means of the theory – frequently attributed to Siger of Brabant, Aquinas's colleague and adversary in Paris – that there exist two independent realms of truth, reason and faith. Much medieval literature, including some religious literature, owed more to pagan philosophy than to faith. It is also hard to imagine that there was nothing serious behind the aesthetic charm – often elegant and mostly fanciful, sometimes delightfully naughty – with which many medieval and early Renaissance authors proposed not a few pagan ideas which, if seriously entertained, would be quite offensive. What comes to mind is the courtly love tradition,[25] and names like Petrarch, Chaucer and Boccaccio; even Dante has not escaped suspicion.[26] The advice of the humanist Clelio Caicagnini ('speak with the many, think with the few') was widely taken long before it was formulated. At least for the record, therefore, it must be noted that real dissent, all the more careful for having to be cautious, was far from unknown in the otherwise very Catholic Middle Ages.

(ii)   First of all, we will probably do well to go on the assumption that there is something universal about the tendency to criticize positive religion, and to reduce it, at least to some extent, to its anthropological dimensions. There are aspects to positive religion that simply ask for, and even provoke, criticism – especially of outsiders.

To mention one example, in positive religion, the response to the divine is very often ingenuous and unstudied. Yet the artlessness of innocence can turn into naiveté, especially when innocence turns stubborn and resists the demands of rationality and sophistication; and hard though it may be to draw the line, there is a decisive difference between ingenuousness and credulity. Hence, when the critique of religion arises, it is often hard to tell which of the two attracts the critique: positive religion in and of itself, or the immaturity of its forms and the irrationality of its adherents. On the other hand it is also true that outside critics of positive religion frequently make their task rather too easy for themselves by declaring that positive religion is, in and of itself, a form of immaturity or prejudice, or, worst of all, insincerity.

(iii)   Yet not all critique comes from outside. As persons and communities mature and get broader realities to face, their very religions tend to give rise to thought, and reflection comes to inhibit the spontaneity of the old-time religion. In this way, like an unstable chemical compound, positive religion gives evidence, it would seem, of a native tendency to find a lower energy-state; it appears spontaneously to want to trade itself in for something a little more 'realistic'.

Martin Buber has laid bare some of the twentieth-century cultural dynamics of this process of reduction, manifested in the development of the modern 'darkening of God', in a book with the same title.[27] But the tendency towards this kind of reduction is probably ubiquitous, witness, for example, the ease with which the early eighteenth-century naturalists' religious wonder at the marvels of nature soon drifted off into mere ethical exhortation,[28] and much further back, the naturalness with which Euripides came to psychologize what had been truly cultic and religious–ethical postures and attitudes in Aeschylus and Sophocles.

(iv) However, positive religion frequently has to face a rather more intentional critique, which at times can turn downright aggressive. Positive religion can indeed be crude and 'unspiritual'. Not only do its deities and its heroes (not to mention the accounts of their exploits) often look dubious; the blind, partisan devotion often shown by its adherents is disconcerting, if not downright repulsive, even if the object of their cult could, perhaps, be considered acceptable or even attractive.

(a) The Christian church had to face this issue from the outset. In the ancient world, the crassness and narrow-mindedness of much positive religion caused as much polite embarrassment as they do nowadays, especially among the motivated intelligentsia. Then as now, the need for sophistication and integrity in believing took a number of forms. The yearning for mystery uncluttered by vulgar detail and shared only with the serious and the select was as apparent in the various forms of ancient religious Gnosticism as it was ever to be among eighteenth-century Freemasons. Philosophic reflection on humanity's natural religiosity produced allegorized, rationalized, liberal and above all tolerant versions of traditional religions. Stoicism, with its tasteful cultivation of disciplined virtue, proved especially attractive. This was partly due to its ability to interpret traditional polytheism in an urbane, reasonable, profound and ultimately monotheistic (if pantheistic) perspective. Other religious movements, mostly of Neo–Platonic extraction, considered positive religion crude beyond recovery, as Plato himself had tended to do. They tended to opt either for an intellectual philosophic monotheism with ecstatic perspectives, or, in the case of the Isis religion, for a mystical–cultic monotheism with clearly universalist perspectives.[29] All these movements in some fashion appealed to an eternal order of reality, accessible either by Reason, or by way of special revelations. Most of them also agreed in criticizing and rejecting particularity in religion as gross and sectarian.

The ancient church shared many of these criticisms. It, too, had a universalist outlook. It was developing an increasing respect for Reason, for it saw in Christ the final revelation of the divine Logos, which had given evidence of itself at other times and in other places. Finally, it rejected the grossness and the busyness of idolatry as an insult to humanity as much as to God. At the same time, it insisted on being particular as well. This was a demanding combination of claims to

271

defend, but the challenge was met, and it produced a series of capable apologists. Eventually, it produced the brilliant mind who was equal to the ancient church's task of intellectually confronting the claims of natural religion: Origen. It took the shape of a lengthy diatribe known as *Contra Celsum* – Origen's elaborate rejoinder to a pointed attack on the Christian church by the late second-century pagan philosopher Celsus, entitled *Alēthēs Logos* ('True Reason').[30]

(b) A substantial part of Celsus's critique of the Christian religion derived from the Stoic elements in his philosophical background. Celsus, therefore, found much to admire in the church, especially the universalism of its *Logos* doctrine. As a result, he was all the more baffled as well as offended by the impenitent insistence, on the part of Christianity (and of the Judaism it arose from: cf. Esther 3:8!) on its particularity.

In Celsus's eyes, absolute claims on the part of positive religions had to be steadfastly denied, and it was a mark of true philosophical intelligence to be able to do so, in a civilized manner. It was best done by interpreting the myths of all religions allegorically. Putting the positive religions in perspective in this way enabled one to view them all together, ultimately, in the light of Reason. Seen in that light, all religions had basically the same import: they were versions of 'an ancient doctrine which has existed from the beginning, which has always been maintained by the wisest nations and cities and wise men'.[31] No positive religion, therefore, presented a serious intellectual problem as long as it did not insist on professing its particularity as divine. From a philosophical point of view, all particular religious forms and observances fitted into a broad picture of humane civilization ultimately governed by Reason. In practice, this meant that they all must agree to being appropriately fitted into the order comprehensively held together by the divinely imperial state.[32]

Yet is was a matter of long, wearisome experience that particular religions, despite their obvious grossness and particularity, tended to insist on absolute claims. Since this could only lead to barbarism, it was in the interest of humane civilization to keep the positive religions literally in their places. There, in their own contexts, their particularity was to be appreciated.[33] There, too, they could be encouraged to do what they did best, namely, to give concrete shape to the worship of 'the greatest God', who benevolently let himself be worshipped by means of the worship extended to his lieutenants, the regional deities and daemons appointed by him.[34]

In regard to (Judaism and) Christianity, therefore, Celsus saw a major problem. What offended him was Christianity's arrogant refusal to let itself be fitted in and thus to become like the other religions, which were happy to be only as particular and as partial as the deities and daemons that were the objects of their observances.[35] Any particular religion that failed to recognize these essential limitations was vulgar; Christianity, then, was the limit of corruption and obstinacy, and deserved nothing but contempt. This explains the violence of Celsus's invective: the details of Judaism and Christianity were so crude, he writes, and so inferior to the mythologies of other nations,[36] that most of them were not even capable of refinement by means of allegory.[37] They could, therefore, only be counted on to mislead illiterate yokels and bumpkins.[38]

Given this background, it is clear why Celsus should have greeted Christianity's claims to newness with special scorn. This claim, especially when coupled with the claim to universal significance, involved the rejection of the authoritative religious and philosophic tradition as an acceptable yardstick to judge Christianity by. In the ancient world, however, immemorial tradition symbolized the perennial order and harmony of things; the ancients were inclined to consider antiquity the single most important and incontrovertible sign of truth. 'I have nothing new to say, but only ancient doctrines', Celsus boasts.[39]

For Christians to come up with the novelty that 'some God or son of God has come down to the earth ... is most shameful'. After all, if God wanted 'to correct men', God did not have to come to earth to 'learn what was going on among men'; God could have corrected them 'merely by divine power, without sending some one specially endowed for the purpose'.[40] The true God does not intervene: 'if you changed any one quite insignificant thing on earth, you would upset and destroy everything'; and if we supposed that God wanted to come to earth to throw his weight around, we would be attributing 'a very mortal ambition' to God.[41] What is also in bad taste is that Christians sully the goodness and holiness of the universal Logos, by bringing forward 'a man who was arrested most disgracefully and crucified'.[42] But what is fundamentally objectionable in all of this is the particularism attributed to God by Christians. Why was it only 'after such a long age' that it occurred to God to redirect the human race? 'Did he not care before?' Also, why should God, after such a 'long slumber', have sent some one 'into one corner'?[43] 'He ought to have breathed [his spirit] into many bodies in the same way and sent them all over the world. The comic poet wrote that Zeus woke up and sent Hermes to the Athenians and Spartans because he wanted to raise a laugh in the theatre. Yet do you not think it is more ludicrous to make the Son of God to be sent to the Jews?'[44]

(c) Origen appreciates the import of what Celsus means. In a slightly different context, he agrees with him on an important point. He concedes that God does indeed intend that 'this world as God's work [should] be made complete and perfect in all its parts ... we should agree that in this point [Celsus] was right'. But then comes the decisive difference: 'God does not take care, as Celsus imagines, only of the universe as a whole, but in addition to that He takes particular care of every rational being'.[45]

In Origen's view, therefore, the world is not a world as the Stoics (whom Celsus is here following) conceive of it. It is not a quiescent place where differences (such as those between the animal world and humanity) do not really count, and where an impersonal divinity permeates all things indiscriminately, like a benign, intelligent gas.[46] Rather, Origen maintains, the world is differentiated and dynamic, and it culminates in humanity; and humanity, in turn, is oriented to God. If, then, God wants to correct the whole world, it is not unreasonable that God should visit humanity in particular, and in a particular time and place. Origen's analysis implies that Christianity as a positive, particular religion is the perfection of natural religion, not its deformation.

(v)   Remarkably, Celsus's critique of Christianity has some characteristic features in common with contemporary theological positions of the 'liberal' kind. While a bit condescending, his appreciation of all positive religions has a familiar ring to it, as does his polite insistence that none of them must make absolute claims. His recommendation that myths and scriptures be interpreted in a sophisticated, allegorical fashion, which will show them to be mutually compatible and harmonious, is reminiscent of modern appeals to demythologize. Even his Stoic refusal to place humanity in a position of eminence over the animal world sounds curiously like some contemporary expressions of ecological concern. Most strikingly modern, however, is his rejection of an 'interventionist' God, and his pointed insistence that the Christian faith in the particularity of the incarnation poses a huge theological problem, since it raises the suspicion that the Christian church is innately intolerant.

Yet there are characteristic differences, too, and it is precisely these differences that should warn us not to equate Celsus's critique of Christianity as a positive religion too readily with the modern, post-Enlightenment critique. In all likelihood, we would be making an error in historical judgement if we were to notice the similarities, and immediately jump to the conclusion that Celsus's critique is but an historic instance of a timeless, meta-historical issue in fundamental theology: the affirmation of the universal character of humanity's innate religiosity. Such a conclusion might also blind us to the distinctiveness of this fundamental theological issue as it presents itself today. The critique of positive religion, and of the Christian faith in particular, has become current in contemporary Western Christianity, and widespread in North America. We must, therefore, somewhat more carefully review its characteristic features. Then we will be in a position to draw conclusions for the further conduct of our argument. The remainder of this essay will be devoted to this task.

3   Christianity as a Positive Religion Today

1   *From Latitudinarian critique to Deist rejection*

(i)   There is something deeply disturbing about the historical antecedents of the modern critique of the Christian faith as a positive religion, namely, that it is the product, not of outsiders like Celsus, but of self-destructive tendencies within Christendom itself.

It arose as a radical reaction, on the part of sincere Christians, to the painful aftermath of the Reformation: the interminable, unprofitable and often murderous confessional debates of the sixteenth and seventeenth centuries, carried out amidst the devastation and confusion of the religious wars.[47] It had been difficult to profess a faith broken by the broad divisions of the first phase of the Reformation; it became almost self-defeating to profess a faith progressively shattered into unnumbered factional confessions. There is a world of painful discord behind George Herbert's harmonious lines:

> Come, my Way, my Truth, my Life: . . .
> Such a Truth, as ends all strife.[48]

In the case of the Roman Catholic Church, the real achievements of the Counter-Reformation were painfully offset by a rash of progressively abstruse theological controversies, as well as by widespread disaffection among the learned. But the problem was not limited to Catholicism. Like malignant growths, overspecialized doctrines were disfiguring the great body of Christian doctrine everywhere and draining it of its energy. What made things worse was that all of them were in various degrees being enforced (or, as the case might be, repressed) by authority, sacred as well as secular. This created, among other things, a steady movement of exiles for conscience's sake, which exacerbated the churches' sickness and metastasized many growths even further. This is the period, it must be recalled, that also witnessed a spectacular spread of Christianity outside Europe; but it was religious exiles as well as missionaries that were joining the conquerors and the traders; Europe was bequeathing to the world a Christendom hardened by division. All denominations and churches, from Popery to Puritanism, came to look more and more like intolerant, sectarian theological systems.

Hence, wearied and worn down, and at a loss for constructive alternatives, many middle and late seventeenth-century Arminians, Latitudinarians, Quakers and quiet agnostics opted out of the churches. In a platonizing vein, they turned to a simple, direct, pietistic biblicism combined with an ardent trust in the authority of Reason as the only way to recover serenity, peace, and sometimes, as in the case of Rembrandt's biblical etchings, extraordinary spiritual and artistic harmony and depth. Eventually, many came to the conviction that it was in the interest of unity to hold that the Christian faith could, and should, be freely judged by Reason.[49]

John Toland's tract *Christianity not Mysterious*, published at Oxford in 1696, comes to mind as a representative early statement of this position. Toland, an Irish Catholic born in Derry, was not a very capable theologian, but he had his finger on the pulse, and he wrote from experience. Having been brought up, 'from my Cradle, in the grossest Superstition and Idolatry',[50] he had travelled, via the Scottish Protestantism of Glasgow and Edinburgh, to the Arminianism of Leyden, from where he moved to Oxford. The little book he wrote there was far from profound, but it startlingly expressed what many people were half thinking, which accounts for its *succès de scandale*.

The preface is the more telling part of the book, for that is where the author shows his hand. Early on, he disarms his reader, 'the well-meaning Christian', with the assurance that he is writing 'with all the Sincerity and Simplicity imaginable'.[51] He implies that those two virtues have long been lost, given the 'foreseen Wranglings of certain Men, who study more to protract and perplex than to terminate a Controversy'.[52] However, what has really gotten lost is Reason, for the contestants inevitably end up having 'Recourse to Railing when Reason fails them'. Along with Reason, what has gotten lost is Religion, and Religion 'is always the same, like God its Author, with whom there is no Variableness, nor Shadow of changing'.[53]

The implication is, of course, that Reason and Religion have a common cause, based on the fact that they are both simple and unchangeable, and that both can be had apart from doctrinal and theological systems. 'A wise and good Man will judge the Merits of a Cause consider'd only in itself, without any regard to Times, Places or Persons.'[54] John Toland, therefore, will appeal to Reason as the tribunal of last resort in matters of Religion. This has the added advantage of also providing a reasonable defence against the 'declar'd Antagonists of Religion'. What he wants to correct, in sum, is 'the narrow bigoted Tenets' of the churches, denominations and sects, as well as 'the most impious Maxims' of the atheists.[55]

What does Toland mean by this reasonable religion between impious atheism and sectarian prejudice? Interestingly, it is simply the gospel: 'They are not the Articles of the East or West, Orthodox or Arian, Protestant or Papist, consider'd as such, that I trouble my self about, but those of Jesus Christ and his Apostles'.[56]

It is in passages like this that Toland shows his mood. His plea for Reason and Religion arises from an understandable frustration with the divisions, from an impatience that has driven him altogether out of that wearying world of controversy. Once he has gained his distance, he can freely denounce; in this way his initial profession of religious sincerity and simplicity begins to degenerate into a scarcely veiled, spiteful petulance. It comes as no surprise when, with more grandiloquence than realism, he announces his intention to publish an 'Epistolary Dissertation ... entitul'd Systems of Divinity exploded'.[57] This is Toland's real agenda. In comparison with this, his other concern – the denunciation of atheism – is no more than a feeble corollary. Could it be that he was taking precautionary measures against accusations of atheism directed at himself?

Toland's advocacy of Reason and Religion, therefore, is governed by a double negative agenda. First, but relatively unimportantly, he does not want to pass for a non-Christian or a heathen. The prevailing cultural climate is still distrustful of Socinianism; Deism is on the horizon, but it is not acceptable yet. Secondly, and most importantly, he has lost faith in the viability of any concrete, historical form of Christianity.

Seventy years before Toland, another former Roman Catholic, John Donne, had still prayed, amidst the disorientation of controversy, for a vision of Christ's spouse, and he had looked among, not above, the churches for an answer to his prayer:

> Show me deare Christ, thy spouse, so bright and cleare.
> What, is it she, which on the other shore
> Goes richly painted? or which rob'd and tore
> Laments and mournes in Germany and here?
> Sleeps she a thousand, then peepes up one yeare?
> Is she selfe truth and errs? now new, now'outwore?
> Doth she, and did she, and shall she evermore
> On one, on seaven, or on no hill appeare?
> Dwells she with us, or like adventuring knights
> First travaile we to seeke and then make love?[58]

Toland no longer prays for any vision of a church; he simply claims he *has* the true religion, 'of Jesus Christ and his Apostles,', 'of the Lord Jesus Christ, who alone is the Author and Finisher of my [!] Faith'.[59] The truth he wants to establish is a deinstitutionalized, essentially private truth – the one reasonable, true Christian religion, harmonious above all divisions, serene above all vicissitudes of place and time.

On this airy foundation, then, Toland outlines his project in writing *Christianity not Mysterious*. In the present volume, he writes, he will 'prove [his] Subject in general', which is 'that the true Religion must necessarily be reasonable and intelligible'. Strikingly but not unexpectedly, he will offer this proof while taking 'the Divinity of the New Testament . . . for granted'.

The second volume will then be devoted to 'a particular and rational Explanation of the reputed Mysteries of the Gospel'; this will show that the 'requisite Conditions' for the true religion, namely rationality and intelligibility, 'are found in Christianity'. The third volume will argue that the 'clear and coherent System' of Christianity was not framed by human 'good Parts and Knowledge', but 'was divinely reveal'd from Heaven'.[60] Technically, therefore, Toland is not a Deist, for he calls the Christian faith revealed, but his case is flimsy. His demonstration, in a projected third volume, of 'the Verity of Divine Revelation' has a negative intention: it is to be directed 'against Atheists and all Enemies of reveal'd Religion'.[61]

But in such a framework, the divine authority of scripture is no more than a voluntarist postulate; there are no cogent reasons, whether communal or intrinsic, why scripture should still be respected as of divine origin. In this context, it can be anticipated that in due course the free, unfettered flight of Reason will become far more attractive than any forced homage paid to scripture. It did in Toland's case, as his fantastical *Pantheisticon* of 1720 showed with a vengeance.[62] Still, Toland's almost total surrender to Reason had been noted earlier, when he had repeated, with approval, a remark made by Benjamin Whichcote, the Cambridge Platonist, to the effect that 'natural religion was eleven parts in twelve of all religion'.[63] Thus, *il n'y a qu'un pas* from Toland to the full Deism of the Enlightenment, whose theologians 'did not reject the Bible; they found in it only natural religion'.[64]

(ii)   A quick glance at the world of the New Learning, which was developing largely apart from the churches, can only confirm this development. Was methodical Reason not proving its ability to provide far more insight and harmony than theological controversy ever had provided, especially in its discovery of the secure laws governing the heavens and the earth – laws that never will be broken, divinely established for the guidance of the universe? Laws of such geometrical purity and harmony that they could not but provide the patterns for the pursuit of all truth and all goodness? Laws which could be discovered by means of one universally applicable method?

(iii)   The theological rationality advocated by Christians like Toland was still residually dependent on confessional Christianity; in fact, that was what entitled them to advertise their critique of divided Christianity. That critique was, at least in the beginning, and quite overtly, their principal agenda.

In a more scholarly vein, the reasonable interpretation of scripture advocated by the German 'Neologians' showed a similar combination of basic rationalism with residual biblical Christianity. However, it did not take long for this unstable alliance between rationalism and faith in biblical revelation to be broken up by the progress of rationalistic Deism, which clearly had the force of logic on its side.

Gotthold Ephraim Lessing, a declared enemy of Christian orthodoxy, yet one who greatly respected its intellectual tradition, had only contempt for the feeble compromises of this residually Christian Socianism and related forms of 'enlightened' Christianity. 'Under the pretext of making us reasonable Christians', he wrote to his brother Karl,

> we are turned into extremely unreasonable philosophers. . . . We are one in our conviction that our old religious system is false. But I cannot say with you that it is a patchwork of bunglers and half-philosophers. I know of nothing in the world upon the study of which human intelligence has been more acutely shown and exercised. What really is a patchwork of bunglers and half-philosophers is

the religious system which they now want to put in place of the old; and with far more influence upon reason and philosophy than the old arrogated to itself.[65]

(iv)   This forced severance of Reason and the Bible led to a real, though relatively minor, change at the level of content: by the time Reason *pur et simple* began to advocate and admire a purely natural Religion, there was not too much orthodoxy left to lose among the liberal Christians. Some fifty years after Toland, the inevitable conclusions of this development were firmly drawn by Lessing, who – so the story goes – wanted a notary at his deathbed (not a priest, like Voltaire, after all!), to certify that he had died 'in none of the positive religions'.[66] In Lessing's view, positive religions are nothing but conventional constructs, made 'out of the religion of nature, which was not capable of being universally practised by all men alike'. In the concrete order, positive religion is indispensable, but this indispensability lies not in its 'modifications' but in 'its inner truth, and this inner truth is as great in one as in another. Consequently all positive and revealed religions are equally true and equally false. The best positive religion is that which contains the fewest conventional additions to natural religion, and least hinders the good effects of natural religion'.[67]

The Deist mood was able to find this natural religion not only in nature, but everywhere: in the Bible, in Islam, and in the religions of China and other foreign parts, which were just beginning to fascinate eighteenth-century Europe. It found it even in Sephardic Judaism, which was experiencing a revival, not in the last place in response to the trail-blazing writings of Spinoza in the previous century.

Deism also showed a fairly fertile literary imagination. Lessing found natural religion, with Nathan the Wise, in a philosophy of universal tolerance that vaguely sounded like Jewish wisdom.[68] Daniel Defoe found it, with Robinson Crusoe, on an off-shore island near the mouth of the Orinoco River, in the company of noble savages whose opinions sounded surprisingly similar to those of the lower-class urban English dissenters.

(v)   It is in Jean-Jacques Rousseau perhaps more than in any other writer that Deism shows its true face. Several factors contribute to Rousseau's rare clarity and suasiveness. An important one is the fact that he does not set Deism in the accommodating context of British liberal Protestantism, but harshly offsets it against a French Roman Catholicism with Jansenist overtones, and cast by Rousseau himself as cold, deliberate and uncompromising, as well as obscurantist and theologically thin. Yet the principal source of the suasiveness of Rousseau's Deism is the sheer fascination that the author's own immoderate personality and his extraordinary talent inspire.

Unlike John Toland, Rousseau is a dazzling stylist. Like Toland, he is not profound. But far more than Toland, he has his finger on the pulse of the intelligentsia of the period, whose sensibility he knows from inside like few others in the century. Like Lessing, he is marvellously versatile – an arguer and sophist rather than a thinker; unlike Lessing, who is ultimately interested in solid positions and ideas, he is the past master of charm, beguiling to the point of being seductive, yet in the most innocent of ways. One of the great prose passages of the century, the 'Profession of Faith of the Savoyard Vicar', in the fourth book of *Émile, or, Education*,[69] is Rousseau's classic statement on Deism.

The fictitious speaker is a suspended priest professing his faith (or making his confession?) to a young man. In the first half of this profession, the priest gives an autobiographical account of the unreliability of all systems of religion and metaphysics. Duped and driven into perplexity by all the established authorities, but sustained by an inner love of truth as his sole resource, he recounts how he had at long last entered into his own soul, with Descartes and Locke as his principal guides. In this way he has succeeded in constructing the truth he was always looking for. That truth is Deism pure and simple, of the kind that resolutely refuses to make any definitive affirmations about God or, for that matter, anything else.[70]

At the end of his monologue, the vicar – presented by Rousseau as the very embodiment of the twin Deist virtues of simplicity and sincerity – abandons himself to the reader's judgement. In doing so, he characteristically appeals only to the sincerity of his unaided effort, and deviously suggests that God is to blame for any errors he may have committed:

> I rightly mistrust myself, and so I ask [God] for only one thing, or rather, I expect it from his justice: that he correct my error if I am wrong and if this error puts me in jeopardy. Much as I am in good faith, I do not believe I am infallible. Those of my opinions which I consider the most true may be so many lies, for which person does not hold fast to his [opinions], and how many people agree on everything? Much as the illusion by which I am deceived may have its roots in me, only he can cure me of it. I have done all I could to attain to the truth, but its Source is too lofty; when the strength to go any further fails me, what can my guilt be? It is up to it [the Truth] to draw near to me. [In the meantime I am happy, because I set little store by all of life's wrongs, and because the price that redeems them is within my power.][71]

This last move introduces the theme of the second half of the vicar's profession of faith. It is a typical example of Rousseau's insidious irony. The vicar himself has raised the issue of the need for incarnation, if God's truth is to be fully known. Yet in reality he has brought up the subject only in order to deny it. Under cover of apparent innocence our priest explains that there are no reasonable grounds to accept the claims of any of the positive religions: 'I consider all the religions as so many salutary institutions, which prescribe, in

every country, a uniform way of honouring God by means of a public cult. . . .
I think all of them are good when people serve God conveniently in them: the
essential cult is that of the heart'.[72]

Consequently, Rousseau implies, those who say that the Source of Truth has
in fact drawn near to humanity are expressing no more than a local opinion.
The supernatural reality of the Christian faith is but an empty claim; all we
really have is Nature. There is more than straightforward unbelief here; this
is the rhetoric of polite scorn, knowingly aimed at a weakened ecclesiastical
establishment only too ready to be infuriated.

(vi)   If, therefore, the Savoyard vicar's profession of faith is a fine statement
of the content of Deism, it is vastly more effective in conveying its agenda, both
the overt and the hidden. The overt agenda of Rousseau's plea in favour of
Nature and Reason is a refutation of Christian orthodoxy. That refutation
incorporates elements of what used to be the critique of Christianity offered
by residually Christian rationalists. But that critique has now been absorbed
into Deism to add up to a complete rejection: the reader is to understand that
Reason positively favours the abandonment of the religion of one's immaturity.

But there is something else going on as well: Reason's plea has the hidden
support of *Sentiment*. The speaker in the book merely professes to have been
awakened from the illusions of his upbringing and education, to set out on an
open-minded search for truth, in simplicity and sincerity; the reader is meant
to feel something else. For Rousseau's agenda encompasses, not just repudiation but hostility, and what is more, unacknowledged hostility. This feature of
the text must be briefly discussed, for it is precisely in this regard that Rousseau
is an especially clear and characteristic representative of classical Deism.

The hostility is conveyed indirectly, by means of savage irony. The entire
profession of faith is a brilliant pastiche. The speaker is a priest who has abandoned
the faith. What he has not abandoned, however, is his clerical style. His confession
is a perverse profession of faith, and he still employs, by turns, the language of
faith, of the manuals of spiritual direction, of the Sunday sermon, of the
confessional, of pious hagiography, and, of course, of Augustine's *Confessions*.[73]
He does so while maintaining a pose of harmless, even pious, innocence.

The vicar confesses that his former life was lacking in full humanity, yet not
the vicar but 'they' are to blame for that. 'I learned what they wanted me to
learn, I said what they wanted me to say, I made the commitment they wanted,
and I became a Priest; but I did not take long to find out that in promising not
to be a man, I had promised more than I could keep'.[74] Those 'they' are, of
course, the church:

> This is what complicated my perplexity. Having been born into a Church which
> decides everything, which permits no doubt whatever, the rejection of one point

caused me to reject everything else, and the impossibility of accepting so many absurd decisions also deprived me of those that were not. By telling me, Believe everything, they prevented me from believing anything, and I did not know where to stop.[75]

These quotations call for a moment of realism. There are some choice rationalizations in this second passage. Even if we grant that totalitarian integralism is the systemic temptation of Roman Catholicism, and that the aftermath of the Reformation had shown excessive reliance on enforced orthodoxy, innocence and blame cannot be apportioned that easily.

What we have here is the presentation of an emotional contradiction. Rousseau's vicar denounces an unacceptably totalitarian, ecclesiastical logic to justify his abandonment of the Christian faith, but by attributing that logic to the church, he covers up the fact that it is also his own. This is nothing but a self-justifying move, which enables him to pose as the advocate of a very different logic – that of truth, simplicity and sincerity.

This contradiction operates entirely at the emotional level. In one move, Rousseau communicates to his reader a double message: hostility towards Christianity and sympathy for himself, all under cover of the advocacy of Reason. In fact, this emotional contradiction accounts to a large extent for the persuasive power of Rousseau's piece: the author expects that his irritation will become contagious and contaminate the reader. On the surface, the vicar's profession appeals to the impartiality of Reason to undergird certain arguments for the rejection of the Christian faith; below the surface, he treats us to a profession of innocence that serves as a cloak for hostility. And precisely because the hostility is denied, or at least not acknowledged, it is all the more virulent. Ingenuous readers feel the impact of that hostility without quite knowing where it comes from; the author, whose prejudice is meant to escape them, conceals his animus behind a front of ingenuous reasonableness.

In this regard, Rousseau is, again, very much a child of his time. It is impossible here to give a full account of the conflicted mood that increasingly came to prevail among the sophisticated in the eighteenth century; a few suggestions, however, are not out of place.

The eighteenth century gave us the first medical treatises on a new class of diseases. William Stuckely's lecture *On the Spleen* of 1722 and George Cheyne's book *The English Malady* of 1733 contain the first descriptions of the 'lowness of spirits' and other 'nervous distempers' which a later age would recognize as neuroses. Cheyne explicitly mentions the fact that it is among 'people of the better Sort' – the sophisticated – that 'this Evil mostly rages'.[76]

The causes are not far to seek; they are related to a new, unsettling way of thinking. The early eighteenth century witnessed the beginning of what is easily the most characteristic feature of modernity: the experimental approach to humanity and the world. But this curiously detached, empirical way of life had consequences. It gave rise to the 'divided self', specifically in the circles whose initiates were on the cutting edge of 'progress'. The eighteenth century saw the first symptoms of the process of dissociation, and even disintegration, of sensibility, that has continued to characterize the social and individual sensibilities of the West down to our own day.[77]

This process of dissociation is curiously paralleled, in the objective order, by the ceaseless cultivation of division of elements as a most characteristic feature of eighteenth-century rationality. In 1740, Abraham Trembley discovered that it was possible overnight to produce two fresh-water polyps by cutting one polyp in half.[78] Around the same time, Carl Linnaeus is working on his division and classification of the vegetable and animal realms.[79] The most intricate mechanical devices are being developed on the basis of a division of operational tasks. Last but not least, there are the first moves in the direction of division of labour – the process that for the first time in history was to turn human beings into parts of an industrial machinery.[80]

The unconditional cultivation of rationality had a curious side-effect. The world of rational objectivity became so mechanical that the worlds of ethical conduct and feeling got cut loose from their anchorage in rationality and objectivity, and began to lead unconnected lives of their own. Christian pietism became the emotional refuge against rationalism. Predictably, ethics flourished. The Deists thought of religion in almost exclusively ethical terms; Christianity, in their eyes, amounted to a 'perfectly simple ethical teaching, merely loving one's neighbour'.[81] This Deist conception is curiously matched, in the eighteenth-century Roman Catholic Church, by a distressing impoverishment of dogmatic theology and an extraordinary interest in moral theology of a very un-doctrinal kind.

All these dissociative tendencies were not without effect. Modernity came at a price: the cultivation of individuality and freedom, and the displacement of traditional authority by free, and allegedly purely rational, enquiry and discovery led to maladjustments in many spheres. Both Deism and Christian orthodoxy suffered from these maladjustments; it is not surprising that many of their encounters have remained downright neuralgic, down to our day.

It would be a mistake to overlook the liberating aspects of these neuralgic developments: they marvellously stretched the range of available human experience, and thus also demonstrated the depth and the breadth of humanity's capacity for fulfilment. To mention only one example, more sophisticated technology and better playing-techniques produced an unprecedented burst of musical invention. It started with the *empfindsamer Stil* ('sensitive style') of the school of Mannheim, spread like wildfire, with a rich variety of talent, and attained its full flower in the splendour of the work of

Haydn, Gluck and especially Mozart.

Yet not all is balance even here. To appreciate the ambiguities of the eighteenth-century soul, one should try, by an exercise of the imagination, to listen to Sarastro's aria in Mozart's *The Magic Flute* with the ears of an orthodox Catholic Christian:

In diesen heilgen Hallen
kennt man die Rache nicht
und ist ein Mensch gefallen
führt Liebe ihn zur Pflicht.
Dann wandelt er an Freundes Hand
vergnügt und froh ins bere Land.

In diesen heilgen Mauern,
wo Mensch den Menschen liebt,
kann kein Verräter lauern,
weil man dem Feind vergibt.
Wen solche Lehren nicht erfreun,
Verdienet nicht ein Mensch zu sein.

In these holy halls
vengeance is unknown,
and if a man has stumbled,
love guides him to duty.
Then he walks, at a friend's hand,
content and glad into the better land.
Within these holy walls,
where man is loved by man,
no traitor lies in ambush,
since enemies are forgiven.
Those not cheered by such precepts
do not deserve to be man.[82]

The figure of Sarastro, high-priest of Isis and Osiris, is Mozart's monument to a man he much admired. He was the versatile Ignaz von Born, who had once, in 1787, apostrophized Mozart – then at the height of his maturity – as 'graced by Apollo', and who had died shortly before Mozart and his friends Schikaneder and Gieseke started work on *The Magic Flute*. Von Born was a representative embodiment of the protean temper of his age. After a brief period as a Jesuit, he had become a widely travelled jurist and mineralogist, and the author of many scientific works. But he had also cultivated more idealistic pursuits: he had founded the Masonic Grand Lodge *Zur wahren Eintracht* ('To True Concord') – though only to resign from it again, five years before he died.

Mozart's music is heavenly; Sarastro's words are an indictment of the

Catholic Church (and the *ancien régime* it was allied with) as inhumane and punitive – an indictment all the more embarrassing for being kept implicit. Even here, in the midst of beauty, the overtones of the conflict between Faith and Reason can be heard.[83]

(vii) It is time to sum up. The principal difference between Deism and the Christian rationalism from which it had sprung was that Deism completed the severance between Reason and the Bible. This involved a small but real difference at the level of content. Deism did acknowledge the existence of God and commended natural religion, but the intent behind these two affirmations was never far to seek: both served to relativize positive religion in all its forms.[84] However, since all other known religions had already been interpreted as forms of natural religion, the only real target of the Deist critique was orthodox Christianity, as it had been for Celsus.

What was far more significant, however, was the change of *agenda* produced by the shift to pure Deism. Critique turned into hostile repudiation. Repudiation had been Celsus's agenda, too, of course. Yet one feature made the Deist rejection of Christianity decisively different from Celsus's: forced by its own logic, Deism attempted to keep its anti-Christian agenda unacknowledged – is Reason not, by definition, impartial and above the fray? In this way, critique and repudiation turned into prejudice. The new tolerance became intolerant of Christianity's alleged intolerance; the modern rejection of all prejudice turned into a prejudice against all alleged prejudice. The advocacy of pure Reason had to resort to repression to keep its claim to impartiality alive. Tacit contempt of orthodox Christianity began to be cherished as the cultural prejudice of the cultivated. By the end of the century, Schleiermacher would know whom to address.

(viii) All of this leads to an important conclusion. The cardinal issue of the relationship between Christianity and natural religion as it has come down to us is not a purely intellectual one; it is charged with deep-seated emotionality.[85] We have close to three centuries of nervous conflict to teach us that the intellectual, thematic aspects of the problem can only be constructively broached if its emotional elements are squarely faced. It is the main object of the present section to recognize the neuralgic, conflicted mood that has been characteristic, both of the Enlightenment and its aftermath and of Christian orthodoxy in the modern era. Both deserve some reflection.

2 *Christianity and modern culture: emotionalities*

(i) As explained, the new authoritative cultural and intellectual climate brought about by the Enlightenment was hostile to Christian orthodoxy. That hostility, however, had a tendency to pose as reasoned impartiality, and many Rationalists acted as if this profession of impartiality sufficed to absolve them from serious intellectual effort. The classical rationalists were dexterous and versatile encyclopedists rather than profound thinkers, and their new-found inventiveness often blinded them to the shallowness of their arguments. But the sad truth is that in dealing with the church, contempt, not argument, had become the accepted, and infuriating, procedure among the sophisticated – something which very much suited the mood of a century that had adopted lighthearted (and sometimes surprisingly vulgar) mockery as one of its favourite genres.[86] Bishop Joseph Butler was being prophetic rather than peevish, when he wrote, in the preface of his *Analogy of Religion* of 1736:

> It is come, I know not how, to be taken for granted, by many persons, that Christianity is not so much as a subject of inquiry; but that it is, now at length, discovered to be fictitious. And accordingly they treat it, as if, in the present age, this were an agreed point among all people of discernment; and nothing remained, but to set it up as a principal subject of mirth and ridicule, as it were by way of reprisals, for its having so long interrupted the pleasures of the world.[87]

The Enlightenment, therefore, had internal weaknesses and instabilities of its own, often masked and even repressed by a superficial faith in progress. Its apparent advocacy of religion, in the shape of natural religion, masked a lot of emotional ambiguity.

From a theoretical point of view, this should not come as a surprise. Natural religion does not actually exist except in a relationship of mutual dependence on, and perichoresis with, some form of positive religion. Only at the price of inner conflict, therefore, can natural religion regard itself as entirely autonomous and unprejudiced, and view positive religion as naive and uncritical. When natural religion locks the front door against positive religion and its 'prejudice', they will enter by the back door, in the form of other biases – usually rather less easily detectable and less tractable. Such biases will arrive and insinuate themselves strangely disguised, sometimes even as substitute religions. History has witnessed plenty of self-deception in this area, and there are numerous instances of surprisingly naive creeds religiously held by the enlightened, with a devotion worthy of an infinitely better cause, and with an intolerance that is all the more stubborn for parading as objectivity and openness.

(ii) Not being taken seriously is neuroticizing, especially when one's weaknesses are exposed. The Christian faith was not taken seriously, and its principal weakness was a serious as well as an immemorial one: Christian theology had forgotten how to deal with educated unbelief.[88]

Theodosius's decrees *Cunctos populos* of AD 380 and *Nullus hereticus* of AD 381 had banned, not only paganism, but even heresy; Nicaea and Constantinople

I had become the law of the land. Over a period of some thirteen centuries, the church had gotten accustomed to relying on Christian orthodoxy as the normative cultural and intellectual climate. It had come out of the late Middle Ages and the Reformation and its aftermath deeply divided. Not surprisingly, the church's (and the churches') sense of theological priorities had gotten seriously weakened by dint of controversy about doctrines most of which were at least once removed from the foundation of the Christian faith. Preoccupation with heresy and specialized doctrine had robbed Christians of the habit of giving a focused, confident account of the really fundamental dimensions of their faith to unbelievers.

Thus, when the Enlightenment became the prevailing intellectual climate, the church's own resolve was wanting, and its perception of its new, elusive adversary lacked theological precision. At times it fought back so fiercely that it did not look carefully just where to land its blows, and it ended up striking out not at enemies but at hidden allies and friends. At other times it sinned by overstatement, discrediting the very truth it meant to uphold. Sometimes, too, it sought refuge in piety and passivity, and bitterly complained when it was being attacked. Much of the time, it drew not only contempt but supercilious ridicule.

(iii) In this way, cultural developments with deep roots in the sixteenth and seventeenth centuries saddled the relationships between the church and the modern world with deep conflict. Church and Culture, Faith and Reason came to be habitually antagonistic, leaving a trail of mutual caricatures throughout recent history.

As usual in such circumstances, voices of authority[89] on every side endeavoured to settle complex issues by enforcing order and hardening boundaries rather than by promoting patient understanding. The conflict became no less painful where it was interiorized: numerous Christians, especially among the well-educated, got torn between orthodoxy and modernity. In the process, a great deal of suffering was caused by a short-sighted anti-intellectualism of far too many leaders in the churches.

The mood of nervous conflict persisted and even deepened when, in the aftermath of the Enlightenment, there was a welcome revival of substantial philosophical and theological reflection. The Romantic era saw the rise of the great humanistic theisms and atheisms as well as the first great renewals of Christian orthodoxy. Liberal compromises were numerous but only few of them, like F. D. Maurice's conciliatory latitudinarianism, were deep and broad enough to last; most were short-lived. The nineteenth century continued to bristle with the conflicts bequeathed to it by the intellectual and socio-political developments initiated by the eighteenth. These conflicts ran too deep to be quickly settled, and in addition, new conflicts kept arising; integration was only very partial and in any case painfully slow. Mutual suspicions and accusations continued to bedevil the theological discussion of the relationship between natural religion and positive religion, between the legitimate demands of human integrity and autonomy on the one hand and the integrity of the Christian faith on the other.

All of this has consequences for theology today. Forgetfullness of history condemns the forgetful to repeating history's mistakes. The eighteenth century witnessed the first moves of what was to be known, in the twentieth century, as secularization: the definitive displacement of Christian orthodoxy, as the sole normative cultural climate, by autonomous human Reason. The church cannot be said to have taken its cultural disestablishment graciously, nor can it be said that it was free enough to extend to the new scientific and socio-political humanism the critical welcome it deserved. Yet on the other hand the new culture of human Reason was not as open and impartial as it often professed to be. Orthodox Christians in the West have long felt that frequently an unfairly heavy burden of proof has been on them. They have felt how their intelligence and their integrity have come under the scrutiny of prejudice, in what is now a thematically non-Christian world. In such a situation, Christians may be tempted to evade the tension by a quick retreat into isolationist integralism, of the militant or the defensive variety, or by looking for cheap modernist compromises.

(iv) Both temptations must be resisted. Contemporary Christian orthodoxy and theology must achieve a true, contemporary integration of the best of the tradition that has come out of the Enlightenment and the best of the Christian faith. They will do so to the extent that they will learn freely to respect the concerns behind the modern advocacy of natural religion and equally freely to profess the positive elements of the Christian faith.

Neither natural religion nor Christianity as a positive religion occur in the abstract; both occur in time and space, in cultures and in the historic Christian tradition. We know the guises the problem has taken on: nature–grace, reason–revelation, Athens–Jerusalem, culture–religion, state–church.

This leads to a conclusion. If the first task of theology is the search for new forms of unity – or integration – between faith and culture, theology must be as patient and diligent in seeking to understand the contemporary cultural shape which the native human religiosity has taken as in giving an intelligible account of the positive Christian profession of faith. The sadness of past conflict can become the wisdom of present understanding. Disintegration does not necessarily lead to permanent degeneration; it may lead up to, and provide the stuff for, broader as well as deeper integration. There are good reasons to think that in the long run convergence is dominant over divergence.[90]

These considerations also serve to put in bold relief the historic significance of the second Vatican Council. In it, the Roman Catholic Church – even though acting later than many other responsible orthodox Christian bodies – succeeded in putting an end to the 'siege mentality' that had long characterized, not only the church's relationships with the world, but also the practice of theology in the church. The council enabled the church to recognize the two great attainments of the modern age – attainments that will ways remain tasks and never turn into achievements.

The first is the recognition of the potential, the integrity and the fundamental rights of the individual human person; the second is the recognition and appropriation of humanity's power to affect the structures of nature and human society by means of the responsible deployment of scientific and technological knowledge and know-how. Both are precious as well as precarious, as Vatican II recognized, especially in the Declaration on Religious Freedom, *Dignitatis Humanae* and in the Pastoral Constitution on the Church in the Modern World, *Gaudium et Spes*. That they are precarious implies that their actualization will be beset with hardship and conflict; that they are precious implies that they are worth suffering hardship and conflict for.

3 Christianity and modern culture: themes

(i)   The observations just made have brought us back to the thematic aspects of the relationship between Christian faith and modern culture. It was suggested, in a previous section, that there might be characteristic differences between the two shapes which the critique of Christianity as a positive religion has taken: Celsus's version and the modern, post-Enlightenment one. Neglect of those differences, it was added, might blind us to some distinctive theological issues today. The section just concluded has cleared the way for a survey of these distinctive issues.

Four themes suggest themselves as crucial to the understanding of the religious dimensions of modern culture. Understandably, they are also the themes around which much modern emotionality has crystallized. The first is the basic quality of the relationship between natural religion and positive religion. The second is the integrity of the individual human person. The third is the authority of the scientific world picture. The fourth is worship as the original act of religion. Interestingly but not unexpectedly, they are also the four points on which the Deist repudiation of Christianity as a positive religion most strikingly differs from Celsus's.

(ii)   The first is that Celsus saw Reason and positive religion as positively related. His position did involve a reservation about the religions; none were to be considered absolute. Yet in Celsus's view, all religions had positive affinities with a supreme absolute, since all of them were forms of an ultimately reasonable, universal cult of the greatest God. Celsus saw universal Reason as encompassing and permeating the whole world; this enabled those who pursued a life of Reason to accommodate and support and even commend all positive religions.

This shows an important aspect of the classic critique of positive religion. Celsus construed the relationship between natural religion and positive religion asymmetrically, in favour of natural religion; but this asymmetry did not commit him to a rejection of positive religion. Celsus's objection to Christianity was not that it was a positive religion, but that it did not accept his reservation.

The Deist critique of positive religion, on the other hand, was, as a matter of principle, negative. In reality, Deism reduced religion to ethics and was unaware of the self-defeating tendencies inherent in its claim to purely natural religiosity. Lessing's professed contempt for positive religion is more consistent and honest in this regard than the religious claims of many Deists. In any case – and this is our first suggestion – contemporary Christian theology should be realistically aware of the anti-religious tendencies which modern humanism has inherited from Deism, and attempt to show that they are unnecessary. This must be done partly by insisting that natural religion does not possess an independent existence. It should also be done by developing an appreciative approach to the non-Christian positive religions, as Vatican II has shown in the Declaration about the Relationship of the Church to Non-Christian Religions, *Nostra Aetate*.

The real contempt of positive religion implicit in Deism is strikingly conveyed by Henry Chadwick. He writes: 'The enlightened thought it morally justifiable to conceal their true opinions behind the mask of orthodoxy. John Toland had made a special study of the practices of ancient philosophers of teaching one thing to the crowd and another to the inner circle of chosen disciples'.[91] The tradition of Christian orthodoxy has always rejected such gnosticizing mental reservations. It has consistently placed the positive elements of the Christian faith in a position of superiority over the claims of natural, reasonable religion, and denied that intellectual independence requires a certain amount of pardonable duplicity.

One characteristic way in which the tradition has put the positive elements of the Christian faith in a position of superiority lies in its taking worship seriously. Geoffrey Wainwright is on the mark when he writes: 'In comparison with the language of theologic reflection, liturgical language is typically and appropriately more poetic, more affective. But this is hardly licence for holding that one may be a trinitarian within the charmed circle of the liturgy and a unitarian in the academic study'.[92]

(iii) Celsus's universalist conception of Reason had a second important consequence. Reason was indeed found in individuals, but only by way of a *logos spermatikos* – a dissemination of the universal Logos. Reason, therefore, connected the individual, not only with the divine world of encompassing

Reason, but also with the whole universe.

The modern, post-Enlightenment critique of religion is based on a very different experience. It is part of modernity to feel that Reason individuates and even isolates. Modernity's characteristic feature, therefore, is the tendency to view individual freedom and self-consciousness as the prime locus of authentic Reason. For many modern persons, the recognition of the full intellectual and conscientious integrity of the individual is the decisive credibility test of any positive religion. This typically modern 'turn to the subject' (*Wende zum Subjekt*) merits recognition as well as a searching, critical welcome in any contemporary catholic theology. It must be added, however, that it urgently raises the issues of community and personal communication and their relationships with personal integrity – which is our second suggestion.

On this point, contemporary catholic theology is most profoundly indebted to Karl Rahner. His insistence that the Christian faith is to be interpreted as the gracious fulfilment of the human subject's deepest integrity has settled a long-standing debt owed by Christian orthodoxy to the Enlightenment. This may very well turn out to be Rahner's most decisive contribution to Christian theology, especially since he has not tired of showing also how the fundamental integrity of the human subject not only individuates, but also opens up to the mystery of God and to the whole world.

(iv) In *Contra Celsum*, Origen repeatedly reminds his readers that Celsus's philosophical interpretation of all positive religions fails to respect an essential claim of Christianity. The Christian faith is vindicated, not by means of suasive philosophical argument, but by 'demonstration of spirit and power' (1 Corinthians 2:4).[93] This demonstration, Origen explains, is especially cogent in the fulfilment of prophecy and in signs and wonders.

Now on these issues, Celsus and Origen did have their differences. Celsus thinks Jesus's miracles were performed by means of the magic Jesus learned in Egypt, whereas Origen thinks they are morally superior to magic; Celsus thinks that the Old Testament prophecies are so obscure that they might have referred to any number of people, whereas Origen thinks they predicted the events of Jesus's life. These differences, however, are undergirded by a basic agreement. Both believe that we live in a world in which God can be encountered: a world in which wonders and miracles occur, and in which divinity manifests itself in oracles, sibyls and seers.[94]

This is where the modern issue is joined. Can the Christian faith fully respect human integrity and the relative autonomy of the world, and at the same time claim that God has been, is being, and will be (and therefore can be) truly encountered in the world – as both Celsus and Origen agreed? Or does human intellectual and conscientious integrity require of us today that we construe the world in a purely scientific fashion? Is Deism right in construing the world as a closed, autonomous system, which implies that God is ultimately marginal and even superfluous? Even if, with Dietrich Bonhoeffer, we agree to the death of ' "God" as a working hypothesis, as a stop-gap for our embarrassments',[95] does that also kill the possibility of encountering the living God? This crucial third theme must be recognized as one of the foundational issues in contemporary fundamental theology.

Lessing is completely aware of this problem, and formulates the difference with characteristic resolve. He deals with the issue in a short commentary whose title he derived from Origen's claim against Celsus: 'On the Proof of the Spirit and of Power'.[96] He writes:

> I am no longer in Origen's position; I live in the eighteenth century, in which miracles no longer happen. If I even now hesitate to believe something on the basis of the proof of the spirit and of the power – something that I can believe on the strength of other arguments more appropriate to my age: what is the problem? The problem is that reports of fulfilled prophecies are not fulfilled prophecies; that reports of miracles are not miracles. These, the prophecies fulfilled before my eyes, the miracles that occur before my eyes, are immediate in their effect. But those – the reports of fulfilled prophecies and miracles, have to work through a medium which takes away all their force.[97]

(v)   There is a fourth and final difference between Celsus and the Deists. Celsus respected cult as the most typical expression of religion and encouraged the cult of the inferior daemons as a vehicle of the worship of the greatest God. Celsus also respected the mythologies of the positive religions, which he wanted to see allegorically understood. His eclectic combination of Stoicism and Platonism understandably gave much prominence to ethics, but it had not completely lost touch with worship and creed. His interpretation of cult and mythology was appreciative, not dismissive.

The Deists, on the other hand, tended to pay lip-service to cult, but were forever reluctant to engage in its practice. Understandably so, for worship is the most nakedly positive element in positive ('organized') religion. To justify their rejection of worship, the Deists (starting a tradition that was to become especially widespread in North America) tended to appeal to two mutually related tribunals.

The first was ethics, to which Deist religion typically reduced itself. What really mattered, so the Latitudinarians had already taught, was simple and sincere virtue, which unites – not worship and doctrine, which divide.[98]

The second tribunal was individual conscience. The Deists liked to appeal to it in the interest of the assertion of moral rectitude. So did the Romantics, whose idea of conscience, however, was considerably more profound: they appealed to conscience as the locus of a person's fundamental awareness of self-identity. Yet both the Enlightenment and Romanticism agreed that it was in the 'inner shrine', whether of moral conscience or of original, unspoiled awareness of self-identity, that true religion – that is, religion independent of doctrine and common worship – was to be practised, or rather, experienced: 'God being with thee while we know it not'.[99]

(vi)   Our analysis so far would seem to suggest that worship is in some way the element that accounts for the coherence of the three traditional elements of all religion: Cult, Conduct and Creed. The neglect of worship in Deism produced an autonomous, individualist ethic of an ultimately non–doctrinal kind. It is to be expected, then, that concentration on worship will prove to be a productive opening move to explore Christianity as a positive religion.

4   Respecting Christianity's Positive Elements

1   Theology and the superiority of the positive elements

(i)   This essay is committed, with the great tradition, to the thesis that Christianity as a positive religion is hierarchically superior to humanity's transcendental orientation to the mystery of God (which is the basis of natural religion), while at the same time essentially related to it and respectful of it. This leads to conclusions for systematic theology. The method of understanding must be determined by the matter to be understood; it follows that systematic theology must show its respect for the Christian faith as a positive religion before setting out to give a theological account of humanity's native, transcendental aptitude to receive the Christian faith. This means at the very least that theology should acknowledge that the former is epistemologically prior to the latter.

Thomas Aquinas explicitly makes this acknowledgement at the outset of the *Summa contra Gentiles*. Even though the first three books will be devoted to discussions based on natural reason, it is the catholic faith that is to be explained.[100] In the same way, the very first article of the opening *quæstio* of the *Summa Theologica* expressly acknowledges the need for, and the actual existence of, revelation.[101]

The epistemological priority of Christianity as a positive ('historic') religion is also what Karl Rahner implies when, dealing with the relationship between humanity's native desire for God's self-revelation in Christ and the actuality of the Christian revelation, he writes:

> The radical human hope in the very self of God, who is the absolute future, looks for an absolute bringer of salvation in history. A transcendental christology as such cannot arrogate to itself either the task or the ability to state that this absolute bringer of salvation can be readily found in history and that he has actually been found in Jesus of Nazareth. Both of these are part of the irreducible experience

of history itself. In our day, however, we would become blind to this factual history, if we failed to approach it with the kind of reflective and articulate hope for salvation that is featured in a transcendental christology. The latter allows one to seek, and in seeking to understand, what one had already found in Jesus of Nazareth in the first place.[102]

(ii)   Consequently, even though theology, as instanced by Aquinas and Rahner, has traditionally opened the systematic exposition of the Christian faith by an analysis of natural religious knowledge, this has never served to deny that the Christian faith is epistemologically prior. Those who fail to realize this fact run the risk of misconstruing the catholic natural theology tradition in Deistic terms.

(iii)   Yet there are good reasons at this point to raise the question if the traditional order of treatment must simply be accepted as normative. We should also question Karl Rahner's thesis that transcendental reflection is the most appropriate starting point for systematic theology today.

It is obvious that integrity of the human person must be fully recognized today, and that the church's mission includes a mission to take the world seriously. Yet it is equally obvious that orthodox Christianity owes, both to itself and the world, an account of the Christian faith that is both true and matured by reflection, and that there are good reasons to assume that such an account is not as readily available as it could and should be. The principal reason for this is that much Christian theology has lost touch with worship, which is the core experience of the Christian faith, and which alone will be able to recall the church to its original and normative nature. Both the liturgical movement and emphasis placed on the liturgy by Vatican II point in the same direction.[103] *There exists, in other words, a present-day need for a positive starting-point of systematic theology.* This will have to consist in a renewed attention to the positive elements of the Christian faith – a concentration which careful attention paid to the worship of the church can be expected to generate and sustain.

Yet it is also clear that the pressure of modernity works against such a positive starting-point. The history of modern theology shows the effects of this pressure in a variety of ways. Working in very different ways but sharing a deep concern, both Karl Barth and Hans Urs von Balthasar have protested that the integrity of the Christian faith is at bottom a matter of God's holiness, and hence, not up for negotiation. They have often expressed their scepticism about tendencies in Christian theology and practice which, in their view, accommodate the world rather than understand it, and look for compromise rather than encounter. They may have overstated their conviction at times, but their very overstatements at least give us an indication of the pressure to accommodate brought to bear on Christian orthodoxy by modern culture. In a very different yet analogous manner, the aggressive, heavy-handed, sectarian intolerance of much contemporary Evangelical fundamentalism is, minimally, an indication to the same pressure.

(iv)   Much of contemporary Western culture likes to flaunt itself as post-Christian, yet curiously does not succeed in dismissing the Christian faith altogether. Rather, it puts pressure on Christianity to conform. Could this be a sign of a real, if apprehensive, thirst for the Christian faith? If it is, the church would betray the world as well as its own mission if it were, in the passionate words of Dietrich Bonhoeffer,

> so to trim down and lop off the message as to make it fit the fixed framework; until the eagle can no longer raise itself and soar up to his true element, but becomes, his pinions clipped, one more peculiar showpiece among the other tame, domesticated animals. Just as the farmer who needs a horse for his land leaves the fiery stallion in the marketplace and buys himself a spunkless, tame horse, so domestication has produced a serviceable Christianity. When this happens, it is only a matter of time and common sense to lose interest in this whole construct and turn away from it. This type of updating leads straight into paganism.[104]

(v)   These are serious words, spoken, in the critical 1930s, by one who had studied the history of liberal Protestantism and found it wanting. Words like these deserve to be taken seriously everywhere.

In the West, especially in Western Europe, this could very well take the shape of a reminder which the prevalent, residually Christian culture has not heard for a long time: not only should the church listen very carefully to the world, but the world should also very carefully listen to the church. Such a reminder could, perhaps, also move the church of the Old World closer to the emergent church everywhere. The present-day mass conversions, especially to Roman Catholicism, in Africa and in some Asian countries, are reminiscent of the spectacular wave of conversions in the late fourth and early fifth centuries, which created the culture of the Christian West. In such circumstances, the church owes it to the world to speak and act with authority. That authority is not primarily magisterial, although those in ecclesiastical office must exercise magisterial authority in its service. It is the authority that comes from the 'demonstration of the Spirit and of the Power' – of the gospel itself, spoken with boldness and lived out with perseverance.

(vi)   Speaking with boldness, or *parrhēsia*, as the New Testament calls it, is mediating: it is done before God (Ephesians 3:12; 1 Timothy 3:13) as well as before people (2 Corinthians 3,:12; Ephesians 6:19). It involves openness to and familiarity with God and openness to and familiarity with the world. But it comes from God. *Parrhésia* comes to the church from the resurrection of Christ, which is the source of Christian worship, and hence, of the Christian faith.

The study of the Christian faith as a positive religion, however, must not lose touch with natural religion. We must remember, therefore, that Schleiermacher suggested that the interpretation of a positive religion must be practised by focusing on its *structures*; our study of Christianity, in other words, must be a study of the coherence of its positive elements. Only to the extent that we will succeed in doing this will the Christian faith, viewed as a positive religion, reveal the inner quality that characterizes it as a true religion. Our study of Christian worship, therefore, must be the first, and decisive, step in a larger project: to show the coherence of all the structural elements that make up the Christian faith. In fact, it will be argued that Christian worship is the originating source of all those elements. In the mind of the present writer, it will be the task of the new generation of catholic theologians to explain and argue this.

Notes

1   F. Schleiermacher, *Über die Religion,* ed. R. Otto (Göttingen: Vanderhoeck and Ruprecht, 1967), pp. 186–7; *On Religion,* tr. J. Oman (New York: Harper and Row, 1958), pp. 234–5.

2   Schleiermacher's discussion, in *The Christian Faith* (Edinburgh: T&T Clark, 1928), §§ 24–5, of what he sees as the distinctive difference between Roman Catholicism and Evangelical Protestantism lends support to this interpretation. That difference lies in contrary appreciations of the role of the *church*: Protestantism, Schleiermacher explains, holds that believers depend, for the relationship to the church, on their relationship to Christ; Catholicism holds that they depend, for their relationship to Christ, on their relationship to the church.

3   It is good to recall Karl Barth's opinion, expressed in the winter of 1923–4, that Schleiermacher 'does intelligently, instructively and generously what the useless folk of more recent times do stupidly, unskillfully, inconsistently and fearfully' (Eberhard Busch, *Karl Barth: His Life from Letters and Autobiographical Texts,* (Philadelphia: Fortress Press, 1976), p. 151.

4   Quoted by G. Meckenstock, in F. Schleiermacher, *Schriften aus der Berliner Zeit, 1796– 1799,* ed. Günter Meckenstock, *Kritische Gesamtausgabe,* I, 2 (Berlin and New York: Walter de Gruyter, 1984), p. lix.

5   Cf. the discussion of Schleiermacher's hermeneutics in Hans Frei, *The Eclipse of Biblical Narrative: A Study in Eighteenth and Nineteenth Century Hermeneutics* (New Haven, CT, and London: Yale University Press, 1974), pp. 282–324.

6   F. Schleiermacher, *Über die Religion,* pp. 41–99; *On Religion,* pp. 26–101; *Der Christliche Glaube,* 7th edn, ed. Martin Redeker, 2 vols. (Berlin: Martin de Gruyter, 1960); *The Christian Faith,* §§ 3–4. Richard R. Niebuhr, *Schleiermacher On Christ and Religion* (London: SCM Press, 1964), pp. 116–34; F. J. van Beeck, *Christ Proclaimed: Christology*

   as Rhetoric (New York, Toronto, Ramsey, NJ: Paulist Press, 1979), pp. 548–66.

7   K. Rahner, *Foundations of Christian Faith: An Introduction to the Idea of Christianity* (New York: Seabury, 1978), p. 150 (slightly altered); *Grundkurs des Glaubens: Einführung in den Begriff des Christentums*, 3rd edn (Freiburg, Basel and Vienna: Herder, 1976), pp. 154–5.

8   *Foundations of Christian Faith*, p. 208; *Grundkurs*, pp. 207–8.

9   Cf., for example, *Foundations of Christian Faith*, pp. 140–2; 178–203; *Grundkurs*, pp. 145–7; 180–202.

10 Cf. Gerald R. Cragg's thumb-nail sketch of one of the forebears of the modern advocacy of natural religion, the Latitudinarians (*The Church and the Age of Reason 1648–1789*, vol. 4 of *The Pelican History of the Church*, revised edition [Harmondsworth: Penguin Books, 1970], p. 72): 'A strong ethical emphasis was characteristic of all the Latitudinarians. They constantly stressed man's moral duty. They not only counselled upright behaviour, they themselves were indefatigable in every good work. Unfortunately their moral zeal lacked dignity and urgency. Everything they did or said was moderate in tone; their religion was genuine but never ardent; they stood for a temper rather than a creed. Their outlook was reasonable and dispassionate, magnanimous and charitable. Their virtues easily degenerated; their good will subsided into mere complacency'.

11 Gerald R. Cragg (*The Church in the Age of Reason 1648–1749*, p. 78) mentions 'the hatred of priestcraft which became so consistent an obsession of the Deists'.

12 *The Autobiography of Benjamin Franklin*, ed. Richard B. Morris (New York: Washington Square Press, 1955), pp. 100–22.

13 Vatican II opted, as a matter of principle, for a form of separation of church and state that includes mutual respect and co-operation (*Gaudium et Spes* 76), and while it did not peremptorily exclude the possibility of an ecclesiastical establishment (*Dignitatis Humanae* 6, par. 3), it gently but firmly denied the right of Catholic civil authorities to direct the affairs of the church (e.g. *Christus Dominus* 20). In these conciliar developments, a crucial contribution came from the American experience, so patiently and ably articulated, in the decades preceding the council, by John Courtney Murray and others.

14 Cf. James Hennesey, 'Séparation de l'église et de l'état: états-unis et france', *Concilium* 114 (*Théologie pratique*) (Paris: Beauchesne, 1976), pp. 65–76.

15 Willem Kloos's sonnet 'Ik ben een god in 't diepst van mijn gedachten'.

16 'Nur das Metaphysische, keinswegs aber das Historische, macht selig.' E. Jüngel, *Gott als Geheimnis der Welt: Zur Begründung der Theologie des Gekreuzigten im Streit zwischen Theismus und Atheismus*, 3rd edn (Tübingen: J. C. B. Mohr [Paul Siebeck], 1978), pp. 170ff., quotation pp. 170–1; *God as the Mystery of the World: On the Foundation of the Theology of the Crucified One in the Dispute Between Theism and Atheism*, trans. Darrell L. Guder (Grand Rapids, MI: Wm. B. Eerdmans, 1983), pp. 128ff.; quotation p. 129, slightly altered.

17 R. Otto, 'Zur Einführung', in F. Schleiermacher, *Über die Religion*, pp. 11–12 (author's translation); *On Religion*, pp. xv–xvi.

18 Esp. pp. 24–89; *Grundkurs*, pp. 35–96.

19 Cf. Dietrich Bonhoeffer 'Vergegenwärtigung neutestamentlicher Texte', in *Gesammelte Schriften*, ed. Eberhard Bethge, III (Munich: Chr. Kaiser Verlag, 1966), esp. pp. 304–5; cf. *No Rusty Swords*, vol. I, ed. Eberhard Bethge (New York: Macmillan, 1967), pp. 303–4. Cf. F. J. van Beeck, *Christ Proclaimed*, p. 248.

20 Flannery O'Connor, *The Habit of Being*, ed. Sally and Robert Fitzgerald (New York:

Farrar, Strauss and Giroux, 1969), pp. 479 (italics added) and 427.

21 *Summa Theologica* I, 1, 8, *ad* 2: 'Since grace does not cancel nature, but perfects it, natural reason must pay homage to faith'. (Cf. *Summa Theologica* I, 2, 2, *ad* 2: 'Faith presupposes natural knowledge, just as grace does nature, and a perfection something capable of being perfected'. *Summa Theologica* I–II, 112, 1 *in c.*; cf. *Summa Theologica* I–II, 114, 2, *in c.*, and 5, *in c.* Note, too, the clarity and ardour with which Aquinas draws his conclusion in *Summa Theologica* I–II, 113, 9, *ad* 2: 'The goodness involved in the grace of one person is greater than the natural goodness involved in the whole universe'.

22 'A moment is an essential constitutive part of a whole [viewed] as a quiescent system, and a necessary transitional phase in a whole [viewed] as a dialectical movement'; 'Das Moment ist ein wesensnotwendiger Bestandteil des Ganzen als ruhenden Sytems und ein notwendiges Durchgangsstadium im Ganzen als dialektischer Bewegung'. Johannes Hoffmeister, *Wörterbuch der philosophischen Begriffe* (Hamburg: Felix Meiner, 1955), p. 408.

23 Cf. Norman Cohn, *The Pursuit of the Millennium: Revolutionary Millenarians and Mystical Anarchists of the Middle Ages*, revd edn (New York: Oxford University Press, 1970).

24 Cf. e.g. Emmanuel Le Roy Ladurie, *Montaillou, The Promised Land of Error* (New York: Vintage Books, 1979).

25 Cf. e.g. C. S. Lewis, *The Allegory of Love: A Study in Medieval Tradition* (London: Oxford University Press, 1936).

26 Cf. e.g. E. L. Fortin, *Dissidence et philosophie au Moyen Age – Dante et ses antécédents. Cahiers d'études médiévales*, 6 (Paris: J. Vrin, 1981).

27 Martin Buber, *Gottesfinsternis: Betrachtungen zur Beziehung zwischen Religion und Philosophie*, in *Werke*, vol. 1, *Schriften zur Philosophie* (Munich: Kösel; Heidelberg: Lambert Schneider, 1962), pp. 503–603; *Eclipse of God: Studies in the Relation Between Religion and Philosophy* (New York: Harper and Row, 1957).

28 J. Bots, *Tussen Descartes en Darwin: Geloof en natuurwetenschap in de achttiende eeuw in Nederland* (Assen: Van Gorcum, 1972).

29 Cf. A. D. Nock, *Conversion* (Oxford: Clarendon Press, 1933), pp. 164–86, 138–55; on the Isis religion, cf. also F. Solmsen, *Isis among the Greeks and Romans*, *Martin Classical Lectures*, 25 (Cambridge, MA: Harvard University Press for Oberlin College, 1979), esp. pp. 49ff., 57ff., 87–113.

30 Celsus's work is lost, but his positions can be reconstructed from the numerous quotations in Origen's *Contra Celsum*. Henry Chadwick's fine edition helpfully prints the quotations in italics.

31 *C. Celsum*, trans. Henry Chadwick, 3rd edn (Cambridge: Cambridge University Press, 1980), I:14.

32 Cf. *C. Celsum* VIII:65.

33 Cf. e.g. *C. Celsum* V:34ff.

34 Cf. *C. Celsum* VII:68.

35 Cf. e.g. *C. Celsum* VIII:33; VIII:55.

36 Cf. *C. Celsum* I:14.

37 Cf. e.g. *C. Celsum*, IV:31–48.

38 Cf. *C. Celsum* VI:12; H. Chadwick, in a note, refers to I:27; III:44, 50, 55, 59, 74, 75; VI:13–14.

39 *C. Celsum* IV:14.

40 Cf. *C. Celsum* IV:2–3.
41 Cf. *C. Celsum* IV:5–6.
42 *C. Celsum* II:32.
43 *C. Celsum* VI:78; cf. IV:36; V:50 ('one corner in the land of Judaea').
44 *C. Celsum* VI:78.
45 *C. Celsum* IV:99.
46 The metaphor is suggested by A. A. Long, *Hellenistic Philosophy: Stoics, Epicureans, Sceptics* (New York: Charles Scribner's Sons, 1974), p. 156. In identifying Christ as the *Logos*–Spirit Incarnate, Tertullian (*Apologeticus* 21, ed. John E. B. Mayor, trans. Alex Souter [Cambridge: Cambridge University Press, 1917], pp. 68–9) quotes the Stoic Cleanthes as maintaining that the Spirit (in which are combined the creative *Logos*, fate, the mind of Jupiter, and the inevitableness of all things) is 'what permeates the universe' ('*Haec Cleanthes in spiritum congerit, quem permeatorem universitatis adfirmat*').
47 Cf. Gerald O'Collins, *The Case Against Dogma* (New York, Toronto, Paramus, NJ: Paulist Press, 1975), esp. pp. 7–13, 20–2, 49–52.
48 'The Call', in *The Works of George Herbert*, ed. F. E. Hutchinson (Oxford: Clarendon Press, 1941), p. 156 (italics added).
49 A fine and very full account of the process in England is John Redwood's *Reason, Ridicule and Religion: The Age of Enlightenment in England 1660–1750* (London: Thames and Hudson, 1976).
50 John Toland, *Christianity not Mysterious*, ed. Günter Gawlick (Stuttgart Bad Cannstatt: Friedrich Fromman Verlag [Günther Holzboog], 1964 [facsimile edition of the original edition of 1696], p. ix.
51 *Christianity not Mysterious*, p. x.
52 *Christianity not Mysterious*, p. xviii.
53 *Christianity not Mysterious*, p. xiii. The reference is to James 1:17.
54 *Christianity not Mysterious*, p. xv.
55 *Christianity not Mysterious*, p. vii.
56 *Christianity not Mysterious*, p. xiv.
57 *Christianity not Mysterious*, p. xxvi.
58 John Donne, *The Divine Poems*, 2nd edn (Oxford: Clarendon Press, 1978), p. 15.
59 Cf. *Christianity not Mysterious*, pp. xiv, xxviii. The reference – in the singular (!) – is to Hebrews 12:2.
60 *Christianity not Mysterious*, pp. xxvi–xxviii.
61 *Christianity not Mysterious*, pp. xxvi–xxvii.
62 John Toland, *Pantheisticon, or, The Form of Celebrating the Socratic-Society*, in *British Philosophers and Theologians of the 17th and 18th Centuries*, ed. René Wellek (New York and London: Garland Publishing, 1976) (facsimile edition of the 1751 translation printed for Sam Paterson and sold by M. Cooper, London).
63 Günter Gawlick, 'Einführung', in John Toland, *Christianity not Mysterious*, p. 28.
64 Thus Henry Chadwick, in a splendid introductory essay, in Gotthold Lessing, *Lessing's Theological Writings*, selected and trans. Henry Chadwick (Stanford, CA: Stanford University Press, 1957), p. 45. Cf. also Chadwick's quotation from Matthew Tindal's *Christianity as Old as Creation* of 1730: 'The Christian Deists ... believe not the Doctrines because contain'd in Scripture, but the Scripture on account of the Doctrines' (p. 18, n. 1).

65   Quoted by Henry Chadwick, in *Lessing's Theological Writings*, p. 13.

66   Cf. Henry Chadwick, in *Lessing's Theological Writings*, pp. 44–5.

67   Cf. G. E. Lessing, 'On the Origin of Revealed Religion', theses 5, 7, and 8; the full text in *Lessing's Theological Writings*, pp. 104–5.

68   Cf. Henry Chadwick's observation, in *Lessing's Theological Writings*, p. 27: 'The theology of Nathan is the familiar eighteenth-century thesis that all the "positive" religions are equally true to those who believe them, equally false to the philosophers, and equally useful to the magistrates: that the only absolute is the "universal religion" of humanity as a whole. What is required of man is not adherence to dogma but sincerity, tolerance, and brotherly love.' He also quotes Lessing's note: 'Nathan's attitude to all positive religions has long been mine' (p. 44, n. 2). It has been suggested that Lessing's Nathan has more than a few touches in common with Moses Mendelssohn, whose *Jerusalem oder über religiöse Macht und Judentum* argued that the power to enforce belongs to the state, not the church, and that the truths contained in Judaism are none other than those God has taught 'by fact and idea' to all rational beings, so that what observances Jews adhere to on the basis of the written Torah are a matter, not of truth but (like all matters of organized religion) of chosen obedience to particular traditions.

69   J. J. Rousseau, *Émile, ou De l'éducation*, vol. 4 of *Oeuvres complètes*, ed. Bernard Gagnebin and Marcel Raymond (*Bibliotèque de la Pléiade*, 208), 4 vols (Paris: Gallimard, 1969), pp. 565–635. In the English translation, *Émile or Education*, by Barbara Foxley, the 'Creed of a Savoyard Priest' is found on pp. 228–78; the translation is to be used with caution.

70   Cf. Lessing: 'If God held all truth in his right hand and in his left the everlasting striving after truth, so that I should always and everlastingly be mistaken, and said to me, "Choose", with humility I would pick on the left hand and say, "Father, grant me that. Absolute truth is for thee alone"'. Quoted by Henry Chadwick, in *Lessing's Theological Writings*, p. 43. It would be a mistake to take these noble sentiments at face value; in the context of the eighteenth century, such statements always have a rather more immediate agenda, too: the rejection of Christian doctrine.

71   *Émile*, pp. 605–6; *Émile or Education*, pp. 257–8. The last, bracketed sentence reads: 'En attendant je suis heureux, parce que je compte pour peu tous les maux de la vie et que le prix qui les rachette est en mon pouvoir' (*Émile*, p. 1569, note [a]); while it was deleted by Rousseau, it proves that he was thinking of the incarnation and the atonement.

72   *Émile*, p. 627; *Émile or Education*, p. 273.

73   Thus the account, in the course of the vicar's confessions, of how he descended into himself (*Émile*, p. 569) recalls a famous passage in *Confessions* VII, 10. The association with Augustine is not surprising in an author who entitled his autobiography *Les Confessions* (*Oeuvres complètes*, I, pp. 1–656); cf. Ann Hartle, *The Modern Self in Rousseau's Confessions: A Reply to St. Augustine* (Notre Dame, IN: University of Notre Dame Press, 1983).

74   *Émile*, p. 566; *Émile or Education*, pp. 228–9.

75   *Émile*, p. 19; *Émile or Education*, p. 230.

76   Quoted by J. H. van den Berg, *Leven in Meervoud: Een metabletisch onderzoek*, 5th edn (Nijkerk: G. F. Callenbach, 1967), pp. 107–10.

77   On this subject, cf. T. S. Eliot's classic essay 'The Metaphysical Poets', in *Selected Essays 1917–1932* (New York: Harcourt, Brace, 1932), pp. 241–50. Cf. also J. H. van den Berg's *Leven in Meervoud* and the copious literature cited there; van den Berg's analyses of *Diderot's Le Neveu de Rameau* and *Le Rêve de d'Alembert*, and of the

sensibility behind the *Encyclopédie* provide particularly insightful introductions to the chaotic tendencies of the civilized eighteenth-century mind.

78 J. H. van den Berg, *Leven in Meervoud*, pp. 162–5; cf. J. H. van den Berg, *'s Morgens jagen, 's middags vissen* (Nijkerk: Callenbach, 1971), pp. 14–15.

79 van den Berg, *'s Morgens jagen, 's middags vissen*, pp. 8–9.

80 J. H. van den Berg, in *Leven in Meervoud* (opp. p. 160), reproduces a plate entitled *Épinglier* ('pin–maker'), found in the fifth volume of Diderot and d'Alembert's *Encyclopédie* of 1755. The text (*Leven in Meervoud*, pp. 170ff.) explains that eighteen distinct operations are needed to make a pin. (Cf. also his *'s Morgens jagen, 's middags vissen*, pp. 60–1.) Adam Smith, in the very first chapter of Book I of *The Wealth of Nations*, relates that he visited a pin-factory in which ten workers produced in excess of 48,000 pins per day, whereas one single pin-maker might produce no more than twenty pins per day. I remember seeing, in a museum in Europe which I no longer recall, an enormously elaborate eighteenth-century machine, powered by a treadmill, on which at one time, it was claimed, a string quartet could be played. The four instruments had mechanical fingers mounted on them, and there were four circular bows that could whir around. One wonders how the music must have sounded. One wonders even more about the sensibility that conceived such contraptions and proceeded to make them. In any case, it is difficult to imagine a more eloquent symbol of the eighteenth century's mechanical mind. Walter J. Ong has shown that Dean Swift's metaphors for thought abound with mechanical images; cf. his 'Swift on the Mind: Satire in a Closed Field', in Walter J. Ong, *Rhetoric, Romance, and Technology: Studies in the Interaction of Expression and Culture* (Ithaca, NY, and London: Cornell University Press, 1971), pp. 190–212.

81 Thus Henry Chadwick in *Lessing's Theological Writings*, p. 28.

82 I have, regretfully, found no satisfactory alternative to translate the inclusive German word *Mensch*, which is in many ways the key word in the text.

83 Cf. Erich Schenk, *Mozart: Eine Biographie* (Munich: Wilhelm Goldmann Verlag, n.d.) pp. 455, 559–63.

84 Pascal had, as usual, been keen enough to notice this while it was happening. He wrote: 'I cannot forgive Descartes; in his entire philosophy he would have liked to do without God; but he was forced to have him flick his finger [*il n'a pu s'empêcher de lui faire donner une chiquenaude*], in order to set the world in motion; after that he had no use for God any more' (*Penseés*, ed. Léon Brunschvicg [Paris: Nelson, 1936], no. 77). Two centuries later, Lessing was to complete the argument: 'Lessing saw that in the scheme of nature that had come to dominate the mind of the age, this transcendent God, who made no special revelations and was only known to all men alike through the book of nature, was no longer necessary. He may have been the first cause of the world, but he had not intervened since the beginning. He might as well be dead' (Henry Chadwick, in *Lessing's Theological Writings*, pp. 45–6).

85 W. H. van de Pol, therefore, was on target when, after a lifetime's devoted ecumenism, he turned to the fundamental question of theology and modern culture, and opened his classic book *The End of Conventional Christianity* (trans. Theodore Zuydwijk [New York: Newman Press, 1968]), with a treatment on an emotional issue, namely *prejudice* (pp. 15–59). Incidentally, the English translation of this book missed the hopeful epigraph that opens the Dutch original and beautifully sums up the author's intentions: 'At evening time there shall be light' (Zechariah 14:7).

86   Cf. chapter VIII ('The Church in Danger – Ridicule Runs Riot'), in John Redwood, *Reason, Ridicule, and Religion*. A quick review of eighteenth-century literature will also bear out the point.

87   Joseph Butler, *The Analogy of Religion, Natural and Revealed, to the Constitution and Course of Nature* (New York: Jonathan Leavitt; Boston: Crocker and Brewster, 1833), p. 5.

88   Cf. F. J. van Beeck, 'Professing the Uniqueness of Christ', *Chicago Studies* 24 (1985), pp. 17–35, esp. pp. 20–2, 31–3.

89   Cf. F. J. van Beeck, *God Encountered*, vol. I (New York: Harper and Row, 1989), paragraph 14, p. 2.

90   Thus Sir Julian Huxley in his introduction to Pierre Teilhard de Chardin's *The Phenomenon of Man*, 2nd edn., ed. Sir Julian Huxley (New York: Harper and Row Torchbook, 1965), p. 11 – a fine example of a constructive encounter between a modern agnostic with impeccable rationalist credentials and a modern Christian scientist devoted to orthodoxy.

91   Henry Chadwick, *Lessing's Theological Writings*, p. 44.

92   Geoffrey Wainwright, *Doxology: The Praise of God in Worship, Doctrine and Life, a Systematic Theology* (New York: Oxford University Press, 1984), p. 57.

93   *C. Celsum*, I:2, 62; III:68; VI:2.

94   Cf. Henry Chadwick, *Lessing's Theological Writings*, pp. 34–35. The references, listed by Chadwick, are to *C. Celsum* I:28, 38; II:28, 48 ff.

95   Dietrich Bonhoeffer, *Letters and Papers from Prison*, revd. edn., ed. Eberhard Bethge (New York: Macmillan, 1967), under 3 August 1944 ('Chapter I, b').

96   Henry Chadwick, *Lessing's Theological Writings*, pp. 51–6.

97   Henry Chadwick, *Lessing's Theological Writings*, p. 52 (slightly adapted after the original; cf. G. Lessing, *Axiomata*, vol. 13 of *Sämtliche Schriften*, ed. Karl Lachmann, revised by Franz Muncher (Berlin: Walter de Gruyter, 1968), p. 4, lines 22–4.

98   Cf. Henry Chadwick, *Lessing's Theological Writings*, p. 44: '"Truth" for [Lessing] does not consist in dogma, except for the dogma that there is no dogma. "Truth" is brotherly love, sincerity, and tolerance rather than a metaphysical interpretation of nature, man, and God. His certainties are moral certainties'.

99   William Wordsworth's sonnet 'It is a beauteous evening, calm and free' (*The Poetical Works of William Wordsworth*, ed. E. de Selincourt and Helen Darbishire, vol. 3 [Oxford: Clarendon Press, 1946], p. 17).

100 *Summa contra Gentiles* I, 2 (*Assumpta igitur*).

101 *Summa Theologica* I, 1, 1, *in c.*

102 Karl Rahner and Wilhelm Thüsing, *Christologie: systematisch und exegisch* (*Quaestiones disputatae*, 55) (Freiburg, Basel and Vienna: Herder, 1972), p. 24; the English translation, *A New Christology*, for which Rahner wrote a revised version of his contribution, does not contain this passage. But the same thought can be found, e.g., in *Foundations of Christian Faith*, pp. 206–7; *Grundkurs*, pp. 206–7.

103 Cf. F. J. van Beeck, *Catholic Identity After Vatican II: Three Types of Faith in the One Church* (Chicago: Loyola University Press, 1985), pp. 61ff.

104 Dietrich Bonhoeffer, *Gesammelte Schriften*, Vol. III, pp. 304–5; *No Rusty Swords*, pp. 303–4.

PART

Criticisms

Feminist Theology: Language, Gender and Power

Mary McClintock Fulkerson

This material is excerpted from the second chapter of *Changing the Subject: Women's Discourses and Feminist Theology*. While the technical language of poststructuralism is difficult, Fulkerson ably introduced the reader to the challenge which poststructuralist feminism can offer to 'taken for granted' notions of subjectivity and experience. This chapter lays the groundwork for the next chapter on an alternate interpretative practice for reading the Bible, and the subsequent study of women's actual reading of the text. Fulkerson offers a sophisticated mediating position between the revisionist trends of some Christian feminist thought and the emphasis on stability and identity in postliberal accounts of Christianity and its traditions of speech.

The feminist theory with the most to contribute regarding the problems with experiential appeals combines liberationist concerns with use of poststructuralist views of language. Other types of feminist theory, particularly liberal and radical or cultural feminism, still depend upon the experiential warrant to make their arguments and elaborate their visions.[1] Here I draw from feminist thinking that employs poststructuralist discourse theory for liberation interests. Discourse theory, which understands language as a (but not the only) signifying process that constructs rather than represents reality, will allow me to sketch an alternative to the experiencing subject of feminist theology. That alternative is the discursively constructed subject position.

The view that discourse constructs subjects brings with it a way of thinking about the work of language to oppress and liberate different from that implied in feminist liberation theologies. It will offer a way to think about the constitutive nature of language and power that is more nuanced to the distinctive and located character of women's situations – the systems of meaning that constitute them – than that found in liberation feminist theological accounts. This alternative – an analytic of women's discourses – provides access to different forms of gender oppression and liberation. It also exposes more serious problems in the experiential expressivism manifested in feminist theological method. It is incomplete as the offering of an analytic for women's faith practice, however, without exploration of an alternative to the sexist or liberating text. Chapter 3 will complete my analytic by proposing the account of biblical texts that results from the turn to signifying processes and the implication of this analytic for processes of liberation and oppression.

First, some clarifications are in order. *Poststructuralism*, as distinguished from the more widely used term *postmodernism*, refers to a theory of language, of which the most well-known example is the practice of deconstruction. Postmodernism, a cultural logic, is typically associated with aesthetics, but often used loosely to refer to a host of reactions to the modern. The issue of women and respecting difference – the problem of the false universal – has to do with the constitutive character of language for 'experience'. Therefore the label *postmodernism* is not a helpful way to identify my analysis, except to say that poststructuralism is a refusal of a view of language (and, by extension, a subject) typically identified with the modern.[2] Thus my critique is not directly postmodern, nor is it directly allied with Jacques Derrida, given the use of the term *theology* in deconstruction for the very language/knowledge practices I am criticizing. My aims are unabashedly liberationist and theological, a term that I will assume can work more transgressively than simply as an exemplary metaphysics of presence.[3]

With these qualifications, is it possible to 'use' poststructuralism for liberationist theological purposes? I think it is, but an apology is in order for what may appear an eclectic proposal. Although long past its prime in France where it originated in the 1960s, poststructuralism was picked up by English-speaking literary and cultural theorists in the 1970s and is still important in feminist theory. One reason for the feminist appropriation of poststructuralist theory is that the use of gender and women's experience to identify patriarchy in the 1970s has produced claims about the universality of phallocentrism – claims that are unnuanced with respect to the complexities of race, class and other identities. 'Women' is simply not a universal state of victimization, as women of colour and so-called Third World women testify.[4] Euro-American feminists have begun to respond in self-critical ways as the deleterious effects of their universalizing claims are exposed. This process has been aided by the radical undermining of unities made possible by poststructuralism and by a recognition of the exhaustively coded (or textual) nature of reality.

The Euro-American feminist self-critical posture generated by poststructuralism has not gone unremarked. Susan Bordo calls it 'gender scepticism', the suspicion of gender as a false universal. Gender scepticism casts a hypercritical and nuanced eye on the differently nuanced meaning of 'woman' through history. A typical book, in fact, bears the question 'Am I That Name?' regarding 'women' as its title.[5] Some feminists raise concerns about what they see as an extremist reaction of self-criticism. Tania Modleski warns of the disappearance of women from feminism, a tendency she observes when the employment of poststructuralism in its deconstructive form appears to aid the conservative backlash against women in culture and the wider social formation of the 1990s.[6] Another feminist points out a certain irony in poststructuralism's ostensible correction of Cartesianism. If the sin of the dualism in the Cartesian subject was the idealizing of a 'view from nowhere' – the essence of male rationality – the movement of poststructuralism is hardly an improvement, the argument goes. Poststructuralism, with its valorization of multiplicity, indeterminacy and heterogeneity, continually displays the instability of any text or any subject. Poststructuralism thus funds the 'view from everywhere'. An erasure of the body is effected when poststructuralism works to celebrate difference and multiplicity. This, Bordo warns, is a dangerous bypassing of the realities of bodied limits of always being somewhere and constrained.[7]

These warnings are well heeded and will shape my use of poststructuralism. Whether it depends upon appeals to women's experience or not, the generative context of feminist theory is commitment to the liberation of women along with conviction of the dominance of patriarchal power in contemporary and past social arrangements.[8] The specifics of these claims about feminism are clearly contested in this wave of criticisms of essentialist tendencies in the use of 'woman'. I will assume, however, that continued self-identification with the term *feminist* indicates a theorist who understands change as the point of theorizing and has the entrenched social forms of male hegemony as a target. The givens of late twentieth-century life are still textured by asymmetries of power and resources that are based on gender as well as class and race. A view from everywhere can never get at such realities. Such a context, as Bordo and Modleski warn, dictates a careful use of poststructuralism.

Moreover, my analysis is a theological reading of the convergence of interest and knowledge, one that views these issues with the grammar of theo/acentric finitude. Thus my agenda for this debate is somewhat more complicated than negotiating loyalty to feminism with the risks of literary theory. Poststructuralist accounts of language help theologians display the embeddedness of readings and practices in networks of meaning (and, by implication, power). My theo/acentric grammar of social finitude focuses on forms of oppression, the possibilities for liberation in those situations, and the way in which traditions of faith are a guiding rubric. The benefit of poststructuralism to these liberation-theological interests is not its potential to defer meaning forever or undermine unities endlessly. The benefit is rather its ability to expose the kind of finitude and danger that attend our transitional unities. This merits elaboration.

I have in some sense mis-spoken when I refer to the 'use' of poststructuralism as if it were a hermeneutical choice that I, a free subject, take up and utilize as one of a number of hermeneutical options. As Jane Tompkins points out, poststructuralism is not one of a number of methods that one can pick up and put down at will. Rather a poststructuralist account of language shows how 'I' am used by a signifying process already operative. It dissolves the discrete 'objects' of subjects, texts, methods and interpretations into 'a single, evolving field of discourse'. This dissolution of everything into discourse or 'textuality' does not mean that we cannot posit unities, such as subjects and texts, but that we must take account of the embedded, constructed and political character of the 'objects' that emerge. According to structuralism (semiotics and poststructuralism alike), the authorizing of any particular discourse, text or signifying process does not come from its referents or its origins, as Wesley Kort points out, but from the discourse itself.[9]

What literary theory says with regard to the unavailability of extra-discursive foundations for knowledge has resonances with a theo/acentric grammar. There is a theological logic that leads to a parallel agreement that theological knowledge is non-foundational as well. The 'must' comes from the logic of a grammar which not only requires that entities be accorded a non-absolute status, but that they be employed to honour the created goodness of the 'neighbour'. It is this embeddedness in processes of meaning that helpfully evokes what Christians mean (or ought to mean) by situatedness and finitude.[10]

A theological analysis carried out by way of the inescapability of the signifying processes or social codes that construct us all is able to portray three features of a liberation theological grammar of finitude. (1) Compared to the notion that language represents or corresponds to reality, it is better suited to display the bondage of sin and how that bondage is enmeshed in those specific processes. (2) Liberating transgressions of that bondage can be identified in the discursive possibilities of the situation, rather than in a freedom external to a situation. (3) The constitutive, embedded character of subjects suggests that Christian perspectives are distinctive, yet not universalizable. They are distinctive because they create subject positions not available to others; conversely, Christians literally are not in the position to articulate hegemonic accounts of 'human experience'. These three aspects of the constitutive character of codes do not legitimate Christian theologizing but neither can they disprove it. While feminist theologians have not displayed these convictions with language theory, it is high time that we, for whom language is such a constitutive reality, did so.

Employment of poststructuralism as an account of language (meaning) has served a number of feminists outside of theological conversations well. As a move away from representational views of language, poststructuralism allows them to identify and destabilize the practices that fall prey to the naturalizing of discourse.[11] It allows the destabilizing of subjects and texts, which will be exactly the two moves feminist theology needs in order to advance toward a position that can respect difference. By recognizing the textual or coded nature of all of reality, we can perceive its conventional or made character, there look at the existing forms of unity granted texts and subjects and the systems of meaning that create them, and discover their cracks and occlusions in order to press the possibilities for change. We may, as it were, pose new kinds of 'objects' or unities whose liberating character will have meaning only in relation to the positions they challenge. We will not expect these 'objects' to escape the fragility and risks of their location, however; they, like any other, cannot be absolutized.

We should look now at the emergence of the notion that everything is textual – 'a single, evolving field of discourse', as Tompkins puts it, in order to show how subjects are not stable sites of meaning. Feminist concern with the existent situations of gender oppression will move the analysis to a question that poststructuralism by itself does not answer. We need to know how specific meanings are produced for a feminist analytic that will enable more radical questioning of the things which constitute gender oppression and liberation. For that I will theorize discourse as a communicative event that can occur even with the destabilized subject, woman. Because my question concerns the possibilities for liberation, we must understand these two seemingly contradictory things: how the subject does not control meaning and also how change occurs through the processes of meaning . . . how subject woman 'produces' emancipatory meanings at the same time that sexist ones are produced 'over her head', so to speak.

In what follows I will argue that an understanding of language as an unstable process of signifying is helpful to feminist thinking about the conventional nature of reality. Reality is coded or textual, rather than constructed out of non-semiotic terms like empirical objects and experience or consciousness. Poststructuralist criticism helps in rethinking three domains that are operative in feminist theologians' inadequate treatments of language, gender and power: (1) the theory of language as representation; (2) the Cartesian/experiencing subject; and (3) the relation of power to discourse. As we move out of modern ways to conceive the three domains, alternative possibilities will emerge for conceiving women as producers of meaning and of the workings of power.

The original text here gives a detailed account of the 'three domains' just mentioned, in eight sections entitled: 'From representing to signifying', 'Repositioning feminist inquiry', 'Textuality and discourse analysis', 'The multiply positioned subject: "woman" as opposition', 'Discourse and the problem of reality', 'Existence versus being', 'The power–discourse relation: hegemonic and local', and 'Patriarchal power as ordinary: incitements, production, and oppression'.

Discourse versus Representation: Stifling Difference

As a theory of power, language and gender, the account of discourse I have proposed differs at a number of points from those earlier identified assumptions of feminist liberation theology on these topics. The view that reality is constituted by signifying shuts off access through language to the thing-in-itself. Discourse theory entails a realism of the sort that requires a look at convention and at the relations of power that define or describe what counts as real. It entails a materialism that avoids dichotomizing the mental and the physical by the incorporation of social processes in an analysis of discursive ordering. At every point terms of oppression and liberation require that the intelligibility of reality be understood in terms of its creative instability – an instability displayed in all discourse. Dominant discursive formations neither silence all dissent nor present themselves with no boundaries or seams for the defining of an entity.

In contrast, the appeal to women's experience in feminist theology can be taken to assume that there is a natural referent, 'woman', the 'we' who share oppression and common humanity. The natural is, according to discourse theory, not a given, a neutral meaning, that may be read off of bodies or actions, but an unarticulated realm already ordered by discursive processes. This problem is not resolved by pointing to feminist experience rather than prediscursive experience. It is not just a problem of experiential grounding, something George Lindbeck has identified in criticizing liberal theology. More than an infelicitous epistemic justification is at stake. The use of women's experience is connected to an account of power that is inadequate for the situation of all women, and may in fact disempower the 'other' woman.

A feminist account of power is problematic when it attributes a virtually monarchical negative force to patriarchy. It is also incompatible with a theological grammar of the bondage of sin. The extreme case of that incompatibility occurs in the treatment of language as the conveyer of harmful information in the form of dominant male-valorizing content. In its simplest form, the inclusive–exclusive language discussion, language works as the conveying of ideas. Its force is cognitive, and the meaning conveyed is negative: language renders women invisible and invalidates them. The simplistic cognitive nature of the language–power relation – the suggestion that understanding is the realm of harm – is mitigated a bit by the notion that language works in the form of networks of symbols that shape experience. That view still relies upon the content of patriarchal traditions, however. Without recognition of conflict and desire, or of the systems of meaning that make every subject, feminists suggest a one-way understanding of the force of power and imply that it is undifferentiated, that ideas have the same impact on everyone. In such a configuration the appeal to women's experience supports a cognitive–communicative view of power that operates with a representative view of language (the view that language points to and can convey a reality) and drastically narrows a feminist theological vision.

It may seem that I have caricatured the way feminists understand power.[12] By focusing only on their identification of the harmful, anti-woman character of much of the content of the tradition, I deflect attention away from the fact that feminists always also recognize the *use* of the tradition against women and structures of power. Continued comparison with discourse theory, however, suggests the problem is more profound. Not only power but a whole way of thinking about power, gender and language is implicated in the appeal to women's experience. In so far as feminist theology is based on the norm of 'women's experience', it risks perpetuating this configuration. Review of the main points of feminist liberation theology as *method* in light of discourse theory gets us closer to a more serious verdict on the problematic account of language, and therefore of power, employed by liberation feminist theology.

Feminist theologies answer the question 'What is language?' with various accounts of its representational character. They rely upon the nominalizing work of language, the view rejected by the poststructuralist theory that language is relations or differences. This work is exemplified in the notion that the dominance of male pronouns and images excludes women and that, conversely, to name the female effects their inclusion. This view treats language as a process of naming, operative outside complex relations of difference. The impact of being named could be utterly negligible if we factor in social relations of class – a subject position of poverty, for example. The metaphorical character of theological reflection in the work of Sallie McFague is relief provided to pursuit of nominalizing accounts of language; however, all share the notion that theological claims, negative or otherwise, 'express human experience', a reinstating of the same problem that bypasses the coded nature of any experience.[13]

To my second question, 'How is language *produced*?', feminist liberation theology points to at least three sites. First, when it does refer to a subjectivity prior to discourse, the privileging of 'women's experience' locates the origin of meaning in subjects. It suggests the illusory notion that 'our speech is our servant', as Foucault says.[14] This appeal is consistent with the view represented by Rosemary Radford Ruether, that even as meaning is social and gets mediated through communal traditions, it is after all an individual consciousness that is the origin of religious traditions and their renewals.[15] We must assume, the logic continues, that the experience which binds women together is just such a realm of consciousness from which new transformative traditions will be generated, or at least confirmed. As the destabilizing of the subject indicated, presenting the subject as the originating site of meaning production universalizes women's experience with an uncoded subject and perpetuates the very practice feminists sought to expose and undermine – the false universal, man.

The methodological pattern of feminist theology accounts for the production of language in its recovery of historical meanings, particularly from scripture.[16] Because the theological task requires more than simply the original contributions of contemporary women's consciousness, feminist theologians also appeal to the Christian tradition, where they show evidence of their assumptions about language. A prominent form of that appeal occurs in the search for the real meaning of a biblical passage, exemplified in feminist defences of women's ministries, and in the references to the histories of patriarchal oppression of women. Whether in the use of biblical–critical tools to get at what the text (usually Paul) meant then, or in the recovery of the women hidden by the texts of the official traditions, the recoverable, decipherable meanings about women in the Christian biblical and postbiblical tradition supply meaning for feminist theologians. This supply is dependent on the tools of historical–critical method. While such an approach is in line with the rules of the theological academy, it is itself a social system of meaning. Subject to a critique of positivism in its reliance upon recovery of 'facts' and 'events', the historical 'what really happened' is reminiscent of the appeal to the 'natural', yet is *not* the system of meaning that orders the biblical text for all women.

The third source for positive meaning is in feminist theologians' recognition of the social structures that create and sustain the conditions of gender oppression. The appeal to the social is definitional to liberation feminist theology. What we do not see, as I have argued, is the connection of the stuff of social structures, actions and practices, with the realm of signifying, of meaning (the connection of social systems of meaning with coded subjects). Instead we find the separation of language/ideas from external reality. Idealist dichotomies of the 'material' and the ideational, the external realm and the internal realm, are perpetuated. The recognition of patriarchal structures is never correlated to the discourses of women in particular subject positions. Even if all women are constructed by the processes of capitalist patriarchy, there are multiple discursive games or totalities that create different subject positions and practices for them.

The gap between the hegemony of capitalist patriarchy, for example, and the discursive practices of the poor woman is not filled in. Her resistances are rendered invisible; the texts of Christian patriarchal scripture and their oppressive power are the only indication of local discourses that liberation feminist accounts leave us. (We must assume they would be the 'same' for women in different social locations.) In short, meaning is produced by history, by the biblical text; it is affected by social structures, but there is no way to theorize its production at the site of utterance by different systems of meaning. There is, consequently, no way to theorize that the convergence of history, biblical text and social structures might need to be conceived in very different terms for women in different subject positions.

Liberation Commitments versus Liberal Modernist Language Theory

The separation of signifying process (in this case language) and the social (or everything else) is possible in liberation feminist theology because the view of language as a conveyor of fixed meaning is more problematic than first appeared. Two metaphors about language help portray what is problematic about that view and show it at odds with liberationist commitments of feminist liberation theology. The most straightforward indication of the view is in feminist theologies' claims that appear to be about the constitutive character of language: language conveys the realities outside of it – patriarchal intentions – in the sexist content of the tradition, and conveys affirmation of women in traditions that recover and name women. I say 'appear', because in light of discourse theory, this no longer is an accurate statement. Rather than constituting reality in the way that patterns of signification do, leaving no unmeaningful 'stuff' outside to be dealt with later, in feminist theologians' accounts, language carries or mediates a reality outside of it, whether that be the divine, women's experience, or patriarchal power.

The primary way the seriousness of gender oppression is articulated via the convergence of language, power and gender in the sexist text – the pernicious tradition – is exemplary of this view of language as mediator. That formulation reduces power and attributes it inappropriately. It is based on a dichotomy between the stuff of social structures, of the external world of economy and state, and the realities of language. The metaphor best capturing the notion of language in this formulation is that language is a vehicle or container that passes information between subjects.[17] Ironically, the notion of the sexist text – the very attempt to indicate the impress of location on knowledge – is implemented with a view of language that leaves virtually invisible the differential processes of signifying which accompany it. This observation connects feminist theological method with a liberalism that is surely contradictory to its liberationist commitments.

What is problematically liberal in this treatment of language as a medium are the features it shares with the epistemic notion of language that Timothy Reiss terms 'modernist'. Herein is found a second metaphor. Modernist accounts of knowledge are characterized by their failure or incapacity to acknowledge the imprint of the enunciating 'subject' on the enunciated.[18] In order to acknowledge complicity in discourse, it is necessary to give up the notion of a free space prior to its discursive ordering, whether that space be found in the imagination, in primal, pre-reflective experience, or in a carefully defended Cartesian notion of founding intuitive self-knowledge. It is this self-defining, autonomous subject that characterizes the liberal notion of the self, as I have already argued. In the light of the linguistic assumptions of modernism, the fact that feminist theologians are critical of liberalism does not extricate them from participating in its practice.

Modernity's dominant metaphor is the telescope and the controlling gaze, according to Reiss. While it is clear that this is an ordering that encompasses far more than liberalism's discourse, it is compatible with the notion under inspection. Within the space of this metaphor, language has the status of a lens that can alternately serve to mediate reality to the cognizing mind or to alter the shape of that reality – by focusing it more sharply or fuzzing its edges. The point is that language's claim to do the former is rendered suspect by the latter. As long as the roles of the lens and the knower on the product are acknowledged, we have a space for the discussion of production and accountability.[19] Once language is allowed to substitute for the reality, to stand in for it, or to re-present it, the role of the lens disappears in the discourse of knowledge.[20] What is more, the control exercised over the product of the technology is elided; one appears to be cognizing reality itself. The claim of neutral access and the option to claim the display of the world as it really is both become possibilities. Both ways of thinking about reflection characterize Enlightenment universalizing reason and obscure the embeddedness of discourse in power.

Recognition of the complicity or the position of the subject in reflection, as I argued in chapter 1, is one of the hallmarks of feminist theology. In it we find neither an assumption of neutral access nor a claim to display the world as it really is. Moreover, because feminist theology participates in the historical consciousness of modernity, it grants that its own voice is limited, partial, experimental and historically relative.[21] Despite these good intentions, feminist theology does not escape the failings of the telescope metaphor when it relies upon this methodological pattern. That is seen more clearly with regard to its own status as a discourse. What feminist theology fails to do is articulate the webs of meaning/power that constitute even its own ostensibly 'natural' claims. Without attention to the kind of discourse in which its reflection is constructed and its institutional location, feminist theology as a kind of liberatory reflection is implicated in some of the features of the modernist grid of intelligibility by virtue of its erasure or occlusion of the full dimensions of that location.

Simply to confess historicality and transitoriness is not enough. Nor are authorial confessions of social location sufficient, since the individual consciousness is not the (sole) source of oppressive formations.[22] This kind of relativity does not flesh out the multiple orderings that create differences in women's positions. Language – sexist language – as currently understood stands in for the realities, such as practices, subject formations and the social relations and desires that construct them. Feminist theology has yet to foreground its linkages with power *as discourse*, and discourse *as power*.

To recount the problems with language: language is, at best, figurative in feminist accounts. There is no way to understand the significations of non-linguistic reality and the social systems of meaning that construct the coded subject. The appeal to pre-discursive experience is one example of this, where women's experience serves as a warrant. Another example is its inability to reflect upon the discursive ordering of bodies and the resulting occlusion of the heterosexist bias in feminist liberation theology. The heterosexist binary is the continually invoked content for oppression and liberation, a practice connected, according to Butler, with compulsory heterosexuality. The discursive ordering of male–female bodies and the formations of heterosexual desire that accompany it make feminist theology an unwitting reinforcer of compulsory heterosexuality with its appeal to women's experience and identity politics.[23]

The linkage of language with power also implicitly silences voices of other women of faith: texts' meanings are fixed, power is monarchical. Those whose experience differs from the model of 'women's experience' are not accounted for, or constitute a lobotomized casualty of patriarchy, one of Mary Daly's 'fembots'.[24] This is not to say that feminist theologians do not want to be challenged by other women's experience or that they do not invite it. It is to say that the methodological pieces are not challenged simply by contrasting experiences, for the epistemic grid is the problem that experience cannot touch. The purveyor of these blindnesses, the 'telescope' or occluding and occluded instrument in feminist liberation theology, is found in the methodological discourse with its indebtedness to modernist liberal notions of subjects and texts.

Feminist method relies upon the warrants and sources of women's experience in convergence with the judgement that certain contents of the tradition are sexist and others liberating. This constellation prevents the kinds of questions that might open up the specific subject positions, desires and technologies of power that construct women in different subject positions. Perhaps those texts are different for other women. Minimally those questions require respect for the complexity and variety of gender oppression and forms of its resistance. That respect requires a move out of the liberal grid of intelligibility regarding experiencing subjects, representational language and oppressive liberating texts.

A way out of these problems is offered by the very discourse theory that brings them into focus. As feminist theologians we will better display our commitment to the situated character of knowledge by finding a feminist way to articulate an opening for other women's practices, women who are not the 'we' of the feminist account. To do this, feminist theology needs to understand itself as constructed in a discursive order – a system of meaning – and as contributing to discursive practices, particularly to women's emancipatory faith practices, not as a partially figurative and multivocal form of reflection and not as reflection on women's experience.

This alteration in definition entails viewing liberation feminist theology as a discursive practice located in a situation of utterance. Discourse, we remember, is a set of statements that get their meaning via networks of differences, intersections with other discursive formations. Discourse has its own stabilities and its own emancipatory thrusts. To admit that feminist theology's appeal to 'women', then, is (as it sometimes acknowledges) to *certain* women's experience – those who work for women's liberation and against all injustices – is not to disqualify liberation feminist theology *as theology*. Rather, it means that this 'experience' must be seen as constructed from converging discourses, their constitution by differential networks, and their production of certain pleasures and subjugations. While it may have practices and insights for women in other social locations, it is not representative of a natural realm of women's consciousness, religious or otherwise.

Feminist theological discourse can be identified and given shape as signifying processes that open up resistance *in a particular way*, as well as participate in forms of oppressive power. This alternative entails identifying feminist theologians as institutionalized academics as well as participants in other social practices, such as ecclesiastical organizations. 'Feminist theologians' occupy subject positions that are constructed out of multiple discursive totalities – from the smaller totalities of the academy and local culture and church, to the larger totality of patriarchal capitalism.

I conclude that until the shift from women's experience to women's faith practices in discursive totalities is accomplished, feminist theology presents its own ruminations as a form of realist representation, not necessarily emancipatory discourse.[25] With realist representation, feminist theology appears to appeal to truth outside of power, to take a position outside the struggle, and thereby to perpetuate the hegemony of the liberal false universal. Feminist theology needs to understand itself as discursive *practice*, meaning in a rather trivial way that it incorporates more than linguistic (oral and written) significations, and in a more significant way that it is co-constituted by the games of the academic institutions that produce it – a discursive totality, by church, and by the social formation of patriarchal capitalism as well.

To proceed in the formation of feminist theology as emancipatory discursive practice, one must offer alternatives to its problematic aspects, the methodological features. In chapter 1, I argued that this account was problematic because it did not presume a coded subject who is constructed out of social systems of meaning. In this chapter, I have identified this methodological problem more specifically as the remnants in feminist theologies of a *liberal discursive order*. I have focused on the importance of the criteriological woman subject placed in relation to the fixed text or its recoverable meanings that harm by virtue of their contents and thus ignore the complexities of desire and conflict in power.

In the next chapter, I will take up the question of biblical texts and the possibilities in a theory of discourse for connecting women's practices of faith with texts so as to provide alternatives to this liberal discursive order. Alternatives will enable us to identify the systems of discourse that constitute women's faith practices relative to different locations in the social formation of patriarchal capitalism. When such differences can be seen, we can better read women's practices as emancipatory and constrained without resorting to a hegemonic notion of women's experience as their common denominator or to fixed texts that oppress or liberate simply by virtue of their contents.

Notes

1   The appeal to women's experience still figures in some Marxist and socialist feminisms. Standpoint theory, the feminist materialist position of Nancy Hartsock, is a case in point. Some of the more recent versions of such theories use poststructuralist work, however, and are not identified with the appeal in the same way as liberal and radical–cultural feminisms are. This may be because these latter two contain views of the essential subject, either 'neutral' in the case of liberalism or 'woman' in the case of radical–cultural feminism. Such a view does not lend itself easily to totally constructionist accounts. For a helpful account of different types of feminist theory (not including poststructuralist feminism), see Alison M. Jaggar, *Feminist Politics and Human Nature* (Brighton: Harvester Press, 1983).

2   The term *postmodernism* is used broadly; frequently, it includes some form of poststructuralism. See Jean-François Lyotard or Fredric Jameson for theorists of the postmodern and Jacques Derrida, Jacques Lacan, Julia Kristeva and Michel Foucault for poststructuralism. See 'Introduction' in *After Philosophy: End or Transformation?* eds. Kenneth Baynes, James Bohman and Thomas McCarthy (Cambridge, MA: MIT Press, 1987), pp. 1–18, for an overview of the linguistic turn and its various forms: poststructuralism, postanalytic philosophy, hermeneutics and critical theory. Regarding the epistemic aspects of the modern, see Timothy J. Reiss, *The Discourse of Modernism* (Ithaca, NY: Cornell University Press, 1982). The relation of the term *modernism* to aesthetics is, of course, entirely different.

3   In Derrida's works and other poststructuralist writings, the term *theological* stands for

practices grounded in the 'transcendental signified' (meanings that are fully present and self-enclosed), for which the sign 'God' is considered exemplary. See Jacques Derrida, *Of Grammatology* (Baltimore: Johns Hopkins University Press, 1974), pp. 49–50; *Position* (Chicago: University of Chicago Press, 1981), pp. 19–20; *Writing and Difference* (London: Routledge and Kegan Paul, 1978), p. 136. There are several accounts of the relationship between Derridean poststructuralism and theology, the practice of religious reflection: Mark C. Taylor, *Erring: A Postmodern A/Theology* (Chicago: University of Chicago Press, 1984); Kevin Hart, *The Trespass of the Sign: Deconstruction, Theology and Philosophy* (Cambridge: Cambridge University Press, 1989). In contrast to Taylor's death-of-God account and the negative theology account of others, Hart (p. xi) offers an account of deconstruction as 'an answer to the theological demand for a 'non-metaphysical theology'.

4   Such writers as Chandra Mohanty, Trinh T. Minh-Ha and Gayatri Chakravorty Spivak employ poststructuralism to expose the colonializing effects of white feminists' use of 'women's experience' to investigate 'Third World women'.

5   Susan Bordo, 'Feminism, Postmodernism, and Gender-Scepticism', in *Feminism/Postmodernism*, ed. Linda J. Nicholson (New York: Routledge, 1990), pp. 133–56. Denise Riley, *Am I That Name? Feminism and the Category of 'Women' in History* (Minneapolis: University of Minnesota Press, 1988).

6   Tania Modleski, *Feminism without Women: Culture and Feminism in a 'Postfeminist' Age* (New York: Routledge, 1991). Modleski brings together the conversation and debate in a helpful way, even if she does not probe the real possibilities of feminist poststructuralist criticism. The use of poststructuralism has been controversial in all the fields where it has been employed: in feminist historical work and philosophy, as well as in feminist cultural and literary studies (domains in which it is most prominent). Feminist historian Joan Scott, for example, has been highly criticized for her use of poststructuralism.

7   Bordo, 'Feminism, Postmodernism', pp. 136–45.

8   For a helpful, brief definition of *feminist* that highlights the political commitment, see Toril Moi, 'Feminist, Female, Feminine', in *The Feminist Reader: Essays in Gender and the Politics of Literary Criticism*, ed. Catherine Belsey and Jane Moore (New York: Blackwell Publishers, 1984), pp. 117–32.

9   Jane Tompkins, 'A Short Course in Post–structuralism', *College English* 50: 7 (November 1988), p. 733. Wesley A. Kort, *Bound to Differ: The Dynamics of Theological Discourses* (University Park: Pennsylvania State University Press, 1992), pp. 30–6.

10   One cannot say here that what poststructuralists mean by the 'différance' that makes distinctions possible *is* the Christian principle of finitude. The former is not a principle or a theory. See Jacques Derrida, 'Différance', in *Margins of Philosophy* (Chicago: University of Chicago Press, 1982), p. 27. Tompkins explains 'différance' in 'A Short Course,' pp. 739–47.

11   As indicated in the earlier discussion, naturalization is one of the functions of ideology. It occurs when the assumptions of a community or social order are allowed to remain invisible as assumptions, making them appear true and beyond question. Beliefs are naturalized when they seem to reflect the very order of things; for example, views that woman has 'natural' domestic duties suited to the 'natural' fit of her body and nature to the needs of the child. One of Derrida's first targets for deconstruction was the

prioritizing of speaking over writing, as he exposed the fallacy of the assumption that the presence of the speaking subject grants transparency to the 'real meaning'. In the denaturalization of the assumption that spoken language provides the full presence of meaning, poststructuralism goes far beyond sociology of knowledge; it requires a sceptical posture toward the assumed transparency of any form of discourse, the investigator's as well, not simply the belief systems of a social order. For feminists, the naturalization of discourse is inimical, for the possibilities of sustaining the status quo and its oppressions lie first and foremost in the assumption that the beliefs that support women's subordination or the unnaturalness of the homosexual are 'transparent to the real'. Derrida, *Of Grammatology*.

12 Feminists articulate other accounts of power, to be sure; the notion of co-creative power is found in most feminist thinking to counter domination. This view is not connected with the operative view of language, however, so it does not get to the problems I am criticizing. I thank Carol Robb for reminding me of this point.

13 This has been discussed in terms of Rosemary Radford Ruether. Sallie McFague, *Models of God: Theology for an Ecological, Nuclear Age* (Philadelphia: Fortress Press, 1987), pp. 29–57.

14 Foucault, *The Order of Things*, p. 297.

15 'Since consciousness is ultimately individual, we postulate that revelation always starts with an individual.' Rosemary Radford Ruether, *Sexism and God–Talk: Toward a Feminist Theology* (Boston: Beacon Press, 1983), p. 13.

16 The focus on scripture is understandable, given the importance of its use in the Christian community to exclude, construct and otherwise shape believers' lives. Occasionally we find a search for meanings generally – in Western culture, such as Catherine Keller's *From a Broken Web: Separation, Sexism, and Self* (Boston: Beacon Press, 1986). But my interest here is the methodological constants of liberation feminism, which focus on scripture. What scripture means with regard to gender is much more important, it would seem, than any other tradition, written or oral.

17 Interestingly Brian Wren rejects this metaphor. Although he perpetuates essentialist notions of feminine and masculine, his work comes the closest to moving away from a communicative account of language. *What Language Shall I Borrow: God-Talk in Worship: A Male Response to Feminist Theology* (New York: Crossroad, 1990). For a discussion of the 'container' metaphor, see George Lakoff, *Metaphors We Live By* (Chicago: University of Chicago Press, 1980).

18 I use quotes around 'subject' to indicate some breadth of interpretation here. I do not want to continue the notion of the imprint of the enunciating subject to the individual, creative consciousness. Reiss, *The Discourse of Modernism*, ch. 1.

19 This premodern stance characterized Galileo's use of the telescope. With it he emphasized the distance between the object and the mind and was able to think about the impact the telescope/lens had on the object of knowledge: what is seen through it is different than that object seen with the naked eye. Reiss, ch. 1.

20 This second move is initiated by Descartes, but finalized most clearly by Cartesianism. It is in Cartesianism that the collapse of the object and the language's capacity to represent it occurs. Reiss's example is the Port Royale Logic. See Reiss, ch. 1.

21 This concession fits Reiss's category of the shift to the process of knowledge and its finitude, a feature of nineteenth-century historicism. Thus we might compare this kind

of acknowledgement to the recognition that theological reflection is a description of the human process, rather than of God-in-Godself, which is how he described historicism. Reiss, pp. 21–37. Also see Reiss's description of Baconian experimental discourse, ibid., p. 34.

22 The logic of poststructuralism makes this problematic. If writing does not express the inner reality of the subject, neither does personal locating get at the discursive economy, for example, of the academic text. See Paul A. Bové on the problem of the humanism perpetuated rather than challenged by oppositional intellectuals who fail to distinguish their role as perpetuator of the status quo due to confusions about the subject. *Intellectuals in Power: A Genealogy of Critical Humanism* (New York: Columbia University Press, 1986).

23 Butler is not the only one making this kind of argument. Although her position is not the same, Eve Kosofsky Sedgwick argues for the ways in which gender and sexuality are best treated as distinct issues, but always with awareness of their co-implication. *Epistemology of the Closet* (Berkeley: University of California Press, 1990), pp. 27–37.

24 See Meaghan Morris's harsh criticism of this category in 'Amazing Grace: Notes on Mary Daly's Poetics', in *The Pirate's Fiancee: Feminism, Reading, Postmodernism* (New York: Verso, 1988), pp. 27–50. It is not the case that feminist theologians develop the implications of this, that women are passive and obliterated by patriarchal power. Elisabeth Schüssler Fiorenza, for example, argued for a recovery of her story, refusing the implication that patriarchal oppression blotted out women's agency; *In Memory of Her: A Feminist Theological Reconstruction of Christian Origins* (New York: Crossroad, 1983). The way oppressiveness is theorized and attributed in relation to language is still problematic, however. Even though there is recognition (especially by Daly) that women internalize patriarchy's sexist views, therefore becoming the vehicles of their own oppression, a more adequate image of power – the dominant model – limits the way the overdetermination of oppression and multiplicity of resistance can be appreciated in feminist theological analysis.

25 Rebecca S. Chopp has argued for the shift to discourse in *The Power to Speak: Feminism, Language, God* (New York: Crossroad, 1989).

Postmodern Theology and the Judgement of the World

Rowan Williams

A sympathetic critic of postliberal theology, Rowan Williams is appreciative of its integration of theology and church, yet remains concerned that it may have an inadequate grasp of the nature of Christian believing as a set of provisional historical projects. In particular, postliberal use of scripture may reinforce a rather introverted ecclesiology and spirituality, in some measure closed against the activities of working out its identity in relation to what lies beyond its borders.

In the nineteenth century, Kierkegaard retold the story of Abraham and Isaac with shattering effect; several generations have grown up spiritually and intellectually in the shadow of this retelling in terms of the 'suspension of ethics', the realm of risk and terror beyond morality. More recently, Jung in his *Answer to Job* reworked the scriptural text into an extraordinary new mythological shape: the blind God of the natural and primal order looks with envy at the creature who has the self-awareness to challenge him; the conflict between Job and his maker shows why that maker himself must at last identify himself with human suffering, must become Jesus Christ. Only as human is God self-aware; only as human is God fully God, the active and transfiguring archetype of the human itself.

What is going on here? Should we call these enterprises translations of the world's experience into biblical categories, or the opposite? It is because I find I am not at all clear about the answer to this that I want to put some questions to the project so persuasively outlined by Professor Lindbeck in his book *The Nature of Doctrine*, the project of inserting the human story into the world of scripture: 'Intra-textual theology redescribes reality within the scriptural framework rather than translating scripture into extra-scriptural categories'.[1] I have no doubt at all of the need to revive and preserve a scriptural imagination capable of deploying decisive and classical narratives in the interpretation of the human world, nor any doubt of the present weakening of such an imagination in our culture. I am both interested and perturbed by the *territorial* cast of the imagery used here – of a 'framework' within whose boundaries things – persons? – are to be 'inserted'. Is this in fact how a scripturally informed imagination works? I believe that the reality is more complex, and that it sits less easily with the picture Professor Lindbeck has outlined of a church heavily committed to the refinement and deepening of a scriptural speech and culture *within* its own territory.

What I shall be proposing is that we may have misunderstood the alternatives before us. The 'world of scripture', so far from being a clear and readily definable territory, is an *historical* world in which meanings are discovered and recovered in action and encounter. To challenge the church to immerse itself in its 'text' is to encourage it to engage with a history of such actions and encounters; and in the era after the disappearance of a unitary Christian worldview, this is to engage with those appropriations of biblical narrative on the frontiers of the church and beyond represented by figures such as Kierkegaard and Jung.[2] If as has sometimes been said, the Bible is itself a history of the *re*reading of texts, our reading of it should not be so different. What we are dealing with is a text that has generated an enormous family of contrapuntal elaborations, variations, even inversions – rather like the simple theme given to Bach by Frederick the Great, that forms the core of *The Art of the Fugue*. When we have listened to the whole of that extraordinary work, we cannot simply hear the original notes picked out by the King of Prussia as if nothing had happened. We can't avoid saying now: '*This* can be the source of *that*' – and that is a fact of some importance about the simple base motif.

The church may be committed to interpreting the world in terms of its own foundational narratives; but the very act of interpreting affects the narratives as well as the world, for good and ill, and it is not restricted to what we usually think of as the theological mainstream. Something happens to the Exodus story as it is absorbed into the black slave culture of America. Something still more unsettling happens to Abraham and Isaac when they have passed through Kierkegaard's hands – or the hands of the agnostic Wilfred Owen, writing in the First World War of how the old man refused to hear the angel 'and slew his son, And half the seed of Europe, one by one'. Where are we to locate this kind of reflection? It is not purely intra-textual, conducted in terms fixed by the primal narrative, nor is it in any very helpful sense a 'liberal' translation into an extraneous frame of reference. It is, much more, a generative moment in which there may be a *discovery* of what the primal text may become (and so of what it is) as well as a discovery of the world. Owen's savage transformation of Abraham's sacrifice points up what we might miss in Genesis: the final drawing back from slaughter is an act of obedience as great as or greater than the first decision to sacrifice Isaac. It also points up the impotence of the narrative in a world that has lost the means to forego its pride. Not sacrificing Isaac is a necessary humiliation; the righteous old men of Europe in 1914 are strangers to such a possibility. This is indeed a discovery of scripture and world, and of the gulf between them; and it is now – or should be – part of what the church reads in Genesis 22. It will have found out *what it is itself saying* in absorbing this scriptural exegesis from its own margins. And part of my thesis is that the interpretation of the world 'within the scriptural framework' is intrinsic to the *church's* critical self-discovery. In judging the world, by its confrontation of the world with its own dramatic script, the church also judges itself: in attempting to show the world a critical truth, it shows itself to itself as church also. All of which means that we are dealing not with the 'insertion' of definable blocks of material into a well-mapped territory where homes may be found for them, but with *events* of retelling or reworking traditional narrative patterns in specific human interactions; an activity in which the Christian community is itself enlarged in understanding and even in some sense evangelized. Its integrity is bound up in encounters of this kind, and so in the unavoidable elements of exploratory fluidity and provisionality that enter into these encounters. At any point in its history, the church needs both the confidence that it has a gospel to preach, and the ability to see that it cannot readily specify in advance how it will find words for preaching in particular new circumstances.

Words like 'preaching' and 'interpretation' have come to sound rather weak; or, at least, they do not very fully characterize the enterprise to which the church is committed. The church exists for the sake of the kingdom of God; it is 'engaged in the same business as its Lord: that of opening the world to its horizon, to its destiny as God's Kingdom'.[3] This means that it is essentially missionary in its nature, seeking to transform the human world by communicating to it in word and act a truthfulness that exposes the deepest human fears and evasions and makes possible the kind of human existence that can pass beyond these fears to a new liberty. The church, in claiming to exist for the sake of opening the world to the fuller life in which God can be deemed as the controlling meaning of things, claims to have something to contribute to all human cultures, all human essays in the construction of meaning. What is contributed is not easily summed up; but it is at least a Christian participation in the whole business of constructing meanings, the business of art and politics in the widest senses of those words, and at most the invitation to a new self-identification, a new self-description, in the categories of Christian prayer and sacrament. Ideally, the Christian sharing in the enterprise of art or politics is working towards the point where these new self-descriptions can be seen as possible and intelligible.

As already intimated, this work involves a passing of judgement; and here we encounter some serious difficulties. In the classical Christian story as presented in John's Gospel, judgement is not effected by uttering words of condemnation but by a quite complex process of interaction. The works and words of Jesus demand choice for or against him; they force to the light hidden directions and dispositions that would otherwise never come to view, and thus make the conflicts of goals and interests between people a *public* affair. The inner rejection of one's own identity as God's creature and the object of God's love, the violence done to human truth *within* the self, becomes visible and utterable in the form of complicity in rejecting Jesus.[4] The inner readiness to come to judgement and to recognize the possibility of truth and meaning becomes visible and utterable in the form of discipleship, abiding in the community created by God's love. The dramatic event of Jesus's interaction with his people – set out in a series of ritual, quasi-legal disputations – is an event of judgement in that it gives the persons involved definitions, roles to adopt, points on which to stand and speak.[5] They are invited to 'create' themselves in finding a place within this drama – an improvisation in the theatre workshop, but one that purports to be about a comprehensive truth affecting one's identity and future. As John hints (for instance in chapter 3), and as Paul more vividly and clearly sees (as in Romans 11), this is far more than a simple separation of the already godly from the already damned: the scope of Jesus's work is the *world* – so, we must assume, the declaration of a newly discovered identity in encounter with Jesus represents a *change* for at least some. You may recognize your complicity in the rejection of Jesus and at the same time accept the possibility of a different role offered by the continuing merciful presence of God in the post-Easter Jesus. In Paul's terms, all may find themselves both prisoners of disobedience and recipients of grace (Romans 11:32).

The gospel, then, is what enables this dual self-discovery in women and in men; and as Matthew 25 suggests, it may prove difficult to give any general account of what a converting event may be, because neither the rejection of Jesus nor the receiving of his grace may readily be identifiable as such. Proclaiming the gospel may have much to do with the struggle to make explicit what is at stake in particular human decisions or policies, individual and collective, and in this sense bring in the event of judgement, the revaluation of identities. I think this is rather different from what Professor Lindbeck suggests is the goal of Christian theology – 'to discern those possibilities in current situations that can and should be cultivated as anticipations or preparations for the hoped for future, the coming kingdom'.[6] I am wholly in sympathy with his challenges to the 'liberal' assumption that this is to be achieved by adjusting theology to current fashion, and what I have already said accords in important respects with his call for discernment on the basis of criteria drawn from the specifically Christian narrative ('an intra-textually derived eschatology').[7] But I want, in contrast, to argue that such discernment is not easily intelligible when divorced from the language of a transformative judgement, enacted in particular *events*, that is the central theme of so many of our foundational texts. In short, I don't think that Christian and theological discernment can ever be wholly 'contemplative' and 'non-interventionist'; I believe it is more importantly exercised in the discernment of what contemporary conflicts are actually *about* and in the effort both to clarify this and to decide where the Christian should find his or her identity in a conflict. The Christian is involved in seeking conversion – the bringing to judgement of contemporary struggles, and the appropriation of some new dimension of the transforming summons of Christ in his or her own life.

Here we come up against the most central issue in the whole of this discussion. How are we to speak of judgement in a fragmented culture? The language of judgement presupposes recognition and communication, the possibility of shared points of reference. To pass judgement is to propose and in certain circumstances (the law court) to effect a definitive 'placing' of who or what it is that is being judged: it affects attitudes towards the object of judgement, it influences the decisions and priorities of others, it shapes what can be claimed by or for the object. All this applies equally to legal, artistic and moral judgement: none of these makes sense as anything other than a public affair. To put it at its weakest: what would be *meant* by saying, I think or 'judge' that the *St Matthew Passion* is the greatest achievement of European music, but I don't care whether it's ever performed again? Judgements take for granted a real or possible community of speaking and responding persons, and a history of concrete decisions and acts.

Hence, in a radically pluralist society, the society as such increasingly withdraws from judgement. It will contain groups who continue to believe that judgement is possible or imperative, but the social system overall sees its job as securing a pragmatic minimum of peaceful coexistence between groups, by a variety of managerial skills and economic adjustments. 'Late capitalist societies are neither coherent nor integrated around a system of common values',[8] according to the sociologist Bryan Turner, who goes on to argue that such coherence and stability as there is are secured by a mixture of diverse factors – the apparatus of modern administration itself, the neutralizing of genuine political dissent, the system of palliative welfare benefits, the reduction of the franchise to an almost passive formality, and the social dependency induced by the nature of economic and employment relations in a technologically advanced multinational economy.[9] Societies that are able to control their populations in such ways do not need the legitimization of 'values'; they do not need myth or religion or morality. To put it in other terms, they can evade the question of why *this* social order should be respected, preserved or defended, because they are not threatened, practically speaking, by their inability to answer it: they have sufficient resources, administratively and technically, to guarantee survival for the foreseeable future. If the price of survival is high (permanent large-scale unemployment, the erosion of public health care or state education, the creation of what has come to be called an 'underclass'), it is still manageable, because the damaging results of the system have the effect of moving the disadvantaged further away from the processes of public decision making.

Societies like this (like the UK and the USA under their present governments) have no problem in tolerating a 'chaos of personal lifestyles' in practice, even where there may be varieties of public rhetoric that commend some lifestyles more than others.[10] In the context of these societies, indeed, *style* is everything: with massive commercial support, cultural options – even when their roots are in would-be dissident groupings – are developed and presented as consumer goods. Religious belief is no exception, whether this process of consumerization appears in the naked crudity of fundamentalist broadcasting or in the subtle ways in which secular media dictate the time and the agenda of the behaviour and utterances of religious leaders; and religious commitment is reduced to a private matter of style, unconnected with the nature of a person's membership in his or her society. Public life continues, whatever style we adopt. And concern with style notoriously detracts from seriousness about what is to be said (a point noted long ago by Augustine and others):[11] a recent series in the London *Guardian*[12] about postmodernism in the arts noted with anxiety the rising popularity of pastiche and pseudo traditionalism alongside anarchic and parodic idioms, a kind of new baroque – two sides of the same coin.

There remains, of course, a nostalgia for 'values', which the church should beware of exploiting. The diffuse discontent that consumer pluralism can engender (although it largely contains and even utilizes it) yields itself readily to any programme that dresses itself persuasively enough in moral rhetoric; but this is something essentially unrelated to how priorities are fixed in government (as recent British and American policies make depressingly clear). The church misconceives its missionary task if it simply latches on to this kind of window dressing and echoes the individualistic and facile language of moral retrenchment that often accompanies a further intensification of administrative control and the attrition of participatory politics. To put it in language lately made familiar by Richard Neuhaus, there may be a 'naked public square', but, before the churches rush into it, they have to ask whether the space opened up is genuinely a *public* one, or is simply the void defined by a system that can carry on perfectly well in the short term with this nakedness.[13]

My worry with Professor Lindbeck's proposal is that it might end up encouraging the continuance of this situation. In *The Nature of Doctrine*, he identifies with admirable precision the danger of reducing faith to a commodity marketed to atomistic selves in a hopelessly fragmented culture, and goes on to defend the idea that a unified future world rescued from the acids of modernity would be more likely to be fostered by 'communal enclaves', concerned with socialization and mutual support rather than with 'individual rights and entitlements', as opposed to religious traditions that eagerly abandon their distinctiveness in favour of a liberal syncretism.[14] This may be so; but unless these 'enclaves' are also concerned quite explicitly with the problem of restoring an authentically public discourse in their cultural setting, they will simply collude with the dominant consumer pluralism and condemn themselves to be trivialized into stylistic preferences once more. The communal enclave, if it is not to be a ghetto, must make certain claims on the possibility of a global community, and act accordingly.

Naturally, this raises for many the spectre of theocratic totalitarianism. But such an anxiety, though quite proper in itself is not necessitated by these 'claims on . . . a global community', for a number of reasons. First of all, theocracy assumes that there can be an end to dialogue and discovery; that believers would have the right (if they had the power) to outlaw unbelief. It assumes that there could be a situation in which believers in effect had nothing to learn, and therefore that the corporate conversion of the church could be over and done with. Second, following from this, theocracy assumes an end to history. The powerful suggestions of Barth and von Balthasar[15] about history between the resurrection and the second coming as the gift of a time of repentance and growth are set aside; instead of God alone determining the end of the times of repentance, the church seeks to foreclose the eschaton. Third, most obviously, theocracy reflects a misunderstanding of the hope for God's kingdom, a fusion of divine and earthly sovereignty in a way quite foreign to the language and practice of Jesus. Theocracy, the administration by Christians of a monolithic society in which all distinction between sin and crime is eroded, is neither a practical nor a theologically defensible goal.

The Christian claim, then, is bound *always* to be something evolving and acquiring definition in the conversations of history: it offers a direction for historical construction of human meaning, but it does not offer to end history. Like the humane Trotskyism of Raymond Williams, it envisages a 'long revolution', at best an asymptotic approach to a condition that history is itself (by definition) incapable of realizing – a perfect communality of language and action free from the distortions imposed on understanding by the clash of group interests and the self-defence of the powerful.[16] The Christian may have no clearer a picture than anyone else of what this would look like, but can at least contribute specific perceptions of what holds back the coming of such a world, and specific possibilities of transforming acts and decisions – conversion in the broad sense already outlined, or what Dietrich Ritschl in his superb new book on *The Logic of Theology* calls the work of the 'therapeutic spirit' in the creative renewal of persons and communities.[17]

Christians in general and theologians in particular are thus going to be involved as best they can in those enterprises in their culture that seek to create or recover a sense of shared discourse and common purpose in human society. This can mean various things. The most obvious is some sort of critical identification with whatever political groupings speak for a serious and humane resistance to consumer pluralism and the administered society. These days, such groupings are less likely than ever to be found within historic mainstream political parties, though there are some countries, happily, where moral imagination has not been so completely privatized. For many, it has been ecological issues, feminism, civil rights and 'peace' networks that have provided a new political language and a sense of the urgency and possibility of human unity. All of these are themselves in constant danger of being marginalized, and all have their fringes of mere style, apolitical and exclusivist posturing. The task of keeping them related to what remains of a democratic public process, to the parties that people actually vote for, is a hard and thankless one: if my suggestions are right, it may well be a major task for the informed Christian. But I have in mind also the work of those artists who have a commitment to the future of language and imagination: here too the Christian's business is engagement and solidarity, a willingness to listen and respond. The English playwright Howard Barker argues in the *Guardian* (10 February 1986) for the necessity of a revival of tragedy, in order to break through the false collectivism of 'populist' theatre (typified by the musical) and put people back in touch with the isolation of their own pain – a paradoxical move towards the *authentically* public by way of intensifying the personal. In Britain the television dramas of Alan Bleasdale and Dennis Potter have perhaps most vividly exemplified such a move. Can the Christian, in whatever way, help to nurture both the production and the reception of these statements? For many people, these are thresholds – perhaps more – of judgement, of 'therapeutic transformation'.[18] And, in a very different way, contemporary scientific and medical practice reflects the struggle between mechanistic, dominating, administrative patterns and a relatively new, tentative, not always very coherent concern for unity and interdependence. Here is a further field for learning and for solidarity.

The late Cornelius Ernst, OP, in a seminally important essay on 'Theological Methodology', argued that the meaning of the world in Christ could only be articulated in a continuing search for a 'total human culture, the progressive discovery of a single human identity in Christ'.[19] The form of this search was quite simply any and every process of human self-definition in response to mass culture, the threat of a 'totalizing' society of technological manipulation and control. 'There is at least a single discernible adversary.' If the essence of the church is missionary, this is precisely the search and the struggle to which the church is committed. Professor Lindbeck suggests that those who give primacy to the question of how the gospel is preached in a post-Christian environment 'regularly become liberal foundationists', preoccupied with translating the gospel into alien terms, or at least redefining it in response to secular questions.[20] I am not so sure. For one thing, as I have argued, preaching is not something extraneous to the identity and integrity of the church; we are not allowed to sidestep the question. But equally, it is not clear that the only alternative to intensive in-house catecheses is translation into a foreign language in a way that sacrifices the distinctiveness of the gospel. I don't see Cornelius Ernst as a 'liberal foundationalist': he is, I think, suggesting not a search for *words* equivalent to our traditional terms (so that we presuppose a more neutral or abstract content), but a search for what recognizably – however imperfectly – shares in the same project that the gospel defines. Can we so *rediscover* our own foundational story in the acts and hopes of others that we ourselves are reconverted and are also able to bring those acts and hopes in relation with Christ for their fulfilment by the recreating grace of God?

This is certainly a potentially riskier task than simple translation either into or out of traditional Christian and scriptural terms. The Christian engaged at the frontier with politics, art or science will frequently find that he or she *will not know what to say*. There can be a real sense of loss in respect to traditional formulae – not because they are being translated, but because they are being tested: we are discovering whether there is any sense in which the other languages we are working with can be at home with our theology. I'd agree entirely, by the way, with Professor Lindbeck that a deeper catecheses in that theology and its images is indispensable, but I think it is so because of the testing it will endure in the process of 'playing away from home', conversing with its potential allies. And to take an obvious political example – if the most plausible allies in a situation are people with similarly global commitments, the encounter is loaded with the possibilities of tragic conflict. If the most plausible ally in the Philippines or Chile or South Africa is a Marxist the Christian may be tested to the uttermost (not every Christian with Marxist or socialist sympathies shares the optimism of many liberation theologians). The Christian woman actively involved in feminism will record the same kind of tension. The paradox of our situation often seems to be that the struggle for Christian integrity in preaching leads us close to those who least tolerate some aspects of that preaching.

The difficulty appears equally in the consequent need to know when to be silent, when to wait. This account of the Christian mission is not a recipe for talkative and confident activism; it requires something like a contemplative attention to the unfamiliar – a negative capability – a reluctance at least to force the language and behaviour of others into Christian categories prematurely, remembering that our understanding of those categories themselves is still growing and changing. The premature and facile use of Christian interpretative categories in fact invites judgement of another kind. My title is deliberately ambiguous: the church judges the world; but it also hears God's judgement on itself in the judgement passed upon it by the world. 'The burden of proof lies on believers and the life they lead', writes Ritschl, pointing out the way in which, when transformation becomes no more than an inflated metaphor, the language of new creation is projected more and more towards the future: present conversion becomes accordingly unreal – verbal or figurative only.[21] Preaching cannot be heard.

But the judgement of the world can cut more deeply. The weightiest criticisms of Christian speech and practice amount to this: that Christian language actually fails to transform the world's meaning because it neglects or trivializes or evades aspects of the human. It is notoriously awkward about sexuality; it risks being unserious about death when it speaks too glibly and confidently about eternal life; it can disguise the abiding reality of unhealed and meaningless suffering. So it is that some of those most serious about the renewal of a moral discourse reject formal Christian commitment as something that would weaken or corrupt their imagination.[22] It may equally be that a church failing to understand that the political realm is a place of spiritual decision, a place where souls are made and lost, forfeits the authority to use certain of its familiar concepts or images in the public arena. Bonhoeffer, in his justly famous meditation for his godson's baptism in May of 1944, speaks powerfully of this loss of authority: 'Our church, which has been fighting in these years only for its self-preservation, as though that were an end in itself, is incapable of taking the word or reconciliation and redemption to mankind and the world. Our earlier words are therefore bound to lose their force and sense.'[23] This is emphatically not a 'liberal' observation or a demand for better translations into modish secularity, but a sober recognition that, in the world as it is, the right to be heard speaking about God must be earned. The Christian is at once possessed by an authoritative urgency to communicate the good news, and constrained by the awareness of how easily the words of proclamation become godless, powerless to transform. The urgency must often be channelled into listening and waiting, and into the expansion of the Christian imagination itself into something that can cope with the seriousness of the world. It is certainly true that, for any of this to be possible, there must be a real immersion in the Christian tradition itself, and to this extent Professor Lindbeck's programme is rightly directed. But if I were devising schemes of Christian education, I should be inclined to set such immersion side by side with an exposure to political and cultural issues that might help to focus doctrinal language in a new way: only so, I believe, can a theological formation be an induction into *judgement* – hearing it as well as mediating it.

In the same meditation for his godson, Bonhoeffer makes one of his celebrated references to the need for a non-religious language in which to proclaim the gospel; 'so to utter the word of God that the world will be changed and renewed by it'.[24] This will not be a conscious modernizing or secularizing of the terminology of dogma and liturgy; it is certainly not something that can be planned. It will be like Jesus's own language (and practice, we must assume) in that it effects the presence of God's peace with his creatures, and so, as Bonhoeffer says in a later letter (July, 1944), it exposes the actual godlessness of the world.[25] It is non-religious in the sense that it is not primarily concerned with securing a space within the world for a particular specialist discourse. Whether or not it uses the word 'God', it effects faith, conversion, hope. Bonhoeffer's paradigm (as the July letter explains) is the encounters in the gospels between Jesus and those he calls or heals: these are events in which people are concretely drawn into a share in the vulnerability of God, into a new kind of life and a new identity. They do not receive an additional item called faith; their ordinary existence is not reorganized, found wanting in specific respects and supplemented: it is transfigured as a whole.

Bonhoeffer might equally well have pointed to the parables of Jesus. These are not religious stories or expositions of a tradition, but crystallizations of how people decide for or against self-destruction, for or against newness of life, acceptance, relatedness. Repeatedly, as the kingdom of God is spoken of, Jesus simply presents a situation, a short narrative: like *this*, he says. The riddle of the parables, the fact that they are seen as hopelessly enigmatic by friends and enemies, lies in making the connection with one's own transformation – that is, encountering God in the parable, receiving that therapy of the spirit that Dietrich Ritschl writes of, becoming open in a certain way. This, of course, is why the Christian does not repeat the gospel parables in isolation. Only as the parables of *Jesus* can they be properly heard. They are part of a life – a language and practice that culminate in events through which a decisive new being emerges, a new community, a new human identity. The parables have their sense *within* the larger parable that is the life, death and resurrection of Jesus: in relation to this man, the transformation or conversion or therapy which the parables narrate becomes concretely possible. Through the community destroyed in betrayal and desertion at the cross, and recreated at Easter, the possibility of such relation is still open. But if this is the context in which the enigmatic and secular parables ultimately make sense, it is no less true that the events opening the door of the kingdom of God only make sense because they are events concerning a man who had told parables, and enacted them. First we are accustomed to the *pattern* of challenge and transformation, the loss and recovery of self that is involved in hearing a parable. (Think of King David listening to Nathan; forgetting himself so far as to be shocked into recognizing himself.) Only then can we see the loss and recovery of God himself in cross and resurrection as the opening to us of comprehensive change and healing, and see the way in which the meanings of love lie beyond the capacity of human beings for virtue, religion and faithfulness, and survive all loss that can be imagined.

The transfiguring of the world in Christ can seem partial or marginal if we have not learned, by speaking and hearing parables, a willingness to lose the identities and perceptions we make for ourselves: all good stories change us if we hear them attentively; the most serious stories change us radically. That is why tragedy is important, especially in a culture of false communality. And if we can accept a very general definition of parable as a narrative both dealing with and requiring 'conversion', radical loss and radical novelty, it may not be too far-fetched to say that the task of theology is the exploration of parable, and so of conversion. The skills for this may be, and should be, learned largely from scripture; yet – as was suggested at the beginning of this chapter – such learning must include those transformations of scriptural narrative that restore to us or open to us the depth of what the narrative deals with, even when these versions do not belong in a mainstream of exegesis. This is perhaps the place to mention the importance of contemporary feminist exegesis as an example of disturbing scriptural reading which forces on us the 'conversion' of seeing how our own words and stories may carry sin or violence in their telling, even as they provide the resource for overcoming that sin and violence. The centre may be localizable, but the boundaries are not clear. Theology should be equipping us for the recognition of and response to the parabolic in the world – all that resists the control of capital and administration and hints at or struggles to a true sharing of human understanding, in art, science and politics. It should also equip us to speak and act parabolically as Christians, to construct in our imagining and our acting 'texts' about conversion – not translations of doctrine into digestible forms, but effective images of a new world like the parables of Christ. Part of the power of T. S. Eliot's *Four Quartets* is its extraordinary reticence about recognizable Christian language. Also the force of the witness of the L'Arche communities is in what they are, collaborations of those we call handicapped and those we call normal, not in the theological articulation that may (and must) be given. *This* is what is involved in speaking parabolically, and it is action nourished by the theological grasp of what the life and death of Jesus are, by scripture and the wrestle with dogmatic and devotional tradition; but not confirmed by it. Such formation in our tradition goes with and presses us further into the disciplines of listening – to our own untheologized memories and context, the particularity of where we are, and to the efforts at meaning of the rest of the human race. Good doctrine teaches silence, watchfulness and the expectation of the Spirit's drastic appearance in judgement, recognition, conversion, for us and for the whole world.

Notes

1 George A. Lindbeck, *The Nature of Doctrine: Religion and Theology in a Postliberal Age* (Philadelphia: Westminster Press, 1984), p. 118.

2 On Abraham and Isaac, it is also worth looking at Eric Auerbach, *Mimesis: The Representation of Reality in Western Literature* (Princeton: Princeton University Press, 1953), ch. 1, especially pp. 8–11, where Auerbach suggests how this and kindred narratives help to construct the notion of character as it typically works in Western culture. This again is an instance of our being returned to the scriptural text afresh by its own legacy as appropriated outside the theological community.

3 *For the Sake of the Kingdom: God's Church and the New Creation*, the report of the Inter-Anglican Theological and Doctrinal Commission (Cincinnati: Forward Movement Publications, 1986), p. 23.

4 See e.g. Sebastian Moore, *The Crucified is No Stranger* (New York: Seabury Press, 1977) as well as later works by the same author, for a fuller account of such a theological option.

5 On the trial motif in scripture generally and in the New Testament in particular, see Ulrich Simon, 'The Transcendence of Law', *Theology* 73 (1970), pp. 166–8; and Anthony Harvey, *Jesus on Trial: A Study in the Fourth Gospel* (London: SPCK, 1976). On the wider issue of self-identification or self-discovery through a dramatic process (to which I shall be returning later), see, above all, Hans Urs von Balthasar, *Theodramatik, Prolegomena*, vol. 1 (Einsiedeln: Johannes, 1973), particularly part 2; discussed briefly in Rowan Williams, 'Balthasar and Rahner', *The Analogy of Beauty*, ed. John Riches (Edinburgh: T&T Clark, 1986), pp. 11–24, 26–7.

6 Lindbeck, *The Nature of Doctrine*, p. 125.

7 Ibid., p. 126.

8 Bryan Turner, *Religion and Social Theory* (London: Heinemann, 1983), p. 197.

9 Ibid., pp. 197–8; cf. pp. 240–1.

10 Ibid., p. 241.

11 It forms the central theme of Augustine's *De Doctrina Christiana*, Book 4.

12 1–3 December 1986.

13 Turner, *Religion and Social Theory*, p. 246.

14 Lindbeck, *The Nature of Doctrine*, pp. 126–7.

15 See Barth's *Church Dogmatics* II/2, and Von Balthasar's *Theology of History* (London/New York: Sheed and Ward, 1963) and *A Theological Anthropology* (New York: Sheed and Ward, 1968).

16 Any echoes of Habermas's notion of the 'ideal speech situation' are deliberate. On this concept, see John Thompson's excellent introduction to Habermas's thought in *Critical Hermeneutics: A Study in the Thought of Paul Ricoeur and Jürgen Habermas* (Cambridge: Cambridge University Press, 1981), especially pp. 92–4.

17 Dietrich Ritschl, *The Logic of Theology* (London: SCM, 1986), p. 240; cf. pp. 231, 275–7.

18 Ibid., p. 231.

19 Cornelius Ernst, 'Theological Methodology', *Multiple Echo*, ed. Fergus Kerr and Timothy Radcliffe (London: Darton, Longman, Todd, 1979), p. 85.

20 Lindbeck, *The Nature of Doctrine*, p. 132.

21   Ritschl, *The Logic of Theology*, p. 237.
22   Angela Tilby (who has for some years done much to deepen the seriousness of religious broadcasting in the UK) writes in an essay entitled 'Spirit of the Age: A Reflection on Ten Years of Theology, Television, Mad Vicars and Magazines' (*Christian*, vol. 5, no. 3 [1980]): 'I am disturbed to discover that the playwright Dennis Potter who has through this decade been intensely aware of the pain and ambiguity of our condition feels he *cannot* enter the community of formal Christian believing because he believes the jollity, the triviality and the half-truths masking suffering would deprive him of his power to write' (p. 12).
23   Dietrich Bonhoeffer, *Letters and Papers from Prison* (enlarged edition) (London: SCM, 1971), p. 300.
24   Ibid.
25   Ibid., p. 362.

The Uneasy Alliance Reconceived: Catholic Theological Method, Modernity and Postmodernity

David Tracy

One of the commanding figures of theological revisionism, Tracy has been both appreciative and critical of postliberal theology. Although critical of the influence of the Enlightenment on mainstream Christian thought, he remains unconvinced that the postliberal project of a non-foundational theology is likely to succeed , and seeks to retain the importance of transcendental, hermeneutical reflection for a theology which is both mystical and ethical–political in orientation.

Every great religion, Friedrich von Hügel once observed, is comprised of three fundamental elements: the mystical, the institutional and the intellectual.[1] Only when all three are flourishing may the religion itself be said to flourish. However limited the applicability of Hügel's observations may be for other religious traditions, it remains, I believe, the most fruitful hypothesis for understanding the Roman Catholic tradition.

The Uneasy Alliance

More exactly, Roman Catholicism is comprised of three elements which tend to clash at times and harmonize at other times. The first element, the mystical, may more exactly be named the religious element. The forms of Catholic piety, myth, ritual, liturgy, religious orders and movements, symbols of popular culture and elite cultures alike are those realities that anthropologists and historians of religion have taught us all to observe in new ways. Indeed, if Catholic studies are to flourish in the multidisciplinary modern academy, it will happen only when we not only possess the more familiar philosophical, theological, social scientific, and historical studies of the Catholic religious element, but also encourage anthropologists and historians of religion to discern the forms, the interrelationships and the history of the entire symbolic religious life of Catholic Christianity. We still await the Clifford Geertz to write *Catholicism Observed* in different cultures, or the Wendy Doniger to illuminate the great myths and symbols of Mexican, Polish, Italian and Irish forms of Catholic life, or the Claude Lévi-Strauss to study the mythemes and binary oppositions typical of a characteristically Catholic analogical imagination across the many different cultures formed by Catholicism.[2] Above all, we need not only philosophers and theologians but historians of religion and anthropologists to study the myths, rituals, symbols and symbolic forms of this amazing, pluralistic and rich Catholic tradition.

Such work has barely begun for Catholic studies – indeed, for the study of Christianity itself. Yet there is good reason to hope that many historians of religion, like their colleagues in anthropology (such as Mary Douglas and Victor Turner),[3] will turn their scholarly attention to such a curiously under-studied phenomenon as Hügel's 'religious element' in Catholicism.

In the meantime we do possess many first-rate historical and social scientific studies of the second and third elements, the institutional and intellectual aspects of Catholicism. Indeed, thanks to the work in social history of scholars like Jay Dolan, Martin Marty and Andrew Greeley in the US, and F. X. Kaufman and Jean Delumeau in Europe, Catholic institutional and intellectual history is no longer confined to studies of great events and personalities (like councils and popes).[4] Rather, social history has forged new ways to clarify the long-term continuities as well as the significant discontinuities in the religious life of Catholic peoples in different cultures and periods. This social scientific and historical work is already affecting the nature of much Roman Catholic thought, especially its ecclesiology.

Such historical, social scientific, anthropological and history-of-religion perspectives, in my judgement, are what are most needed to challenge, enrich and change the familiar forms of Catholic studies, including Catholic theological method. Such work is at its beginnings in the modern academy, but that beginning is real and promising. No student of Hügel's third element, the intellectual, can afford to ignore that work. For Catholic thought, both philosophy and theology, will become more and more the locus where the challenges posed by the study of the religious element and the institutional element will come home for reflection on where we have been and where we may wish to go.

In the meantime, of course, those thinkers and scholars principally involved in understanding the intellectual element of Catholicism have further tasks of their own. For in so far as philosophy and theology are reflective and correlational disciplines, they attempt, in properly general terms, to correlate critically an interpretation of the tradition and an interpretation of the contemporary situation.[5] Philosophy and theology inevitably pay attention to the shifts not only in the tradition but in the contemporary situation itself.[6] Here the recent explosion of interest across the disciplines in the categories 'rationality' and 'modernity' are two principal candidates for new philosophical and theological study.[7] To argue that our age is better characterized as postmodern than as modern is admittedly to solve very little. But it is to acknowledge that radical plurality and a heightened sense of ambiguity, so typical of all postmodern movements of thought with their refusal of premature closure and their focus upon the categories of the 'different' and the 'other', are here to stay.[8] A major element in that acknowledgement is the abandonment of any claim of traditional and modern forms of philosophy and theology that cannot account for their own linguistic and thereby historical character. In the modern period, positivism has been the principal but not sole intellectual bearer of strictly ahistorical claims. But however powerful positivism still is as a cultural force, it is intellectually a spent force.[9] Neither the natural sciences nor the social sciences nor the humanities any longer linger over the false promises of this last modern Western outpost of the quest for ahistorical certainty.

The Western temptation to believe in its own intellectual superiority and thereby certainty is dying as slowly, and admittedly as dangerously, as the Western colonial period itself.[10] Hence the interest across the disciplines in the exact nature of Western 'rationality'. Hence the insistence in theology to cease our Eurocentric ways and learn to interpret the polycentric[11] theologies of a global church. Western thinkers, including theologians and philosophers, now feel obliged not merely to study but to learn from non-Western traditions of reason. Western thinkers are also deeply involved in recovering the more modestly conceived premodern resources of Western reason in such classics of reason as the nature of rational dialogue in Plato, the nature of rational argument in Aristotle, and the development of scholastic method among the medievals.[12] At the same time as these retrievals of the classic Western resources on reason are occurring, new and strong hermeneutics of suspicion on modern Enlightenment notions of rationality continue: those proposed by the 'others' in the other great civilizations; those proposed by the marginalized and oppressed 'others' in the Western tradition itself; those occasioned by the acknowledgement of the omnipresent relationships of power in all claims to knowledge; and those occasioned by the hermeneutical and pragmatic turn in Western thought

– all focused, in sum, on the postmodern concern with 'otherness' and 'difference'.[13] As a single example of these developments, this congeries of issues on our notions of rationality can be seen clearly in contemporary Western feminist theory, which at its best is the most ethically challenging and intellectually sophisticated exposure of the full dilemmas of our pluralistic and ambiguous postmodern moment.[14]

Whether it wills to or not, Catholic theology is a part of all this. To think otherwise is to deny the often ironic and occasionally tragic Catholic history in modernity.[15] The neo-scholastic thinkers of the late nineteenth and early twentieth centuries, for example, used all their considerable intellectual gifts to try to refute modernity in its Cartesian form. Ironically, in this very attempt at refutation they imposed Cartesian forms and an ahistorical quest for certainty on the quest for understanding of classical Catholic theology, like that of their own presumed hero, Thomas Aquinas. But this irony only provoked a greater intellectual tragedy for Catholic theology in the early twentieth century. Just when an alliance, however uneasy, was being forged between Catholic thought and modernity, the institutional church intervened. The silencing of the Catholic Modernists was not merely intellectually self-defeating and ethically and religiously unsettling; it was also unnecessary, as the parallel history of liberal Protestant thought in the same modern period shows. Critical inquiry, left to the self-correcting power of the entire community of inquiry, can and should be trusted to provide whatever corrections it may eventually need. As Wilhelm Pauck observed, Protestant neo-orthodox thought, despite its strong criticism of Protestant liberal theology, was not a return to a premodern, orthodox model for theology. Protestant neo-orthodoxy was, rather, a self-corrective moment within the same post-orthodox theological paradigm first developed by the great liberal theologians from Schleiermacher forward.[16]

Pauck seems to me exactly right about the history of Protestant theology in the modern period. His insight renders all the more poignant the fate of Catholic Modernism. For what that event meant, for Catholic thought, was that many of the best theologians and philosophers of that period retired to purely historical work. This historical vocation was and is a noble calling, surely, and one which in the long run proved eminently enriching to understanding the fuller tradition of Catholic thought and practice. Indeed, the great generation after the Modernist debacle – the generation, after all, which produced the self-reforming movements that issued in the Second Vatican Council – spent most of their early years as scholars retrieving the classic resources of the Catholic tradition in institutionally bleak times; the great *ressourcement* or 'return to the sources' of French Catholic thought of Chenu, Congar, de Lubac, Bouyer and the Swiss Hans Urs von Balthasar and others concentrated on the patristic, liturgical and scriptural resources of the tradition. Others, like Gilson,

Grabmann and Lottin, focused on the historical recovery of the history of the methodologically sophisticated scholastic thought of the high medieval period. Yet others, like Maréchal, Rahner, Lonergan, Schillebeeckx and Chenu, led in forging new, post-Modernist alliances with modern thought by rethinking the theological programme of Thomas Aquinas in modern terms. Joseph Komonchak has observed – justly, I believe – that if you follow the intellectual journeys of the generation that produced Vatican II after Vatican II, you will understand much of the development of Catholic thought in the last twenty-five years. For most of the theologians who spent their early years trying to rethink Aquinas's thought in modern terms – Chenu, Congar, Rahner, Lonergan, Schillebeeckx – remained, after Vatican II, open to the continuing self-reform of Catholic thought, Catholic institutional life and Catholic religious life. Many of these same generations that had spent their early years retrieving either patristic thought (especially Origen) or, among the medieval classics, Bonaventure rather than Aquinas, began after Vatican II to pull back from continuing intellectual and institutional self-reform. The alliance, even the *entente cordiale*, established at Vatican II between modernity and Catholicism, in their judgement, had failed.

It was Rahner, Lonergan, Schillebeeckx and others, after all, who helped encourage the further reforming and correlational theological proposals of correlational theologies of all kinds: Anglo-American empirical theologies, European political theologies, Latin American liberation theologies and North American feminist theologies.[17] All these different theologies, in their Catholic forms, remain committed, despite their otherwise strong differences, even conflicts with one another, to what can only be named some version of a method of correlation for theology.[18] This method the Catholic generations after Vatican II learned initially from Rahner and Lonergan, who argued that they had learned its basic form from Aquinas. This method of correlation they were happy to learn anew and in importantly new ways from the Protestant tradition from Schleiermacher through Tillich and their successors.

In the meantime alternative scenarios were proposed for the post-Vatican II period. For example, Catholic theologians like Metz in Germany or Segundo in Uruguay now call Vatican II the 'bourgeois revolution' in modern Catholicism.[19] They do not mean a desire to return to a pre-Vatican II period, any more than secular postmodernists long for a return to romanticism, much less medievalism. Radical political and liberationist theologians mean, rather, that the kind of correlation between Catholicism and modernity needs to be far more radical, on both sides of the correlation, than Vatican II envisaged.[20] Hence the emergence of political and liberation and other postmodern theologies as major new forms of contemporary post-Vatican II Catholic correlational theology. Catholic feminist theologians continue to radicalize that same post-Vatican II scenario and correlational model – now, of course, with strongly feminist concerns directed to rethinking both the Catholic tradition and modernity.[21]

A second reading of the uneasy alliance also began to unfold after Vatican II. This interpretation of Catholic theology, especially since the pontificate of John Paul II, takes a quite different form. Led by some of the theologians who also helped bring Vatican II about (de Lubac, Balthasar, Bouyer and Ratzinger), this reading, in effect, claims that the alliance between modernity and Catholicism forged by theologians like Rahner, Lonergan, Schillebeeckx, Kung and others had not yielded a new Catholic unity-in-diversity; rather, these kinds of correlational theologies threaten to destroy even the earlier uneasy alliance between Catholicism and modernity of Vatican II itself. For Balthasar and Ratzinger, Bonaventure rather than Aquinas provides the best classical model for Catholic theology.[22] For Bonaventure is interpreted by Balthasar and Ratzinger (but not by others, including myself) as envisioning that Catholic theology, above all, needs to clarify and affirm its own unique identity as such and not in correlation with the ever-shifting and dangerous contours of the contemporary situation. Such theology can make great use of any extra-ecclesial thought: as Bonaventure clearly did with Neoplatonism; as Balthasar and Ratzinger clearly do with German idealism.[23] But such correlations should be present only in an ad hoc, not systematically correlational manner.[24] The effect should not be any attempt to correlate systematically a Catholic self-understanding with that of modernity. Bonaventure's famous colleague at the University of Paris, Thomas Aquinas, did attempt such a correlation with his interest in the new Aristotelianism (the modernity) of that period.[25] Historically, Bonaventure may have been as fearful of what was happening among the radical Aristotelians of the liberal arts faculty at the University of Paris as Ratzinger was at what happened at the University of Tübingen in the late 1960s.[26] But Aquinas, who did not hesitate to argue against the radical Aristotelians when it seemed appropriate, remained committed to what can be justly described as the attempt to correlate the best of Aristotle and Plato with the best of the Catholic tradition.

Indeed, this new kind of post-Vatican II Catholic theology of Balthasar and Ratzinger is remarkably similar in method to the claim in American Protestant theology proposed by the neo-Barthian anti-correlational theology.[27] As Lindbeck makes clear, theology should be intra-textual and not correlational.[28] At its best, as in Karl Barth, theology, for Lindbeck, does not engage in a deliberately apologetic task at all. Therefore theology should not use revisionary methods of correlation like Tillich's, but intra-textual methods like Barth's. The questions recur: who are the true heirs of Calvin? Schleiermacher and Troeltsch or Barth? Who are the true heirs of Luther? Tillich or Lindbeck? Who are the true heirs of Aquinas? Rahner or Balthasar? Who is the true heir of Bonaventure? The early Ratzinger or the later? And perhaps, lurking beneath all these questions, who are the true heirs of that most puzzling, pluralistic and important theologian of them all, Augustine?[29]

In my judgement, some revisionary method of correlation for theology, as Aquinas and Schleiermacher, Rahner and Tillich, Lonergan and Gilkey insist, is the only hope for a way forward for theological method. But if such revisionary methods are not to become trapped in an unwelcome complacency in their own revisionary and correlational methods, they too must be continually open to critique and revision. Hence my need to insist upon the full force of the 'reconceived' in the title of this essay. For I share the sense expressed by Schillebeeckx when he observed: 'After two centuries of resistance, Catholics embraced the modern world just at the moment when the modern world began to distrust itself'. There are, in fact, some good reasons, as I suggested above and have argued elsewhere, for modernity to distrust itself.[30] There are also good reasons for Catholic thought to be open to constant revision as the acknowledgement of the fuller plurality and often radical ambiguity of all three of Hügel's elements comes more clearly into view.

Catholic Methods of Correlation in Fundamental Theology

In theology at the moment there is occurring, across the traditions, a great divide. Many theologians insist that the modern paradigm of some form of a revised correlational model for theology has reached the end of its usefulness. One basic reason for that claim is, paradoxically enough, a typically correlational move: the claim that in our situation we should now acknowledge – as modernity itself lingers over its own self-distrust – that modern theology by the very attempt to correlate an interpretation of the tradition (usually by some candidate for the heart of the tradition) with an interpretation of the ever-changing modern situation (usually by some candidate for the principal religious questions posed by modernity or postmodernity) has lost its distinctively theological centre by attempting to be correlational at all.[31] This methodological loss has also occasioned a substantive loss; for every tradition is in danger of losing its distinctiveness through the subtle erosions of all particularities by the illusory claims to universality of Western Enlightenment modernity. On this scenario it is time to call theology back to its own task – something like a 'thick description' of the tradition for the tradition's own sake. Hence anti-correlational theologians appeal to Geertz-like understandings of theology as, in effect, a kind of descriptive religious anthropology, or they appeal to intra-textual enterprises like literary criticism's ability to provide close readings of the details (character, plot, point of view, metaphor, narrative) of the Christian founding biblical narratives.[32] Hence the anti-correlational theologians employ the later Wittgenstein and the word 'foundationalism' sometimes to cover ground all the way from any Cartesian or neo-scholastic quest for certainty to any claim for the self-transcending character of reason at all.[33] Hence the return, in Protestant theologies, to Barth's theological method and his reading of Protestant theological history. Hence the equally strong interest, in several Catholic theologies, in the theological method of Balthasar as an alternative to Rahner, Lonergan and their successors.[34]

It is a puzzling scene. On the one hand, correlational theologians are informed that their concern with analyses of modernity and postmodernity (under the rubric of the 'situation') has caused the problem. On the other hand, they are given a typically situational analysis: that the loss of identity by all traditions in modernity is the central *situational* question facing all theologians who can see our present situation clearly.

On the Hügel model proposed above, there is no good reason to reject the genuine gains which such new anti-correlational theologies promise. Those gains include disciplinary ones like the greater use in theology of anthropology and literary criticism. They include substantive gains like the insistence on the need to pay closer intra-textual attention to the biblical narratives for Christian self-identity and to defend the centrality of a concern with Catholic ecclesial identity and the centrality of 'visible form' for Catholic theology.[35] Correlational models of theology, after all, also insist on the need for criteria of appropriateness to the tradition.[36] They should, therefore, be fully open to all proposals for assuring an appropriately Christian identity, including the fruitful intra-textual studies of the anti-correlational theologians. There is also much gain in the philosophical anti-foundationalist enterprise in so far as it may help not only to expose the quest for certainty but to recover the classical notions of reason as dialogue and argument.[37] For once any thinker admits the linguistic and historical character of all models of rationality, the aims of reason must be more modest than many formulations of transcendental thought suggest.

Indeed, on the basis of the revised Hügel model proposed earlier, the gains provided by these new interdisciplinary moves within theology remain considerable. The use of anthropology and especially history-of-religions methods (the latter curiously lacking in most of the new intra-textual proposals) could greatly challenge, enrich and render 'thicker' the construals of both the religious life of a people (Hügel's mystical element) and thereby the theological interpretations of the tradition (the intellectual element). There is much to be gained and little to be lost in following Kenneth Burke's sage advice: use all there is to be used. In reconceiving Catholic studies in this pluralistic manner, the gain could be great. For then one would find, in the modern academy and in fidelity to the academy's highest standards,[38] a multidisciplinary study of Catholicism within which the element of thought would be related, in interdisciplinary fashion, to the wider field of descriptive Catholic studies. The central methodological question posed by these new challenges to correlational models of theology is clear: what is the role of fundamental theology in the wider task of theology? Alternatively, should apologetics play an intrinsic and systemic role in theology or merely an ad hoc one?[39]

It is this role of fundamental theology which all the now familiar attacks on any revised correlational method for theology must oppose, by denying any systemic (as distinct from ad hoc) role to apologetics. Fundamental theology (the modern correlational form of apologetics) has been a familiar focus for modern Catholic theology, both as a distinct sub-discipline within theology and as a necessary element in both systematic theology and practical theology.[40] To reject fundamental theology as a basic theological discipline is the logical implication of all anti-correlational moves. For to the anti-correlationalist any announcement of a critically reflective role for theology sounds suspiciously like foundationalism. In one sense such suspicions are inevitable and in some cases justified. Theologians may sometimes function as if they were unaware of the historicity of all modes of critical reflection, including transcendental ones. They may also be too quick to provide too general, abstract, 'thin' descriptions of both the tradition and the situation in their rush to move on to the task of critical philosophical reflection.[41]

A correlational method open to these kinds of anti-correlationalist suspicions is always in need of re-examining its mode of inquiry. Such re-examination is exactly what has been occurring for the last twenty years across all the major forms of revised correlational method. That some form of transcendental reflection is needed by theology seems as clear now as it was twenty years ago, and that for the same reason: if one understands the logic of the claim Jews, Christians and Muslims make when they affirm their belief in a radically monotheistic God, transcendental reflection is that mode of rational inquiry appropriate to considering that claim.[42] And yet, to have this insight is not necessarily to be able to redeem it. Here the full force of modernity's self-doubt hits home. In so far as all modes of reasoning are linguistically rendered (as they are), they are historically embedded. Any transcendental method needs to pay greater attention to that fact than many forms of theology, both classical and modern, characteristically do. If such attention is not forthcoming, theology will quietly but inevitably drift away from the apologetic and situational elements of the correlation in fundamental theology.[43]

If theology can reconceive its mode of inquiry in a manner that does not violate its acknowledgement of its own linguisticality and thereby historicity, the method of correlation, once again revised, will continue to hold the field as an ever revisionary and ever self-critical mode of inquiry. Like Husserl in his constant rethinking of phenomenology, fundamental theologians aware of these difficulties must always be beginners; for each step forward seems to expose new difficulties that force one back again to rethink the beginnings of that peculiar mode of inquiry that is fundamental theology. Like Husserl's own enterprise, correlational fundamental theology could end in a failure that has all the marks of classic tragedy: witness that great tragic text of and on modernity, Husserl's *Crisis of the European Sciences.*[44] Any transcendental mode of inquiry like Husserl's will function well if, and only if, it can account for its own linguistic and historical essence. This was the principal reason for the turn to hermeneutics among Husserl's successors (Scheler, Heidegger, Gadamer, Merleau-Ponty, Ricoeur, and even, in his odd way, Derrida). This, too, is the reason for the retrieval of pragmatism and the new alliance of pragmatism with hermeneutics among so many contemporary Anglo-American philosophers (Putnam, Bernstein, Toulmin, Charles Taylor, and even, in his odd way, Rorty).[45]

Criteria for Fundamental Theology in the New Postmodern Situation

If theology is to continue to have a systematically apologetic task, and if that task is to prove adequate to the contemporary postmodern situation, then new criteria for the task are needed. Traditional modern fundamental theologies relied too exclusively on transcendental inquiry – and, too often, models of that inquiry not explicitly related to the questions of language (and thereby plurality and historicity) and questions of history (and thereby ambiguity and postmodern suspicion, not merely modern critique).[46] One way to try to clarify the present state of fundamental theology (short of abandoning it with the anti-correlationists) is to clarify anew the tripartite set of criteria needed in order to allow fundamental theology to fulfil its correlational task.[47] In properly general terms, the question of meaning and truth is a question of clarifying: first, the hermeneutical notion of truth as manifestation; second, how a given claim to manifestation coheres or does not cohere with what we otherwise consider reasonable; third, the ethical–political implications of these claims.[48] All three sets of criteria revise, even as they allow for, the kind of transcendental reflection proper to theological inquiry. All three criteria, moreover, clarify how these hermeneutic–pragmatic–transcendental concerns of the apologetic (or correlational) element in fundamental theology have distinct affinities to the various proposals for a mystical–prophetic model for systematic and practical theologies.[49] Such, at least, is one way to read the present conflict of interpretations on theological method in contemporary Catholic theologies: fundamental, systematic and practical. By concentrating on the need for new criteria for fundamental theology, one may hope to illuminate the fundamental element in systematic and practical theology as well.[50] This kind of reflection has impelled me in recent years to try to rethink the character of the criteria needed for correlational theology in the new situation. Those methodological criteria, I further believe, can not merely account for but, if properly open to learning anew, can also appropriate the genuine gains of the new anti-correlationalists in Catholic and Protestant theology alike.[51]

First, the hermeneutical criteria of truth as manifestation.[52] The central hermeneutical category is 'possibility'. In so far as hermeneutics is grounded in the reality of conversation with the claim to attention of the other, and in so far as hermeneutics is fashioned to relate experience directly to language and history, hermeneutics proves one fruitful philosophical tradition for the present dilemma. Moreover, as post-Gadamerian hermeneutics has yielded its own history-of-effects, there is now available, *pace* Gadamer, a greater role both for explanatory methods (Ricoeur), ideology-critique (Habermas) and even plurality than an earlier hermeneutics envisaged.[53] A notion of dialogue that has no place for these central intellectual, moral and even religious demands is one tempted by too easy notions of similarity or even sameness, and too sanguine a notion of the complementarity of all differences.

Granted these important caveats, hermeneutics shows that the model of conversation remains the central hope for recognizing the possibilities which any serious conversation with the claim to attention of the other and the different yields.[54] It matters relatively little whether the hermeneutical dialogue is through person-to-person dialogue or through that peculiar form of dialogue we call close reading of texts, rituals, symbols, myths or events. To acknowledge the claim to attention of the other as other, the different as different, is also to acknowledge that other world of meaning as in some manner a genuine possibility for myself. The traditional Catholic language of analogy may still prove, in admittedly new forms, one way to formulate how, after any genuine dialogue, what once seemed merely other now seems a real possibility. Thereby that otherness, now rendered hermeneutically as possibility, is in some manner analogous to what I have already experienced. I acknowledge that I and others who are trying to formulate an analogical imagination as one strategy for understanding the pluralism within Catholicism, the greater pluralism of the inter-religious dialogue, and the kinds of correlations likely between an interpretation of the situation and an interpretation of the tradition, must be not only wary but downright suspicious of how easily claims to analogy or similarity can become subtle evasions of the other and the different.[55] Similarity cannot be a cover word for the return of the same. Hence we need to remind ourselves linguistically of this danger by speaking not of analogies simply as similarities, but as always already similarities-in-difference.

The concept 'correlation' in correlational theology does not entail a belief in harmony, convergence or sameness.[56] Correlation logically entails only the notion that *some* relationship is involved. That relationship may (rarely) be one of identity – as in some of the proposals of liberal Protestant 'culture

Christianity' and some of the Catholic Modernists. That relationship may also be one of non-identity (existentially, confrontation) – as in the challenge of correlational theology to much of secular modernity's interpretation of secularity as secularistic and thereby non-religious or anti-religious.[57] The relationship may also be one of similarity-in-difference – as in analogical theologies; or identity-in-difference – as in dialectical theologies. The point of correlation is the need to relate critically interpretations of both tradition and situation.[58] The method of correlation, like all good method, provides only a heuristic guide to the inquiry. The inquiry is always hermeneutically determined by the question, the subject matter. No theologian can decide before the actual inquiry whether identity or non-identity or identity-in-difference or similarity-in-difference should obtain. Method is always and only a heuristic guide: a useful, critical guide which, if allied to flexible criteria, can aid but never replace the actual theological inquiry.

But whatever the fate of the strategy of an analogical imagination for rendering possibilities into similarities-in-difference, the larger issue is elsewhere: in the category of possibility itself. All possibilities can be understood more accurately as suggestive possibilities. The adjective 'suggestive' serves as a reminder that 'possibility' need not be a 'live, momentous, and forced' option in order to prove a genuine possibility.[59] As reception theory in hermeneutics reminds us, a whole spectrum of responses to any classic is available.[60] That spectrum can range all the way from a shock of recognition (in aesthetic terms) or faith (in religious terms) to a sense of tentative response to a genuine, i.e. live and suggestive, possibility on the other end of the spectrum. The spectrum remains a real spectrum (and not a mere chaos of responses) in so far as any genuine *possibility* evoked by the hermeneutical conversation is produced. What little I understand of Buddhist 'compassion' I do not understand on inner-Buddhist grounds of enlightenment. Yet I can respond to that classic Buddhist notion with a resonance to the challenge it poses to my own Catholic understanding of love as *caritas*.

A further advantage of the hermeneutical category of suggestive possibility is its rethinking of the primordial character of truth as manifestation. The hermeneutical tradition from Heidegger through Gadamer and Ricoeur defends the primordial notion of truth as event of manifestation. This notion of truth as manifestation has some singular advantages for this first general set of criteria for correlational theology. The primary advantage is that the notion of truth as manifestation (and recognition on the side of the subject) more closely fits both notions of revelation as event of God's self-manifestation and the response of faith as gifted recognition.[61] The truth of religion, like the truth of its nearest analogue, art, is primordially a truth of manifestation (more exactly, disclosure–concealment and human recognition).[62] Hermeneutical thought, with its philosophical and non-romantic defence of truth as manifestation, is well suited to defending anew this primal insight of both art and religion. In that sense hermeneutical thought is useful for reopening the highly complex philosophical and theological questions of the nature of revelation and the graced response of recognition named faith.

The mystical strands of Catholic Christianity are the best, but not sole, candidates for this mode of hermeneutical reflection in any mystico-prophetic Catholic theology. The wisdom traditions of the Hebrew scriptures and, in the New Testament, the Gospel and Letters of John evoke this kind of mystical meditative reflection. The marginalization in Catholic theology of the great mystical traditions – the image mysticism of Gregory and Origen, the trinitarian mysticism of Augustine and Ruysbroeck, the love mysticism of Bernard or the Victorines and Teresa of Avila and John of the Cross, and even the radically apophatic mysticism of Pseudo-Dionysius, Scotus Eriugena and Meister Eckhart – must surely end. Thanks to the labours of many scholars,[63] the import – aesthetic, religious and theological – of these too often theologically marginalized mystical traditions is now available for serious theological attention. Indeed, here too lies the import of the great work of Balthasar for Catholic theological attention. The classics of Bonaventure and Dante and all the other classic and too often ignored mystical Catholic theologies of the visible form manifesting the Beauty and Glory of God, so well rendered in Balthasar's *Herrlichkeit*, can be appropriated anew by correlational theology by being rendered as hermeneutical possibilities and thereby as new theological resources.[64] Karl Rahner and Bernard Lonergan knew instinctively this singular truth of the need for hermeneutical reflection. For, however great the turn to the mystical was in both the later Rahner and Lonergan (and it was),[65] they never abandoned the theological need to render these classic possibilities available to those non-mystics (including theologians) whose sense of religious possibility can be heightened by hermeneutical dialogue with the mystics.

The future of serious Catholic theology lies with its ability to recover these classic resources of the mystical tradition without forfeiting the need to retrieve them critically. Hermeneutical thought, with its grounding in the notion of truth as manifestation, provides one promising way to achieve this necessary substantive rethinking of Catholic theology. Moreover, as Gershom Scholem has observed in the case of kabbalism, the re-emergence of mystical readings in all prophetic traditions is also the re-emergence of the repressed archaic traditions.[66] Such seems to be the case with many forms of Catholic mysticism as well. As Eliade's work makes clear (with its grounding in a hermeneutics of manifestation), the so-called 'pagan' roots of Christianity need constant retrieval.[67] Such retrieval is available for all those willing to take the mystics' readings of our prophetic heritage seriously again.

And yet, even these hermeneutical criteria need further testing. They provide us with an ability to understand truth as primordially an event of manifestation and thereby to understand anew the kind of truth claim in the event of revelation and the gifted response – recognition of faith. At the same time, they provoke further questions on how these manifestations cohere with what we otherwise know or, more likely, believe to be the case. The second set of criteria may be described, generically, as a rough coherence with what we otherwise know or, more likely, believe to be the case. The danger is that this set of criteria (under rubrics, e.g. like strict verification and strict falsification) will so quickly take over that the notion of truth as event of manifestation will quickly become a distant memory.

However, several recent Western philosophical discussions of reason are helpful for fighting that rationalistic and scientistic (not scientific) temptation. In an intellectual situation where philosophers of natural science like Toulmin have challenged earlier reigning paradigms of scientism and rationality, many in the philosophical community have far more flexible notions of truth and reason than was once the case in the days of positivism.[68] Science itself is now also acknowledged as a hermeneutic enterprise.[69] What one now finds is a historically and hermeneutically informed philosophy of science (often named, interestingly enough, postmodern science)[70] as well as a philosophically informed history of science. It is not merely the case, as Hegel insisted, that the fact that reason has a history is a problem for reason. It is also the case that the history of reason includes the history of relatively adequate (e.g. Aristotle and postmodern science) and inadequate (e.g. positivism) accounts of reason. I do not pretend by these brief references to imply that the problem of an adequate notion of reason is readily available for use in fundamental theology. Of course, there is no *de facto* consensus among contemporary philosophers on what rational consensus is. But this, for present purposes, is not necessarily unfortunate. If, in fact, philosophers can continue to show a genuinely rational way to recover the classical resources of reason (e.g. Platonic dialogue, Aristotelian *phronesis*, and Peirce's 'community of inquiry'), then, minimally, the discussion of reason and faith should be freed from what Richard Bernstein nicely labels both 'objectivism' and 'relativism'.[71] The two options, so familiar in the recent past and so fatal for critical reflection on religious manifestations, have proved inadequate on strictly philosophical grounds. Rather, we are left with more flexible but no less rational criteria for the rough coherence of what truths-as-manifestations we may hermeneutically learn from revelation with what we otherwise know reasonably from science and all other uses of reason.[72]

The most persuasive attempt in modern Catholic thought to defend the reality of reason without capitulating to foundationalist notions of rationality remains that of Bernard Lonergan. If reformulated in linguistically informed terms, Lonergan's masterwork, *Insight*, retains its power to persuade.[73] It is, above all, the self-correcting character of reason that needs careful defence.

This Lonergan provides in recognizably empirical, Anglo-American terms: we reach, in every act of judgement, whether that of common sense, historical scholarship or scientific theory, the point where, for the present inquirer faithful to the demands of the inquiry itself, no further relevant questions emerge. This is why Lonergan named every judgement not an absolutely unconditioned but a virtually unconditioned. The judgement is unconditioned, since it answers the questions relevant to the subject, the criteria and the evidence now available to competent inquirers. Such judgement, as dependent upon the present community's available evidence and modes of inquiry, is also only virtually unconditioned, since every judgement is by definition open to further revision as further questions emerge.[74] And further questions will always eventually emerge. I have elsewhere reformulated Lonergan's defence of the self-correcting and thereby partly history-transcending character of reason under the rubric of judgements of relative adequacy: adequate to the question at hand and relative to the evidence presently available.

This is the same kind of modest but real defence of reason which Hilary Putnam[75] means when he insists that on any given question, if you demand everything, you will not succeed; on most questions enough is enough, enough is not everything. More importantly, for Catholic thought at least, this is the same kind of defence of reason which Aquinas defended with his insistence, thanks to his study of Aristotle, that we can only have the kind of certitude that a given subject matter allows. The classic Western resources of reason, especially those first articulated by Plato and Aristotle, remain, with appropriate revisionary modifications, our central resources. Descartes, Hegel or Husserl may have been guilty of foundationalism, as may indeed much modern Western thought that succeeded them. But neither Plato's notion of dialogue nor Aristotle's notion of argument is foundationalist.[76] The more careful proponents of communication theory in our day continue that Platonic–Aristotelian line.[77] As did Lonergan and, before him, Aquinas.

What the theologians add to such inquiry on reason – and it is, to be sure, no minor addition – is the further relevant question, the strictly transcendental question, of the nature of ultimate reality. Above all, it is the self-correcting and unrestricted character of inquiry itself which demands a posing of this question for rational inquirers unwilling to stop the inquiry arbitrarily.[78] What theologians need to be willing to continue to argue is the reasonableness of this question and what reasonable, relatively adequate answers we might have as inquirers on that question – a question provoked by inquiry itself for any thoughtful inquirer. If theologians expect certainty in their answers to these limit questions of reason, they are doomed to failure. But if theologians are faithful to the logic of the subject matter they presume to study (the nature of ultimate reality) and the coherence of the self-manifestations of God and the logic of inquiry itself with what we otherwise reasonably hold, they cannot avoid asking this question of ultimate coherence. Apologetics must always be an intrinsic aspect of all Christian theology.[79] Alternatively, both systematic theology and practical theology need fundamental theology. Even the explicit and implicit cognitive claims of the mystics should be inquired into in order to see how they cohere or do not cohere with what we otherwise know or believe to be the case.[80] To abandon that critical correlational task of theology is to abandon, within theology, its reflective task and to abandon as well the claims of all the prophets and mystics to speak directly and purposively to the human search for meaning and truth. It is indeed important in thought, as Wittgenstein insisted and the anti-correlationalists love to repeat, to know when to stop. But the anti-correlationist theologians stop too soon, or more exactly, will not even begin the reflective questions on hermeneutical manifestation as possibility and the coherence of those possibilities to reason–questions which theologians like Aquinas and Lonergan show is also the non-foundationalist question of inquiry itself, the question Christians and Jews name the question of God. A systematic or practical theology that refuses its own need for a fundamental theology is a truncated vision of the fuller task of theology. For theology at its best is not an exercise in the quest for certainty at all, but includes the difficult, necessary exercise in the quest for some understanding of how all claims to meaning and truth in the revelatory and salvific manifestations of faith cohere with the character of the self-correcting, unrestricted nature of inquiry itself.[81]

As any participant in contemporary theology soon discovers, moreover, a further set of criteria will and should emerge from the inquiry itself – generically ethical–political criteria.[82] These criteria, so familiar to the prophetic core of Christianity and Judaism, will continue to enter the theological conversation in several routes. First, the religions themselves, especially but not solely in their prophetic strands, demand them. Secondly, our very nature as human beings demands ethical assessment.

There is no manifestation disclosure that is not also a call to transformation. There is no revelation without salvation. There is no theological theory without praxis. There need be no hermeneutic without pragmatics. There need be no divisions between the mystical and prophetic strands of the great tradition unless we arbitrarily impose them. The pragmatic turn of hermeneutics itself – as indeed of much contemporary discourse philosophy – fully shares in this insistence on the need for ethical–political criteria. In that sense we are all the heirs of William James's insistence on the criteria of ethical, humane fruits, or consequences for action, for praxis, both individually and societally. Even here, however, our situation is more difficult and more parlous than the situation faced by early modernity or even the classical pragmatists. On the individual side the rampant problems of possessive individualism have become a major ethical dilemma for modern Western societies.[83] More puzzling still, the very notion of the self, so cherished in almost all Western philosophies and theologies (even those, like process thought, highly critical of earlier substantialist notions of the self, has become a central problem in inter-religious dialogue where several highly sophisticated Buddhist and Hindu notions of 'no-self' enter, along with several postmodern critiques of the self (e.g. Kristeva and Lacan), to radicalize all more familiar Western revisionary notions of self.[84]

The ethical–political criteria must meet further challenges: above all from the discovery of the inevitability of concrete social–political realities embedded in all discourse and the theological reformulations of the prophetic strands of these traditions into several distinct political and liberation theologies. In the meantime the recovery of pragmatic criteria of personal ethical and political consequences for action remains a necessary set of general and flexible criteria for serious theology today – as the feminist, liberation and political theologians, as well as the new pragmatists, argue; as the new insistence on the centrality of praxis justly insists.[85]

That all these criteria themselves need further reflection and refinement beyond the brief analysis given above is obvious. For even if these criteria are, on the whole,[86] sound, they still cannot replace the actual task of theological inquiry on particular questions but only inform it with the kind of questions and some general heuristic criteria for asking those questions.

On this reading the pragmatic turn of European hermeneutics, like the hermeneutic turn of Anglo-American analytical pragmatics, is merely the expression of the drive of contemporary inquiry to demand a fuller set of criteria for all inquiries. The systematic and practical theological analogues of this hermeneutic–pragmatic turn in fundamental theology is the new search in many Christian theologies for both mystical and prophetic readings of the rich and pluralistic tradition.[87] The future, I believe, belongs to those mystico-prophetic systematic and practical theologies. But the future will belong best even to these great emerging and global options if the traditional theological concerns of apologetics, reformulated in the modern period as correlational theologies, continue to be reformulated when the need is clear. As Hügel knew as well as Husserl, in such reflectively methodological questions we must always be beginners. And that willingness to begin always anew is at least as important an injunction as the knowledge of when to stop.

Notes

1   Friedrich von Hügel, *The Mystical Element in Religion*, 2 vols (New York: Dutton, 1923). In another form the core of this paper was given as my inaugural lecture for the

Andrew Thomas Greeley and Grace McNichols Greeley Chair in Catholic Studies at the University of Chicago in spring 1988. The critical comments of Anne Carr, Andrew Greeley, Mary Jule Durkin, and especially (on Bonaventure) Bernard McGinn allowed me to develop and revise positions. I should also like to thank colleagues at St John's University (Collegeville), Georgetown University, and the University of Dallas for their reflections on different parts of this study.

2 See Clifford Geertz, *Islam Observed* (Chicago: University of Chicago Press, 1971); Wendy Doniger O'Flaherty, *Other People's Myths* (New York: Macmillan, 1988); Claude Lévi-Strauss, *The Jealous Potter* (Chicago: University of Chicago Press, 1988). I have suggested myself how a Catholic analogical imagination may endure across Catholic cultures: 'The Catholic Theological Imagination', *Catholic Theological Society of America Proceedings* 32 (1977), pp. 234–44. For a social scientific study here, see Andrew Greeley, *Religious Change in America* (Cambridge, MA: Harvard University Press, 1989). The further need is for a semiotic and hermeneutic study of the similarities and differences of such an analogical imagination in different Catholic cultures.

3 See e.g. Mary Douglas, *Purity and Danger* (London: Routledge, Chapman and Hall, 1984); Victor Turner and Edith Turner, *Image and Pilgrimage in Christian Culture* (New York: Columbia University Press, 1978).

4 Jay Dolan, *American Catholic Experience* (New York: Doubleday, 1985); Martin E. Marty, *Modern American Religion: The Irony of It, 1893–1919* (Chicago: University of Chicago Press, 1986).

5 For a brief statement of this position, see David Tracy, 'Tillich and Contemporary Theology', in *The Thought of Paul Tillich*, ed. J. Adams, W. Pauck and R. Shinn (San Francisco: Harper and Row, 1985).

6 The category 'situation' is used here in Paul Tillich's sense in his *Systematic Theology* 1 (Chicago: University of Chicago Press, 1951): 'Theology, as a function of the Christian church, must serve the needs of the church. A theological system is supposed to satisfy two basic needs: the statement of the truth of the Christian message and the interpretation of this truth for every new generation. Theology moves back and forth between two poles, the eternal truth of its foundation and the temporal situation in which the eternal truth must be received' (p. 3).

7 For two representative studies, see: on rationality, Bryan R. Wilson, ed., *Rationality* (Oxford: Blackwell Publishers, 1970); on modernity and postmodernity, Alan Wilde, *Horizons of Assent: Modernism, Postmodernism and the Ironic Imagination* (Philadelphia: University of Pennsylvania Press, 1987).

8 I have argued for this in *Plurality and Ambiguity* (San Francisco: Harper and Row, 1988), esp. pp. 47–66 (on plurality) and pp. 66–82 (on ambiguity).

9 The cultural power of positivism is especially evident in the debates over technology and its extraordinary force on all our culture and thought.

10 See Langdon Gilkey, 'Der Paradigmenwechsel in der Theologie', in *Das neue Paradigma von Theologie*, ed. Hans Küng and David Tracy (Einsiedeln: Benziger, 1986).

11 The expression 'polycentric' as distinct from 'pluralistic' is that of Johann Baptist Metz.

12 Bernard Lonergan, *Grace and Freedom* (New York: Herder and Herder, 1970).

13 For contrasting approaches see Michael Theunissen, *The Other* (Cambridge, MA: MIT Press, 1984); Gilles Deleuze, *Difference et repetition* (Paris: Presses Universitaires de France, 1981); Jean-François Lyotard, *The Differend: Phrases in Dispute* (Minneapolis:

University of Minnesota Press, 1988).

14 For three examples see Jeffrey Allen and Iris Marion Young, eds, *The Thinking Muse: Feminism and Modern French Philosophy* (Bloomington: Indiana University Press, 1989); Toril Moi, ed., *French Feminist Thought* (London: Blackwell Publishers, 1987); and Janet Todd, *Feminist Literary History* (London: Routledge, Chapman and Hall, 1988).

15 See James Hennessey, 'Leo XIII's Thomistic Revival: A Political and Philosophical Event', in David Tracy, ed., *Celebrating the Medieval Heritage, Journal of Religion* 58 (supplement 1978), pp. 185–97; Bernard M. Reardon, *Roman Catholic Modernism* (Stanford: Stanford University Press, 1970).

16 See the individual studies of Wilhelm Pauck on Harnack, Troeltsch, Barth and Tillich.

17 That several of these theologies do not call themselves 'correlational' is less important than the methodological-as-correlational character of the theologies themselves. For representative examples of these theologies, see Hans Küng, David Tracy, eds, *Theologie Wohin?* (Einsiedeln: Benziger, 1984).

18 Representative examples of those differences and conflicts within a basically correlational model may be found in Kung and Tracy, eds, *Das neue Paradigma* (n. 10, above).

19 See Johann Baptist Metz, *The Emergent Church* (New York: Crossroad, 1986); Juan Luis Segundo, *The Liberation of Theology* (Maryknoll, NY: Orbis, 1976).

20 The dialectical character of political and liberation theologies assures that the 'correlation' will not prove a merely harmonious, 'liberal' one.

21 See Anne Carr, *Transforming Grace: Christian Tradition and Women's Experience* (San Francisco: Harper and Row, 1988); Rosemary Radford Reuther, *Sexism and Godtalk* (Boston: Beacon Press, 1983); Elisabeth Schüssler-Fiorenza, *In Memory of Her* (New York: Crossroad, 1985).

22 The readings of Bonaventure as, in effect, non-correlational are nicely challenged by the work of Ewert Cousins, *Bonaventure and the Coincidence of Opposites* (Chicago: Franciscan Herald, 1978). Ratzinger's own, earlier reading of Bonaventure (on history and revelation) lends itself to a more 'correlational' reading of Bonaventure than Ratzinger's more recent readings suggest: see Joseph Ratzinger, *The Theology of History in Bonaventure* (Chicago: Franciscan Herald, 1971). Perhaps in following the suggestion of Gerrish on Schleiermacher as providing (in the *Glaubenslehre*) 'Theology within the Limits of Piety Alone', we can call major aspects of Bonaventure's position 'Theology within the Limits of Spirituality Alone'. As with Schleiermacher, however, and unlike Barth and Balthasar, Bonaventure clearly also possessed what can only be named 'correlational' interests.

23 The influence of Hegel on Balthasar merits further study – as does, indeed, the influence of Neoplatonism on Hegel.

24 For a fine study of the various meanings of ad hoc apologetics, see William Placher, *Unapologetic Theology* (Louisville, KY: Westminster/John Knox, 1989), pp. 166–70. A clear and systematic statement of the alternative ad hoc apologetics may be found in William Werpehowski, 'Ad hoc Apologetics', *Journal of Religion* 66 (1986), pp. 282–301. Placher's book is notable for showing the nuances in both the intra-textual and the correlational positions on the issue of apologetics. It is also notable for its noble attempt to find a *via media*.

25 See Marie Dominique Chenu, *Introduction à l'étude de saint Thomas d'Aquin* (Montreal: Institut d'Études Mediévales, 1974); James A. Weisheipl, *Friar Tommaso d'Aquino*

(New York: Doubleday, 1974).

26   The influence of particular historical events on the thought of theologians is rarely as clearly illustrated as in the differing responses of Bonaventure and Aquinas to the crisis of radical Aristotelianism and the responses of Ratzinger and Küng to the crisis of the German universities.

27   The differences are also, of course, notable: the Protestant theologians, in fidelity to the theology of the Word, emphasize the intertextual developments; the Catholics, in fidelity to the sacramental vision of Catholicism, emphasize the 'ecclesial sense' (Ratzinger) or the importance of the incarnational–sacramental 'visible form' (Balthasar).

28   George Lindbeck, *The Nature of Doctrine* (Philadelphia: Westminster Press, 1984).

29   The contrast of all Western Christian (Augustinian) theology with Eastern Orthodox theology remains largely a matter of how to interpret Augustine.

30   In *Plurality and Ambiguity* (n. 8, above).

31   See Lindbeck's penetrating observations on the dangers, in a consumerist culture, of an emphasis on 'experience' in *The Nature of Doctrine* (n. 28, above).

32   See Hans Frei, *The Eclipse of Biblical Narrative* (New Haven, CT: Yale University Press, 1974), and *The Identity of Jesus Christ* (Philadelphia: Fortress Press, 1975).

33   On the ambiguities of the word 'foundationalism' see Placher, *Unapologetic Theology* (n. 24, above).

34   See the helpful study on Balthasar by Robert Louis, *The Theological Aesthetics of Hans Urs von Balthasar* (Washington, DC: Catholic University of America, 1987).

35   Here the magisterial works of Hans Frei and Hans Urs von Balthasar merit the primary attention. Both have much to teach all correlational theologians on new and fruitful ways to provide 'close' theological readings of the classics.

36   For a clear presentation of these criteria, see Schubert Ogden, *The Point of Christology* (San Francisco: Harper and Row, 1982), p. 4.

37   See John Dewey, *The Quest for Certainty* (Carbondale: Southern Illinois University Press, 1988); Stephen Toulmin, *Cosmopolis: The Hidden Agenda of Modernity* (Chicago: University of Chicago Press, 1990).

38   The emphasis here on the academy is not intended to disallow the necessary theological attention to the other publics of theology: church and society; see my *The Analogical Imagination* (New York: Crossroad, 1981), pp. 1–46.

39   The use of philosophy in traditional natural theologies and apologetic theologies as well as in contemporary fundamental theologies lends itself to a systemic rather than ad hoc reading. For a recent and good example of this tradition, see John Macquarrie, *In Search of Deity: An Essay in Dialectical Theism* (New York: Crossroad, 1987). For this ad hoc option, see n. 24 above.

40   For one clarification of these terms, see my *Blessed Rage for Order* (New York: Seabury Press, 1975), on fundamental theology, and *The Analogical Imagination* (n. 38, above), on systematic theology; and my essay 'The Foundations of Practical Theology' in Don Browning, ed., *Practical Theology* (San Francisco: Harper and Row, 1983). Although I continue to believe in the aim of transcendental reflection proposed in *Blessed Rage for Order*, the need for more careful attention to the linguistic–historical character of all such claims seems far more urgent to me now than it did then (1975) – as the remainder of this essay may serve to testify.

41   See Gary Comstock, 'Two Types of Narrative Theology', *Journal of the American*

Academy of Religion 55 (1987), pp. 687–717.

42 It is to be noted that this demand is formulated by the intra-textual needs of the logic of the Christian understanding of God, and not only from modern situational needs. On the latter, the approach of limit questions to inquiry itself remains a fruitful one. On the former, I can see no way, on purely inner–Christian grounds, to deny the universality and necessity of the Christian understanding of God. A lesser 'god', for the Jew, Christian and Muslim, is not God.

43 More exactly, in so far as the situational analysis is an *intrinsic* part of the theological task, apologetics will remain intrinsic and thereby systemic rather than an ad hoc part of that same task.

44 Edmund Husserl, *The Crisis of the European Sciences* (Evanston, IL: Northwestern University Press, 1970).

45 Hilary Putnam, *Reason, Truth and History* (Cambridge: Cambridge University Press, 1981); Richard Bernstein, *Beyond Objectivism and Relativism* (Philadelphia: University of Pennsylvania Press, 1981); Stephen Toulmin, *The Uses of Argument* (Cambridge: Cambridge University Press, 1958); Charles Taylor, *Philosophical Papers* 2 vols (Cambridge: Cambridge University Press, 1985); Richard Rorty, *Consequences of Pragmatism* (Minneapolis: University of Minnesota Press, 1982).

46 See Paul Ricoeur, 'Hermeneutics and the Critique of Ideology', in *Hermeneutics and the Human Sciences* (Cambridge: Cambridge University Press, 1981).

47 I here revise William James's criteria for assessing religion in *The Varieties of Religious Experience* (New York: New American Library, 1958), pp. 32–4, for a more properly theological task.

48 The criteria are not intended to be cumulative but demand a coherence of all three in order to function properly.

49 This would need to be shown in each case – not only, as in the present essay, in the case of the second set of criteria. On the hermeneutical–transcendental issues, see Rudiger Bubner, *Essays in Hermeneutical and Critical Theory* (New York: Columbia University Press, 1987). On the ethical–transcendental issue, see Karl-Otto Apel, *Understanding and Explanation: A Transcendental Pragmatic Perspective* (Cambridge, MA: MIT Press, 1984), and the critique of Apel by Franklin I. Gamwell, in *The Divine Good: Modern Moral Theory and the Necessity of God* (San Francisco: Harper, 1990).

50 This remains the case even if one chooses to have the criteria of praxis dominant, as in the effort by J. B. Metz to develop a practical fundamental theology in *Faith in History and Society* (New York: Seabury Press, 1980).

51 Those gains are real, especially in the exceptional work of Hans Frei and Balthasar.

52 For a fuller discussion, see *Plurality and Ambiguity*, ch. 2.

53 Paul Ricoeur, *Interpretation Theory* (Fort Worth: Texas Christian University Press, 1976); Jürgen Habermas, *Knowledge and Human Interests* (Boston: Beacon Press, 1971).

54 For a defence of the model of conversation, see *Plurality and Ambiguity*, ch. 1.

55 See *The Analogical Imagination*.

56 This seems to be a common misconception of the logic of the term 'correlation': see e.g. the criticisms of the term by Francis Schüssler Fiorenza, *Foundational Theology: Jesus and the Church* (New York: Crossroad, 1984), esp. pp. 276–84, and Elisabeth Schüssler Fiorenza, *Bread Not Stone: The Challenge of Feminist Biblical Interpretation* (Boston: Beacon Press, 1985). On my present reading, both these books are examples

of the broad model of correlational theologies, even if Francis Schüssler Fiorenza's 'reflective equilibrium' model leads more to the pole of similarity, and Elisabeth Schüssler Fiorenza's model heads more to the pole of dialectical difference. In their substantive proposals, both these exemplary theologians always allow the particular question and not any general method (correlational or anti-correlational) to determine the results of their inquiries.

57   See the exchange of Peter Berger, Langdon Gilkey, Schubert Ogden and David Tracy in *Theological Studies* 37 (1977), pp. 39–56, and 39 (1978), pp. 486–507.

58   See *The Analogical Imagination*, pp. 405–46.

59   The expression 'live, momentous and forced' is William James's in 'The Will to Believe', in *Essays on Faith and Morals* (New York: New American Library, 1974).

60   For one example see Hans Robert Jauss, *Toward an Aesthetics of Reception* (Minneapolis: University of Minnesota Press, 1982).

61   The analogy is an analogy of proportionality: revelation : faith :: manifestation : recognition.

62   Manifestation is the general term; as all manifestation-oriented thinkers (e.g. Heidegger, Ricoeur, Eliade) observe, the disclosure is also a concealment. The response evoked by the disclosure is recognition and always involves a call to transformation.

63   See especially the excellent Paulist series on Western spirituality and the Crossroad volumes on spirituality. I am especially indebted to the work of Louis Dupré and Bernard McGinn here.

64   Balthasar's highlighting of a theology of beauty has clear analogues to the manifestation orientation in hermeneutics. His great contribution, in my judgement, is his Christian incarnational and sacramental insistence on the centrality of the 'visible form' for Christian revelation and salvation.

65   Recall Rahner's 'mystagorical turn' in his later work, e.g. his essay on 'The Incomprehensibility of God according to St Thomas Aquinas', in *Celebrating the Medieval Heritage, Journal of Religion* 58 (supplement, 1978), pp. 107–25.

66   See Gershom Scholem, *Major Trends in Jewish Mysticism* (New York: Macmillan, 1961).

67   E.g. Mircea Eliade, *The Myth of the Eternal Return* (New York: Harper and Row, 1959).

68   I.e. we may reasonably believe (e.g. Einstein's relativity theory) even when we do not fully understand (i.e. mathematically) and thereby do not strictly know it. Most of our 'knowledge', in fact, is of the 'reasonable belief' type.

69   Note Gadamer's change here in *Reason in the Age of Science* (Cambridge: Cambridge University Press, 1981).

70   See David Roy Griffin, ed., *The Reenchantment of Science: Postmodern Proposals* (Albany: State University of New York Press, 1988).

71   Bernstein, *Beyond Objectivism and Relativism* (n. 45, above).

72   This, in sum, is one of the major concerns of an appropriately reformulated fundamental theology.

73   Bernard Lonergan, *Insight* (London: Darton, Longman and Todd, 1957).

74   Ibid., pp. 279–326.

75   Putnam, *Reason* (n. 45, above).

76   On Plato see Hans-Georg Gadamer, *Dialogue and Dialectic: Eight Hermeneutical Studies on Plato* (New Haven, CT: Yale University Press, 1980). On Aristotle see Toulmin, *Beyond Modernity* (n. 37, above).

77   This is especially true of the more recent work of Jürgen Habermas: see e.g. *Theory of Communicative Action* (Boston: Beacon Press, 1984).

78   See Lonergan, *Method in Theology* (New York: Seabury Press, 1972).

79   This is on intra-textual (i.e. the logic of the claims of the reality of God) as well as situational grounds: see Tillich, *Systematic Theology* 1 (n. 6, above) .

80   See Louis Dupré's *The Other Dimension* (New York: Seabury Press, 1979).

81   Lonergan's magisterial work here may be called representative of this paradigm shift from certainty to understanding: see e.g. his essay 'Aquinas Today: Tradition and Innovation', in *Celebrating the Medieval Heritage* (n. 15, above), pp. 1–17.

82   In theology these are often promoted under the rubric of praxis: see Matthew Lamb, *Solidarity With Victims* (New York: Crossroad, 1982).

83   Robert Bellah et al., *Habits of the Heart* (Berkeley: University of California Press, 1985).

84   Most fruitful here is Julia Kristeva's postmodern notion of the subject-in-process-on trial.

85   See e.g. Metz, *Faith in History and Society* (n. 50, above).

86   The reference is to William James's sane description of the need for 'on the wholeism'.

87   See Edward Schillebeeckx, *Jesus in Our Western Culture: Mysticism, Ethics, and Politics* (London: SCM, 1987).

PART

Afterword

Toward a Postliberal Theology

George A. Lindbeck

This final excerpt is from the book which more than any other is identified as a classic statement of theological postliberalism, Lindbeck's *The Nature of Doctrine*. The closing chapter of that book offers a sketch of a way of doing theology whose primary task is descriptive, namely giving an explication of the meaning of a religion for its adherents. Lindbeck's provocative remarks fuelled an entire decade of debate, and most of the earlier materials in this reader are explicit or implicit responses to his proposal.

This final chapter is an addendum to the main argument of the book, but a necessary one. If the theory of religion we have been exploring is useful only for understanding church doctrine and not also in other theological areas, it will ultimately prove unacceptable even to specialists in doctrine. In this chapter, therefore, we shall discuss the implications for theological method of a cultural–linguistic approach to religion, starting with some preliminary observations on the meaning and difficulties of assessing, as we shall afterward do, the faithfulness, applicability and intelligibility of fundamentally different types of theology.

The Problem of Assessment

Systematic or dogmatic theology has generally been thought of in the Christian West as especially concerned with faithfulness, practical theology with applicability, and foundational or apologetic theology with intelligibility; but each of these concerns is present in every theological discipline. When dogmaticians attempt faithfully to describe the normative features of a religion, they are also interested in applicability and intelligibility. Similarly, practical and foundational theologians seek not only to apply and make the religion intelligible but also to be faithful.

Further specification of the meaning of these terms depends on the contexts in which they are employed. Theologies of a given type, whether this be preliberal propositionalist, liberal experiential–expressivist, or postliberal cultural–linguistic, can combine formal similarities with radical material differences in their understanding of faithfulness, applicability and intelligibility. Spanish inquisitors and Enlightenment theologians disagreed radically in creed and practice and yet agreed on the formal point that propositional truth is the decisive test of adequacy. Similarly, Anglo-Catholics such as the authors of *Lux Mundi*, Lutheran confessionalists of the Erlangen school, and some 'death of God' theologians shared the liberal commitment to the primacy of experience but differed on the material question of what kind of experiences are religiously crucial. Analogously, a Christian postliberal consensus on the primarily cultural–linguistic character of religions would not by itself overcome substantive disagreements between conservatives and progressives, feminists and anti-feminists, Catholics and Protestants. The debates would turn more on conceptual or grammatical considerations than on experiential or propositional ones, but they would also involve disagreements on where proper grammar is to be found, on who are the competent speakers of a religious language. The progressives would appeal to rebels, the conservatives to establishments, and Catholics and Protestants would continue to differ in their understanding of the relation of scripture and tradition. Nevertheless, the common framework would make possible, though not guarantee, genuine arguments over the relative adequacy of specifiably different positions.

Such arguments are difficult, however, when theologies have formally different views of religion. The problem, as we have noted in earlier chapters, is that each type of theology is embedded in a conceptual framework so comprehensive that it shapes its own criteria of adequacy. Thus what propositionalists with their stress on unchanging truth and falsity regard as faithful, applicable and intelligible is likely to be dismissed as dead orthodoxy by liberal experiential–expressivists. Conversely, the liberal claim that change and pluralism in religious expression are necessary for intelligibility, applicability and faithfulness is attacked by the propositionally orthodox as an irrationally relativistic and practically self-defeating betrayal of the faith. A postliberal might propose to overcome this polarization between tradition and innovation by a distinction between abiding doctrinal grammar and variable theological vocabulary, but this proposal appears from other perspectives as the worst of two worlds rather than the best of both. In view of this situation, the most that can be done in this chapter is to comment on how faithfulness, applicability and intelligibility might be understood in postliberal theologies,[1] and then leave it to the readers to make their own assessments.

Faithfulness as Intratextuality

The task of descriptive (dogmatic or systematic) theology is to give a normative explication of the meaning a religion has for its adherents. One way of pursuing this task that is compatible with a cultural–linguistic approach is what I shall call 'intratextual', while an 'extratextual' method is natural for those whose understanding of religion is propositional or experiential–expressive. The latter locates religious meaning outside the text or semiotic system either in the objective realities to which it refers or in the experiences it symbolizes, whereas for cultural-linguists the meaning is immanent. Meaning is constituted by the uses of a specific language rather than being distinguishable from it. Thus the proper way to determine what 'God' signifies, for example, is by examining how the word operates within a religion and thereby shapes reality and experience rather than by first establishing its propositional or experiential meaning and reinterpreting or reformulating its uses accordingly. It is in this sense that theological description in the cultural–linguistic mode is intrasemiotic or intratextual.

In an extended or improper sense, something like intratextuality is characteristic of the descriptions of not only religion but also other forms of rule-governed human behaviour from carpentry and mathematics to languages and cultures. Hammers and saws, ordinals and numerals, winks and signs of the cross, words and sentences are made comprehensible by indicating how they fit into systems of communication or purposeful action, not by reference to outside factors. One does not succeed in identifying the 8:02 to New York by describing the history or manufacture of trains or even by a complete inventory of the cars, passengers and conductors that constituted and travelled on it on a given day. None of the cars, passengers and crew might be the same the next day, and yet the train would be self-identically the 8:02 to New York. Its meaning, its very reality, is its function within a particular transportation system. Much the same can be said of winks and signs of the cross: they are quite distinct from non-meaningful but physically identical eye twitches and hand motions, and their reality as meaningful signs is wholly constituted in any individual occurrence by their intratextuality, by their place, so to speak, in a story.

Meaning is more fully intratextual in semiotic systems (composed, as they entirely are, of interpretative and communicative signs, symbols and actions) than in other forms of ruled human behaviour such as carpentry or transportation systems; but among semiotic systems, intratextuality (though still in an extended sense) is greatest in natural languages, cultures and religions which (unlike mathematics, for example) are potentially all-embracing and possess the property of reflexivity. One can speak of all life and reality in French, or from an American or a Jewish perspective; and one can also describe French in French, American culture in American terms, and Judaism in Jewish ones. This makes it possible for theology to be intratextual, not simply by explicating religion from within but in the stronger sense of describing everything as inside, as interpreted by the religion, and doing this by means of religiously shaped second-order concepts.

In view of their comprehensiveness, reflexivity and complexity, religions require what Clifford Geertz, borrowing a term from Gilbert Ryle, has called 'thick description',[2] and which he applies to culture, but with the understanding that it also holds for religion. A religion cannot be treated as a formalizable 'symbolic system . . . by isolating its elements, specifying the internal relationships among these elements, and then characterizing the whole system in some general way – according to the core symbols around which it is organized, the underlying structures of which it is the surface expression, or the ideological principles upon which it is based. . . . This hermetic approach to things seems to me to run the danger of locking . . . analysis away from its proper object, the informal logic of actual life.' The theologian, like the ethnographer, should approach 'such broader interpretations and abstract analyses from the direction of exceedingly extended acquaintances with extremely small matters.' 'As interlocked systems of construable signs . . . culture [including religion] is not a power, something to which social events, behaviours, institutions, or processes can be causally attributed; it is a context, something within which they can be intelligibly – that is, thickly described.' Only by detailed 'familiarity with the imaginative universe in which . . . acts are signs' can one diagnose or specify the meaning of these acts for the adherents of a religion. What the theologian needs to explicate 'is a multiplicity of complex conceptual structures, many of them superimposed or knotted into one another, which are at once strange, irregular and inexplicit, and which he must contrive somehow first to grasp and then to render.' In rendering the salient features, the essential task 'is not to codify abstract regularities but to make thick description possible, not to generalize across cases but to generalize within them.' If this is not done, one may think, for example, that Roman and Confucian *gravitas* are much the same, or that atheistic Marxism more nearly resembles atheistic Buddhism than biblical theism. This is as egregious an error as supposing that uninflected English is closer to uninflected Chinese than to German.

Thick description, it should be noted, is not to be confused with Baconian empiricism, with sticking to current facts. It is rather the full range of the interpretative medium which needs to be exhibited, and because this range in the case of religion is potentially all-encompassing, description has a creative aspect. There is, indeed, no more demanding exercise of the inventive and imaginative powers than to explore how a language, culture or religion may be employed to give meaning to new domains of thought, reality and action. Theological description can be a highly constructive enterprise.

Finally, in the instance of religions more than any other type of semiotic system, description is not simply metaphorically but literally intratextual. This is true in some degree of all the world's major faiths. They all have relatively fixed canons of writings that they treat as exemplary or normative instantiations of their semiotic codes. One test of faithfulness for all of them is the degree to which descriptions correspond to the semiotic universe paradigmatically encoded in holy writ.

The importance of texts and of intratextuality for theological faithfulness becomes clearer when we consider the unwritten religions of non-literate societies. Evans-Pritchard[3] tells of a Nuer tribesman who excitedly reported to him that a woman in the village had given birth to twins, both dead, and that one was a hippopotamus and had been placed in a stream, and the other a bird and had been placed in a tree. There are in that society no canonical documents to consult in order to locate these puzzling events within the wider contexts that give them meaning. Is the equation of dead twins with birds and hippopotami central or peripheral to Nuer thought and life? Would the religion and culture be gravely disturbed if this equation were eliminated? Even the wisest of Evans-Pritchard's informants might not have understood these questions, and even if they did, they presumably would have had no idea of how to reach a consensus in answering them. In oral cultures there is no transpersonal authority to which the experts on tradition can refer their disputes. This helps explain why purely customary religions and cultures readily dissolve under the pressure of historical, social and linguistic change, but it also suggests that canonical texts are a condition, not only for the survival of a religion but for the very possibility of normative theological description. In any case, whether or not this is universally true, the intrasemiotic character of descriptive theology is inseparable from intratextuality in the three Western monotheisms – Judaism, Christianity and Islam. These are pre-eminently religions of the book.

We need now to speak in more detail of how to interpret a text in terms of its immanent meanings – that is, in terms of the meanings immanent in the religious language of whose use the text is a paradigmatic instance. On the informal level this is not a problem; it becomes so, as we shall see, only when theology becomes alienated from those ways of reading classics,[4] whether religious or non-religious, which seem natural within a given culture or society. Masterpieces such as *Oedipus Rex* and *War and Peace*, for example, evoke their own domains of meaning. They do so by what they themselves say about the events and personages of which they tell. In order to understand them in their own terms, there is no need for extraneous references to, for example, Freud's theories or historical treatments of the Napoleonic wars. Further, such works shape the imagination and perceptions of the attentive reader so that he or she forever views the world to some extent through the lenses they supply. To describe the basic meaning of these books is an intratextual task, a matter of explicating their contents and the perspectives on extratextual reality that they generate.[5]

These same considerations apply even more forcefully to the pre-eminently authoritative texts that are the canonical writings of religious communities. For those who are steeped in them, no world is more real than the ones they create. A scriptural world is thus able to absorb the universe. It supplies the interpretative framework within which believers seek to live their lives and understand reality. This happens quite apart from formal theories. Augustine did not describe his work in the categories we are employing, but the whole of his theological production can be understood as a progressive, even if not always successful, struggle to insert everything from Platonism and the Pelagian problem to the fall of Rome into the world of the Bible. Aquinas tried to do something similar with Aristotelianism, and Schleiermacher with German romantic idealism. The way they described extra-scriptural realities and experience, so it can be argued, was shaped by biblical categories much more than was warranted by their formal methodologies.

In the case of Aquinas especially, however, the shaping was in part methodologically legitimated. Traditional exegetical procedures (of which he gives one of the classic descriptions)[6] assume that scripture creates its own domain of meaning and that the task of interpretation is to extend this over the whole of reality. The particular ways of doing this depend, to be sure, on the character of the religion and its texts. One set of interpretative techniques is appropriate when the Torah is the centre of the scripture, another when it is the story of Jesus, and still another when it is the Buddha's enlightenment and teachings. For the most part, we shall limit our observations on this point to the Christian case.

Here there was a special though not exclusive emphasis on typological or figural devices, first to unify the canon, and second to encompass the cosmos. Typology was used to incorporate the Hebrew scriptures into a canon that focused on Christ, and then, by extension, to embrace extra-biblical reality. King David, for example, was in some respects a typological foreshadowing of Jesus, but he was also, in Carolingian times, a type for Charlemagne and, in Reformation days, as even Protestants said, for Charles V in his wars against the Turks. Thus an Old Testament type, filtered through the New Testament anti-type, became a model for later kings and, in the case of Charlemagne, provided a documentable stimulus to the organization of the educational and parish systems that stand at the institutional origins of Western civilization. Unlike allegorizing, typological interpretation did not empty Old Testament or post-biblical personages and events of their own reality,[7] and therefore they constituted a powerful means for imaginatively incorporating all being into a Christ-centred world.

It is important to note the direction of interpretation. Typology does not make scriptural contents into metaphors for extra-scriptural realities, but the other way around. It does not suggest, as is often said in our day, that believers find their stories in the Bible, but rather that they make the story of the Bible their story. The cross is not to be viewed as a figurative representation of suffering nor the messianic kingdom as a symbol for hope in the future; rather, suffering should be cruciform, and hopes for the future messianic. More generally stated, it is the religion instantiated in scripture which defines being, truth, goodness and beauty, and the non-scriptural exemplifications of these realities need to be transformed into figures (or types or anti-types) of the scriptural ones. Intratextual theology redescribes reality within the scriptural framework rather than translating scripture into extra-scriptural categories. It is the text, so to speak, which absorbs the world, rather than the world the text.

There is always the danger, however, that the extra-biblical materials inserted into the biblical universe will themselves become the basic framework of interpretation. This is what happened, so the Christian mainstream concluded, in the case of Gnosticism. Here Hellenism became the interpreter rather than the interpreted. The Jewish rabbi who is the crucified and resurrected Messiah of the New Testament accounts was transformed into a mythological figure illustrative of thoroughly non-scriptural meanings. Nor did the mainstream wholly escape the danger. It creedally insisted that the Jesus spoken of in scripture is the Lord, but it often read scripture in so Hellenistic a way that this Jesus came to resemble a semi-pagan demigod. The doctrinal consensus on the primacy of scripture, on the canonical status of the Old as well as the New Testament, and on the full humanity of Christ was not by itself enough to maintain an integrally scriptural framework within which to interpret the classical heritage which the church sought to Christianize. Better theological and exegetical procedures were needed.

Up through the Reformation, this need was in part filled through the typological methods we have already noted. As one moves in the West from Augustine, through Aquinas, to Luther and Calvin, there is an increasing resistance to indiscriminate allegorizing and an insistence on the primacy of a specifiable literal intratextual sense. Whatever the failures in actual execution, and they were many, the interpretative direction was from the Bible to the world rather than vice versa.

In the Reformers, it should be noted, the resistance to allegorizing and the greater emphasis on intratextuality (*scriptura sui ipsius interpres*) did not diminish but heightened the emphasis on proclamation, on the preached word. Scripture, one might say, was interpreted by its use,[8] by the *viva vox evangelii*. In the intratextual context, this emphasis on the living word involves applying the language, concepts and categories of scripture to contemporary realities, and is different in its intellectual, practical and homiletical consequences from liberal attempts, of which Ebeling's is the most notable,[9] to understand the Reformation notion of the word of God in terms of an experiential 'word event'.

As the work of Hans Frei shows,[10] the situation has changed radically in recent centuries, and new difficulties have arisen. Typological interpretation collapsed under the combined onslaughts of rationalistic, pietistic and historical–critical developments. Scripture ceased to function as the lens through which theologians viewed the world and instead became primarily an object of study whose religiously significant or literal meaning was located outside itself. The primarily literary approaches of the past with their affinities to informal ways of reading the classics in their own terms were replaced by fundamentalist, historical–critical and expressivist preoccupations with facticity or experience. The intratextual meanings of scripture continue informally to shape the imagination of the West (even atheistic Marxists think of history as the unfolding of a determinate pattern with an ultimately ineluctable outcome), but theologians do not make these meanings methodologically primary. Instead, if they are existentially inclined, they reinterpret the notion of providential guidance, for example, as a symbolic expression of confidence in the face of the vicissitudes of life; or, if they objectivize, they might, as did Teilhard de Chardin, interpret providence in terms of an optimistic version of evolutionary science. Whether it will be possible to regain a specifically biblical understanding of providence depends in part on the possibility of theologically reading scripture once again in literary rather than non-literary ways.

The depth of the present crisis is best seen when one considers that even those who doctrinally agree that the story of Jesus is the key to the understanding of reality are often in fundamental theological disagreement over what the story is really about, over its normative or literal sense.[11] Is the literal meaning of the story the history it is on some readings supposed to record, and if so, is this history that of the fundamentalist or of the historical critic? Or is the real meaning, the theologically important meaning, the way of being in the world which the story symbolizes, or the liberating actions and attitudes it expresses, or the ethical ideals it instantiates, or the metaphysical truths about God-manhood it illustrates, or the gospel promises it embodies? Each of these ways of construing the story depends on a distinct interpretative framework (historical, phenomenological, existential, ethical, metaphysical, doctrinal) that specifies the questions asked of the text and shapes the pictures of Jesus that emerge. These pictures may all be formally orthodox in the sense that they are reconcilable with Nicaea, but their implications for religious practice and understanding are radically divergent. Nothing better illustrates the point made in earlier chapters that for most purposes theological issues are more crucial and interesting than doctrinal ones.

The intratextual way of dealing with this problem depends heavily on literary considerations. The normative or literal meaning must be consistent with the kind of text it is taken to be by the community for which it is important. The meaning must not be esoteric: not something behind, beneath or in front of the text; not something that the text reveals, discloses, implies or suggests to those with extraneous metaphysical, historical or experiential interests. It must rather be what the text says in terms of the communal language of which the text is an instantiation. A legal document should not be treated in quasi-kabbalistic fashion as first of all a piece of expressive symbolism (though it may secondarily be that also); nor should the Genesis account of creation be turned fundamentalistically into science; nor should one turn a realistic narrative (which a novel also can be) into history (or, alternatively, as the historical critic is wont to do, into a source of clues for the reconstruction of history). If the literary character of the story of Jesus, for example, is that of utilizing, as realistic narratives do, the interaction of purpose and circumstance to render the identity description of an agent, then it is Jesus's identity as thus rendered, not his historicity, existential significance or metaphysical status, which is the literal and theologically controlling meaning of the tale.[12] The implications of the story for determining the metaphysical status, or existential significance, or historical career of Jesus Christ may have varying degrees of theological importance, but they are not determinative. The believer, so an intratextual approach would maintain, is not told primarily to be conformed to a reconstructed Jesus of history (as Hans Küng maintains),[13] nor to a metaphysical Christ of faith (as in much of the propositionalist tradition),[14] nor to an abba experience of God (as for Schillebeeckx),[15] nor to an agapeic way of being in the world (as for David Tracy),[16] but he or she is rather to be conformed to the Jesus Christ depicted in the narrative. An intratextual reading tries to derive the interpretative framework that designates the theologically controlling sense from the literary structure of the text itself.[17]

This type of literary approach can be extended to cover, not simply the story of Jesus, but all of scripture. What is the literary genre of the Bible as a whole in its canonical unity? What holds together the diverse materials it contains: poetic, prophetic, legal, liturgical, sapiential, mythical, legendary and historical? These are all embraced, it would seem, in an overarching story that has the specific literary features of realistic narrative as exemplified in diverse ways, for example, by certain kinds of parables, novels and historical accounts. It is as if the Bible were a 'vast, loosely structured, non-fictional novel' (to use a phrase David Kelsey applies to Karl Barth's view of scripture).[18]

Further, it is possible to specify the primary function of the canonical narrative (which is also the function of many of its most important component stories from the Pentateuch to the gospels). It is 'to render a character ... offer an identity description of an agent',[19] namely God. It does this, not by telling what God is in and of himself, but by accounts of the interaction of his deeds and purposes with those of creatures in their ever-changing circumstances. These accounts reach their climax in what the gospels say of the risen, ascended and ever-present Jesus Christ whose identity as the divine–human agent is unsubstitutably enacted in the stories of Jesus of Nazareth. The climax, however, is logically inseparable from what precedes it. The Jesus of the gospels is the Son of the God of Abraham, Isaac and Jacob in the same strong sense that the Hamlet of Shakespeare's play is Prince of Denmark. In both cases, the title with its reference to the wider context irreplaceably rather than contingently identifies the bearer of the name.

It is easy to see how theological descriptions of a religion may on this view need to be materially diverse even when the formal criterion of faithfulness remains the same. The primary focus is not on God's being in itself, for that is not what the text is about, but on how life is to be lived and reality construed in the light of God's character as an agent as this is depicted in the stories of Israel and of Jesus. Life, however, is not the same in catacombs and space shuttles, and reality is different for, let us say, Platonists and Whiteheadians. Catacomb dwellers and astronauts might rightly emphasize diverse aspects of the biblical accounts of God's character and action in describing their respective situations. Judging by catacomb paintings, the first group often saw themselves as sheep in need of a shepherd, while the second group would perhaps be well advised to stress God's grant to human beings of stewardship over planet Earth. Similarly, Platonic and Whiteheadian differences over the nature of reality lead to sharp disagreements about the proper characterization of God's metaphysical properties, while anti-metaphysicians, in turn, argue that no theory of divine attributes is consistent with the character of the biblical God.

Yet all these theologies could agree that God is appropriately depicted in stories about a being who created the cosmos without any humanly fathomable reason, but – simply for his own good pleasure and the pleasure of his goodness – appointed Homo sapiens stewards of one minuscule part of this cosmos, permitted appalling evils, chose Israel and the church as witnessing peoples, and sent Jesus as Messiah and Immanuel, God with us. The intention of these theologies, whether successful or unsuccessful, could in every case be to describe life and reality in ways conformable to what these stories indicate about God. They could, to repeat, have a common intratextual norm of faithfulness despite their material disagreements.

Intratextual theologies can also, however, disagree on the norm. They can dispute over whether realistic narrative is the best or only way to identify the distinctive genre and interpretative framework of the Christian canon, and, even if it is, on how to characterize the divine agent at work in the biblical stories. More fundamentally, they could disagree on the extent and unity of the canon. If Revelation and Daniel are the centre of scripture, as they seem to be for Scofield Bible premillennialists, a very different picture of God's agency and purposes emerges. Further, as current debates over feminism vividly remind us, past tradition or present consensus can serve as extensions of the canon and deeply influence the interpretation of the whole. These extensions can on occasion go beyond the specifically Christian or religious realm. The philosophical tradition from Plato to Heidegger operates as the canonical corpus for much Western reflection on God or the human condition; and when this reflection is recognized as operating with a peculiarly Western rather than trans-culturally available idiom, it begins to acquire some of the features of intratextuality.[20] In short, intratextuality may be a condition for the faithful description and development of a religion or tradition, but the material or doctrinal consequences of this self-evidently depend in part on what canon is appealed to.

It must also be noted that intratextuality in a post-critical or postliberal mode is significantly different from traditional pre-critical varieties. We now can make a distinction (unavailable before the development of modern science and historical studies) between realistic narrative and historical or scientific descriptions. The Bible is often 'history-like' even when it is not 'likely history'. It can therefore be taken seriously in the first respect as a delineator of the character of divine and human agents, even when its history or science is challenged. As parables such as that of the prodigal son remind us, the rendering of God's character is not in every instance logically dependent on the facticity of the story.

Further, historical criticism influences the theological–literary interpretation of texts. A post-critical narrative reading of scripture such as is found to some extent in von Rad's work on the Old Testament[21] is notably different from a pre-critical one. Or, to cite a more specific example, if the historical critic is right that the Johannine 'Before Abraham was, I am' (John 8:58) is not a self-description of the pre-resurrection Jesus but a communal confession of faith, then even those who fully accept the confession will want to modify traditional theological descriptions of what Jesus was in his life on earth. They may agree doctrinally with Chalcedon, but prefer a Pauline *theologia crucis* to the Christological *theologia gloriae* that is often associated with Chalcedon (and that one finds even in great exponents of the theology of the cross such as Luther). Nevertheless, in an intratextual approach, literary considerations are more important than historical–critical ones in determining the canonical sense even in cases such as this. It is because the literary genre of John is clearly not that of veridical history that the statement in question can be readily accepted as a communal confession rather than a self-description.

Finally, and more generally, the post-critical focus on intratextual meanings does involve a change in attitude toward some aspects of the text that were important for premodern interpretation. The physical details of what, if anything, happened on Mount Sinai, for example, are no longer of direct interest for typological or figurative purposes, as they often were for the tradition, but the basic questions remain much the same: what is the nature and function of Torah? It is in the New Testament custodial in Israel and fulfilled in Christ, but what does this imply for later Christianity and its relations to Judaism? Is not Torah by analogical extension both custodial and fulfilled for Christian communities in this age before the end when fulfilment is not yet final; and does this not make Christians much closer to Jews than they have generally thought? What, furthermore, does the Holocaust have to do with Mount Sinai, on the one hand, and another mountain, Calvary, on the other? As these questions indicate, a postliberal intratextuality provides warrants for imaginatively and conceptually incorporating post-biblical worlds into the world of the Bible in much the same fashion as did the tradition. But the consequences inevitably will often be very different because of changes in the extra-biblical realities that are to be typologically interpreted and because of the more rigorous intratextuality made necessary by a critical approach to history.

In concluding this discussion, it needs to be reiterated that the practice of intratextuality is only loosely related to explicit theory. Just as good grammarians or mathematicians may be quite wrongheaded in their understanding of what they in fact actually do, so also with theologians. There is no reason for surprise if an apparent propositionalist, such as Aquinas, or an undoubted experiential–expressivist, such as Schleiermacher, were more intratextual in their actual practice than their theories would seem to allow. Their performance would perhaps have improved if their theories of religion had been different, but this is true only if other conditions remained equal. Native genius and religious commitment are helpful, but in order to convert these into theological competence one also needs a supportive environment, the tutelage of expert practitioners, and assiduous practice in a complex set of unformalizable skills that even the best theoretician cannot adequately characterize. Where these conditions are lacking, even good theory cannot greatly enhance performance, and where they are present, poor theory may be relatively harmless.

The implications of these observations do not bode well, however, for the future of postliberal theology. Even if it were to become theoretically popular, the result might chiefly be talk about intratextuality rather than more and better intratextual practice. The conditions for practice seem to be steadily weakening. Disarray in church and society makes the transmission of the necessary skills more and more difficult. Those who share in the intellectual high culture of our day are rarely intensively socialized into coherent religious languages and communal forms of life. This is not necessarily disastrous for the long-range prospects of religion (which is not dependent on elites), but it is for theology as an intellectually and academically creative enterprise capable of making significant contributions to the wider culture and society. Further, theology (in the sense of reflection in the service of religion) is being increasingly replaced in seminaries as well as universities by religious studies. There are fewer and fewer institutional settings favourable to the intratextual interpretation of religion and of extra-scriptural realities.[22] Perhaps the last American theologian who in practice (and to some extent in theory) made extended and effective attempts to redescribe major aspects of the contemporary scene in distinctively Christian terms was Reinhold Niebuhr. After the brief neo-orthodox interlude (which was itself sometimes thoroughly liberal in its theological methodology, as in the case of Paul Tillich), the liberal tendency to redescribe religion in extra-scriptural frameworks has once again become dominant. This is understandable. Religions have become foreign texts that are much easier to translate into currently popular categories than to read in terms of their intrinsic sense. Thus the fundamental obstacles to intratextual theological faithfulness may well derive from the psycho-social situation rather than from scholarly or intellectual considerations.

Applicability as Futurology

We began this chapter by noting that theologies are assessed by their applicability as well as their faithfulness. They are judged by how relevant or practical they are in concrete situations as well as by how well they fit the cultural–linguistic systems whose religious uses they seek to describe. In this section we shall deal, first, with the relation of judgements of faithfulness and applicability and, second, with some specific issues that are of special concern today.

All-embracing systems of interpretation possess their own internal criteria of applicability: they can be judged by their own standards. This is evident when we consider how views of present practicality are shaped by visions of reality that encompass more than the present. A Marxist and a non-Marxist, for example, may agree in their factual descriptions of current trends and on the general principle that these trends should be evaluated in terms of long-range consequences, and yet they may differ sharply in their extrapolations. What seems to one the wave of the future will seem to the other a mere eddy in the river of time, and judgements of applicability or practicality will vary accordingly. The difference will be even greater if the non-Marxist is, for example, an Advaita Vedantist for whom the course of history is religiously irrelevant; but this kind of devaluation of the temporal future has not generally been characteristic of Western faiths.

Concern for the future has traditionally been associated in biblical religions with prophecy. Prophets proclaim what is both faithful and applicable in a given situation, and they oppose proposals that, whatever their apparent practicality, are doomed because of their unfaithfulness to God's future. To be sure, as biblical scholars remind us, prophetic utterances are not predictions in the ordinary sense. Jonah was disappointed by the non-fulfilment of his prophecies against Nineveh, but this did not make him doubt that God had spoken. The repentance that averted the destruction of the city was, so to speak, the point of the prophecy. Similarly, the non-fulfilment of expectations of an imminent Parousia have rarely been taken by those who shared them as evidence that Christ would not return. A similar logic operates in much non-religious forecasting. The failure of Marxist and other secular anticipations of the early demise of religion does not disconfirm secularism, and the predictive inadequacies of contemporary futurology[23] have not discouraged its practitioners. In all these cases, the purpose is not to foretell what is to come, but to shape present action to fit the anticipated and hoped-for future.

Theological forms of this activity are more like contemporary futurology than biblical prophecy. Unlike prophecy, futurology does not depend on first-order inspiration or intuition, but is a second-order enterprise that draws on the full range of empirical studies in an effort to discover 'the signs of the times'.[24] As we have noted, these signs vary greatly from one overall pattern of interpretation to another – from, for example, Marxist to non-Marxist views. In the case of Christian theology, the purpose is to discern those possibilities in current situations that can and should be cultivated as anticipations or preparations for the hoped-for future, the coming kingdom. In brief a theological proposal is adjudged both faithful and applicable to the degree that it appears practical in terms of an eschatologically and empirically defensible scenario of what is to come.

In the construction of such scenarios, the crucial difference between liberals and postliberals is in the way they correlate their visions of the future and of present situations. Liberals start with experience, with an account of the present, and then adjust their vision of the kingdom of God accordingly, while postliberals are in principle committed to doing the reverse. The first procedure makes it easier to accommodate to present trends, whether from the right or the left: Christian fellow travellers of both Nazism and Stalinism generally used liberal methodology to justify their positions. When, in contrast to this, one looks at the present in the light of an intratextually derived eschatology, one gets a different view of which contemporary developments are likely to be ultimately significant. Similar practical recommendations may at times be advanced, but for dissimilar theological reasons. A postliberal might argue, for example, that traditional sexual norms should be revised because the situation has changed from when they were formulated or because they are not intratextually faithful – but not, as some liberals may be inclined to argue, on the grounds that sexual liberation is an advance toward the eschatological future. Postliberalism is methodologically committed to neither traditionalism nor progressivism, but its resistance to current fashions, to making present experience revelatory, may often result in conservative stances. Yet there are numerous occasions in which the intratextual norm requires the rejection of the old in favour of the new.

These comments on method, however, leave untouched the question of the possible contemporary relevance of postliberalism. Earlier chapters suggested that a cultural–linguistic approach is supported by intellectual trends in non-theological disciplines, and that it can in its own way accommodate some of the main religious concerns that make experiential-expressivism appealing. Yet we also noted that the present psycho-social situation is more favourable to liberalism than to postliberalism. Sociologists have been telling us for a hundred years or more that the rationalization, pluralism and mobility of modern life dissolve the bonds of tradition and community. This produces multitudes of men and women who are impelled, if they have religious yearnings, to embark on their own individual quests for symbols of transcendence. The churches have become purveyors of this commodity rather than communities that socialize their members into coherent and comprehensive religious outlooks and forms of life. Society paradoxically conditions human beings to experience selfhood as somehow prior to social influences, and Eastern religions and philosophies are utilized to support what, from a cultural–linguistic perspective, is the myth of the transcendental ego. Selfhood is experienced as a given rather than as either a gift or an achievement, and fulfilment comes from exfoliating or penetrating into the inner depths rather than from communally responsible action in the public world. Thus the cultural climate is on the whole antithetical to postliberalism.

One can argue, furthermore, that there is little likelihood that the cultural trends favouring experiential-expressivism will be reversed in the realistically foreseeable future. If the nations are to avoid nuclear or environmental destruction, they will have to become ever more unified. What the world will need is some kind of highly generalized outlook capable of providing a framework for infinitely diversified religious quests. Experiential-expressivism with its openness to the hypothesis of an underlying unity can, it would seem, better fill this need than a cultural–linguistic understanding of religion with its stress on particularity. Western monotheisms especially appear to be disqualified because, on an intratextual reading, these religions cannot without suicide surrender their claims to the universal and unsurpassable validity of very specific identifications of the Ultimate with the God of Abraham, Isaac and Jacob; of Jesus; or of the Koran. The future belongs, on this view, to liberal interpretations of religion.

In the speculative domain of futurology, however, it is easy to mount counter-arguments. It can be pointed out that the indefinite extrapolation of present trends is a questionable procedure because any given tendency, if carried far enough, destroys the conditions for its own existence. When liberation from constraints produces chaos, the result is new bondage, and law and order are once again experienced as conditions for freedom. Law and order when unchecked, however, create rigidities that harbour the seeds of their own destruction. Similarly, the viability of a unified world of the future may well depend on counteracting the acids of modernity. It may depend on communal enclaves that socialize their members into highly particular outlooks supportive of concern for others rather than for individual rights and entitlements, and of a sense of responsibility for the wider society rather than for personal fulfilment. It is at least an open question whether any religion will have the requisite toughness for this demanding task unless it at some point makes the claim that it is significantly different and unsurpassably true; and it is easier for a religion to advance this claim if it is interpreted in cultural–linguistic rather than experiential–expressive terms. Thus it may well be that postliberal theologies are more applicable than liberal ones to the needs of the future.

These considerations gain in force when one considers what may be necessary for the viability, not of a world order, but of cultural traditions such as the Western one. If the Bible has shaped the imagination of the West to anywhere near the degree that Northrop Frye, for example, has argued,[25] then the West's continuing imaginative vitality and creativity may well depend on the existence of groups for whom the Hebrew and Christian scriptures are not simply classics among others, but the canonical literature *par excellence*, and who are also in close contact with the wider culture. Much the same argument could be advanced in reference to the Koran and Islamic culture, and perhaps something analogous applies to the religions and cultures of the Far East despite their lack of equally well-defined pre-eminent canons. The general point is that, provided a religion stresses service rather than domination, it is likely to contribute more to the future of humanity if it preserves its own distinctiveness and integrity than if it yields to the homogenizing tendencies associated with liberal experiential-expressivism.

This conclusion is paradoxical: religious communities are likely to be practically relevant in the long run to the degree that they do not first ask what is either practical or relevant, but instead concentrate on their own intratextual outlooks and forms of life. The much-debated problem of the relation of theory and praxis is thus dissolved by the communal analogue of justification by faith. As is true for individuals, so also a religious community's salvation is not by works, nor is its faith for the sake of practical efficacy, and yet good works of unforeseeable kinds flow from faithfulness. It was thus, rather than by intentional effort, that biblical religion helped produce democracy and science, as well as other values Westerners treasure; and it is in similarly unimaginable and unplanned ways, if at all, that biblical religion will help save the world (for Western civilization is now world civilization) from the demonic corruptions of these same values.

These arguments for the applicability of postliberal approaches cannot be neutrally evaluated. Those who think that religions are more the sources than the products of experience will regard a loss of religious particularity as impoverishing, while others will consider it enriching. Comprehensive frameworks of interpretation provide their own standards of relevance, and thus both liberal and postliberal outlooks have no difficulty in reading the signs of the times in such a way as to justify their own practicality.

Intelligibility as Skill

The case for applicability that has just been outlined is incomplete. It does not discuss whether postliberal theologies would help make religions more intelligible and credible. This is a practical as well as a theoretical question, and it can be formulated in terms of two closely related problems. First, intratextuality seems wholly relativistic: it turns religions, so one can argue, into self-enclosed and incommensurable intellectual ghettos. Associated with this, in the second place, is the fideistic dilemma: it appears that choice between religions is purely arbitrary, a matter of blind faith.

These may not be mortal weaknesses in other times or places where communal traditions are relatively unbroken and faiths are transmitted from parents to children in successive generations, but they are, so it can be argued, obstacles to the survival of religions in pluralistic situations where religiousness usually involves decisions among competing alternatives. It seems essential in our day to adopt an apologetic approach that seeks to discover a foundational scheme within which religions can be evaluated, and that makes it possible to translate traditional meanings into currently intelligible terms. The postliberal resistance to the foundational enterprise is from this perspective a fatal flaw.

The great strength of theological liberalism, it can be argued, lies in its commitment to making religion experientially intelligible to the cultured and the uncultured among both its despisers and its appreciators. It is in order to clarify the gospel in a world where it has become opaque that liberals typically choose the categories in which to expound their systematic theologies; and it is by their success in communicating to the modern mind that they assess the faithfulness of their endeavours. This same concern accounts for the liberal commitment to the foundational enterprise of uncovering universal principles or structures – if not metaphysical, then existential, phenomenological or hermeneutical. If there are no such universals, then how can one make the faith credible, not only to those outside the church but to the half-believers within it and, not least, to theologians? The liberal programme is in one sense accommodation to culture, but it is often motivated by missionary impulses no less strong than those which send Wycliffe evangelicals overseas to translate the Bible into aboriginal tongues.

Postliberals are bound to be sceptical, not about missions, but about apologetics and foundations. To the degree that religions are like languages and cultures, they can no more be taught by means of translation than can Chinese or French. What is said in one idiom can to some extent be conveyed in a foreign tongue, but no one learns to understand and speak Chinese by simply hearing and reading translations. Resistance to translation does not wholly exclude apologetics, but this must be of an ad hoc and non-foundational variety rather than standing at the centre of theology. The grammar of religion, like that of language, cannot be explicated or learned by analysis of experience, but only by practice. Religious and linguistic competence may help greatly in dealing with experience, but experience by itself may be more a hindrance than a help to acquiring competence: children, at least in Jesus's parabolic sense, have an advantage over adults. In short, religions, like languages, can be understood only in their own terms, not by transposing them into an alien speech.

Yet this approach, as was noted in earlier chapters, need not confine the theological study of religion to an intellectual ghetto, but can free it for closer contact with other disciplines. The spread of a cultural–linguistic orientation in history, anthropology, sociology and philosophy increases interest in intratextuality, in the description of religions from the inside. Liberal attempts to explain religions by translating them into other conceptualities seem to appeal chiefly to theologians or to other religious people. As modern culture moves ever farther away from its religious roots, these translations become more strained, complex and obscure to the uninitiated. Relativism increases and foundational appeals to universal structures of thought, experience or *Existenz* lose their persuasiveness. Tillich communicated to a wide range of intellectuals a generation ago, but it is doubtful that his numerous liberal successors could now match his record even if they had his talent. Scholarly non-theologians who want to understand religion are concerned with how religions work for their adherents, not with their credibility. Their interest, one might say, is in descriptive rather than apologetic intelligibility. The result, paradoxically, is that a postliberal approach, with its commitment to intratextual description, may well have interdisciplinary advantages, while liberal theology, with its apologetic focus on making religion more widely credible, seems increasingly to be a nineteenth–century enclave in a twentieth–century milieu.

These considerations, however, leave unresolved the problem with which we started this section. The question is whether intratextual descriptive intelligibility is helpful for religious and not simply interdisciplinary purposes; but if intratextuality implies relativism and fideism, the cost for most religious traditions is much too high. If there are no universal or foundational structures and standards of judgement by which one can decide between different religious and non-religious options, the choice of any one of them becomes, it would seem, purely irrational, a matter of arbitrary whim or blind faith; and while this conclusion may fit much of the modern mood, it is antithetical to what most religions, whether interpreted in liberal, preliberal or postliberal fashion, have affirmed.

Anti-foundationalism, however, is not to be equated with irrationalism. The issue is not whether there are universal norms of reasonableness, but whether these can be formulated in some neutral, framework-independent language.[26] Increasing awareness of how standards of rationality vary from field to field and age to age makes the discovery of such a language more and more unlikely and the possibility of foundational disciplines doubtful. Yet this does not reduce the choice between different frameworks to whim or chance. As T. S. Kuhn has argued in reference to science, and Wittgenstein in philosophy, the norms of reasonableness are too rich and subtle to be adequately specified in any general theory of reason or knowledge. These norms, to repeat a point often made in this book, are like the rules of depth grammar, which linguists search for and may at times approximate but never grasp. Thus reasonableness in religion and theology, as in other domains, has something of that aesthetic character, that quality of unformalizable skill, which we usually associate with the artist or the linguistically competent. If so, basic religious and theological positions, like Kuhn's scientific paradigms, are invulnerable to definitive refutation (as well as confirmation) but can nevertheless be tested and argued about in various ways, and these tests and arguments in the long run make a difference. Reason places constraints on religious as well as on scientific options even though these constraints are too flexible and informal to be spelled out in either foundational theology or a general theory of science. In short, intelligibility comes from skill, not theory, and credibility comes from good performance, not adherence to independently formulated criteria.

In this perspective, the reasonableness of a religion is largely a function of its assimilative powers, of its ability to provide an intelligible interpretation in its own terms of the varied situations and realities adherents encounter.[27] The religions we call primitive regularly fail this test when confronted with major changes, while the world religions have developed greater resources for coping with vicissitude. Thus, although a religion is not susceptible to decisive disproof, it is subject, as Basil Mitchell argues,[28] to rational testing procedures not wholly unlike those which apply to general scientific theories or paradigms (for which, unlike hypotheses, there are no crucial experiments). Confirmation or disconfirmation occurs through an accumulation of successes or failures in making practically and cognitively coherent sense of relevant data, and the process does not conclude, in the case of religions, until the disappearance of the last communities of believers or, if the faith survives, until the end of history. This process certainly does not enable individuals to decide between major alternatives on the basis of reason alone, but it does provide warrants for taking reasonableness in religion seriously, and it helps explain why the intellectual labours of theologians, though vacuous without corresponding practice, do sometimes make significant contributions to the health of religious traditions.

Most premodern theological views of the relation of faith and reason are consistent with this outlook. Even Luther's attacks on 'whore reason' are not fideistic: he affirms the importance of reason (at times including scholastic logic) in expounding Christian truth against both heretics and pagans.[29] On the other end of the spectrum, Aquinas's use of reason does not lead to foundational or natural theology of the modern type. Even when he is most the apologist, as in demonstrating the existence of God, his proofs are, by his own account, 'probable arguments' in support of faith rather than parts of an independent foundational enterprise.[30] Both these thinkers, despite their material differences, can be viewed as holding that revelation dominates all aspects of the theological enterprise, but without excluding a subsidiary use of philosophical and experiential considerations in the explication and defence of the faith. Similarly, a postliberal approach need not exclude an ad hoc apologetics, but only one that is systematically prior and controlling in the fashion of post-Cartesian natural theology and of later liberalism. As Aquinas himself notes, reasoning in support of the faith is not meritorious before faith, but only afterward;[31] or, in the conceptuality employed in this book, the logic of coming to believe, because it is like that of learning a language, has little room for argument, but once one has learned to speak the language of faith, argument becomes possible.

Yet, though postliberal anti-foundationalism need not imply relativism or fideism, the question remains of how to exhibit the intelligibility and possible truth of the religious message to those who no longer understand the traditional words. How, as modern Christians often put it, does one preach the gospel in a dechristianized world? Those for whom this problem is theologically primary regularly become liberal foundationalists. The first task of the theologian, they argue, is to identify the modern questions that must be addressed, and then to translate the gospel answers into a currently understandable conceptuality. If this is not done, the message will fall on deaf ears inside as well as outside the church; and unless postliberal theology has some way of meeting this need, it will be adjudged faithless and inapplicable as well as unintelligible by the religious community.

The postliberal method of dealing with this problem is bound to be unpopular among those chiefly concerned to maintain or increase the membership and influence of the church. This method resembles ancient catechesis more than modern translation.[32] Instead of redescribing the faith in new concepts, it seeks to teach the language and practices of the religion to potential adherents. This has been the primary way of transmitting the faith and winning converts for most religions down through the centuries. In the early days of the Christian church, for example, it was the Gnostics, not the catholics, who were most inclined to redescribe the biblical materials in a new interpretative framework. Pagan converts to the catholic mainstream did not, for the most part, first understand the faith and then decide to become Christians; rather, the process was reversed: they first decided and then they understood. More precisely, they were first attracted by the Christian community and form of life. The reasons for attraction ranged from the noble to the ignoble and were as diverse as the individuals involved; but for whatever motives, they submitted themselves to prolonged catechetical instruction in which they practised new modes of behaviour and learned the stories of Israel and their fulfilment in Christ. Only after they had acquired proficiency in the alien Christian language and form of life were they deemed able intelligently and responsibly to profess the faith, to be baptized.

Later, when Christianity became socially dominant, this kind of catechesis disappeared, but similar results were obtained, though in diluted form, through the normal processes of maturation. In both cases, whether through catechesis or socialization, an intimate and imaginatively vivid familiarity with the world of biblical narrative was produced that made it possible to experience the whole of life in religious terms. The popular versions of the biblical world may often have been gravely distorted, but they functioned intratextually.

Western culture is now at an intermediate stage, however, where socialization is ineffective, catechesis impossible, and translation a tempting alternative. The biblical heritage continues to be powerfully present in latent and detextualized forms that immunize against catechesis but invite redescription. There is often enough Christian substance remaining to make the redescriptions meaningful. Marxism, as is often noted, is a secularized form of biblical eschatology, and existentialism and depth psychology develop themes from Reformation anthropology divorced from Reformation theology.[33] The experience and self-identity of even the unchurched masses remain deeply influenced by the religious past. They often insist to sociological investigators, for example, that they are just as genuinely Christian as the pious folk who go to church; and they sometimes make this claim, interestingly enough, even when they deny life after death and consider the existence of a creator God unlikely. Jesus Christ is not the Son of God for them, and their picture of him may be drastically unscriptural, but his name is part of their being.[34] They are immunized against catechesis, but are sometimes interested in translations of the gospel into existential, depth-psychological or liberationist language that articulates their latent Christianity.

The impossibility of effective catechesis in the present situation is partly the result of the implicit assumption that knowledge of a few tag ends of religious language is knowledge of the religion (although no one would make this assumption about Latin). More important, however, is the character of churches during times of progressive dechristianization. In the present situation, unlike periods of missionary expansion, the churches primarily accommodate to the prevailing culture rather than shape it. Presumably they cannot do otherwise. They continue to embrace in one fashion or another the majority of the population and must cater willy-nilly to majority trends. This makes it difficult for them to attract assiduous catechumens even from among their own children, and when they do, they generally prove wholly incapable of providing effective instruction in distinctively Christian language and practice. Those who are looking for alternatives to, for example, the American way of life turn instead to Eastern religions or to deviant offshoots of the Christian mainstream. This situation is not likely to change until dechristianization has proceeded much farther or, less plausibly, is fundamentally reversed.

When or if dechristianization reduces Christians to a small minority, they will need for the sake of survival to form communities that strive without traditionalist rigidity to cultivate their native tongue and learn to act accordingly. Until that happens, however, catechetical methods of communicating the faith are likely to be unemployable in mainstream Christianity. The by no means illegitimate desire of the churches to maintain membership and of theologians to make the faith credible, not least to themselves, will continue to favour experiential–expressive translations into contemporary idioms.

Conclusion

This chapter ends on an inconclusive note. Postliberal theologies employing a cultural–linguistic understanding of religion can be faithful, applicable and intelligible. There is thus no theological, just as there is no doctrinal, reason for rejecting them. Yet the intratextual intelligibility that postliberalism emphasizes may not fit the needs of religions such as Christianity when they are in the awkwardly intermediate stage of having once been culturally established but are not yet clearly disestablished.

Those of postliberal inclinations will be undeterred. They will argue for intratextuality on both religious and non-religious grounds: the integrity of the faith demands it, and the vitality of Western societies may well depend in the long run on the culture-forming power of the biblical outlook in its intratextual, untranslatable specificity. Theology should therefore resist the clamour of the religiously interested public for what is currently fashionable and immediately intelligible. It should instead prepare for a future when continuing dechristian-ization will make greater Christian authenticity communally possible.

Those who hold that religious faithfulness is first of all the presentation of the religious message in currently intelligible forms will, of course, disagree. Their liberal premise, furthermore, can be canonically defended. There is much in scripture and tradition to suggest that preaching the gospel understandably is a necessary part of faithfulness. In short, as was said at the beginning of this chapter, the case for the theological viability of a cultural–linguistic view of religion can only be presented, not proved. Field–encompassing interpretative frameworks shape their own criteria of adequacy.

The ultimate test in this as in other areas is performance. If a postliberal approach in its actual employment proves to be conceptually powerful and practically useful to the relevant communities, it will in time become standard. It was thus that the theological outlooks of Augustine, Aquinas, Luther and Schleiermacher established themselves. There is no way of testing the merits and demerits of a theological method apart from performance.

The present chapter, however, is not a theological performance but at most a fragment of ad hoc apologetics. It discusses theology, but there is, by intratextual standards, scarcely a single properly theological argument in it. Such arguments in defence of its theses can, I think, be found in sources as diverse as Aquinas, the Reformers, and Karl Barth, but these have simply been mentioned, not deployed.

Yet, like most programmatic proposals, the present one is not simply an invitation to future work but is also dependent on past performances. The reader will recall that the stimulus for this book comes from the conviction that the doctrinal results of the ecumenical discussions of the last decades make better sense in the context of a cultural–linguistic view of religion and a rule theory of doctrine than in any other framework. Like the subjects of the Postman-Bruner card experiment mentioned in the Foreword, I have repeat-edly had the experience of seeing that old categories (such as propositional or symbolic construals of doctrine) simply do not apply to what is now happening, but that light dawns when one uses a new category (church doctrines as instantiations of regulative principles within a cultural–linguistic system). Further, on the specifically theological side, Karl Barth's exegetical emphasis on narrative has been at second hand[35] a chief source of my notion of intra-textuality as an appropriate way of doing theology in a fashion consistent with a cultural–linguistic understanding of religion and a regulative view of doctrine.

It remains an open question, however, whether the intratextual path will be pursued. There is much talk at present about typological, figurative and narrative theology, but little actual performance. Only in some younger theologians does one see the beginnings of a desire to renew in a post-traditional and postliberal mode the ancient practice of absorbing the universe into the biblical world. May their tribe increase.

Notes

1   The type of theology I have in mind could also be called 'postmodern', 'postrevisionist' or 'post-neo-orthodox', but 'postliberal' seems best because what I have in mind post-dates the experiential–expressive approach which is the mark of liberal method. This technical use of the word is much broader than the ordinary one: methodological liberals may be conservative or traditionalist in theology and reactionary in social or political matters (as the reference in this essay to the pro-Nazi *Deutsche Christen* is meant to indicate).

2   Clifford Geertz, *The Interpretation of Cultures* (New York: Basic Books, 1973), pp. 3–30. The quotations that follow in this paragraph are taken in order from pp. 17, 21, 13, 10 and 26.

3   E. E. Evans-Pritchard, *Nuer Religion* (Oxford: Oxford University Press, 1956), p. 84. This 'notorious ethnographic example' is cited by T. M. S. Evans, 'On the Social Anthropology of Religions', *Journal of Religion* 62/4 (1982), p. 376.

4   Unlike David Tracy, *The Analogical Imagination* (New York: Crossroad Publishing, 1981), I am using 'classic' to refer to texts that are culturally established for whatever reason. Tracy's model, in contrast to mine, is experiential–expressive. For him classics are 'certain expressions of the human spirit [which] so disclose a compelling truth about our lives that we cannot deny them some kind of normative status' (p. 108).

5   This and the following descriptions of intratextuality were composed without conscious reference to deconstructionism, but, given the current prominence of this form of literary theory, some tentative comments on similarities and dissimilarities may be desirable in order to avoid misunderstandings. First, intratextualism, like deconstructionism, does not share the traditional literary emphasis on a text as that which is to be interpreted, whether (as in the now-old 'New Criticism') as a self-contained aesthetic object or 'verbal icon', or as mimetic, or as expressive, or as pragmatic. (For the meaning of these terms, see Meyer H. Abrams, *The Mirror and the Lamp: Romantic Theory and the Critical Tradition* [Oxford: Oxford University Press, 1953]; cited by M. A. Tolbert, *Religious Studies Review* 8/1 [1982], p. 2.) Instead, intratextualism treats texts – to use a phrase applied to languages in earlier chapters – as 'mediums of interpretation', and thus shares the deconstructionist emphasis on texts as constituting the (or a) world within which everything is or can be construed. Related to this, in the second place, is a common concern (as will later become apparent) with what Christopher Norris, speaking of Paul de Man, calls 'the play of figural language', 'the grammar of tropes' and 'the rhetoric of textual performance' (Christopher Norris, *Deconstruction: Theory and Practise* [Methuen, 1982], pp. 106, 108). In the third place, however, the great difference is that for the deconstructionists there is no single privileged idiom, text or text-constituted world. Their approach is *inter*textual rather than intratextual – that is, they treat all writings as a single whole: all texts are, so to

speak, mutually interpreting. One result is that what in the past would have been thought of as allegorizing is for them an acceptable mode of interpretation. In an intratextual religious or theological reading, in contrast, there is (as this chapter later notes at length) a privileged interpretative direction from whatever counts as holy writ to everything else. Other differences as well as similarities are discussed by Shira Wolosky in a treatment of Derrida's relation to Talmudic modes of interpretation ('Derrida, Jabes, Levinas: Sign Theory as Ethical Discourse', *Journal of Jewish Literary History* 2/3 [1982], pp. 283–301). It should incidentally be noted, however, that Derrida's understanding of Christian interpretative method as presented in this article is quite different from the typological approach, which I shall argue was historically dominant. It may be that Derrida's view of what is characteristically Christian in these matters has been influenced by the experiential–expressive hermeneutics of Paul Ricoeur, whose student he once was.

6   Thomas Aquinas, *Summa Theologica* I.l.10.

7   For the structure, though not all the details, of my understanding of typological interpretation, see Hans Frei, *The Eclipse of Biblical Narrative* (New Haven, CT: Yale University Press, 1974), esp. pp. 1–39.

8   Charles Wood, *The Formation of Christian Understanding* (Philadelphia: Westminster Press, 1981), pp. 42, 101, and passim.

9   See my review of Gerhard Ebeling's *Dogmatik des Christlichen Glaubens*, in *Journal of Religion* 61 (1981), pp. 309–14.

10   Frei, *The Eclipse of Biblical Narrative*, pp. 39ff.

11   For the general way of looking at the problem of scriptural interpretation presented in this paragraph, though not for all the details, I am indebted to David Kelsey, *The Uses of Scripture in Recent Theology* (Philadelphia: Fortress Press, 1975).

12   This way of putting the matter is dependent on Hans Frei's *The Identity of Jesus Christ*.

13   In addition to Hans Küng's *On Being a Christian* (tr. Edward Quinn [New York: Doubleday, 1976]), see his 'Toward a New Consensus in Catholic (and Ecumenical) Theology', in Leonard Swidler, ed., *Consensus in Theology?* (Philadelphia: Westminster Press, 1980), pp. 1–17.

14   This is the focus of attack in Hick, ed., *The Myth of God Incarnate* (Philadelphia: Westminster Press, 1977).

15   Edward Schillebeeckx, *Jesus: An Experiment in Christology*, tr. Hubert Hoskins (New York: Seabury Press, 1979).

16   David Tracy, *Blessed Rage for Order* (New York: Seabury Press, 1975).

17   Karl Barth's way of doing this is described and critically but sympathetically assessed in David Ford, *Barth and God's Story* (Frankfurt: Peter Lang, 1981). See also D. Ford, 'Narrative in Theology', *British Journal of Religious Education* 4/3 (1982): 115–19.

18   David Kelsey, *The Uses of Scripture in Recent Theology*, p. 48.

19   Ibid.

20   Richard Rorty partly illustrates this possibility of doing philosophy intratextually, but the inevitable vagueness of his canon of philosophical texts makes him verge on a philosophical version of deconstructionism. See his *Consequences of Pragmatism* (Minneapolis: University of Minnesota Press, 1982), esp. essays 6 (on Derrida), 8 and 12, and the Introduction.

21   Gerhard von Rad, *Old Testament Theology*, tr. D. M. G. Stalker, 2 vols (New York:

Harper and Row, 1962, 1965).

22 I have elsewhere discussed the growing dominance in North America of 'generic' approaches (which for the most part use experiential–expressive models) to the study of religion. See *University Divinity Schools: A Report on Ecclesiastically Independent Theological Education* (New York: Rockefeller Foundation, 1976), esp. pp. 1–6, 35–41.

23 For example, the pioneering work *Toward the Year 2000*, edited by Daniel Bell (Boston: Beacon Press, 1969), now seems extraordinarily dated.

24 George Lindbeck, 'Ecumenism and the Future of Belief', *Una Sancta* 25/3 (1968), pp. 3–18; and 'The Sectarian Future of the Church', in Joseph P. Whelan, ed., *The God Experience* (New York: Newman Press, 1971), pp. 226–43.

25 Northrop Frye, *The Great Code: The Bible and Literature* (New York: Harcourt Brace Jovanovich, 1982).

26 For the argument of this paragraph, see George Lindbeck, 'Theologische Methode und Wissenschaftstheorie', *Theologische Revue* 74 (1978), pp. 267–80. This article has not been published in English. See also George Lindbeck, *The Nature of Doctrine*, chapter 3, section iv, for a discussion of the status of religious truth claims.

27 What I have in mind here might be called 'assimilation by interpretation' and is to be distinguished from what Cardinal Newman, using the same name, listed as the third mark of authentic doctrinal development. The analogies he used were organic, not interpretative: for example, a plant assimilates foreign material from its environment. (John Henry Newman, *An Essay on the Development of Christian Doctrine* [New York: Doubleday, 1960], pp. 189–92, 338–60.)

28 Basil Mitchell, *The Justification of Religious Belief* (London: Macmillan, 1973).

29 Brian Gerrish, *Grace and Reason: A Study in the Theology of Luther* (Oxford: Oxford University Press, 1962), esp. pp. 168–71; Philip Watson, *Let God Be God! An Interpretation of the Theology of Martin Luther* (Muhlenberg Press, 1947), pp. 73ff.

30 Thomas Aquinas, *Summa Theologica* I.1.8, *ad* 2.

31 Ibid., II–II.2.I0.

32 Cf. n. 26, above.

33 See George Lindbeck, 'An Assessment Re-assessed: Paul Tillich on the Reformation', *Journal of Religion* 63/4 (1983), pp. 376–93, esp. pp. 391ff.

34 Such attitudes are also widespread in Europe, where church attendance is much smaller than in the United States. See H. Hild, ed., *Wie stabil ist die Kirche? Bestand und Erneuerung. Ergebnisse einer Meinungsbefragung* (Gelnhausen: Burckhardthaus-Verlag, 1974). See also Gerhard Szeczesny, 'Warum ich als Nichtchrist Weihnachten feiere', in H. Nitschke, ed., *Was fällt ihnen zu Weihnachten ein?* (Gütersloh: Gütersloher Verlagshaus Gerd Mohn, 1978), pp. 50ff.

35 Cf. Kelsey, *The Uses of Scripture in Recent Theology*, pp. 39–50 and passim; also Ford; but I have learned to think about Barth in this way above all from conversations with Hans Frei.

Index